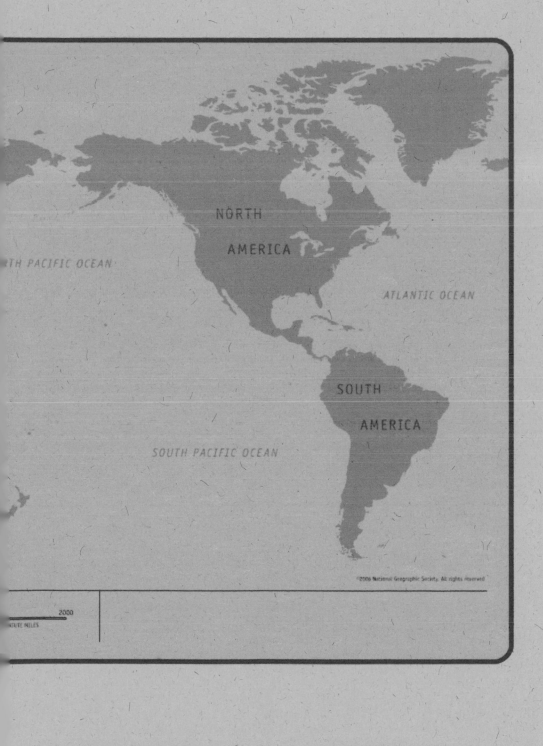

NORTH

AMERICA

TH PACIFIC OCEAN

ATLANTIC OCEAN

SOUTH

AMERICA

SOUTH PACIFIC OCEAN

2000

NUTE MILES

EXCEPTIONAL PEOPLE

EXCEPTIONAL PEOPLE

How Migration Shaped Our World
and Will Define Our Future

IAN GOLDIN,
GEOFFREY CAMERON,
AND
MEERA BALARAJAN

PRINCETON UNIVERSITY PRESS
PRINCETON AND OXFORD

Library of Congress Cataloging-in-Publication Data
Goldin, Ian, 1955–
Exceptional people : how migration shaped our world and will define our
future / Ian Goldin, Geoffrey Cameron, Meera Balarajan.
p.   cm.
Includes bibliographical references and index.
ISBN 978-0-691-14572-3 (hardcover : alk. paper) 1. Emigration and
immigration. I. Cameron, Geoffrey. II. Balarajan, Meera. III. Title.
JV6035.G65 2011
304.8—dc22
2010022368

British Library Cataloging-in-Publication Data is available

Figure 2.1 taken with permission from David Eltis and David Richardson, *An
Atlas of the Transatlantic Slave Trade*. New Haven: Yale University Press, 2009.

Endpapers of Ian Goldin's maternal and paternal ancestors
© 2010 National Geographic Society,
https://genographic.nationalgeographic.com/genographic/index.html
THE GENOGRAPHIC PROJECT, NATIONAL GEOGRAPHIC, and
Yellow Border are trademarks of NGS. All rights reserved.

This book has been composed in Aldus

Printed on acid-free paper. ∞

Printed in the United States of America

1 3 5 7 9 10 8 6 4 2

To Tess, Olivia, and Alex, who have suffered most
from my migration impulse, and to Andrew Glyn and
Stan Trapido, who had a formative influence on my
thinking and yet left this world
as I was entering theirs.
Ian Goldin

❧

To Mom and Dad, for everything, and to Lita, for
keeping new frontiers in our sights.
Geoffrey Cameron

❧

Dedicated with love to my parents.
Meera Balarajan

"It is hardly possible to overrate the value, in the present low state of human improvement, of placing human beings in contact with persons dissimilar to themselves, and with modes of thought and action unlike those with which they are familiar. . . . Such communication has always been, and is peculiarly in the present age, one of the primary sources of progress."

— John Stuart Mill

Contents

PART III: FUTURE

Illustrations and Tables

ILLUSTRATIONS

TABLES

Acknowledgments

This book has been written during our time at the James Martin 21st Century School at the University of Oxford. The School has provided an extraordinary, rich intellectual home, and engagement with our colleagues from across the University has provided a wonderfully vibrant environment in which to think. We have been most fortunate to be able to draw on the Oxford Martin School's International Migration Institute and its successive directors, Professors Stephen Castles and Robin Cohen, who have been tremendously generous intellectually and in offering up their precious time to comment on the entire manuscript. In writing this book, our colleagues at the Oxford Martin School, and particularly Laura Lauer and Verity Ross-Smith, have cheerfully accommodated challenging schedules and created a vibrant environment in which to work.

We have been fortunate to be able to rely on the work of a number of particularly able research assistants. Alan Gamlen provided an incisive fresh look at the structure and content of this book, and his contributions remain evident in the organization and a number of elements of the book. Ted Maxwell and Emma Menell provided help with particular sections, working on the historical chapters and the legal and regulatory environment, respectively. We have Wolfgang Lutz to thank for his expert comments on chapter 7. Tom King created several of the book's illustrations on very short notice. Others who have lent their time and ideas include Alessio Cangiano, Peter Healey, Miles Hewstone, Jaco Hoffman, Judith McNeill, Kathleen Newland, Michael Oppenheimer, Bob Sutcliffe, Darshan Vigneswaran, and two anonymous referees. Princeton University Press has been an ideal publishing partner. Richard Baggaley from our first discussions provided enthusiastic guidance. We are grateful for the tremendous support of Peter Dougherty and all of his colleagues at

Princeton for shepherding the book through its final phases of editing and publication.

(IG) This book has evolved over five years and has its gestation in a life-long interest in migration that was forged out of my own, my parents', and my grandparents' escape from oppressive regimes and productive settlement in new lands. Francis Wilson first helped me translate this fascination into economic analysis while I was completing my under-graduate studies. Decades later, at the World Bank, I was fortunate to work with Nick Stern and to enjoy his support as I sought to develop a program on migration and development. Jim Wolfensohn allowed me to pursue this interest while vice president, and with excellent research assistance from Andrew Beath, I was able to develop a framework for migration that first appeared as a chapter in the book Globalization for Development, which I coauthored with Kenneth Reinert. Finally, this book would not have been possible without the contributions of my research assistants. Meera Balarajan provided a wealth of foundation materials that were invaluable building blocks for this book, reflecting her broad knowledge and dedication to migration research. Geoffrey Cameron subsequently developed these and an amazing amount of other materials. With a writing style that I was delighted to mesh with my own, he has proven himself a most engaging and effective collaborator, without whom this book would not have been completed.

I am deeply grateful to a number of colleagues at Oxford University, not least Laura Lauer, and to Peter Dougherty at Princeton University Press for their remarkable professionalism and support through the challenging birth pains of this book.

My biggest debts are to my family, who endured what must have seemed like endless nights and weekends when I have been preoccupied with the book.

(GC) I have my parents to thank for an enriched childhood growing up in three countries, movement that was born out of their desire to see the world's diversity with open eyes. As I grew up studying Baha'i texts, these experiences helped to prompt deep reflection about the future of world development. I thank Laura Lauer and Ian Goldin for bringing me into the School, where thinking about the future is a vocation for its vibrant research team. Ian was not only a stimulating and encouraging collaborator on this book, he also constantly reminded me of our ethical obligations to humanity—especially those who appear to be different from us. I thank him for that, most of all.

I owe my deepest gratitude to my wife, Lita, for entertaining so many conversations about the research and thinking that went into this book. I also have her to thank for giving us a reason to stay in Oxford long enough to advance this project.

While this book was completed after I took a position with Foreign Affairs and International Trade Canada, the views expressed do not necessarily reflect those of the Government of Canada.

(MB) My contribution to this book was written during my time with the James Martin 21st Century School. It was a privilege to be at the School at its inception, and exciting to work with Ian at this creative time. My contribution would not have been possible without the help of my colleagues at the Centre on Migration, Policy and Society (COMPAS) in Oxford, and especially the support of Professor Steve Vertovec and Dr. Nick Van Hear. Also, I wish to thank several scholars and friends all round the world who have shaped my academic development in migration studies, especially Dr. Frank Pieke and Dr. Rachel Murphy.

Finally, I am greatly indebted to my parents who themselves are exceptional people—migrants, who experienced many challenges and created a wonderful and supportive platform for me, and my family.

Ian Goldin, Oxford (UK); Geoffrey Cameron, Ottawa (Canada);
Meera Balarajan, London (UK)
December 2010

EXCEPTIONAL PEOPLE

Introduction

❧

We live in a dynamic age of global integration, where the reconnection and mixture of the world's people is challenging dominant norms and practices in many societies. Disintegration and integration are simultaneous and interwoven. Cultural codes adapt. New economies emerge. Innovation prospers. Social institutions struggle to adapt.

To many, the challenges associated with migration are characteristic of our age of postmodernism, multiculturalism, and aspiring cosmopolitanism. Some are nostalgic for an illusory past when people had more in common. While the scale, pace, and intensity of human movement may be greater today, the habits of migration and its disruptive effects are as old as humanity itself. Outsiders have always encountered opposition from their adoptive societies. Nevertheless, the direction of history points to the persistent expansion in the boundaries of community. Our cultural and political frontiers have gradually receded.

In most parts of the world, the old distinctions between clans and tribes are now of less significance than are national boundaries. Whereas at one time a "migrant" may have been one who married into a neighboring village, "migration" now generally refers to moving across a national border, often with the purpose of settling for a period of time. The names "immigrant" and "asylum seeker" have acquired negative connotations in many societies, echoing the ancient fear of the "barbarian." Our governments and societies retain an antiquated suspicion of outsiders, who were born in one nation-state and seek to make their life in another one. The result is a conventional view that a high rate of international migration should be prevented.

In the current period, "migration" is defined as cross-border movement, and it has come to be seen as something to be managed—a cost to be minimized rather than an opportunity to be embraced. Our view is that it is a key driver of human and economic development and that our future will be strongly influenced by policies regarding migration.

How governments craft and coordinate migration policy will determine whether our collective future is defined by a more open and cosmopolitan global society or one that is unequal, partitioned, and less prosperous. This book aspires to set contemporary debates about policy within a wider context. Public debates about migration are limited by a lack of perspective of its historical role, contemporary impacts, and future prospects. This book aims to address these gaps and to contribute to advancing the discourse about the role of migrants and migration in world development.

We seek to shift discussion on international mobility away from narrow national-level immigration debates, toward a more global view of migration. The terms "immigration" and "immigrant" can obscure more than they reveal, because they imply that people move once, permanently—from outside the country to inside—when migration for the most part is temporary, repeated, or circular. This perspective also ignores the dynamism of human movement: countries that accept large numbers of migrants also typically send similarly large numbers across their borders. Migrants are uncommon people, and they often move several times in search of opportunity and safety. Viewing cross-border movement simply in terms of immigration limits a broader appreciation of how networks and economies function in an increasingly integrated world.

In this book, we question the received wisdom that an increase in the flow of international migrants is undesirable. We offer fresh insights into the past, present, and future role of migration. We begin by reviewing the historical role of migrants and migration in advancing human progress and world development. Second, we analyze the contemporary period of managed migration. Drawing upon a rapidly growing field of multidisciplinary scholarship on the dynamics, flows, and impacts of migration, we make the case that current ad hoc regulations are poorly suited for a world economy that thrives on openness, diversity, innovation, and exchange. Last, we look to the future, presenting projections of demographic, environmental, and social trends that highlight how the number and diversity of migrants will grow over the next fifty years.

PART I: PAST

Throughout history, as remains the case today, people have moved under conditions that are not typically of their own choosing. Even those under the most restrained and difficult circumstances have navigated new social and cultural settings with determination and ingenuity. By adapting, innovating, and combining knowledge across cultural barriers, migrants have advanced the frontier of development since humans departed from Africa, some 50,000–60,000 years ago. The emergence of early civilizations around 4000 BCE drew people from scattered settlements into dense patterns of complex social life. The first civilizations, like social magnets, brought people from the hinterlands into the life of the cities—as labor, merchants, traders, and administrators—and propelled city-dwellers into the frontiers to find resources and trading partners.

The growth of civilizations quickened the pace of exchange and the commerce of ideas and technologies. As increasingly complex societies developed in Eurasia, traders, adventurers, missionaries, and conquering armies broke down the frontiers separating distant empires. Valuable technologies and commercial and other practices, which at times took many centuries to develop, were shared over ever-increasing distances. Migrants carried with them religious teachings, agricultural techniques, and commercial practices. The scourge of war and the lure of commerce propelled people across old frontiers, reconnecting communities from eastern China to West Africa, which had developed distinct cultures over tens of thousands of years.

The expansion of seafaring trade during the second millennium brought new levels of prosperity to China and Europe, which both saw the launch of ambitious voyages into uncharted waters to find new markets for their goods. As China suddenly terminated its explorations near the turn of the fifteenth century, Portugal was beginning to fund open-ended expeditions across the Atlantic Ocean; the coincidence of these two developments would precipitate European contact with the Americas and a seismic shift in global power. The European "Age of Discovery" (also termed the "Age of Gunpowder Empires")[1] between the fifteenth and seventeenth centuries completed the process of reconnecting humanity. European ships were now dominating trade within the Indian Ocean and extracting resources in New World plantations. Regional mercantile trading networks became knitted into a global power structure with force and control projected across vast distances.

With the emergence of global networks and the development of a world economy, the pace of economic development began to drive migratory flows, most significantly in the form of chattel slavery. International trade and the industrial revolution fueled competition, promoting innovation and expanding production in Europe. Many people traveled across oceans or continents, some in search of a better life. Millions more, particularly from Africa, were forced to move under the tyranny of slavery or indentured labor. In this new era of globalization, free and forced migrants were the causes and consequences of economic growth.

The twentieth century has witnessed the proliferation of states and the extension of government bureaucracies into the management of migration. The introduction of passports, strict border controls, immigration quotas, guest-worker programs, and the distribution of rights on the basis of nationality are all features of the new era of highly managed migration. Passports and border controls are relatively new innovations, and their increasingly strict enforcement in the twentieth century dramatically changed the dynamics of migration. International migration became regulated at the level of the nation-state. Apart from measures to protect refugees, international cooperation has largely neglected the vital dimension of migration.

PART II: PRESENT

Despite the obstacles inherent within highly regulated national migration systems, people continue to move for many of the same reasons that have driven migrants throughout history: to seek new opportunities and to escape economic and political distress. Many factors related to family, wages, security, values, and opportunities influence migration decisions. Migration confounds simplistic analysis, as the decision to migrate is nested within relationships, networks, and structures. People frequently move more than once, and migration has evolving social dynamics that take into account economic cycles, immigration policies, and political conditions. Despite the complexity of decisions to migrate, a number of factors associated with the most recent wave of globalization, including transportation and communication technologies, have collapsed social distances and make it easier to move than ever before.

Immigration regulations aim to manage flows to meet public policy goals. These regulations have evolved from earlier practices of using nation based quotas to encompass a range of migration "channels." Economic channels bring in students and highly skilled migrants, as well as low-skilled workers to meet temporary labor demands. Families and particular ancestral groups are recognized through social migration channels. Those who have been compelled to move because of civil conflict, persecution, or intense pressure move as refugees or as asylum seekers. In strictly limiting the conditions under which one may legally migrate, states spend heavily on a sprawling architecture of enforcement and control. The effectiveness of new regulatory mechanisms in meeting their objectives of controlling migrant flows remains a matter of considerable debate.

Despite the efforts of many states to halt permanent settlement by certain migrants and to distinguish "their" citizens from foreigners, the constant movement of people has continually changed the concept of what it means to be a foreigner. Multiculturalism and cosmopolitanism are now celebrated features of many societies. Yet the contribution of migrants to economic and other aspects of life is severely underestimated. As a result, the focus of governments and public opinion often is on managing the perceived threats posed by migrants, rather than assisting them to fully participate in mainstream society.

International migration pays dividends to sending countries, receiving countries, and migrants themselves. In receiving countries, it promotes innovation, boosts economic growth, and enriches social diversity, and it is a boon for public finance. Sending countries have their economies stimulated by the financial and social feedback of migrant networks. Migrants reap the welfare benefits of higher wages, better education, and improved health when they move to relatively more developed countries. High rates of migration do, however, produce costs that are carried unevenly by particular localities and countries. These costs are often short-run, and they can be reduced through resource transfers and by building the capacity of public institutions to manage the social and administrative changes presented by higher rates of migration.

PART III: FUTURE

The forces that have propelled migration in the past are continuing to intensify, and the sheer pressure of human movement requires that more attention be paid to domestic policy and global migration governance. In the next fifty years, the supply of potential migrants will expand alongside economic growth, urbanization, and rising educational attainment in low-income countries—especially in sub-Saharan Africa and Central Asia. As always, people will move to seek better opportunities, higher wages, and security, concerns that will become more salient as intercountry inequality widens and climate change threatens livelihoods. Demand for migrants will also increase dramatically in most developed countries and in many developing countries. Population decline and population aging will create new demands for labor, both skilled and less-skilled. National competitiveness is already leading countries to dismantle barriers to mobility for high-skilled workers. Migration is a vital source of dynamism in economies and will become even more important as societies age and fertility tumbles.

The twentieth century assumption that migration is a strictly national problem to be handled independently by nation-states is no longer valid. A twenty-first century approach to international migration demands that we come to terms with the social and economic forces propelling people across borders and that the instruments of governance equip countries to reap the full benefits of global mobility. Both national and international policy reform is required to achieve objectives that meet evolving national needs, as well as the aspirations of migrants themselves.

At the domestic level, public policy should reflect the understanding that migration is a social process that cannot be turned on or off. Pragmatic policy choices are needed to accommodate the new dynamics of international mobility and to draw collective benefit from the processes of migration and cross-border exchange. Important lessons can be learned from those regions that have open borders (such as within parts of the

European Union) as well as those that have tried to prevent all migration. In the light of our analysis of past and current practices, we outline the key objectives for a global migration agenda. For both ethical and economic reasons, we argue that the most desirable future scenario involves freer movement across borders. A global migration agenda ought to be framed around principles that guide pragmatic steps toward a more open global economy that serves our collective interest.

Reforming migration policy at the national level needs to be complemented by coordinated approaches to global migration governance. Migration is the orphan of the global institutional architecture. The international institutional and legal framework is silent on systemic migration issues, other than refugees. Responsibility for migration falls chaotically between several international agencies that currently have neither the mandate nor the capacity to address key global concerns regarding migration.

The twenty-first century will bring major new challenges to migration policy with demographic, economic, and environmental changes leading to fundamental shifts in the flows of migrants. The global community is becoming connected in a manner not experienced since our small-world evolutionary origins in Africa. Our ability to meet the challenges of the twenty-first century requires a better understanding of our deep migration impulse and its impact on our future.

PART I

❦

PAST

1

❧

Migration from Prehistory to Columbus

We begin the story of human migration where our collective history began—in Africa, the cradle of humanity. Migrants have
propelled the advancement of human communities since these early
days, some 150,000 to 200,000 years ago. Our biological evolution cul-
minated in the *homo sapiens* species, whose capacity for language and
propensity for trading accelerated a new stage of social evolution that
allowed humans to displace other hominids and eventually to develop
advanced civilizations.[1] The human gift for cooperation and collective
learning made our ancestors particularly adaptive to new environments,
and incremental migration gradually populated the earth with human
settlements. People continued to move. Merchants, soldiers, adventurers,
and religious teachers carried new ideas and technologies between human
settlements and civilizations, creating dynamic patterns of growth.

Early in human history, a pattern of cross-community migration appeared. Groups of people would move to new regions, leading to differentiation between the old and newly established communities: subtle
variance in language, technology, and beliefs would develop among these
groups. Concurrent with this process of differentiation, however, was
that of interaction. The diverse ways of doing things were shared across
communities by migrant brides, traders, farmers, and herders. Differentiation between communities and regular interaction among them is a
historical pattern that continues to this day.[2] Migrants have driven forward the development of society and civilization by serving as conduits
for the transmission of new ideas, accelerating learning and innovation.

The history of human communities and world development highlights the extent to which migration has been an engine of social progress. By viewing our collective past through the lens of migration, we can appreciate how the movement of people across cultural frontiers has brought about the globalized and integrated world that we inhabit today. We refer to globalization not only in economic terms, but also in relation to social and political transformations and the emergence of global currents of thought. Of course, migrants are rarely the bright-eyed entrepreneurs that this narrative may unintentionally imply, and migration has often been driven by conflict, exploitation, and poverty. More often than not, people have moved out of necessity and under arduous conditions. Human suffering has accompanied migration; nevertheless, societies have been enriched by the dynamism of migration. As people have moved, they have encountered new environments and cultures that compel them to adapt and innovate novel ways of doing things. The development of belief systems and technologies, and the spread of crops and production methods, have often arisen out of the experiences of, or encounters with, migrants.

Early human migrations can be roughly divided into two stages. In the first, humans spread out. "It is safe to assume," says to William H. McNeill, "that when our ancestors first became fully human they were already migratory."[3] Migrants initially moved throughout Africa, before leaving the continent between 50,000–60,000 years ago to populate the world.[4] As populations of hunter–gatherer groups grew to their geographical limits, members moved to settle new groups, and the process of expansion across the world continued.[5] The development of agriculture and sedentary communities prompted the second stage in migration: connecting humanity. Despite the global dispersion of humans, communities remained connected through trade networks and conquest. Diversity emerged through the separate development of populations, but cross-cultural contact ensured continuing interaction between scattered human communities.

EARLY MIGRATION

Out of Africa

Every one of us has migrant blood running through our veins. As Spencer Wells put it, "We all have an African great-great ... grandmother who lived approximately 150,000 years ago."[6] Around 80,000 years ago, the archaeological record of *homo sapiens* grows vague, and Wells argues that the human population dwindled to around 2,000 people. Genetic mutations within this small group of humans led to rapid brain development, giving us the power of abstract thought. With new capacities for innovation and adaptation, populations began to increase and expand, first throughout Africa and eventually into Asia and beyond. Migrants moved within their cultural group; they settled new areas, colonized their neighbors, or just sojourned to foreign areas.[7] Movement spread knowledge, new capabilities, and belief systems, but it could also spread disease and stimulate conflict.

The earliest migrations followed a pattern of "extensification": people spread out, but as they migrated, there was limited growth in the size and density of human communities. There were evolutionary advantages to this "roving pattern of behaviour" exhibited by humans, notes McNeill: "Their restless movements continually probed for new possibilities and tested old barriers, usually finding nothing of importance to other human beings, but every so often opening the way for critically important technological, geographical and/or social breakthroughs."[8] In addition to the natural inclination for "roving," people also moved in response to social conflict or overpopulation.[9]

Within Africa, people initially moved beyond the savannahs of eastern and southern Africa into the east–west belt of the northern savannah between Ethiopia and Senegal.[10] Human communities spread farther north and east in Africa. About 60,000 years ago, men and women moved from Africa's Nile Valley across the strait of Bab el Mandeb into the Arabian Peninsula. This movement initiated a series of coastal migrations that slowly spread human settlements across to the Indian subcontinent and beyond (see figure 1.1).

Flows of cross-community migration continued to connect members of the slowly expanding human species as people inhabited new ecologies. Patrick Manning suggests that young people "left their home community to visit or join other communities . . . learning as well as introducing ideas about technology, culture and social relations."[11] Among the most influential of these young people were migrant brides—some of whom would have been captured—by virtue of their complete integration into foreign societies. Knowledge about stone technology, weaving, hunting and fishing techniques, raft and boat construction, and other

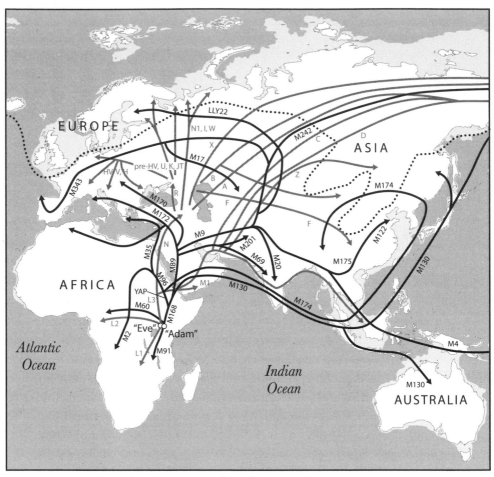

Migration Patterns of Early Humans

→ Y Chromosome Markers   (thousand years ago)

M 91	(60)	M 9	(40)	M 201	(20)
M 60	(50)	M 175	(35)	M 242	(20)
M 168	(50)	M 45	(35)	M 3	(10)
YAP	(50)	M 173	(30)	M 172	(10)
M 174	(50)	M 20	(30)	M 17	(10)
M 130	(50)	M 69	(30)	M 122	(10)
M 96	(45)	M 170	(25)	M 4	(10)
M 89	(45)	M 2	(20)	LLY 22	(10)

Figure 1.1. The genetic pathways of human migration. Courtesy of Spencer Wells. ©2005–2010 National Geographic Society. THE GENOGRAPHIC PROJECT, NATIONAL GEOGRAPHIC, and Yellow Border are trademarks of NGS. All rights reserved.

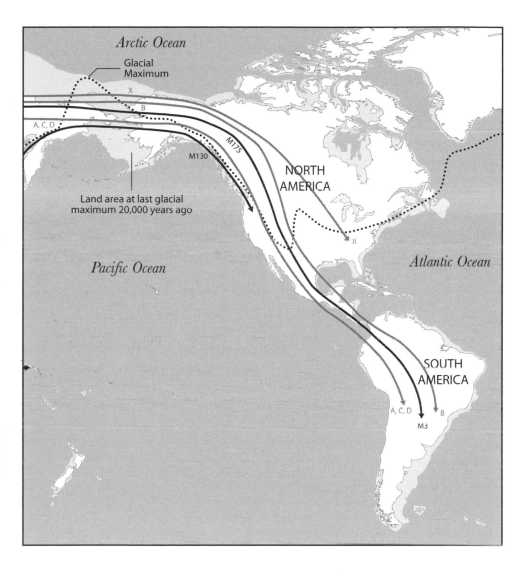

Arctic Ocean

Glacial
Maximum

X

B

A, C, D

M175

M130

Land area at last glacial
maximum 20,000 years ago

NORTH
AMERICA

Pacific Ocean

Atlantic Ocean

X

SOUTH
AMERICA

A, C, D   B

M3

mtDNA Markers   (thousand years ago)

L 1	(>100)	F	(50)	Z	(30)
L 2	(80)	R	(50)	HV	(30)
L 3	(70)	D	(45)	H	(30)
M	(60)	pre-HV	(40)	N 1	(30)
M 1	(60)	U	(40)	I	(30)
N	(50)	K	(40)	X	(30)
B	(50)	JT	(40)	W	(30)
C	(50)	A	(30)	V	(15)

adaptive creations developed by humans in their new environments, all
traveled between communities through cross-community migration.
Archeological evidence of seashell jewelry found far from coastal regions
and stone tools made out of nonlocal material indicate that humans were
also trading over great distances at least 40,000 years ago.[12]

Migrants Inhabit the Earth

After moving beyond Africa, migrants initially stuck to tropical climates
by working their way overland into Eurasia and moving through water's-edge expansion along the coastline into Southeast Asia and Australia. By 50,000–60,000 years ago, people populated the shores of the
Indian Ocean and Red Sea.[13] The group that initially moved to southwest Asia may have initially been as few as 50 people, and it has been
estimated that only 500 or so people made the journey over the next
200 years.[14] And 10,000 years later, human communities could be found
along the tropical belt from the coastal and inland areas of West Africa
all the way to Australia.

The settlement of Australia around 40,000–50,000 years ago was undertaken through a series of audacious seafaring expeditions from Indonesia to Australia. Indonesia was separated from Sahul (a continent
that connected Australia and New Guinea) by less than 100 kilometers,
and the first settlers would have sailed in reed or bamboo boats with the
intention of establishing a permanent colony.[15] David Christian writes:
"Any humans traveling to Sahul . . . had to be superb sailors. And they
had to be careful planners, for populations that drifted to Sahul by chance
would not have been large enough to form permanent colonies. So, settling Sahul required technologies that we do not find in any previous
hominine species . . ."[16] Moving to Australia was the first human movement into an ecology that was substantially different from the tropical
zones they had previously inhabited.

Around 40,000 years ago, people began to occupy the relatively colder,
though still temperate, regions of Europe and inner Eurasia through
several different routes. One involved movement along the rivers and
valleys of the Himalayas from South China into the Eurasian steppes.
Another would have followed the Pacific shore before turning inland. A
final western route may have come more directly out of Africa toward

the Black Sea. An ice age between 30,000 and 15,000 years ago, however, led human populations that had initially settled the warmer parts of Eurasia to retreat farther south.

The evidence for how humans occupied northern Eurasia and the Americas is unclear, and there are many competing accounts based on genetic tracing, linguistics, and archaeology. Human settlements were restricted to Africa, Asia, and Oceania until about 40,000 years ago, in part by the formidable mountain ranges of Asia. During the next 10,000–20,000 years, people populated all of Eurasia (including the northern regions) and parts of North America.[17] Several important innovations would have preceded movement into colder regions: hunting techniques and technologies—such as spears and throwing sticks—were developed, along with methods of sewing heavier clothing.[18] As with other such migrations, movement into a new ecology prompted the development of tools to assist human adaptation.

The movement of humans from northern Eurasia into the Americas was a particularly impressive migration. Recent research proposes that several thousand people survived the last ice age on the former Bering Land Bridge, a grassland steppe that connected Russia and Alaska, protected from glacial expansion by Pacific currents. These migrants later populated the Americas as the glaciers melted around 16,500 years ago.[19] We now know them as Native Americans; the First Nations, Inuit, and Innu of Canada; the Caribs and Arawaks of the Caribbean basin; and the indigenous peoples of Central and South America. There were probably several waves of migration across the Land Bridge, possibly including early journeys by boat around the glaciers. The dates of migrations across the Bering Land Bridge are disputed by archeologists (within the range of several thousand years), but this pattern of migration from what is now Russia into the Americas is by now widely upheld. Despite some past speculation that sailors living in what is now China or Japan crossed the Pacific to the Americas, the most recent genetic evidence shows that all ancient migrants to the Americas came across Siberia.[20]

The extraordinary challenge of crossing large expanses of the Pacific Ocean did not stop Polynesians from settling extremely remote islands. Humans set off from Southeast Asia in seafaring vessels, progressively populating the South Pacific. Fiji was populated about 3,600 years ago, Hawaii 2,000 years later, and New Zealand 1,000 years ago.[21]

Less than 50,000 years after humans departed from Africa, they had settled on all of the world's continents (aside from Antarctica). By 10,000 years ago, humans had adapted to live in vastly different ecologies across the earth: from West Africa to Siberia, and from Australia to Tierra del Fuego.[22] The culmination of this vast enterprise to occupy the planet in all of its diverse climes and ecologies represents humanity's great migratory feat. No sooner had this massive expansion been completed than the first developments in agriculture and horticulture began to generate new energy for migrants to spread technological and social innovations across thousands of miles. As human communities followed separate trajectories of social and cultural evolution, they remained connected by the unceasing movement of people.

CONNECTING HUMANITY

The Agricultural Revolution

Around the time that humans completed their great migration, the ice age also ended and the earth entered into the Holocene period. The Holocene was marked by radical changes in climate, retreating ice sheets, shifting vegetational zones, and rising sea levels.[23] The environment became more unpredictable in many parts of the world. These pressures contributed to the emergence of the first sedentary communities in the Middle East, which adapted to environmental changes through more intensive exploitation of food sources, food storage, and more permanent settlement.[24] While sedentism did not immediately produce recognizable agriculture, as Christian notes, it was "a vital, unplanned step toward agriculture."[25]

From 15,000 to 10,000 years ago, people living in six regions of the world experimented with harvesting and fishing techniques. In what is today called the Fertile Crescent—which extends from the eastern Mediterranean shoreline along the Syrian Desert to the Persian Gulf— people in settlements began to harvest wild grasses and other plants and to build permanent structures.[26] Similar experiments with planting and harvesting grains, grasses, and tubers were simultaneously happening in Southeast Asia, Yunnan (China), New Guinea, West Africa, and

Mesoamerica.[27] Archaeological finds in Britain indicate that farming was introduced about 6,000 years ago by migrants from France. This allowed the hunter–gatherers to settle, leading to a quadrupling of the population in just 400 years.[28]

As a result of population growth and intensive exploitation of local resources, sedentism placed increasing pressures on the local ecology. Resource scarcity forced these communities to either innovate with new farming technologies—often focusing on a few crops—or to revert back to more nomadic lifestyles.[29]

The farming innovations produced by successful sedentary communities spread through interregional networks of exchange. Christian explains: "Exchanges of valued goods between foraging communities . . . were particularly intense in the early Holocene along the Levantine corridor, between Anatolia and the Red Sea; they might have stimulated communities already exploiting natural stands of cereals on well-watered highlands to try encouraging their growth in lowland regions crossed by flourishing 'trade' routes."[30] Sedentism became increasingly prevalent through gentle population pressure, local abundance, and growing networks of exchange. The transmission of new farming technologies anticipated the central role that networks of traders and migrants would play in the development of agrarian civilizations.

The domestication of plants and animals was associated with intensified production, which greatly increased the caloric production in these areas. As farmers settled near fields and orchards, their sedentary lifestyle was associated with the development of more complex fixed abodes. Fertility became higher as mothers were able to care for more children than was possible in constantly moving hunter–gatherer communities. Reduced birth-intervals and higher survival rates generated further increases in population.

While it is important not to exaggerate the distinction between sedentary groups and hunter–gathering groups (in practice, these groups often overlapped),[31] sedentary food production became more prevalent over time. Population growth and improved hunting technologies led to overhunting and the declining availability of wild game. At the same time, improvements in the selection of seeds, the development of sickles and other implements, and the successful domestication of animals for farming all made sedentary life more viable. In the Fertile Crescent and elsewhere, the balance between the benefits of hunter–gathering and food production had by 10,000 years ago tipped in favor of settled farming.

Around 7,000 years ago, improved agricultural technologies had reached many parts of the settled world, and gains in productivity led to an increasing division of labor and urbanization. The spread of agriculture was partly through colonization by the early agricultural pioneers, but it was equally the result of the spread of ideas of agriculture; ideas spread more quickly than agricultural communities could move.[32] Only a minority of Europeans have been shown to possess genetic markers from the Middle East of 10,000 years ago, which strongly suggests that agricultural and other innovations traveled without the need for large numbers of people to move.[33] A small number of travelers and migrants served as the couriers for big ideas, launching a virtuous cycle: as people moved, they carried ideas that facilitated income and population growth—eventually prompting further movement.

As agricultural technology and the variety of crops proliferated, populations became more concentrated, and a division of labor and social hierarchy developed in regions such as Mesopotamia, Nubia, Egypt, highland Mexico and the lands of the Mayans, Peru, Ethiopia, and the valleys of the Indus, Yangzi, Huang He, Nile, and Niger rivers. Religion became more sophisticated, and priests assumed greater influence. Handicrafts and pottery were improved, and homes were increasingly built to endure. In addition to facilitating specialization, food production was associated with the development of full-time bureaucracies, along with administrative systems and politicians.[34] Inequality in such societies grew as leadership minorities diverted their attention from hunting and gathering to ruling dense food-producing groups and developing standing armies for exploration, conquest, and defense.

Settled life did have disadvantages, however—in a sense, it would have been healthier to keep moving. Settlements reduced the breadth of the resource base, making it more difficult to cope with dramatic climactic shifts. For example, people were more vulnerable to famines when societies were stuck in one place, whereas hunter–gatherers could move to pastures greener. Infectious diseases such as smallpox or typhoid require threshold numbers to survive, and they became more prevalent among settled communities.[35] Denser populations with accumulated wealth and possessions were also more vulnerable to warfare and raiding.

More positively, greater population density allowed for faster information sharing and more powerful "collective learning."[36] Christian identifies collective learning, or the ability of humans to pool and share knowledge, as "the most important distinguishing feature of human history."[37] Two factors are critical to collective learning: the volume and variety of information being pooled, and the speed with which information is shared. In this respect, increasingly dense sedentary communities expanded the possibilities for creativity and innovation. As city economies developed, the proliferation of trade routes connecting them to other communities served to transmit learning and promote the spread of superior technologies. Sedentism accelerated the production and spread of significant knowledge about how to manipulate the natural world.

The development of early cities not only brought people closer together, it also generated high population mobility. Rural-urban markets developed. Wealthy elites promoted intellectual exchanges among scholars. Merchants traveled to acquire trading information. Newcomers married locals to tap into existing social networks. This increasing tempo of movement required roads and bridges, as well as guides and translators. Cities were slowly connected with the sinews of social and physical infrastructure.[38]

Long-Distance Trade and Agrarian Civilizations

While the concept of "civilization" has acquired a negative connotation in some corners of academia, it can be used more neutrally to describe societies characterized by occupational specialization among relatively large numbers of people.[39] Specialization promotes the refinement of skills, and a division of labor increases production and wealth, necessitating the development of markets and trade routes. The first civilizations emerged where societies could establish control over food sources and manage the distribution of food for a large number of people. The existence of dense agrarian populations was thus a necessary precondition for the development and spread of the first civilizations.[40] Religion and governance in these civilizations were impressively integrative forces, but powerful rulers also launched destructive campaigns of imperial warfare.

The earliest known civilization was established by Sumerian seafarers on the Tigris-Euphrates floodplain around 4000 BCE. These warrior–migrants subjected the region's scattered inhabitants to their rule, eventually developing several large temple-centered cities. Under Sargon of Akkad (who ruled from ca. 2350 BCE), Sumerian civilization expanded to include about a dozen cities, each with 20,000 to 50,000 people. Sargon created a standing army and conquered neighboring cities, incorporating them into his expanding empire. Sargon's rule marked one of the first appearances of state formation, where multiple hinterland cities were governed by a central ruler.

This emerging empire also supported growing trade networks that connected Sumer with the rest of Mesopotamia and extended as far as central Asia, the Indus Valley to the east, and south into Egypt and sub-Saharan Africa.[41] Sumerian civilization led to unprecedented technological innovation: the Sumerians developed wheeled vehicles, bronze metallurgy, writing, monumental buildings, and irrigation.[42] Sumerian cities were also the first to practice year-round agriculture, which would have been necessary to feed their relatively dense populations.

Sumer relied on a continuing flow of migrants from its frontiers to sustain population levels in the city. Because cities brought people into close proximity with each other, they were characterized by much higher mortality rates than the countryside. Demographically significant epidemic infections became routine aspects of urbanism in Sumerian civilization, a pattern that would continue in cities until the development of modern public health programs.[43] The depopulation of the Sumerian-speaking city required increasing in-migration from the Akkadian-speaking countryside. The volume of replacement migration from the countryside eventually led to the Akkadian language displacing Sumerian in administration and record keeping.

The maintenance of civilized life not only depended on a continual flow of migrants into cities, it also required the regular movement of people out beyond the civilizational frontiers to secure raw materials. Early civilization in Mesopotamia needed timber, metals, and stone, which were unavailable near river valley cities. Trade expeditions and raids carried city elites to far-away emerging cities and court centers in order to locate these materials, which were needed for early civilized technologies.[44]

Trade diasporas emerged concurrently with the development of urban life in these first civilizations. Philip D. Curtin describes these early forms of cross-cultural trade:

> Commercial specialists would remove themselves physically from their home community and go to live as aliens in another town, usually not a fringe town, but a town important in the life of the host community. . . . The result was an interrelated net of commercial communities forming a trade network, or trade diaspora—a term that comes from the Greek word for scattering, as in the sowing of grain.[45]

Archeological findings suggest that trade diasporas developed as early as 3500 BCE. Clay tablets dating back to 2000 BCE show commercial records of an Assyrian trade settlement in Cappadocia (modern Turkey)—hundreds of miles away from home.[46]

Early riverine civilizations in Mesopotamia, Egypt, and the Indus Valley appeared around the same time, probably because trade networks stretching between modern Egypt and Pakistan carried ideas about culture and technology.[47] Mesopotamian-style artifacts have been found in modern Iran, the Indus Valley area, and Syria, suggesting a relatively sophisticated system of exchange in the region. Similarly, gemstones mined in modern Afghanistan around 3000 BCE have been found in archeological sites in Mesopotamia and Egypt.

The development of long-distance trade in this period was enabled by innovations in transportation technology. Around 3200 BCE, central Asian nomads domesticated the horse, and Arabians did the same with camels several hundred years later. Egyptians also developed new sailing vessels to enable travel up and down the Nile and to carry on trade in the Red Sea area. By 2000 BCE, donkey caravans were carrying goods between Mesopotamia and Asia Minor. Early merchants and traders were responsible for establishing roads, sea routes, and communication networks that set the stage for increasing cross-cultural contact between civilizations.[48] This pattern recurs throughout history: the exploration of merchant–migrants paves the way for the larger flow of people and ideas across cultures and civilizations.

Pulsing trade networks circulated people, goods, and ideas, which nourished the growth of agrarian civilizations. McNeill observes that migrant-powered exchange between civilizations "provided a major— perhaps *the* major—stimulus to change within civilized communities."[49] The influence of the Orient on the ancient Greeks is recorded in the works of Herodotus (484–425 BCE), and the Sima Qian's (ca. 145–86 BCE) *Shiji* documents early Chinese contact with ancient Middle Eastern civilizations. These cross-cultural encounters "drastically altered patterns of cultural growth and often accelerated developments or turned them into new paths," adds McNeill.[50]

A Migrant Alphabet

The lineage of our modern alphabet illustrates the significance of these early trade routes for the cross-cultural transmission of new ideas. Western script is based on the Phoenician alphabet, which was developed around 1000 BCE in the area of modern Israel and Lebanon. Phoenicians were active seafarers, and they dominated trade in the Mediterranean region for several hundred years, even venturing to the British coast and possibly even around the African continent.[51] In the process of their travels, they spread their alphabet, which has influenced the Greek, Aramaic, and Brahmi writing systems that form the basis for Latin, Arabic, Hebrew, and scripts in India and Mongolia. The English language acquired its Phoenician influence by way of Greek adaptations that were augmented by the Romans.

Where growing communities were clustered closer together, the efficient movement of people and ideas produced dynamic centers of innovation and growth. The ability to establish significant settlements led to the creation of some of history's most famous cities and civilizations in the first century BCE: the Nubian and Egyptian kingdoms, the Achaemenid Empire of Persia, the Greek and Hellenistic states, the Qin and Han states in what is now China, the Roman Empire surrounding the Mediterranean, and the Mauryan and Gupta states in what is now India.[52]

The histories of these "ancient" or "classical" times are replete with examples of wealth and power of the great cities and the threats posed by foreigners. The concept of the "barbarian"—the odd-looking foreigner, baying at the gates of the city—featured prominently as threats to civilization in ancient folklore and political discourse. Cities and towns developed gates and walls to protect themselves from outsiders. The term "barbarian" referred to one who did not speak Greek, and it came to refer to the general inferiority of outsiders.[53]

A close look at history, however, shows that "barbarian" populations were often essential for the growth and maintenance of these civilizations.[54] The Mesopotamian, Persian, Indian, and Chinese civilizations coexisted autonomously with an amorphous buffer of nomadic barbarians between them. They would extend their loosely defined frontiers through emigration into the peripheral areas, or their territory would contract when these migrants could no longer be sufficiently accommodated and incorporated into the civilization.[55] The frontiers of civilization were geographically and administratively vague; nevertheless, this cyclical pattern of expansion and contraction produced "indistinct frontiers and polyethnic social composition" within the empires.[56] It also served as the basis for technological and cultural borrowing among civilizations: military technologies would often be developed by borrowing from other civilizations through encounters with nomadic barbarians shared by them all.[57]

Although these civilizations were polyethnic, laws and rights were unevenly applied on the basis of ethnicity. Certain groups would work in particular occupations, and slaves often served as a primary source of labor. Rey Koslowski observes, however, that "some cities became so dependent on slavery for replenishing their populations that the slaves eventually took over political control."[58] Although history is sometimes presented as a "clash of civilizations," these civilizations tell a story of constant movement and engagement providing the "oxygen" for innovation and development.

By 500 CE, major routes facilitated commerce and migration between the principal population centers. Well-traveled interregional routes included the Silk Road, which connected the Mediterranean and Black Seas to the Huang He Valley in northern China; the south Asia route, linking southern China with Bengal; and the cross-Sahara routes connecting the

Niger basin with the Mediterranean. In the Mediterranean and Red Seas and Indian and Pacific Oceans, boats played a key role in ferrying cargo and people.

The energy running through the dynamic corridor between Mesopotamia and China gradually pushed these arterial trade networks even farther into Europe, Southeast Asia, and sub-Saharan Africa. By 300 CE, camel-riding pastoralists and traders were connecting West Africa with the Mediterranean—they carried gold, copper, and sometimes slaves into the north. The wealth and traffic along these trade routes eventually fostered the growth of cities and states where farmers had settled to produce sorghum and millet.[59] Near the end of the millennium, the trading empire of Kanem had developed near Lake Chad, and the Wagoudu (or Ghana) Empire emerged near contemporary Mali and Mauritania.

The development of the Silk Road trade routes corresponded with the consolidation of vast empires between 400 and 200 BCE. Prior to this time, merchants faced significant threats of banditry along trade routes. An increased tempo of long-distance trade required the security that was provided by large Eurasian states and the nomadic barbarians in between. The Qin and Han dynasties in China, the Mauryan Empire in India, the Greek Empire of Alexander the Great, and the Parthian and Roman states helped to provide the stable political order necessary for a new era of cross-civilizational trade. As Bentley notes, "Beliefs, values, and cultural traditions traveled the silk roads alongside the merchants and ambassadors who opened them."[60] The Han Empire sent Sima Qian as an imperial envoy to western Asia, and he returned with reports about military technologies, agriculture, and trade possibilities. Emperor Ashoka of Maurya sent representatives to Greece to spread Buddhism and gather knowledge about the Hellenic kings.[61]

Patrick Manning has called the expansion of trade among these states and empires between 1000 BCE and 500 CE a "commercial revolution."[62] Long-distance trade and travel fostered the transformation of commerce from informal exchange into rudimentary systems that are now familiar elements of modern economies: money, specialized merchants, organized marketplaces, ports, loans and credit, and commercial taxes. States also funded the infrastructure of canals, roads, bridges, and ferries necessary for more efficient trade. In the Mediterranean, maritime commerce between 300 BCE and 200 CE drove technical progress in shipping, scales, warehouses, and dock facilities, which allowed for long-distance seafaring trade to expand.[63] Families from particular ethnic groups, like Armenians, Jews, and Mandé-speaking West Africans, forged long-distance trading diasporas. Languages like Greek and Aramaic spread far beyond their home communities because of their utility as common trading languages. As Manning notes, "new ideas came not only from geniuses and brilliant inventors, but also from the commerce of ideas and the linkage of innovations in the course of daily life."[64]

Whereas nomad tribesmen often carried military technology between cities, long distance traders were more knowledgeable and socially embedded. As such, they transported influential cultural and political ideas. These traders "moved back and forth between regions of high and low skills, and in doing so they tended to spread skills more uniformly."[65] Universal religions, such as Buddhism and Islam, often spread through trade routes. The migration of religious missionaries, secular teachers, and medical experts spread great spiritual and ethical traditions that, among other things, addressed new social and moral problems associated with the large-scale organization of society.[66]

The period between 800 BCE and 200 BCE is now widely known as the "Axial Age," so named by Karl Jaspers, who described the simultaneous emergence of universal religions within the great agrarian civilizations of Mesopotamia, Persia, China, and India. In urban and imperial societies, new religions promoted social order with abstract moral principles and codes. Religion and society developed through dynamic interaction. During this historical window, Socrates and Plato emerged in Greece, Buddha appeared in India, Confucius and Lao Tzu in China, Zoroaster in Persia, and the Hebrew Prophets in Palestine. Jaspers remarks on the similarity in the thought of these religions and in the lives of their founders. As he famously argued, "the spiritual foundations of humanity were laid simultaneously and independently. . . . And these are the foundations upon which humanity still subsists today."[67] The emergence of these faiths also gave rise to a new class of religious scholars, many of whom traveled to teach and study. Many Indian merchants were Buddhist, and the nomads at trading outposts they visited along their journeys often embraced Buddhism, planting the seed for the later spread of the religion into China.[68]

While the Mesoamerican region still remained disconnected from Eurasia and Africa, the first civilization began to develop there between 1200 BCE and 400 CE, with many similar patterns to the early Eurasian agrarian civilizations. Within the central region of modern Mexico, the Olmecs established city-temple complexes within an area irrigated by the Coatzacoalcos River basin. The production and distribution of food permitted the development of social complexity, and an elite class emerged. An extensive trading network in the area allowed these elites to accumulate valuable artifacts made of jade and obsidian that were mined as far afield as modern Guatemala.

Social and scientific innovations developed by the Olmecs, such as human sacrifice, a calendar, the famous Mesoamerican ballgame, writing, and the invention of zero, traveled to other surrounding cultures and later civilizations. Some persisted long after the Olmec culture died around 400 BCE. Olmec artistic renditions of a feathered serpent God are the earliest appearance of what would become a widespread religious figure in pre-Columbian civilization.

Throughout the development of agrarian civilizations and the emergence of the first states and empires, borders were porous, and cross-cultural encounters were intermittent but far from uncommon. Cross-cultural interaction was a primary stimulus for the growth of commerce, the spread of ideas and religion, and the advancement of civilizations. This interaction was not yet happening on a massive scale, however—it was primarily limited to nomads and occupation-specific migrants, such as soldiers, merchants, seafarers, religious teachers, and ambassadors. Innovations often passed through multiple people before crossing civilization thresholds. As such, the pace of "collective learning" across cultures was still relatively slow. Wars, conquest, and the quickening pace of commerce would progressively dismantle the geographical and social barriers that remained between peoples. In societies open to new influences, the increasing flow of information would challenge conventional wisdom and stimulate economic growth and social transformation.

Empire and Conquest

While the relationship between conquest and civilization has been ambivalent throughout history, war has often led to the expansion of political dominions and the increased movement of migrants, goods, and ideas within these new territories. Between 500 and 1500 CE, the Chinese dynasties and Islamic caliphates extended their control over much of Eurasia and North Africa, together opening new possibilities for long-distance trade and the cross-cultural transmission of ideas.[69] The Mongol invasions during the thirteenth century CE—and the subsequent Mongol Empire—shattered the social and geographical obstacles that had limited contact between the Chinese civilization and those in the Middle East, Europe, and Africa.

The military migrants at the helm of these expanding empires accelerated the transmission of ideas and technology across cultures, laying the foundations for modern navigation, mathematics, and even art. At the dawn of the second millennium, the "globalization of science, technology, and mathematics was changing the nature of the old world," notes Amartya Sen, and "the principal currents of dissemination then were typically in the opposite direction to what we see today."[70] The Roman Empire had fallen in Europe, and innovation and learning between 500 and 1500 CE was primarily centered in the Islamic world. The later "rise of the West" depended on the transmission of these new ideas and technologies across civilizational frontiers.

Following the Prophet Muhammad's death in 632 CE, horse- and camel-mounted Arab armies launched a massive conquest of territory that would eventually stretch from Egypt and Mesopotamia to today's Iran and Afghanistan. The Islamic Caliphate encompassed a territory as large as that once conquered by Alexander the Great, and Arabs moved into major cities to establish Islamic rule.[71] Successive Arab conquests brought about cultural changes associated with the spread of Islam, and Arab elites and the Arabic language exerted a unifying influence throughout the region.[72]

By the eighth century CE, the Abbasid Caliphate had established Islam as the core civilization for the entire "Old World."[73] Drawing from the knowledge within its extensive territory, the intellectual achievements of the Roman, Indian, Chinese, Persian, Egyptian, Greek, and Byzantine civilizations became the focus of Islamic scholarship. This "Golden Age" of Islamic civilization drew the cultural resources of the world into an age of discovery and advancement in science, medicine, and mathematics. Positional value notation was adapted from the Indians in the creation of Arabic numbers (which are still used today), and Chinese inventions like the compass passed through the Arabs to Europe.

Trade routes linking Europe, Africa, and Asia became increasingly significant during the Abbasid Caliphate. Islam spread widely through trade, establishing Muslim populations where Arab armies never trod—such as Indonesia and China, where the world's largest Muslim populations currently live.[74] The improved security of long-distance trade routes under the Caliphate led to the expansion of trade diasporas, among the most important of which was the Jewish *Radaniyya*, which means "those who know the way" in Persian—the dominant trade language. The Radanites shared a single culture and controlled a system of trade that extended from Europe to China, lasting until nomadic Tatars from Asia began to imperil the overland routes to China in the early ninth century.[75]

It was not only merchants who traveled the trade routes within the Muslim realm; soldiers, slaves, administrators, diplomats, pilgrims, missionaries, and refugees also flowed between India, the Mediterranean, and Africa.[76] The increased tempo of movement among regions spread new crops, including staples, like wheat and sorghum; vegetables, like spinach and eggplant; and tropical fruits, such as lemon, lime, banana, and mango. Such crops could be planted in hot weather, which allowed land in the Mediterranean, Africa, and southwest Asia to acquire an extra growing season during the summer. The increased agricultural yields improved peoples' diet within the Caliphate and led to significant increases in the populations of Baghdad, Merv, Nishapur, Isfahan, Basra, and Damascus.[77]

The ascent of Islamic civilization increasingly brought it into cultural and military contact with the expansionist Chinese dynasties. The rise of China in the first millennium was propelled by the Tang Dynasty, which ruled between 618 and 917 CE. The Tang restored political unity to China's fractured regions, and they established the rule of law, developed a system of public administration, and extended the Great Canal of China. While the canal system was initially intended to promote rice paddy irrigation, its use by small-scale traders—many borrowing bazaar trading techniques from the Middle East—led to the expansion of a market-based economy.[78]

To secure the Silk Road trading routes and subdue Inner Asian nomads, the Tang Dynasty conscripted hundreds of thousands of men into a professional army to enlarge China's territory and sphere of influence. Allied with Turkic nomads, the Chinese military extended its reach into

Tibet and regions north of modern Kashmir. The western expansion of Chinese territory brought these cultures into intimate contact with innovations from China. In fact, the transmission of Chinese papermaking into the West is traced to contact associated with the Battle of Talas in 751 BCE between the Abbasid Caliphate and the Tang Dynasty.

The meeting of these two dynasties on the battlefield brought together powers that together controlled territory from modern Mauritania to North Korea. Curtin observes that "the long reach of Tang control to the west made it possible for many foreigners to visit China, including Muslims, Jews, and Nestorian Christians from India and Mesopotamia."[79] The simultaneous rise of the Abbasids and the Tang opened new possibilities for travel from Asia to North Africa, and at the height of its power, the Tang court received ambassadors and tribute from Persia, Arabia, and Antioch.

A series of battles waged by Genghis Khan between 1206 and 1227 CE ultimately served to demolish the remaining barriers within Eurasia. In their rapid conquest of territory roughly the size of the African continent, the Mongols relied upon Turkish soldiers, adapted Chinese military techniques, exploited local knowledge, and followed the historical routes of mounted warriors in the region. They produced the best attempt yet to conquer the world by conquering most of East Asia, half of the Islamic world, and virtually all of the Eurasian steppes.[80]

Following the death of Genghis Khan, his son Obedei extended these conquests to annex all of China and establish control of Korea, Persia, Russia, Hungary, and Poland. The security provided by the Empire allowed the Silk Road between Asia and Europe to flourish, and the volume of overland trade increased.[81] The Mongols accorded merchants a more dignified place in society than did their predecessors, and under the Mongol Empire, European merchants, missionaries, and diplomats traveled more than ever throughout Eurasia.[82] Some scholars trace the birth of the European Renaissance to the printing press, gunpowder, astronomy, musical instruments, paper money, art, and systems of government that were imported by the Mongols and spread to the West through European contact.[83]

On the other side of the earth, the rise of powerful civilizations was also connected to the processes of conquest and movement. The Aztec civilization was founded by several groups of Nahuatl-speaking migrants, likely from northern Mexico, whose long migration occupied a central place in their cosmology. The mythological cause of their migration was domination by tyrannical elites called the Azteca Chicomoztoca, and upon moving to central Mexico, they adopted the name *Mexica*— abandoning the Aztec name (with which they were later relabeled by historians).[84]

This group of migrants arrived in the Basin of Mexico between 1195 and 1248 CE, and their descendants established the famed city of Tenochtitlan in 1325.[85] They established alliances with the Texcoco and Tlacopan and soon subdued much of Mesoamerica under their rule, with the scattered city-states obliged to pay regular tribute to the Mexica. Before its fall to the Spanish conquistadors led by Hernán Cortés—about whom more will be said later—the migrant-led Mexica Empire was the wealthiest and more powerful in the region.

Commercialization and Convergence

Somewhere around 1000 CE, world history began to shift from a pattern of divergence—or separate development of civilizations—toward a pattern of global convergence. Up until this time, migration had virtually always meant a permanent departure from the home community. Around the turn of the millennium, however, the accelerating tempo of cross-civilization commerce was launching transoceanic journeys and satellite communities that were the first tremors of globalization.[86] Italian merchants in the West and Chinese ports in the East developed as two poles around which global trade diasporas gravitated. The rise of long-distance overland and sea trade, under the umbrella of imperial expansion in first-millennium Eurasia, set the stage for a "new era— roughly 1000 to 1350 CE—when trade increased dramatically and continued to bring people and civilizations into contact with each other."[87] In the process, relatively uniform economic institutions and practices spread across Eurasia, laying the foundations for a global market-based system of commerce.

At the dawn of the second millennium, the Mediterranean coast was a cosmopolitan mosaic of merchant communities. Constantinople, the Byzantine capital, served as a principal port on the north coast, where different merchant communities clustered. In 1060, Benjamin of Tuleda, a Spanish Jew, listed the origins of these communities as the following: Babylon, Sennar, Media, Persia, Egypt, Canaan, Russia, Hungary, and Spain, in addition to about 2,000 Jewish merchants.[88] The Muslim center of the Mediterranean trade was Alexandria, where the Byzantines, Turks, and Franks had their own trading diasporas, along with others from Yemen, Iraq, and Syria.[89] While these diverse communities tended to live in their separate localities, they are reported to have dealt with each other on cordial terms; despite social barriers, partnerships often flourished across the lines separating Hindu, Muslim, Jew, and Christian.[90]

During the fourteenth century, even England began to open up to foreign merchants and migrant labor. Edward I welcomed foreign merchants into England with the *Carta Mercatoria* ("the charter of the merchants"), which gave them legal protections and exemption from various transport tolls. In 1334, Edward III extended a special charter to the Hanseatic League, which linked trading posts in northern European port cities. Some local merchants resented the privileged treatment afforded to foreign traders, but the Crown welcomed the flow of goods and wealth brought by the League.

The treatment of the Hanseatic League reflected a broader trend in England, where immigration and trade were encouraged by the Crown, despite a measure of popular resentment toward foreigners. The English elite was awakening to the need to draw on expertise from continental Europe, which was increasingly developing and absorbing knowledge through cross-cultural contact with the Chinese and Muslim civilizations. Robert Winder remarks that "[i]n official circles immigration was encouraged. England was intent on remedying its palpable lack of industrial expertise, and the quickest way to do this was to inspire a brain drain from the continental centres of excellence."[91]

Growing commercialization created a tension within many civilizations between a people who increasingly self-identified as "homogenous" and the migrant traders, laborers, and moneylenders on whom the economy relied. The strangers that populated major cities were sometimes looked upon with mistrust and dislike, but they were rarely driven out because of the essential services they provided by connecting cities to the world trading network. McNeill reflects that "doing without such connections was costly, and few communities were really prepared to revert from commercial production to local self-sufficiency, with all the constrictions of supply and consumption that such a reversion implied."[92] Ultimately, these migrants performed the indispensible functions of intensifying and enlarging "the diversities of skills and culture that were characteristic of civilization itself."[93]

The pace of trade and cross-cultural contact in the Mediterranean drove convergence toward similar commercial practices in both Muslim and Christian ports. One example is the widespread use of checks—where a banker would pay money held on account for a third party. The origins of the term are Arabic (*sakk*), although the practice was carried from Roman Palestine to Byzantium, and then to Egypt.[94] These trade practices spread farther as the intra-European trade connected with Muslim-managed trade networks throughout the Middle East and Indian Ocean. Commercial links, observes McNeill, "tied all the diverse peoples of the ecumene [civilized world] more and more closely together between the eleventh and the fifteenth centuries."[95]

The accelerating pace of Mediterranean trade was accompanied by greater risk of raids on valuable cargo. In this climate, the navy-backed Venetian shippers leveraged their coercive guarantee to slowly dominate trade from the late tenth century. What began as a merchant diaspora grew by the early thirteenth century into a trading-post empire with control over key ports throughout the Mediterranean. Venetian shippers provided transportation for Roman Catholic soldiers in the Fourth Crusade, which eventually toppled the Byzantine Empire in 1204 and allowed the Italians to capture ports in Greece, Acre, and the Black Sea. With these ports, the Italians established new contacts with overland traders traveling on the Silk Road to China. The increasing strength of Italy and the Holy Roman Empire marked the beginnings of the slow ascent of western European civilization.[96] Italy's trading empire would provide the economic underpinning, the cross-cultural resources, and the artistic and intellectual stimuli to foster a culture that would eventually produce the Renaissance.[97]

Long-distance trade across the Asian continent was also shifting from slow and risky overland routes to swift seafaring passage. Advances in maritime technology opened the way for bulk commodities to be transported between East and West. The caravans trekking across the Silk Road were usually restricted to high-value and low-bulk items, such as aromatics and spices. Now, Venetian galleys, Indian dhows, and Chinese junks—all appearing around the twelfth century—could transport hundreds of tons of cargo, such as textiles, spices, pepper, timber, sugar, rice, and salt.[98] The spread of the Chinese magnetic compass also allowed these ships to navigate more easily and accurately. As the Mongol empire deteriorated in the late thirteenth century, maritime trade provided the most secure means to transport goods across Eurasia.

Under the Ming Dynasty in China, maritime trade grew rapidly until the mid-fifteenth century. Chinese trading settlements were established around Southeast Asia, along the coast of Java, and in Malay, Sumatra, Timor, and the Philippines. Merchant diasporas proliferated among islands and towns serving as key ports in the trade between Persia, Africa, India, and China. Thirty to forty stone-built towns could soon be found dotted along the African coastline from Somalia to Zimbabwe, where Persian and Arab merchants shipped and traded gold, silver, and slaves. An important trading center, which connected merchants from the Indian Ocean, Southeast Asia, and China, developed in the strategically located town of Malacca (in modern Malaysia).

Founded in the fourteenth century by a Hindu prince, Malacca emerged as a key commercial city by virtue of its secure location (at the end of a narrow strait) and the enlightened policies of its rulers. Other port cities sought to take advantage of their location by providing security for maritime merchants and taxing them heavily. In Malacca, however, political neutrality and low duties (in addition to protection against piracy) were offered as a way to attract merchants. Initially ruled by Hindus, Malacca later became Muslim, helping to spread the religion throughout Malaysia and Indonesia. As a Sultanate, the city attracted Muslim, Indian, and Chinese merchants. A list of Malaccan residents from the early 1500s shows people from nearly three dozen cities—from Cairo, Ethiopia, Armenia, Java, Siam, Gujarat, China, and the Maldives, among others. As this cosmopolitan mélange illustrates, the Indian Ocean and Southeast Asia formed "a zone of ecumenical trade . . . larger than any that had been created before."[99]

Similar to what occurred in the Mediterranean trade, close contact between migrant communities drove convergence in commercial practices. One such practice was collective price bargaining, where a ship's captain would bargain on behalf of all of the merchants on board. The accelerating pace of cross-cultural trade also attuned more general patterns of behavior in the region toward trade, augmenting "the everyday routines of life" through the growth of specialization and the spread of the price mechanism.

While Europeans would be the first to open up the Atlantic route to the Americas, in the early fifteenth century, the Chinese first established contact over the Indian and Pacific Oceans. Between 1403 and 1433, Admiral Zheng He, under the patronage of the Ming Emperor Zhu Di, undertook a series of explorations with fleets that at times numbered up to 300 ships, carrying 20,000 men. These sailed from China, through Southeast Asia across India to Eastern Africa, and some accounts even suggest that he rounded the Cape of Good Hope almost a century before Bartolomeu Dias did—heading in the opposite direction.[100] The ships used by Zheng He were about ten times the average size of the largest ships then built in Europe.

On these voyages, the admiral established trade relations, created practical maps and sailing directions, and sought out exotic goods for the emperor. The admiral himself was an outsider to the Chinese Confucian elite—he was a Muslim of Mongol ancestry, a migrant. Zhang He was known for his diplomatic skills, and during his fourth voyage, he brought emissaries from about thirty states to the court of the emperor. After the emperor passed away, however, his successors stopped these ambitious ocean journeys.[101]

Scholars have speculated about why China would have stopped its explorations only decades before the great voyages of Columbus and Vasco da Gama. The death of the emperor ushered a new conservative Confucian elite into power, who were reluctant to support expensive and ostentatious overseas journeys. Zhang He's Mongol origins and Muslim religion also cast him as a foreigner, and the new officials distrusted things foreign. Perhaps more importantly, China's primary threat existed across the land frontier; with Japan still relatively weak, China saw less reason to dedicate resources to maritime power. According to McNeill, "the issue ... became a choice between an offensive as against a defensive military policy."[102]

The decision to turn inward would be a tragic mistake for China, foreshadowing its later eclipse by an increasingly powerful and innovative European civilization. While some scholars have emphasized geographical or material reasons for Europe's ascent,[103] others have located the reasons for China's decline in its cultural insularity and progressive isolation from developments in the rest of the world.[104] Despite China's exposure to foreign influences during the height of its economic power, a widespread perception of the superiority of Chinese culture held back social and economic innovation. Technologies developed in China, such as gunpowder, the compass, and the printing press, were used to emphasize stability. Europe, meanwhile, was rapidly assimilating foreign ideas and technologies drawn through accelerating cross-cultural contact. Whereas the printing press advanced social change in Europe by popularizing novel ideas, in China it was used to propagate ancient Chinese thought. Chinese economic decline, relative to Europe, would still be centuries away, but the same cultural forces that halted Zhang He's explorations withheld China from the sources of economic growth and social transformation.

MIGRATION AND HUMANITY

Human migration tells the story of our essential oneness as a species and the great diversity of human communities. Every person can trace his or her genetic lineage to Africa, and yet our different appearances and social habits speak to the distinct physical and cultural adaptability of people. As our ancestors spread out across the earth, they innovated slowly in response to their environments, developing basic technologies that were necessary for survival. The emergence of civilization only 5,000–6,000 years ago began to draw people from scattered settlements into a dense pattern of complex social life. The first civilizations, like social magnets, drew people from the hinterlands into the life of the cities—as workers, merchants, traders, and administrators—and propelled city-dwellers into the frontier regions to find resources and trading partners.

The rise of civilizations quickened the pace of exchange and the commerce of ideas and technologies. As increasingly complex civilizations developed in Eurasia, trading networks, traveling religious teachers, and conquering armies broke down the frontiers separating distant empires. Valuable military technologies and commercial and social practices passed through these brief and limited cross-cultural encounters. Carried by the great forces of religion, war, and commerce, migrants connected human communities from eastern China to West Africa.

By the fifteenth century, cross-civilization trade networks had fueled the growth of Chinese and European fleets of ships capable of long voyages. China appeared to be on the cusp of reuniting the human race when Zhang He undertook increasingly ambitious journeys at the service of the Ming Dynasty. The termination of these adventures, however, would closely coincide with European explorations for a seafaring route into the Indian Ocean trading system. These journeys eventually shifted the balance of economic power toward Europe and prefigured the development of an increasingly global economy.

2

♦

Global Migrations: Toward a World Economy

The previous chapter narrated the pioneering role of migrants over the long arc of history, from the emergence of modern humans to the first intimations of globalization in the early second millennium. We now turn to look at the global networks of production, trade, and migration that grew in scale and density following the European "Age of Exploration" (after 1492) to reconnect human communities around the world. Some communities tried to turn inward, attempting to shield themselves from foreign contact, but the forceful intensity of movement around the world assured the rise of a new global economy.

In 1492, with Columbus's successful voyage across the Atlantic, it was opened as a new highway for people, goods, and ideas.[1] The growing complexity of maps from the fifteenth and sixteenth centuries shows the rapid development of a worldwide system of trade and production. "The breakthrough of the 1490s," Felipe Fernandez-Armesto comments, "was a concentrated phenomenon, in the course of which a handful of voyages transformed the Atlantic into a potential arena of long-range cultural transmission."[2]

The intensifying series of encounters and interactions between Europeans and the rest of the world opened a new era of economic growth and global inequality. As Karl Marx observed, "World trade and the world market date from the sixteenth century, and from then on the modern history of Capital starts to unfold."[3] The extension of European economic and military power around the world produced massive voluntary and forced migrations of people. European plantations, mines, and markets were connected by a global network of human movement.

The development of modern capitalism between the nineteenth and twentieth centuries generated newly disruptive "push" and "pull" factors that launched millions of migrants from villages to cities, from hinterlands to coastal regions, and from port cities across oceans. People were often compelled or coerced to move under circumstances that were not of their own choosing. The movement of people was central to the process of "creative destruction" that revolutionized the economic and political structure of the world, binding humanity into an integrated (though uneven) global economy.

THE AGE OF EXPLORATION

Gunpowder Expeditions

Only decades after the Ming rulers terminated Zhang He's great voyages, the increasingly lucrative seafaring trade from Europe helped to fund exploratory journeys across the Atlantic. Bankers and merchants derived financial rewards from Portuguese contact with and increasing control of gold- and slave-trading West African ports, and the idea of finding the source of the spice trade was sufficiently enticing for some to fund open-ended voyages.[4] Christopher Columbus's discovery that there was gold in the Americas and the suggestion that indigenous people could be evangelized encouraged the support of both Church and State for continued European journeys.

Less than thirty years after Columbus's voyage, Hernán Cortés led an expedition into the Mexican highlands to bring about the Spanish conquest of the Aztec civilization. Although Cortés is known as a controversial conquistador, his most notable legacy is arguably that of closing another gap between great civilizations:

> Until [Cortés's expedition] Spanish outposts in the New World had been of marginal importance: only modestly productive, barely significant for the lives of most people in Eurasia. Cortes put them in touch with one of the world's most populous and productive regions. The great belt of rich sedentary civilizations that stretched

across Eurasia could now begin to exchange culture ... with those in the Americas. A line of communications—still imperfect, still precarious—was beginning to bind the world together.[5]

Tragedy accompanied this historical accomplishment of connecting together the civilizations of America and Eurasia, as American populations were decimated by forced labor and the spread of disease.

Shortly after Columbus's historic westward journey, Vasco da Gama led a much longer voyage east around the Cape of Good Hope into the Indian Ocean. He left Lisbon in July 1497, and by the following year he had established contact with busy ports in East Africa. Da Gama returned to Lisbon with only half of his men and little in the way of exotic goods. The voyage, however, was epochal; it established a more permanent link between Europe and India.[6] In the five years after da Gama returned, 7,000 men were sent out in trading expeditions involving as many as thirteen ships.[7] Initially, they were forced to adapt to the existing framework of trade, serving regional markets and suppliers.[8]

In their effort to dominate Indian Ocean trade, the Portuguese engaged in numerous violent struggles.[9] Eventually, a militarized European presence in the Indian Ocean and East African coast initiated a shift in African trade away from the Islamic world and toward European goods and markets.[10] This shift was accompanied by a global move away from "peaceful mercantile protocols of trade" toward "armed warrior–merchant rule" that enabled the ascendancy of Europe.[11] The "Age of Exploration" became the "Age of Gunpowder Empires."

More voyages of the sixteenth and seventeenth century would extend the reach of European power: Ferdinand Magellan, Jacques Cartier, John Cabot, Giovanni da Verrazzano, James Cook, and others laid the foundations for the development of global commercial networks. Explorers' voyages were supported by early capitalists—financiers, merchants, and entrepreneurs—who produced a system of exchange that linked markets in sub-Saharan Africa, Eurasia, the Americas, and later Melanesia, Australia, and Polynesia into a worldwide network of trade and production.

European trade settlements soon dotted the North American and South Asian coasts. England established colonies in Virginia and Massachusetts, the Dutch did the same in New York, and France colonized Quebec. The Dutch and English East India Companies (established around 1600) served as continent-spanning mercantile organizations for the commercial interests of the two countries in Java (Indonesia), Malaysia, and Ceylon (Sri Lanka). European traders, often organized into large and well-armed companies, increasingly wrested control of large-scale commerce.[12] They slowly altered patterns of production and consumption through their accelerating trade in Indian indigo and cotton goods; Chinese silks, tea, and porcelains; Arabian coffee; and Persian carpets.[13] The introduction of hardy American crops (including maize, peanuts, and potatoes) into China, Europe, and Africa changed diets and led to population booms.[14]

The globe-spanning reach of European traders and military was soon matched by developments in international law, which defended the free movement of people. Francesco de Vitoria (1492–1546), considered by many to be the founder of international law, wrote that "[i]t was permissible from the beginning of the world, when everything was in common, for anyone to set forth and travel wheresoever he would." Similar ideas appeared in the works of other great jurists of the time, including Hugo Grotius (1583–1645), Samuel von Pufendorf (1634–1692), and Christian Wolff (1679–1754), who argued that the state possessed a duty to allow the transit (and sometimes residence) of migrants.[15]

The networks created by migrant explorers and traders brought into circulation an unprecedented amount of wealth, as well as crops, technologies, and people. Whereas the hub of commercial exchange was previously located in the Middle East, Europe was now situated at the center of new flows of information, people, and goods—within Europe, and with Asia and the New World. By repositioning itself at the heart of the global exchange system, Europe benefited from a "torrent of new information," which made it "a sort of clearinghouse for geographical and cultural lore" that opened new opportunities for innovation.[16] Europe drew on tremendous cultural resources from around the world to propel its Renaissance. While European production remained relatively traditional—it had not yet reached the scale and sophistication of the industrial revolution—the new global system presaged accelerating innovation and capitalist development, which would draw virtually the whole population of the world into its vortex.

Diseases

The transmission of diseases has accompanied cross-cultural contact throughout history. The initial biological exchange was often terribly destructive and tragic. Although seldom more than a few hundred people were engaged in European maritime expeditions, these journeys often brought infectious diseases (such as smallpox, measles, influenza, and typhus) to the Americas, Pacific Islands, and parts of Africa. The result was a devastating decline in indigenous populations from about 100 million in 1500 CE to fewer than 10 million in 1650 CE.[17] "Diseases introduced [by] Europeans," writes Jared Diamond, "spread from tribe to tribe far in advance of the Europeans themselves, killing an estimated 95 percent of the pre-Columbian Native American population."[18]

Soon after Columbus landed on Hispaniola in 1493, indigenous people began to die from smallpox passed through limited contact with his crew. The spread of the virus led the population to decline from about one million people to only ten thousand. In Cuba, smallpox ravaged the population; two-thirds of the survivors of this epidemic were killed by a subsequent measles outbreak in 1529. The Mississippi chiefdoms, some of the most populous and highly organized indigenous societies of North America, were eliminated in the sixteenth century with the spread of new infectious diseases.[19]

The devastation wrought by new diseases was not limited to indigenous Americans. In 1713, a smallpox epidemic in Southern Africa decimated the Khoi and San people. Many of the survivors subsequently abandoned their pastoral and nomadic lifeways to work in wage labor.[20] Following Captain Cook's exploration of the Polynesian Islands in the 1770s, the population of Hawaii rapidly declined because of exposure to European diseases. Cook reported that the population decreased from approximately 500,000 people to 50,000. In Fiji, shipwrecked European sailors brought infectious diseases when they landed in 1806: Paul Gauguin, the artist, wrote in 1891, "day by day the race vanishes, decimated by the European diseases."[21] The fact that Europeans appeared to be immune to these diseases had a demoralizing effect on indigenous populations, who became more compliant and dependent on the new arrivals.[22]

Europeans also encountered deadly tropical diseases in their explorations, and the threat of disease shaped and limited European settlement in new territories.[23] "Early British expectations for settlement in West Africa were dashed by very high mortality among early settlers, about half of whom would be expected to die in the first year," note Acemoglu, Johnson, and Robinson.[24] "In the first year of the Sierra Leone Company (1792–1793), 72 percent of the European settlers died . . . in 1805, 87 percent of Europeans died during the overland trip from Gambia to Niger, and all the Europeans died before completing the expedition."[25] Dramatic press reports ensured that the risk of disease was widely known among potential migrants. In fact, the early settlers of Plymouth Colony in America initially considered migrating to Guyana but changed their minds because of the high mortality rates due to disease. Similarly, the British government sent convicts to Australia rather than Gemane Island on the Gambia River, because of the high risk of disease in the Gambia.[26] The inhospitality of West Africa provided opportunities for the relatives of African slaves to later move to Sierra Leone and Liberia.[27]

Ending the biological isolation of parts of the world would eventually make it possible for people to travel easily between countries and climates—and it would also enable the rapid spread of global pandemics—but during the sixteenth and seventeenth centuries, the devastation wrought by disease had wide-ranging consequences. The traumatic depopulation of the Americas opened the way for the gradual European settlement and domination of the continent. In Africa, the lower indigenous susceptibility to European diseases (because of historical contact) and the inhibiting presence of yellow fever and malaria meant that African populations and culture retained their integrity in the absence of overwhelming European domination.[28] However, it also meant that African slaves were preferred to European convict and indentured labor in the Caribbean, because of their resistance to tropical diseases.[29] Until the 1830s, forced African migrants outnumbered both free and indentured Europeans in the Americas.[30]

Between 500 BCE and 1200 CE, Eurasia experienced a process of what epidemiologists term "viral reservoir integration" as contact between civilizations intensified; most of the "historically significant biological exchange" in Afro-Eurasia had occurred by 1400 CE.[31] The "pathocenosis" (or the codevelopment of disease and populations, including their immunity) in Eurasia was quite separate from that which occurred in the Americas centuries later. While the biological exchange between European explorers and American populations had devastating effects, the result was the unification of "every nook and cranny of the humanly habitable earth into a biologically interactive unit."[32] The first step often had disastrous consequences for indigenous people. It meant that as economic growth in Europe accelerated, wealth was increasingly mobilized to fund productive enterprises and trade in distant lands decimated by diseases brought by the earlier military and merchant invaders.[33]

IMPERIALISM AND COERCION

Merchants and missionaries soon followed the adventurers, who mapped the global ocean and land travel routes. As European traders extended their global reach, they occupied land and crowded out powerful trading competitors, inevitably calling upon state support to protect their interests. The influence of mercantilist thinking led states to promote exports, limit imports, and seek to accumulate precious metals. European powers increasingly established political and administrative control over the new sources of their wealth. By the mid-eighteenth century, the Age of Exploration initiated by Columbus had grown into a world ringed by European political and economic power.

Impelled by the mercantilist quest for gold and silver accumulation, European powers in South America used superior military technology and Machiavellian tactics to conquer the Aztec and Inca civilizations in Central and South America. As these empires fell, their Spaniard conquerors assumed control over their populations, which rapidly became at least superficially Christian. Indigenous labor was quickly mobilized (often coercively) for Spanish architectural and commercial projects. Baroque churches were built and mines and plantations established in Mexico and Brazil. Meanwhile, along the Brazilian coast and on Caribbean islands, new plantations had already been started through the use of indigenous slave labor. The exposure of these slaves to diseases, however, rapidly depleted the workforce. A similar process of depopulation was affecting the wage labor workforce in Peru and Mexico.

In the villages, the Spaniards compelled more of the population into wage labor by offering credit to villagers, which eventually turned into debt bondage that could be worked off only in the mines or on plantations. On the coast, however, different rules applied. John Hawkins, an Englishman, brought the first shipment of African slaves in 1562–1563. Sugar cultivation expanded to become increasingly lucrative in the seventeenth century, and African slaves were coerced to supply the necessary labor.[34]

On the other side of the world, Portuguese, Dutch, and then English traders increasingly dominated trading networks in the Indian Ocean. Despite the tense relationship between Muslims and Christians—particularly in the wake of the expulsion of Muslims from Iberia in 1496—new commercial relationships opened up technological, trade, and cultural exchange between civilizations.[35] Along the Indian coast, English traders organized commercial manufacturing of cotton, where few such entrepreneurs had previously succeeded because of strong craft guilds and heavy government taxation.

The Dutch introduced similar commercial operations in modern Indonesia, where coffee (from Arabia), tea (from China), and sugar cane (from India) were grown.[36] Companies were granted trade monopolies in particular regions of the world, and the Dutch East and West India Companies were two of the largest of such enterprises. They were "armed politico-commercial organizations of unprecedented scope and resources" in the scale of their operations and use of military power.[37] Around half of the soldiers and sailors employed by the Dutch East India Company in the seventeenth and eighteenth centuries, in fact, were not Dutch but from poor areas of Germany.[38] The accumulation of wealth in European centers—particularly in Antwerp and London—relied on the projection of coercive power around the world.

Extracting resources overseas increasingly required both military power and an effective administrative apparatus. The dawn of the industrial revolution in the late eighteenth century was accompanied by a growing demand for natural resources to feed economic growth in Europe. Mercantilist thinking declined in favor of the classical market-based economic theories by which states aimed to expand their production capacity and output through specialization and free trade, rather than to simply accumulate precious metals. The new economic logic drove European states to strengthen their control over foreign territories and increase their productivity. The development of colonialism was accompanied by massive labor migrations—free, coerced, and forced—that increasingly drove rural peasants into wage (or forced) labor to meet the demands of plantations, mines, and industry at home or overseas.

UNFREE MIGRATIONS: SLAVERY AND INDENTURED LABOR

The story of an emerging global economy can be narrated through the unprecedented movement of people across continents and oceans. The pace of transatlantic migration accelerated between 1700 and 1900, driven by labor shortages in the old empires and new colonies. The role of coercion in labor recruitment and forced work gradually fell away, to be replaced by the ideal of free labor and, for a time, free migration. As David Northrup comments, the past two centuries have been characterized by "almost continuous raising of the threshold of acceptable labor conditions."[39]

The Rise and Fall of the Transatlantic Slave Trade

In the early fifteenth century, chattel slavery became a key component of an increasingly global economy. Slaves were another "commodity" bought and sold by specialized traders and transported over great distances. Slavery was not new—as the stories of the slaves of Egypt and of the Roman Empire attest—but maritime advances and the growth of British naval power enabled a sharp increase in the scale and impact of the systematic intercontinental transport of slaves. The African slave trade was not limited to the transatlantic routes. African slaves were increasingly transported across Africa and to the Middle East, Russia, around the Indian Ocean, and to China and the Pacific Rim (see table 2.1 and figure 2.1). Whereas men accounted for over 60 percent of the transatlantic slave trade, the trade within Africa itself and from northeast Africa to the Middle East and Arabia was predominantly female—African women were sold as domestics and concubines.

TABLE 2.1
TOTAL SLAVE EXPORTS FROM AFRICA, 1400–1900.

Slave trade	1400–1599	1600–1699	1700–1799	1800–1900	1400–1900
Transatlantic	230,516	861,936	5,687,051	3,528,694	10,308,197
Trans-Saharan	675,000	450,000	900,000	1,099,400	3,124,400
Red Sea	400,000	200,000	200,000	505,400	1,305,400
Indian Ocean	200,000	100,000	260,000	379,500	939,500
Total	1,505,516	1,611,936	7,047,051	5,512,994	15,677,497

Source: Nathan Nunn. 2008. "The Long-Term Effects of Africa's Slave Trade," *The Quarterly Journal of Economics* 123(1): 139–176, appendix, p. 20, table 1.

In the fifteenth century, slavery was mainly concentrated around the Mediterranean, drawing captives from Central Asia and the periphery of Europe. As the system grew, so did the brutality and suffering of the coerced individuals and their societies. By 1700, tens of thousands of Africans were being captured each year and transported in chains to the Caribbean, Brazil, and North America to working to produce cotton, coffee, sugar, tobacco, indigo, gold, and silver for an emerging world market.[40] More than ten million Africans had been brought to the New World by the end of the nineteenth century, with mortality rates averaging 12 percent during the Atlantic crossing.[41]

Once slaves arrived in the New World, they were frequently moved between plantations. Between 1800 and 1860, over a million slaves were moved from tobacco plantations on the mid-Atlantic seaboard of North America to newly established sugar and cotton plantations further south. Similarly large numbers of slaves that had been brought to work on the sugar plantations of Bahia, Brazil, were later moved farther south to establish coffee and other plantations.[42] Others escaped and moved or were freed, occasionally finding passage to Africa, but more often establishing independent settlements in Brazil and elsewhere.

The dramatic escalation of the transatlantic slave trade in the seventeenth and eighteenth centuries was related to other movements connected to Europe's ascendance. Economic growth in Europe drove colonizer migrations; these merchants and soldiers mobilized and controlled local labor for production; and the expansion of mines and plantations

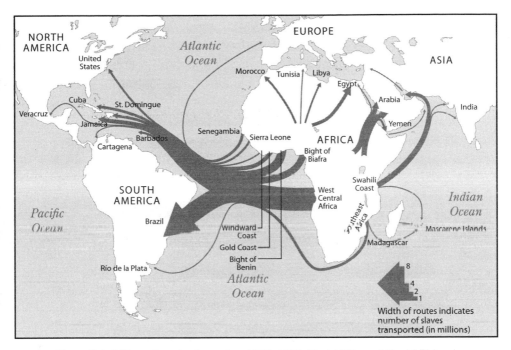

Figure 2.1. African slave trade routes, 1500–1900. David Eltis and David Richardson. 2009. *An Atlas of the Transatlantic Slave Trade.* New Haven, CT: Yale University Press.

generated demand for external labor.[43] This demand was initially met with a steady and increasing supply of slaves.

Once slave shipments started in the early seventeenth century, the high profitability of tobacco, cotton, and sugar plantations increasingly depended on slaves. Annual slave shipments increased fourfold between 1650 and 1800 (see figure 2.2).[44] In Africa, valuable European imports (such as cotton, salt, knives, brassware, and liquor) were offered as incentives for the creation of a highly organized system of slave-raiding, internal trade, and transportation in the West African states of Asante, Dahomey, Benin, and Oyo (in present-day Ghana, Benin, and Nigeria, respectively). The influx of flintlock firearms into Africa in the mid-seventeenth century gave slave raiders the tools of coercion to carry out their trade.[45]

The transatlantic slave trade was one element of a trade network that European powers used to ensure a balance of payments—that their imports would be roughly equivalent to their exports. Exported manufactured goods would be traded at African ports for slaves. Slaves would be

Number of slaves (thousands)

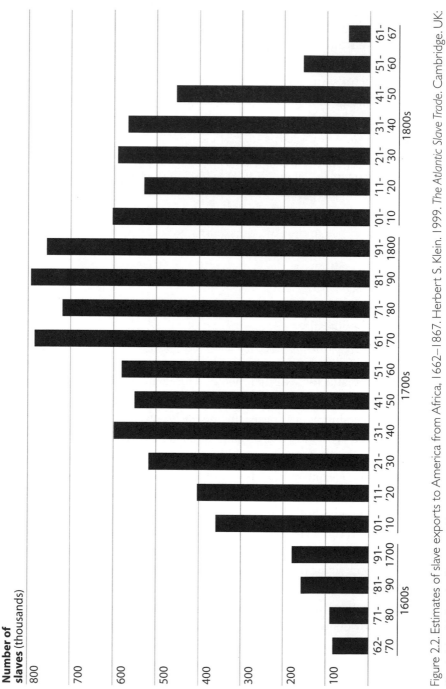

Figure 2.2. Estimates of slave exports to America from Africa, 1662–1867. Herbert S. Klein. 1999. *The Atlantic Slave Trade*. Cambridge. UK: Cambridge University Press, p. 208, appendix table A.1.

sold in the plantation regions of the Americas, and sugar, tobacco, and other agricultural goods would be shipped either to New England or to Europe. Rum from New England could then be traded for slaves. Or, alternatively, the agricultural produce could be returned to Europe and traded for more manufactures. These "triangular trade" routes fueled the growing economies of England and France, boosting development that would ignite the industrial revolution. "The comparative advantage enjoyed by England and France in manufactures during the eighteenth century," notes Barbara L. Solow, "was reinforced by the comparative advantage of slave labour over free labour in the production of certain tropical crops."[46]

The economic impacts of the transatlantic slave trade were devastating for Africa. The transatlantic slave trade moved more than 10 million African slaves to the Americas, making it the largest in history; the Roman Empire comes a distant second, having transported four to six million slaves over four centuries.[47] Slaves were usually exported from the most developed areas of Africa, but the internal warfare, raiding, and kidnapping that comprised the African supply of slaves has contributed to weak and politically fragmented states, ethnic fractionalization, and poor judicial institutions in affected modern African states.[48] The corrosive effect of the trade on social and political institutions in Africa has undermined the long-term economic performance of these areas.[49]

Britain's Role in Forced Migration

In 1713, with the Treaty of Utrecht, Spain's leading role in the slave trade was given to Britain. Over the next century, British traders in over 11,000 ships transported more than two and a half million slaves.[50] The profits generated from the slave trade and the plantations brought new wealth to Britain, generating a new class of wealthy traders, as well as a range of new products, which as production increased became entrenched in the British diet, such as sugar, potatoes, tea, coffee, and tobacco.[51]

Only a small fraction of the African slaves were brought to Britain—an estimated 40,000 by the 1770s—and although they were legally free in Britain, they were barred from engaging in work and therefore dependent on the bonded contracts with their employers.

The British Slave Trade Act of 1807 made the transportation of slaves on British ships illegal, but it was the Slavery Abolition Act of 1833 that banned slavery within the British Empire. The Abolition Act was the product of decades of political campaigning, which started in earnest with the formation in 1787 of the Society for Effecting the Abolition of the Slave Trade—primarily involving humanitarian-minded British Quakers and Anglicans. The Society used public meetings, newspaper articles, popular boycotts, and political lobbying to press their humanitarian message, best incarnated in their logo of a chained kneeling slave asking, "Am I not a man and a brother?"

Britain's economic dependence on slave labor was a major obstacle to the abolition of slavery within its empire. While abolitionists advanced economic arguments in favor of free labor, they were also careful to allay the fears of plantation owners. "The great problem to be solved in drawing up any plan for the emancipation of slaves in our colonies," wrote Lord Howick, a leading abolitionist, in 1832, "is to devise some mode of inducing them when relieved from the fear of the driver and his whip, to undergo the regular and continuous labor which is indispensable in carrying out the production of sugar."[52] The Slavery Abolition Act was accompanied by a provision allowing slaves to continue serving as "apprentices" (although essentially still in bondage), and a £20 million compensation package for plantation owners to help them transition to the use of free labor. Former slaves by and large left the plantations, eschewing offers of wages, and owners were left to begin recruiting from India and China.

While many historians in the twentieth century argued that the end of the slave trade was influenced by British economic decline, it is now generally accepted that rising social consciousness and political pressures to end slavery were far more important.[53] This pressure, however, gained strength from the economic imperatives of European industrial production, which required a free, mobile labor force that could not be provided by coercion.[54]

The anti-slave-trade campaign of the eighteenth and nineteenth centuries drew heavily from moral and political arguments about basic liberties and free labor in a market economy. Despite the continued profitability of slavery, the campaign skillfully used modern political propaganda to launch a moral crusade that eventually led Britain to

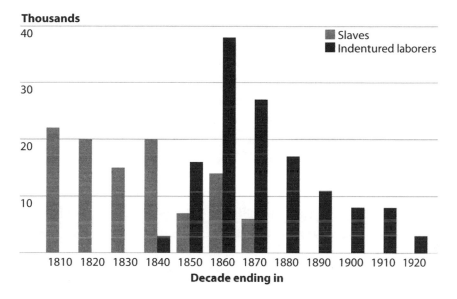

Thousands

Figure 2.3. Annual average slave and indentured labor imports (by thousands) into the Caribbean and Mascarenes, by decade, 1801–1810 to 1911–1920. David Northrup. 1995. *Indentured Labour in the Age of Imperialism: 1834–1922.* Cambridge, UK: Cambridge University Press, p. 21.

abandon the practice and then pressure other nations to abolish slavery.[55] The anti-slave-trade movement did not promote European equality with Africans; rather, it appealed to a widely held belief in the importance of free labor in a modern economy. The idea that labor should be free resonated with the beliefs of both workers and capitalists in Europe, who were in the throes of a modernizing economy and society based on wages and the ideal of self-determination.[56] As Britain first moved to abolish the slave trade, it then pressured other governments to abandon the practice, leading to higher slave prices and illegal slave trafficking. Plantation owners could sense the end of slavery, and they increasingly moved to locate new sources of inexpensive foreign labor (see figure 2.3).

Indentured Labor

In the early nineteenth century, indenture contracts were a relatively common way for poor Europeans to migrate to the Americas. A worker would accept a contract to work for an employer for a set number of years, in exchange for the employer paying certain expenses (often including passage, housing, food, clothing, and other essentials). The worker would be free after the period of work had been completed. Almost a quarter of the 2.6 million Europeans who moved to the New World before 1820 came under indenture.[57] In the mid- to late nineteenth century, the number of migrant indentured laborers—by then primarily from India and China—increased dramatically.

While the rise of international indentured labor coincided with the British abolition of slavery, other economic, technological, and social factors were also important. The falling cost and increased speed of ocean travel in the nineteenth century made it feasible to profitably recruit labor from halfway around the world. The West's "informal" empire of financial and commercial networks also meant that world trade became increasingly important to fueling economic growth in Europe.[58] The volume of world trade multiplied tenfold between 1850 and 1913.[59] China and India experienced rapid population growth and rising poverty, leading many people to search for work in cities and regional centers. From there, some made the leap to international migration. The growing global migration of indentured labor was only a portion of much greater local and regional movement.[60]

The enterprise of indentured labor continued to be driven by the same economic forces as slavery: the need for cheap foreign labor on European-held enterprises around the world. John X. Merriman, the Commissioner for Crown lands in the Cape Colony, wrote in 1876: "In the Cape, the government is called upon to survey mankind from China to Peru in the hope of creating and maintaining a cheap class of labourers who will thankfully accept the position of helots and not be troubled with the inconvenient ambition of bettering this condition."[61] The term "helots" describes the intermediate status of indentured laborers as somewhere between slavery and full citizenship. The mortality rates on ships transporting indentured laborers were similar to those of slaving ships; 17 percent of workers traveling to the West Indies in 1856 died en route.[62] Housing and health conditions were also poor, and heavy penal sanctions were used to discipline workers.[63]

The Recruitment of Indian Indentured Labor

The *Kangani* system, used to recruit Indian labor for nearby plantations in Ceylon (Sri Lanka), Burma, and Malaya (Malaysia), exemplified the cycle of bondage experienced by many indentured laborers. A headman, the *kangani*, would recruit a group of laborers from Indian villages when export prices for crops were high. Although the laborers recruited under this system were initially considered free, in practice they were bound to their employers through a cycle of cash advances and debt bondage.[61] Between 1852 and 1937, 1.5 million Indians traveled to Ceylon, 2 million to Malaya, and 2.5 million to Burma.[65] In Sri Lanka, the descendants of the Tamil population recruited during the nineteenth century still constitute the majority of the labor force in the highland tea plantations.

By the mid-nineteenth century, people were recruited from India and China to work three- to five-year indenture contracts in the Caribbean, Mauritius, Peru, South Africa, Australia, Hawaii, and Fiji (see figure 2.4). New technology and investments in sugar production and mining created new demand for labor; Western imperial power in India, China, and the Pacific Islands provided the means of recruitment; and the surge in population in these countries generated the supply. China's population had increased from 150 million in 1700 to 430 million in 1850, and rural overcrowding and internal conflicts were driving peasants to cities and overseas. India's population grew from 100 million to 185 million during the nineteenth century. The wage gaps between unskilled work at home and at overseas plantations were substantial. In 1870, an Indian laborer could make almost five times as much working in the West Indies, or nine times as much working in Hawaii.[66] A combination of desperation and ambition made workers more amenable to the offers of plantation labor recruiters, many of whom adopted unscrupulous practices.

Assisted and nonassisted migration from India played a major role in the development of sugar, tea, coffee, and other export industries in the British colonies. By 1945, about 80 percent of emigrants from India were agricultural laborers with little or no education.[67] The balance was made up of commercial migrants, such as merchants and financiers. Indians

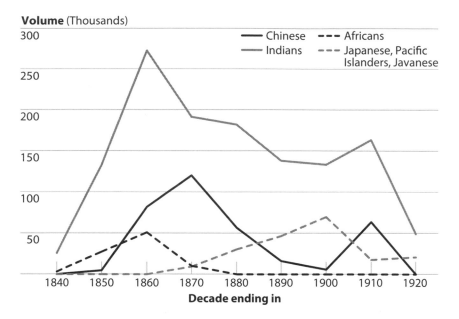

Volume (Thousands)

Legend:
— Chinese   - - - Africans
— Indians   - - - Japanese, Pacific Islanders, Javanese

Decade ending in

Figure 2.4. Gross migration of indentured workers by origin, 1840–1920. Northrup, 1995: 159–160, table A.1.

also proved invaluable in the clerical and technical services of colonial services, and Indian Sikhs were sought after for military duties and as caretakers.

Reports of abuse within the system of intercontinental labor recruitment led to political pressure for the abolition of the practice in European and source countries. In its early days, the trade was not effectively regulated, especially in China, where both European and Chinese recruiters used coercive and deceptive recruitment methods.[68] Kidnapping was also widely reported.[69] Even as the trade became more closely monitored, the line between voluntary and involuntary migration was blurred, and reports of abuses in China continued to spark controversy.[70] The trade was more regulated in India because of British colonial interests, and Indian migrants were disproportionately drawn from the margins of society— sometimes making the difficult conditions of work overseas a relative improvement over those at home.[71]

In the eighteenth and nineteenth centuries, international migrants were mobilized to build new transport infrastructure, including roads and bridges, railroads, trains and stations, ports and steamships, and canals.

Railroad construction began in England in the 1830s, and within a hundred years, railroads were being constructed on every continent, often by indentured laborers. Chinese workers built the links to the western states of North America; Indian workers built the railroad in East Africa; Irish workers the South African mainline and parts of the United States system; and Russian workers the Trans-Siberian network. As Chinese faced political obstacles to entry into Canada and the United States in the late nineteenth century, Japanese workers were brought in to replace them. Significant numbers of Japanese migrants moved to Brazil, Peru, the United States, and Canada in the late nineteenth century—as both indentured and free workers—after the 1868 Meiji Restoration opened Japanese borders for emigration.

Indentured workers were used by all the major colonial powers to work in over 40 countries, and the system only gradually came to an end in the early twentieth century.[72] It is estimated that 12 to 37 million people worked on indenture contracts between 1834 and 1941.[73] The majority of indentured laborers returned home—about 80 percent of Indians, for example—but many remained, as witnessed in large permanent populations of ethnic Indians in Uganda, Kenya, Malaysia, Fiji, Guyana, and elsewhere.[74] Ultimately, the trade ended, as China, Peru, Cuba, and the United States moved to ban it in the late nineteenth century, a decision that was finally supported by Britain in 1916. The general end in the indentured labor trade arose from widely publicized humanitarian concerns, which converged with new racially tinged migration policies (particularly in the United States and Canada), falling prices for tropical primary products, and a shipping shortage on the eve of World War I.[75] Labor for world-spanning enterprises in the future would be mobilized using less coercive methods.

GLOBAL "FREE" MIGRATIONS (CA. 1840–CA. 1914)

The economic forces that led impoverished Indians to accept indenture and seek their fortunes abroad also prompted Europeans and Asians to journey to new lands in search of prosperity. These "free" migrants moved voluntarily (unlike slaves) and without debt bondage (unlike indentured laborers), although they would have been constrained by social and economic circumstances. This first era of globalization was accompanied by tectonic movements of people, who took advantage of global transportation networks to search for greater opportunity and security. These movements usually relieved population pressures and improved economic conditions at home, while meeting labor demands and producing economic growth in rapidly developing parts of the world.

A doctrine of economic liberalism prevailed in the new, global economy: it was believed that people, goods, and capital should be free to move where they would produce the highest returns. Despite the erection of selective barriers to Chinese immigration to Australia, the United States, and Canada in the mid- to late nineteenth century, advocates for open migration remained influential. In 1889, the International Emigration Conference defended the freedom of movement as a natural right: "We affirm the right of the individual to the fundamental liberty accorded to him by every civilized nation to come and go and dispose of his person and his destinies as he pleases."[76] International migration may have been fiercely contested from some corners and for some people during the late nineteenth century—particularly the Chinese, and also southern Europeans and Slavs—but an ideology of economic openness and liberalism prevailed overall.

Transatlantic Migration

The period between 1840 and 1914 is commonly referred to as the "age of mass migration" because of the rapid increase in free mobility during this time.[77] Mass migration raised the labor force of the United States and Australia by one-third, and reduced the labor force in Europe by about one-eighth. The average number of Europeans migrating to North America increased from about 300,000 per year in 1850 to around 600,000 per year in the 1870s, and then almost doubled again to over 1 million migrants annually at the beginning of the twentieth century. Migration to the New World peaked soon afterward at over three million migrants per year. The movement of millions of Europeans across the Atlantic during this period was unprecedented in terms of its size and speed.

Several factors contributed to this emigration from Europe: a demographic bulge in Europe, political upheaval and persecution, changes in the labor market, an exodus from rural life due to factors ranging from hunger (the potato famine in Ireland) to new taxes, the erosion of rights to common land, as well as lower risks and relative costs of the sea passage.[78] As the sail gave way to steam engines, the new ships crossing the Atlantic were safer, more reliable, and faster—they took about ten days to cross the Atlantic, compared to what could be months on a older sailing vessel. Competition between companies drove the price of fares down by 70 percent in the late 1800s. Friends and relatives who had previously arrived in the Americas also made it easier to migrate—they often helped to finance the passage and provided networks for employment.[79]

The patterns of migration during this period reflected economic cycles in source and destination countries. A close study of emigration rates from individual European countries during the nineteenth century shows peaks and valleys, suggesting that the appeal of migration changed with economic conditions (see figure 2.5). Volatility in mid-European migration was related to changes in employment rates and labor supply dynamics both at home and abroad.[80] Political violence and repression was also a significant factor, particularly in the case of the Jewish refugees who fled persecution in Russia from 1880 onward.[81]

The primary sources of migrants to the New World in the late 1800s changed from earlier in the century. The peak of the industrial revolution was the main period of British and German migration to North America: between 1800 and 1860, two-thirds of migrants to the United States were from Britain, and a further 22 percent were from Germany. From 1860 to 1920, most of the 30 million migrants to the United States came from Scandinavia, Ireland, Italy, Spain, and Eastern Europe. By 1920, 13 percent of the population was foreign-born.[82] Entry to the United States remained free for Europeans and Latin Americans, but Asians and Chinese were excluded from the 1880s—an exception to the promotion of free movement that had prevailed in the West since the 1860s.[83]

In the late nineteenth century, Canada, Argentina, and Brazil also received significant flows of migrants. Smaller flows continued from the United Kingdom to Australia, New Zealand, and South Africa and from Germany, Portugal, and France to its African and other colonies. After reaching their initial destinations, the current and subsequent generations of migrants often moved elsewhere. For instance, following the Revolutionary War, Canada had received many British loyalists and about 40,000 former slaves.[84]

**Emigrations per
thousand of population**

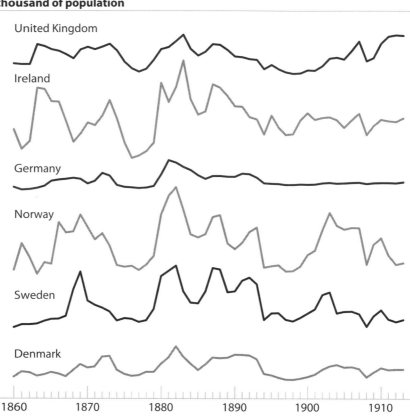

United Kingdom

Ireland

Germany

Norway

Sweden

Denmark

| 1860 | 1870 | 1880 | 1890 | 1900 | 1910 |

Figure 2.5. Annual emigration rates, 1860–1913 (absolute deviations from trend). Timothy J. Hatton and Jeffrey G. Williamson. 2005. *Global Migration and the World Economy: Two Centuries of Policy and Performance*. Boston: MIT Press, p. 20, figure 2.3. By permission of The MIT Press.

The flow of migrants in the age of mass migration was not one-way across the Atlantic. About half of Europe's migrants to the Americas returned to their home countries, although the proportion that returned differed greatly by country of origin.[85] Around half of Spanish and Italian migrants returned home, but only about 5 percent of the Russian, Irish, and Scandinavians returned. Meanwhile, about half of all migrants going to Argentina returned home, while less than a third of those heading for the United States returned to their home countries. The share of return migrants and seasonal migrants and travelers increased as the cost of the Atlantic sea passage declined.

Britain's Role as a Transit Country

Britain provided the cheapest and easiest gateway to North America, and from the middle of the nineteenth century, many came to Britain in anticipation of a new life across the Atlantic. Following the 1840 potato famine, one and a half million Irish fled to Britain. In 1847, 300,000 made the crossing to Liverpool, about half of whom were in transit to North America.[86]

In 1885, Prussia expelled all Russians from its territory, and many of these were Russian Jews who had fled pogroms at home. In 1890, Jews were banned from Moscow. By the 1890s, six ships a week were evacuating Jews from the Baltics, with many coming to Britain as a stop-over on the voyage to North America. Between 1881 and 1914, despite a series of measures designed to reduce this flow, some 120,000 Jews sought refuge in Britain.[87]

While seeking protection and security, refugees and other migrants brought new political ideas, as well as art, culture, and new ways of doing things. The development of ideas of racial purity and the rise of the ideology of Empire supported a growing rejection of Jewish and other foreign settlement. In 1905, Britain passed the Aliens Act, which for the first time sought to systematically control entry into Britain.

The number of migrants led to significant demographic changes for both the sending and receiving countries. On average, 5 percent of the populations of Britain, Ireland, and Norway emigrated every decade between 1850 and 1910, which increased to 14 percent of the Irish population emigrating between 1890 and 1900. By the turn of the century, Italy, Portugal, and Spain recorded similar emigration levels, with over 10 percent of the Italian population emigrating in the decade 1901–1910. The Swedish population fell by 44 percent in the twenty-year period from 1871–1890.[88]

Massive immigration dramatically impacted the economies of countries in the New World, which had relatively small populations. Between 1880 and 1910, Argentina received the equivalent of about 20 percent of its population per decade; the United States between 5 and 10 percent per decade; and Canada between 5 and 15 percent per decade. Immigration in this age of mass migration accounted for around 50 percent of

Argentina's population increase, and about a 30 percent increase for the United States and Australia.[89]

Argentina experienced a boom in immigration from 1870 to 1930, which was the product of government policy to attract "hardworking, thrifty and orderly European farmers" to transform the pampas region into a leading agriculture producer for the British market.[90] The recruitment of migrants to Argentina did not achieve the stated aim, however. Rather than northern Europeans, those who arrived were primarily Spanish, Italian, Poles, and Russian Jews. Only about 30 percent of migrants moved to rural areas—far less than what was expected. Still, the policy of recruiting free migrants (most of them unskilled) yielded unexpected dividends for Argentina. By the early twentieth century, migrants owned more than 80 percent of the "commercial establishments" and 60 percent of the "artisan shops and light industries" in Buenos Aires.[91] In 1920, Argentina was among the six richest countries in the world, and about 30 percent of its population was foreign born.[92]

Brazil adopted a similar policy to Argentina in the mid-nineteenth century to replace departing slaves with free labor. The influx of migrant labor to Brazil's rural areas allowed the economy to triple coffee output in the decade after the abolition of slavery. In the 1880s, the government developed the *colono* system, which subsidized the passage of families to Brazil—an effort to keep migrants from returning to Europe. Between 1889 and 1900, about 750,000 subsidized migrants arrived in São Paulo alone, and over four million migrants had arrived by 1936. In 1920, when only 5 percent of the male population was foreign born, these migrants owned 16 percent of Brazil's farmland; migrant farms were worth, on average, double those owned by native-born farmers.[93] By 1934, foreigners owned 44 percent of São Paulo's factories and shops.[94]

Between 1820 and 1920, about sixty million Europeans ventured to the resource-abundant and labor-scarce Americas.[95] This unprecedented movement of people was a product of new conditions created by the first era of globalization, such as falling transportation costs, booming international trade, and the development of transatlantic migrant networks, which relayed information and finance. In Europe, the industrial revolution raised wages to a level where people could afford to migrate, and a liberal migration regime meant that the regulations were either minimal or supportive of migration. Migrants to the Americas led the expansion of agriculture and industry and linked production into the global economy through European-oriented export industries.

Intra-Europe Migration

Until the 1890s, migration within Europe mirrored the scale of emigration from Europe. The relative ease of movement between countries meant that people migrated in response to Europe's economic and political upheavals in the second half of the nineteenth century.[96] The shift from small- to large-scale enterprises in Europe prompted new levels of competition for foreign workers, and the development of modern industry relied heavily on intra-European migration.[97] Over half of Belgium's emigrants went to neighboring France and Netherlands, and of the fifteen million Italians who emigrated between 1876 and 1920, approximately seven million went to other European countries.[98] Comments by a German observer in the early twentieth century capture the role of migrants in European industrial growth:

> Because in recent times the position of foreigners has grown much different than before . . . most modern states have, with but a few exceptions, abolished their passport laws or at least neutralized them through non-enforcement . . . [Foreigners] are no longer viewed by states with suspicion and mistrust but rather, in recognition of the tremendous value that can be derived from trade and exchange, welcomed with open arms and, for this reason, hindrances are removed from their path to the greatest extent possible.[99]

Britain experienced the highest levels of immigration, with migrants from across Europe escaping unemployment, poverty, famine (such as the Irish), or persecution. The Ruhr mining and heavy industrial region of Germany also became a major magnet for agricultural workers in Prussia and elsewhere in central and Eastern Europe. By 1907, Germany had registered 950,000 foreign workers through a sophisticated system that served as a precursor for the "guest worker" regime of subsequent years.[100]

Faced by labor shortages because of Germany's economic boom, Prussian landlords recruited Poles and Ukrainians to work as replacement agricultural workers. In 1885, due to concern that Polish settlement in the eastern provinces could weaken German control, the Prussian frontier was closed and about 40,000 Poles were deported—despite the protests of the landowners, who lost up to two-thirds of their labor force.[101] By 1890, Poles were allowed to return under a tightly administered scheme for temporary workers. Along with the Poles, increasing numbers of Italian, Belgian, and Dutch workers were admitted.

Growing anti-Semitism in Eastern Europe was associated with violent attacks on Jews who fled to the relative safety of Britain. By the 1890s over six refugee ships a week arrived from the Baltics. Although many suffered discrimination and deprivation on arrival, among those fleeing were individuals who later would become icons of the British establishment, including Michael Marks (Marks and Spencer), Isaac Moses (Moss Bros), Montague Ossinsky (Burtons), and Samuel Montague the renowned banker. In this period, the Franco-Prussian war also prompted over 50,000 Germans to flee to Britain. The influx of Eastern European Jews and Germans brought entrepreneurs, intellectuals, and activists to Britain. Two Bavarians, Hirst and Byng, established the General Electric Company and Joseph Beck developed the largest coal-gas works, bringing electricity to northeast England. These Jewish and German migrants contributed significantly to Victorian culture, sensibility, and industry.[102]

In France, birth rates declined over the nineteenth century, leading to labor shortages in urban areas and seasonal shortages in agricultural regions. The number of foreign workers increased over the second half of the century, from 381,000 in 1851 to 1 million in 1881 and 1.2 million by 1911. Migrants contributed about 15 percent of the urban labor force, and they later served to bolster military conscription during World War I.[103]

Asian Migrations

The flow of European migrants was not the only great migration of the time. During the age of mass migrations, there were comparable population movements from China, Russia, and India into Southeast Asia and North Asia (see table 2.2). Adam McKeown argues that it is not coincidental that Asian population movements were contemporaneous with massive emigration from Europe: "Developments in transportation

TABLE 2.2

MAJOR LONG-DISTANCE MIGRATION FLOWS, 1846–1940.

Destination	Origin	Number	Auxiliary origins
Americas	Europe	55–58 million	2.5 million from India, China, Japan, Africa
Southeast Asia, Indian Ocean Rim, South Pacific	India, southern China	48–52 million	4 million from Africa, Europe, northeastern Asia, Middle East
Manchuria, Siberia, central Asia, Japan	Northeastern Asia, Russia	46–51 million	

Adam McKeown. 2004. "Global Migration, 1846–1940," *Journal of World History* 15(2): 155–189, p. 156, table 1.

technology, such as steamships and railways in all of these areas facilitated the growth in migration. In turn, increased migration facilitated more industrial expansion, which encouraged more migration."[104]

About 50 million Indians and Chinese moved throughout Southeast Asia, often as free migrants. Most of 29 million Indians migrated to British colonies in Malaysia, Ceylon, and Burma, and they were often assisted by colonial authorities or obtained the means to migrate through debt obligations. Less than 10 percent, however, were indentured laborers. In fact, migration from India increased when indentured labor became restricted. Over 19 million Chinese migrants spread out over this period into Thailand, French Indochina, the Dutch Indies, and the Philippines. Only about 750,000 Chinese migrated through indenture contracts; most worked for Chinese employers under various forms of contract, debt obligation, wage labor, or profit sharing. The development of extensive Chinese merchant networks throughout Southeast Asia helped to channel labor within the region.[105]

In the mid-nineteenth century, Russia and China began encouraging migration into north Asia around the same time, leading to an influx of settlers in the hinterlands of Manchuria and Siberia. The Qing government relaxed restrictions on movement in 1860, and in 1880, it actively encouraged resettlement through homesteading policies. In the following century, between 28 and 33 million Chinese moved from north China. Russia emancipated its serfs in 1861, and partly in fear of encroachment by the movement of Chinese, it adopted similar homesteading policies around 1880. About 13 million Russians moved into central Asia and Siberia in the late nineteenth century and early twentieth century. In this same period, about 2 million Koreans and 500,000 Japanese also moved to Manchuria and Siberia. The population in North Asia grew from 22 million in 1850 to 104 million in 1950.[106]

Russia, India, and China also experienced high rates of internal migration. In each region, an estimated 20 million journeys took place.[107] In Russia, migrants relocated to booming cities and agricultural areas. Indians moved to tea plantations, cities, and the mining and textile regions of Bengal. Chinese increasingly moved into coastal cities, the Yangtze basin, and the western borderland.[108]

Early in the Meiji period of rapid modernization (1868–1912), the Japanese government actively discouraged emigration, but near the turn of the century, overpopulation and deflation created new migration pressures. The government initiated a carefully planned emigration process. Compared to other Asian migrations, smaller numbers of Japanese moved in the early twentieth century. In fact, more Japanese moved to Brazil than to China and Russia combined. Between 1868 and 1941, the United States and Brazil received the highest numbers of Japanese migrants.[109] They were recruited to work on coffee plantations, but many subsequently left for São Paulo or Buenos Aires. Similarly, Peru recruited Japanese workers for sugar and cotton plantations, but within a couple of decades, most could be found in Lima and Callao working in small businesses like barbershops and restaurants.

Over 150,000 children from Britain are now thought to have been forced to migrate to Australia, Canada, New Zealand, and other British colonies in a practice that was initiated over 350 years ago and stopped only in 1967. In 1618, about 100 vagrant children were sent to Virginia Colony. Over the next 250 years, it is estimated that over 50,000 children were shipped to the colonies. The Child Migration scheme established in 1869 created an institutional framework and accelerated this practice, with over 100,000 poor, orphaned, and destitute children forced to emigrate over the next century. The extent to which children were forced to migrate has recently become the focus of parliamentary and other inquiries in the United Kingdom and Australia and in 2009 led to a public apology from Prime Minister Rudd in Australia.

BUILDERS OF THE MODERN WORLD

Before the Age of Exploration, small numbers of migrants had been on the vanguard of the advancement of civilization. Their movement fertilized distant lands with new ideas, expanding and accelerating processes of collective learning. With the emergence of global networks and the development of a world economy, the pace of economic development now began to drive much larger migratory flows. International trade and the industrial revolution fueled competition, promoting innovation and the expansion of the scale of economic production in Europe. In the process, struggling rural peasants migrated or became drawn into urban wage labor, and laborers disillusioned with the bleak conditions of industrial Europe sought new beginnings overseas. Governments and industry competed for labor around the world—first fueling a grotesque trade in slaves, then aggressively recruiting contract labor and even subsidizing mass immigration. In the words of Harzig, Hoerder, and Gabaccia, free and forced migrants were builders of the modern world: "Such migrants, bound or self-willed, from and in all segments of the globe, exploited or seizing options, built the urban and industrialized Worlds that had come into being at the turn of the twentieth century."[110]

In 1882, the United States began to apply new regulations aimed at keeping out Chinese laborers while allowing in other classes of Chinese migrants (such as merchants, diplomats, and students). This represented a new experiment in migration administration: to assess individual cases through the application of macro-categories of race, nation, age, class, etc. McKeown remarks, "the original lawmakers had little premonition of the difficult task they were creating, and the resulting administrative behemoth expanded far beyond anything they had ever imagined."[111] The development of bureaucratic regulations to calibrate the flow of migrants became increasingly common throughout the world in the early twentieth century, reversing the trend toward liberalism.

The twentieth century would witness rising nationalism accompanied by a system of states increasingly capable of monitoring their borders. As migrant destination countries received people from ever more diverse locations—and often with fewer skills—native residents demanded greater management of migration flows by the state. Opposition to migration was commonly xenophobic or racist, and prejudices toward foreigners were inflamed by economic downturns and unemployment. The defense of perceived national interests through rising economic protectionism in the early twentieth century was extended to migration control. Once the state increased its bureaucratic capacity to regulate migration, it became difficult to reverse its aspirations for control. The following chapter looks at the development in the twentieth century of systems for regulating migration.

3

⊛

"Managed" Migration in the Twentieth Century (1914–1973)

The dramatic international population movements of the nineteenth century were gradually eclipsed as war, nationalism, and increasingly effective state bureaucracies led to the introduction of new restrictions on migration. States introduced quotas, passports and tighter border restrictions in attempts to "manage" migratory flows.[1]

Managed migration meant that states tried to control how many people entered the country, where they came from, and what rights and resources they could access. Political issues of national security, culture, language, and race became as influential for immigration policies and migrant flows as the economic forces that had been dominant throughout the nineteenth century. New political constituencies, including trade unions, formed to defend the right of existing workers, at times at the expense of foreign or migrant workers. As states increasingly allocated citizenship rights on the basis of nationality, belonging to a state became necessary to be officially recognized and able to move, work, and live. The modern state system elevated the importance of the individual's national identity, and it created new problems for those whose status was unclear.

The growing availability and reach of transportation, communications, and capital in the twentieth century made it more feasible to migrate than ever before. At the same time, governments have sought to reduce this potential for most citizens, by introducing a host of policies and regulations that attempt to "optimize" the flow of migrants. These policies have evolved over time in many countries, and have in recent decades become less overtly racial and more focused on skills. Despite the increase in control, regulation, and the use of increasingly sophisticated technologies for surveillance, effective control over the movement of people remains an elusive goal.[2]

THE END OF THE LIBERAL PERIOD

Borders, Passports, and Citizenship

In the late nineteenth century, the debate about the merits of passports in liberal Europe had been temporarily resolved, and their use was primarily limited to feudal regimes such as Russia (which used them internally).[3] The prevailing wisdom was that passports were unnecessary obstacles to movement and that open borders would promote economic growth. States' attitudes toward migration went through a "liberal interlude" between restrictive periods. Twentieth-century passport controls are not a new invention; during the French Revolution, the merits of passports were hotly debated, with legislation going back and forth about regulating movement. The primary weakness of early passport controls, however, was always the capacity of the state to enforce its ambitious regulations.

As John Torpey writes in his history of border control, during the nineteenth century "passports fell away throughout Western Europe, useless papers to a world in prosperous motion."[4] Advocating for passports was seen as a defense of outmoded systems of feudalism—where people were tied to the land they tilled—and mercantilism—in which the wealth of a nation was measured by its stock of capital rather than by what it produced and traded.[5] A leading Italian legal commentator, Giovanni Bolis, argued in 1871 that passports should be eliminated "as a measure of great importance for economic relations, favouring commerce, industry, and progress, facilitating the relations among the various countries, and liberating travelers from harassment and hindrances."[6] In a liberal world, borders were imaginary lines crossed by moving labor, goods, and capital.

As liberal ideas became more widespread in the late nineteenth century, the reasons to stop people from moving became less and less convincing. Adam Smith, the great laissez-faire economist, objected to anything that obstructed "the free circulation of labour from one employment to another."[7] While free movement was valued instrumentally to permit the natural allocation of labor to booming industry, it also came to be valued intrinsically—as a human right. Giovanni Bolis added to his economic defense of free movement that "the surest thermometer of the freedom of a people is to be found in an examination of its legislation concerning passports."[8] The eminent Institute of International Law in 1892 voiced its collective opinion that "the free entrance of aliens into the territory of a civilized state should not be curtailed in a general and permanent manner other than in the interest of public welfare and for the most serious of reasons."[9] England, which had called for the use of passports in its 1836 Aliens Restriction Act, reversed its course. Earl Granville, the Secretary of State, declared in 1872 that "by the existing law of Great Britain all foreigners have the unrestricted right of entrance and residence in this country."[10]

Although some countries introduced tentative measures to slow migration in the early twentieth century, the advent of World War I marked the end of the "liberal interlude" of free cross-border movement—at first temporarily, and then permanently. Leading up to the war, European states reinstituted passports and border controls as national security measures used to distinguish between citizens and foreigners. In April 1917, France required all foreigners to carry an identification card with a photograph, indicating the bearer's nationality and occupation. Germany and Britain introduced similar regulations to identify foreigners and control their borders. America had already started to police its borders more aggressively, and in 1917 it introduced a literacy test that had to be passed by all migrants. Australia had implemented a "dictation test" more than a decade earlier, given in Gaelic to nonwhite applicants.[11] These controls were initially accepted as a wartime emergency response, and they were perceived to be temporary and provisional measures.[12]

States that had attempted to limit migration before had often done so on racial/ethnic lines, but the introduction of mandatory passports coincided with growth in the capacity of states to effectively police their borders. Selective "country of origin" limits on immigration were introduced as early as 1855 in Australia (to limit Chinese migration) and Canada, the United States, and the UK followed suit several decades later. The emerging labor movements and their struggles for workers' rights in the early twentieth century were accompanied by pressure to limit access to social services. Unions also lobbied governments to limit immigration that was seen to lead to competition for jobs. Democratic states, responding to popular demand, sought to extend the reach of government to seek to identify those who were nationals, entitled to full access to the labor market and social services, and those who by virtue of being foreign were not.

The peace that followed World War I was fragile, and nationalism and economic insecurity defined the priorities of European states. Trade protectionism returned with a vengeance, and economic and political failure was often blamed on foreigners. At the same time, states pushed forward an "identification revolution," whereby passports and other forms of identification were used to mark national subjects as citizens of the state. The passions of nationalism consumed European societies, and states increasingly sought to identify "who was in" and "who was out" of the nation.[13] Alan Dowty writes of this period: "As national loyalty came to be perceived as the cement of society, emigration was increasingly regarded as deviant behavior. This became especially true as international differences sharpened along ethnic or ideological lines, making migration seem almost traitorous."[14] In 1919, Germany and the United States made passport requirements permanent, and Britain did the same in 1920.

Passports and citizen identification became hallmarks of the modern nation-state. By the time decolonization took place in the mid-twentieth century, the norm of issuing passports and visas was widespread—it was something that states "did," so new states did it too. This legal norm found itself institutionalized in the new international order, and most people can no longer imagine attempting to cross a border without a document that carries their photo, birthplace, and nationality. The development of the modern passport system and the near-universal requirement to possess national identification very quickly created problems, however, when groups of people found themselves without a state. As Hannah Arendt pointed out in the mid-twentieth century, one had no rights, in practice, without a state to protect them.

The Death Ship

The ease with which people were able to move within Europe and the shock at the introduction of tighter regulations was captured in fiction by the author B. Traven. In his book, *The Death Ship*, the lead character is a sailor from the United States, who, on leaving France shortly after World War I, is surprised when asked for papers. He responds:

"I have no passport. Nor have I any identification card of the French authorities. No immigration stamp. No customs-house seal. I have no papers at all. Never in all my life did I ever have any papers."

On being threatened with arrest, he quarrels:

"Every age has its Inquisition. Our age has the passport to make up for the tortures of medieval times."

"You ought to have some papers to show who you are," the police officer advised.

"I do not need any paper: I know who I am," the traveler responded.

"Maybe so. Other people are also interested in knowing who you are" the policeman said . . . and sent him on his way to Germany.[15]

Resurgent Chauvinism: Race, Ethnicity, and Nationalism

States' preoccupation with documenting their citizens was influenced by—and in turn reinforced—social tendencies to assert homogenous identities linked to race, ethnicity, and nation. The resurgence of chauvinism on the heels of the age of mass migrations could be considered paradoxical: "Even as worldwide movement multiplied opportunities for the cultural and biological mixing of groups hitherto separated and thereby enhanced the unity of humankind," writes Aristide Zolberg, "the retrenchment of nations behind their self-made walls helped foster a cultural construction of 'societies' as self-contained population entities with a common and homogenous ancestry."[16] The perceived economic threat posed by immigrants combined with pseudoscientific theories of race and deeply rooted cultural prejudices to generate a widespread suspicion of "foreigners" in western countries during the early twentieth century. The result was the introduction of discriminatory immigration policies in some countries and outright expulsion and brutal purges in others.

Notions of racial identity increased in significance from the nineteenth century, and they shaped discriminatory immigration policies throughout the twentieth century.[17] The ideology of social Darwinism and its related pseudoscientific practice of eugenics influenced changes in U.S. immigration policy and also had a powerful influence in South Africa.[18] In the late nineteenth century, the United States already restricted immigration on the basis of race: the 1882 Chinese Exclusion Act was repeatedly renewed to keep out Chinese laborers. After a national census revealed significant changes in the composition of the U.S. population, however, restrictionist lobby groups formed, using eugenic arguments about racial hierarchy to push for more selective migration controls. They drew their inspiration from evolutionary biology and spurious techniques in anthropology—such as skull measurements—to make connections between race, intelligence, and human capacity. Prescott Hall, the Secretary of the influential Immigration Restriction League (IRL), asked whether U.S. citizens "want a country to be peopled by British, German, and Scandinavian stock, historically free, energetic, progressive, or by Slav, Latin, and Asiatic races, historically downtrodden, atavistic, and stagnant?"[19]

Eugenists publicized their views on inherited sources of intelligence and ability, and they tried to shape public policy on immigration. In 1917, the IRL successfully pushed mandatory literacy tests for immigrants through Congress, ultimately overriding President Wilson's veto.[20] Around the same time, the Supreme Court ruled that Chinese, Japanese, Indians, and other Asians were ineligible for naturalization in the United States, and land ownership by these groups was limited in some states.[21]

The debate over immigration controls was connected to a broader movement in the United States around "Americanization," or the process of assimilating immigrants. Both were characterized by racial animosity and a desire to preserve the "white" complexion of the United States. The Chair of the House Committee on Immigration, Congressman Albert Johnson, maintained a close relationship with the "eugenic proselytizer" Dr. Harry Laughlin, providing a conduit into Congress for eugenic research and arguments.[22] The Johnson-Reed Immigration Act of 1924 explicitly differentiated between immigrants on the basis of race. It introduced a controversial system of immigration quotas determined by the estimated national origins distribution of the white population in the 1920 census.[23]

Race also became an increasingly salient factor for immigration policy in Australia and South Africa. One of the first Acts of the Australian Federal Parliament in 1901 was the introduction of the White Australia Policy.[24] "Populate or Perish" was the slogan made popular by Australian Prime Minister Billy Hughes, referring to the need to increase European migration or risk being "overrun" by Asians, principally Chinese. Not surprisingly, the number of Chinese in Australia declined from about 30,000 in 1901 to about 5,000 in 1947.[25] Opinion polls conducted in Australia in 1947, however, revealed that Chinese were not at the top of the list that Australians chose to "keep out." While 26 percent of the Australian respondents indicated that Chinese should be blocked from immigrating, 39 percent wished to keep Jews out and 68 percent to exclude Negroes.[26]

Britain also adopted racially discriminatory restrictions during the early twentieth century, but it did so in a more subtle and selective way. The official policy of the government until 1962 was that any member of the Commonwealth was a citizen and could freely move to Britain. The government repeatedly debated introducing racial restrictions on immigration but was held back by a reluctance to challenge the imperial ideal of equality among all members of the Commonwealth.[27] This ideal was not openly challenged, but racial discrimination occurred nonetheless. Britain took special measures to actively discourage emigration from "New Commonwealth" countries (in Asia, Africa, and the Caribbean) without openly changing its immigration policy.[28]

During World War I, millions of colonial subjects were recruited for the war effort. Over 1.4 million Indians and other South Asian soldiers fought for the Allies in World War I. Canada, the Caribbean, South Africa, Australia, and other parts of the British Empire sent an additional million or more men to fight for the Allies. Following the war, however, the Indian and Caribbean soldiers who had fought for Britain found they were "shooed off home with undisguised alacrity" after being officially purged from representation in the grand London victory parade.[29]

Population Separation

While certain states sought to limit migration on the basis of race, others promoted migration in order to "unmix" their populations. In some African colonies, white minorities maintained economic and political power by displacing native Africans from farmlands, often forcing them to occupy marginal areas. Tribal land in Kenya was confiscated and sold to white settlers, who would select particular families among the displaced native tenants to recruit as workers while the rest were expelled.[30] Similarly, in South Africa, the former inhabitants of land occupied by white settlers were offered the right to live on the farm in exchange for three months of free labor.[31] Between 1902 and 1940, Chinese contract laborers were expelled from the country, Indians faced new restrictions, and pass laws and labor controls were imposed on Africans.[32]

Notions of racial superiority and white nationalism in South Africa prompted the passage of the Native Land Act in 1913, which further advanced the system of segregation which later became entrenched in apartheid. The government established "reserves" to segregate the black population. The system of was further formalized in 1951 with the Bantu Authorities Act and the 1959 Bantu Self-Government Act, which disenfranchised blacks from South African citizenship.

Modern Turkey, emerging from the vanquished Ottoman Empire, used brute force and international agreements to consolidate the ethnic Turkish population—previously spread throughout the Empire—within the boundaries of the modern state. The 1923 Treaty of Lausanne between Greece and Turkey initiated a large-scale compulsory "population exchange": 1.25 million Greeks were "repatriated" from Turkey, and 400,000 Turks were relocated from Greece. The treaty followed a war with Greece, during which Turkey had declared that it would no longer tolerate Greeks on Turkish soil—hundreds of thousands of Greeks fled to the Turkish port of Smyrna to be rescued by Greek ships (but not after a massacre that occurred right in front of the British naval forces in Smyrna harbor).[33] Two years after the Treaty of Lausanne, another treaty with Bulgaria opened the way for an estimated one million Turks to move voluntarily; more than 300,000 would move in the next thirty years.[34] "All of the transfers to "un-mix" peoples," observes Dirk Hoerder, "sprang from projects of the new nationalist governments and their population planners, who viewed ethnocultural and ethnoreligious lifestyles as badges of personal allegiance."[35]

Russia produced the largest flow of refugees during World War I and following the 1917 Bolshevik Revolution.[36] As the German army advanced during the war, Russian troops uprooted villages and forced peasants to flee. They had produced about 2.5 million refugees by December 1915.[37] Germans living in Russian territory were deported in cattle cars to Siberia and Central Asia, and both sides sought to deport Jews within their territory.[38]

As the Germans advanced across the Pale of Settlement—the western frontier of Russia where Jews were permitted to live—Jewish communities were raided for labor and requisitions; about 35,000 were deported to Germany to work in farms and factories.[39] The war scattered the Jewish communities into Europe and Russia, where they encountered further violence. Michael Marrus estimates that between 1917 and 1921, "there were more than 2000 anti-Jewish riots in the affected regions. In Russia and Ukraine alone, these made about half a million Jews homeless, destroyed 28 percent of Jewish homes, killed more than 30,000 people, and may have been responsible for five times that many deaths."[40]

As Jews fled Russia, other states closed their borders. Britain had already passed the 1905 Aliens Act to restrict migration in response to the arrival of Jews from Eastern Europe, and the Aliens Order extended its provisions in 1919.[41] Canada passed an Order in Council in 1923 imposing immigration restrictions on Jews, and the 1924 Johnson-Lodge Act in the United States quickly followed suit. As these options ran out, Jewish refugees increasingly moved to Palestine. In the early twentieth century, "only a small minority chose Zionism," comments Gershon Shafir. "Territorial nationalism, as it were, was imposed on Jews as a last resort."[42] Prior to 1914, less than 3 percent of Jewish emigrants moved to Palestine, but in 1925, about 30 percent embraced Zionism. As Jewish displacement from Europe became increasingly severe in the mid-1930s, the number of refugees arriving in Palestine rose to 200,000 between 1933 and 1936.[43] The systematic murder, persecution, and displacement associated with Hitler's Third Reich in Germany would increasingly propel Europe's Jews toward Palestine—despite restrictions by the British Mandate government—and ultimately pave the way for the creation of the state of Israel, accompanied by the forced displacement of the Palestinian people.

THE INTERWAR PERIOD: ECONOMIC DECLINE AND REGULATED MIGRATION

Following World War I, the Treaty conference at Versailles involved negotiation over the creeping exclusions that signaled the end of open borders. Australia, Canada, New Zealand, and the British Empire all insisted on their right to limit migration (often on the basis of race). Despite Japanese, Chinese, and Indian demands for the free movement of labor, the new League of Nations did not include any institutional support for international migration.[44] Efforts advanced through the League to liberalize or abolish the new passport system were ultimately unsuccessful.[45]

Government opposition meant that the International Labour Organization stayed away from the issue of migration, and the efforts of the International Federation of Trade Unions to create an International Office on Migration failed.[46] Instead, within a climate of nationalism and economic stagnation, states reserved their right to increasingly regulate migration and impose restrictions on the rights of foreigners within their borders. Of course, the movement away from free migration to regulation did not occur suddenly around World War I, but the failure of international negotiations after the war to reopen borders allowed piecemeal government regulation to become systematic and permanent.

New limits on migration were reinforced by the global economic downturn that started around 1929. In many countries, high levels of unemployment unleashed popular resentment against foreigners and focused political attention on immigration policy.[47] Foreign workers were increasingly blamed for economic hardship, and demands rose for protection of domestic workers against foreign competitors. The closure of borders during the interwar period assumed the dynamic of an arms race—as the first countries erected barriers, others became more nervous about increasing pressure on their own borders, and an "upward spiral of restriction" resulted.[48] By the early 1930s, nearly every country in northwestern Europe had introduced policies designed to restrict the inflow of all but a limited number of self-supporting migrants.[49] Furthermore, as social welfare legislation expanded, most countries included provisions that discriminated against foreigners.[50]

After World War I, the United States increasingly regulated migration, and the number of documented migrants entering the country plummeted. Following reports by the U.S. Immigration Commission led by Senator William P. Dillingham, Congress enacted legislation that introduced national quotas and literacy tests for immigrants.[51] The 1917 Immigration Act doubled the head tax on immigrants, and it extended the restrictions on Japanese and Chinese immigration to completely exclude Asian immigration.[52] Several years later, the Emergency Quota Act

Number of immigrants (thousands)

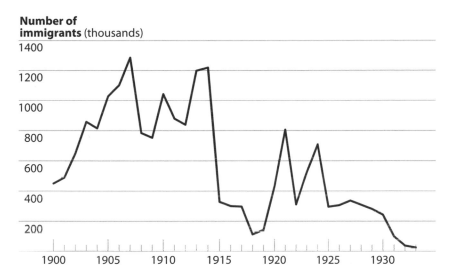

Figure 3.1. Immigration to the United States for selected years, 1900–1933 (thousands). U.S. Government. 1993. *Statistical Yearbook and Naturalization Service.* Washington, DC: U.S. Government Printing Office.

(1921) limited the total number of immigrants each year to 350,000. This number was further reduced to 150,000 by the 1924 Johnson-Reed Act, and by the 1930s, it fell to an average of 50,000 per year (see figure 3.1).

In northwestern European economies, industrial development and declining birth rates meant that these countries were now migrant destinations rather than source countries. While migrants had previously come from the more developed countries in Europe to the undeveloped regions of the New World and colonies, an increasing proportion of those leaving by 1915 came from the less developed areas in southern and eastern Europe and settled elsewhere in Europe or in Canada, Australia, Argentina, Brazil, and New Zealand.[53]

In Europe, France faced labor pressures following World War I because of low birth rates and the high number of casualties suffered during the war—1.4 million dead and another 1.5 million permanently handicapped.[54] In response to labor demands, farm and mining interests set up a private recruitment agency, Société Générale d'Immigration (SGI), to bring in about 560,000 migrants. The migrants brought into France through SGI were about a quarter of roughly two million workers who entered France between 1920 and 1930. By 1931, there were 2.7

million foreigners in France, and they accounted for 6.6 percent of the population. Italians (808,000), Poles (508,000), Spaniards (352,000), and Belgians (254,000) were the largest migrant groups.

During the 1920s in France, there was some opposition to the influx of foreign workers, but this was usually restricted to "nativists," who complained that the immigration of foreigners led to the "pollution of French culture." French immigration policy was dominated by the SGI and the National Alliance for the Growth of the French Population, who argued that large-scale recruitment of workers from Spain and Italy would give France a chance to catch up with the more powerful European competitors, primarily Germany and Britain.

By January 1933, however, France had fallen victim to the global depression, and over one million people were unemployed. New arrivals found work permits almost impossible to obtain. This exclusionary trend went alongside a policy of expulsion whereby thousands of working foreigners were sent back to their country of origin. Failure to comply with an expulsion order could result in imprisonment.[55] By 1936, the foreign population of France had declined by over half a million from its peak.[56]

The economic crisis in Germany was more long-lasting and had been associated with an even sharper restriction on foreign workers. After World War I, relatively few foreigners worked in Germany, with numbers declining to about 100,000 in 1932 after reaching about a million in 1907.[57] Foreign laborers were highly regulated through "strict state control of labour recruitment, employment preference for nationals, sanctions against employers of illegal immigrants and unrestricted police power to deport unwanted foreigners."[58] The Weimar Ordinance on Foreign Workers, which centralized a restrictive admission and control policy, was later implemented by the Nazi regime.

With the appointment of Adolf Hitler as German Chancellor in 1933, the ideal of racial purity initially precluded the use of foreign labor. Economic interest quickly overrode ideology, however. In 1936, the Nazi government negotiated with Poland for agricultural workers, and within several years, tens of thousands of Italians, Yugoslavs, Hungarians, and Bulgarians were working in German agriculture.[59]

By the end of 1937, however, rising anti-Semitism had led approximately 165,000 German Jews to emigrate, and the number of refugees displaced by the German Reich doubled again between the beginning of

1938 and 1939. The outbreak of the war in September 1939 reinforced the reluctance of many countries to receive refugees from Germany. At an intergovernmental conference organized by the High Commission for Refugees Coming from Germany in 1938, all the participants stated that they could not accept any additional refugees, and the League of Nation's efforts were increasingly limited to humanitarian aid. As receiving countries tightened up their immigration policies, however, Germany's initial policy of expelling unwanted populations was superseded by institutionalized genocide.[60]

While Europe was in political and economic upheaval, Japan extended its imperial reach into Korea and China. Rather than sending unskilled laborers or farmers—as Europe had sent to the New World—Japan aimed to export traders, artisans, shopkeepers, and "adventurous merchants," who gravitated toward the cities in China and Korea. Between 1900 and 1930, two million moved to Taiwan and another ten million moved to Korea.[61] The number of Japanese living in Manchuria increased from 180,000 in 1933 to 820,000 in 1940, and Japanese-run coal mines and construction projects pulled in hundreds of thousands of Chinese migrants— many displaced from their homes by drought, famine, and civil war.[62]

The movement of Japanese throughout the region was part of a national modernization program that involved securing control over Chinese and Korean labor. In 1920, Japan's population was 56 million, while those laboring in its colonies added up to 21 million.[63] Japanese managerial personnel directed the production of industrial and military supplies within the colonies.[64]

Japanese colonial policy in Korea led to the dispossession of peasants, who were then recruited as labor for Japan's industrial economy. They were assigned to menial jobs left unfilled by nationals.[65] After 1939, the process turned into forced recruitment to fuel the Japanese war economy, and the numbers of Koreans living in Japan increased dramatically (see figure 3.2). By 1945, around 10 percent of Korea's population worked outside of the country.[66] In Japan, however, they were not accorded full citizenship—few were promoted to middle-class positions, and they faced systemic repression out of Japanese fear of nationalist activities. The Koreans working in Japan were later designated as "third-party nationals," and following World War II, the majority of them were compelled to leave the country.

Number of Koreans (millions)

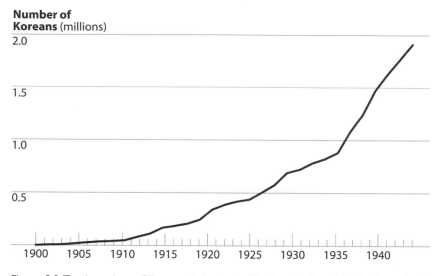

Figure 3.2. Total number of Koreans in Japan, 1900–1944 (millions). Lydia Potts. 1990. *A World Labour Market: A History of Migration.* London: Zed Books, p. 152.

The interwar period showed that national politics, government policies, and the uneven distribution of citizenship rights would shape the patterns and character of international migration in the twentieth century. "The contrast between the policy patterns of the liberal age and those of our own time is very sharp," concludes Zolberg. "Starting around the turn of the twentieth century, one after the other the states of destination began to close their gates, restricting access to relatively small numbers of people of the receivers' choosing, and . . . this still remains the basic stance of the affluent liberal states today."[67]

Nansen Passports and the International Refugee Regime

The reintroduction of passports, strengthened border controls, and greater state regulation of migration all led to a more rigid interstate system in Western Europe.[68] Saskia Sassen calls this period "the beginning of modern refugee history." The modern concept of the refugee is a product of European history related to "the rising importance of borders and of sovereignty over national territories, the increasingly long arm of the state, and the ascendance of variously conceived constructions of national identities as part of the nation state."[69] Serbs expelled from the Balkans, Jews fleeing persecution in Russia, and Italians escaping fascism—along with many other groups—challenged the new international regime.

Widely accepted rules, norms, and institutions to deal with refugees only really developed after the 1917 Bolshevik Revolution in Russia led to the displacement of more than one million people into continental Europe.[70] The newly created League of Nations established a High Commissioner for Refugees (HCR) in 1921 as a temporary agency that could deal with the Russian refugees. The High Commissioner office, headed by Fridthof Nansen, was intended to address a specific and time-bound problem, and it relied heavily on nongovernmental organizations for supplies and personnel. Because the legal problem posed by refugees was related to their lack of passports and identification, the High Commissioner created "Nansen passports" for the refugees, and European states agreed to recognize the documents. The goal of Nansen's program was repatriation and resettlement. However, as with passports themselves, the temporary League of Nations program became more permanent. Soon, Nansen passports were granted to Armenians, Turks, Assyrians, Syrians, Assyro-Chaldeans, and Kurds.

World War II placed new strains on the nascent international refugee regime. As Jews began to flee Germany in the 1930s, some states—such as the Netherlands—refused to accept them without proof that they faced an "immediate danger to life."[71] The divergence between states' recognition of refugees as such and their unwillingness to assume special responsibility for their well-being often rendered the actions of the HCR ineffective in practical terms.[72] During the depression, many European states were more reluctant to assume financial responsibility for destitute Jews,[73] so many were ultimately returned to face persecution in Germany, while about 10,000 others remained unsettled at the outbreak of World War II.

World War II made the problem of refugees even more complicated. At the end of the war, about 30 million people were displaced, including about 12 million ethnic Germans who were expelled from the USSR.[74] The establishment of the United Nations following the war dissolved the League's HCR, and the United Nations created two successive organizations to deal with the status of those displaced by the war. The United

Nations Relief and Reconstruction Agency (UNRRA) had a mandate to simply "assist victims of war in any area under the control of the United Nations."[75] When its mandate ran out in 1947, its refugee responsibilities were assumed by the International Refugee Organization (IRO), which adopted a case-by-case approach to identify and determine the status of refugees. Whereas the UNRRA focused exclusively on repatriation (it helped over seven million return to their home countries), the IRO repatriated about 70,000 more and relocated about a million refugees to Israel, Canada, the United States, and Australia.

The United Nations High Commissioner for Refugees (UNHCR) was finally created as a permanent body in December 1950, quickly followed by the passage of the UN Convention Relating to the Status of Refugees. The Convention clearly defined the concept of a "refugee," and this definition is still considered one of the most widely accepted international norms. Later amended in 1967 to apply to refugees after WWII and outside of Europe, the Convention defines a refugee as:

> Any person . . . who owing to a well-founded fear of being persecuted for reasons of race, religion, nationality, membership of a particular social group or political opinion, is outside the country of his nationality and is unable or, owing to such fear, is unwilling to avail himself of the protection of that country; or who, not having a nationality and being outside the country of his former habitual residence as a result of such events, is unable or, owing to such fear, is unwilling to return to it.[76]

The founding statute of the UNHCR provides the institution with a dual mandate: to ensure that refugees have access to both protection and durable solutions. "Access to protection" means that refugees are assured of certain rights, and "durable solutions" include returning to their home country or resettlement in a new country.

In its early stages, the UNHCR focused primarily on putting together international treaties on refugees and promoting the rights and obligations pertaining to refugees.[77] These actions reflected the early east–west flow of refugees in the context of the Cold War. As refugee flows have dramatically increased in the past several decades, their causes and characteristics have also become more complex. The UNHCR now interprets its mandate much more broadly to include internally displaced persons and returning refugees. As refugee flows increasingly move from south to north, originating from contexts of civil wars, communal violence, and civil disorder, the UNHCR has shifted focus from protection toward humanitarian assistance and repatriation.[78] No longer simply providing Nansen passports, the UNHCR now works more generally at the level of assistance, conflict prevention, and persuading and helping host countries to meet their international obligations.

POST-WWII MIGRATIONS

Another Age of Migration

World War II was, in the words of Charles Tilly, "one of the greatest demographic whirlwinds to sweep the earth."[79] Approximately 30 million people were displaced by World War II—in addition to the millions executed, gassed, and starved by the Nazi regime or killed in combat—and 11 million of these were outside of their country of origin at the end of the war.[80] The Nazi regime had (often forcibly) recruited about 7.5 million foreign workers (including 1.8 million prisoners of war) to replace the 11 million Germans conscripted for military service; a quarter of its industrial production was carried out by foreign labor in conditions comparable to slavery.[81]

Many of those displaced by the war later returned to their country of origin or moved in search of new homes. The largest numbers of displaced people went to the United States (329,301), Australia (182,159), and Canada (123,479), and Israel financed and organized the settlement of 132,000 displaced Jewish people.[82] Between 1946 and 1952, postwar recovery in Europe was slow, and the International Refugee Organization and the International Committee for European Migration helped a combined 3.2 million refugees and "voluntary" migrants to relocate overseas. About 823,000 moved to Latin America.[83] As the numbers of European migrants to Brazil and Argentina show, immigration from Europe spiked between 1948 and 1952, before falling rapidly as European reconstruction accelerated and more jobs became available closer to home (see figure 3.3).

Number of migrants (thousands)

Figure 3.3. European immigrants into Argentina and Brazil after World War II (thousands). Norman Plotkin. 1987. "Latin America after World War II," in Sidney Klein (ed.), *The Economics of Mass Migration in the Twentieth Century.* New York: Paragon Books, pp. 117–150, tables A and B.

As the European economy began to recover in the 1950s, the demand for foreign labor picked up again. Refugees, displaced peoples, and returnees from the colonies ended up providing the labor needed for reconstruction.[84] Europe was returning to pre-WWI levels of demand for foreign labor, and countries devised new systems that aimed to prevent the permanent settlement of migrants.

Decolonization coupled with economic recovery in Europe also prompted the large-scale migration of white colonials and "non-White auxiliaries."[85] From 1945 to 1973, between 5.5 and 8.5 million migrants moved to Italy, Britain, France, Belgium, and the Netherlands from their respective colonies. They were not welcomed home with open arms. Dirk Hoerder notes: "Metropolitan populations saw no reason to have their taxes allocated to the support of settler and planter 'returnees'; mixed-origin families and their children faced racism; 'coloured' auxiliaries often ended up in camps or substandard housing."[86]

Foreign worker programs in Europe drew in additional migrants from Asia, Africa, and Latin America. In Germany, the number of foreign workers grew from 95,000 in 1956 to 2.3 million by 1973, primarily as a result of rapid industrial expansion that drove a demand for large numbers of unskilled workers.[87] Between 1945 and 1960, the Netherlands recruited about 300,000 workers from Indonesia (its former Dutch West Indies colony). A similar number of Africans moved to France from its former colonies by 1972.[88] The United States also loosened it national origins immigration restrictions in 1965, leading to a surge in migration to the United States from Asia and Latin America.[89]

In the United States, the need for additional labor to produce "food to win the war" during World War II led Congress to introduce the *Bracero* guest-worker program to bring in migrants from Mexico and Central America to work as temporary agricultural laborers. During the period from 1943–1965, 4.6 million "braceros" from Mexico were admitted on temporary work permits to do farm work, many of them returning year after year.[90]

Britain required foreign migrants to fill labor shortages after the war, and as early as 1946, it had identified displaced persons as a possible solution. Initially, Britain recruited about 90,000 (primarily male) workers from refugee camps and Italy through a European Voluntary Worker scheme.[91] Workers were tied to a specific job, they could not bring their families to join them, and they could face summary deportation in cases of indiscipline.[92] Over 345,000 Europeans were ultimately recruited on restricted work permits, but the continued shortage of labor meant that British recruiters searched farther afield. By 1958, 115,000 West Indians, 55,000 Indians, 25,000 West Africans, and 10,000 Cypriots had been brought to the UK.

West Germany's temporary guest-worker program, called *Gastarbeiter*, became one of Europe's largest and most sophisticated. Germany signed bilateral agreements with Italy (1955), Greece (1960), Turkey (1961), Portugal (1964), and Yugoslavia (1968) to recruit unskilled labor for jobs in the rapidly growing industrial sector. The Federal Labour Office set up recruitment offices in these countries, and they would test occupational skills, provide medical examinations, screen police records, and transport groups to Germany—after which, employers would provide initial accommodation.[93] Stephen Castles and Mark Miller comment that under the *Gastarbeiter* program, "German policies conceived migrant workers as temporary labour units, which could be recruited, utilized and sent away again as employers required."[94]

Like other European guest-worker programs, however, many of the initially "temporary" migrants eventually had families and established roots in Germany. Settlement and the formation of migrant and ethnic communities was an unanticipated consequence of recruiting foreign labor.[95]

The End of the *Gastarbeiter* Program in Germany

By 1973, 11.9 percent of the entire workforce in Germany was foreign-born, employed in low-skill jobs either in expanding industries, such as automobile factories, or in unattractive trades, such as steel mills. The total foreign population numbered 4,127,400 by 1974. However, with the "oil crisis" at the end of 1973, recruitment of foreign workers was stopped, and the German Federal Government prohibited all further entries of workers from outside the European Economic Community. The permits of foreign workers already in Germany were to be extended only if no German had applied for the job. Moreover, work permits were denied to dependants who entered after 1 December 1974.[96]

This change in policy was the immediate result of the oil crisis but also of the fact that by the early 1970s, the "guest-worker system" was being widely questioned. Migrant laborers had supplied replacement labor for German nationals moving out of low-status, low-skilled jobs, a need that had declined with the economic downturn. In addition, labor-intensive production processes were increasingly being moved to developing countries. Moreover, the scarcity of labor during the boom period of the 1960s had brought about improvements in the rights concerning residence status and family reunification. It became clear that Germany would need foreign workers indefinitely, and this realization led to policy changes toward encouraging greater integration. As result of being granted residence and family reunification rights, workers became less mobile, and the "rotation" principle no longer applied. Germany then had to start addressing the social costs of the labor and supply housing and schooling and undertake steps to facilitate integration, steps never envisaged under the concept of a "guest-worker."

The global economic downturn in the wake of the 1973–1974 oil crisis slowed Western recruitment of foreign labor, and escalating oil prices turned countries in the Gulf region—and to a lesser extent Venezuela and Nigeria—into new regional migrant centers.[97] The Gulf economies initially required that Western oil companies employ local labor, and by 1950, less than 30,000 foreign workers—most of them skilled—were employed in the region. At first, foreign labor was recruited from the region, and about 650,000 Palestinians, Lebanese, Sudanese, Iranians, Egyptians, and others worked in infrastructure and public services.

When oil prices tripled in 1973, the demand in oil exporting countries for labor quickly escalated, and Gulf economies increasingly drew mobile temporary workers from South and Southeast Asian countries. In 1975, 1.7 million guest-workers were employed, and this increased to 3 million by 1980. In 1985, the 8 million guest-workers in the Gulf composed more than half of the labor force; 4.4 million of these workers were drawn from India, Pakistan, and Southeast Asian countries.[98] These "visible minorities" were preferred in part because they are less able to integrate than the Arabic-speaking Muslims from the Middle East.

As they had during earlier economic downturns, western European countries restricted migration in response to the recession following the 1973–1974 oil crisis. By this time, however, large foreign-born populations lived in France, Germany, and the UK. In Germany, these migrants came largely from Turkey, Yugoslavia, Italy, Spain, Greece, and Portugal; Algerians, Portuguese, Spaniards, Italians, and West Africans went to France; and Britain received migrants from former colonies in South Asia and the Caribbean.[99] Substantial migrant populations also lived in Belgium (coming from Spain, Greece, Morocco, and Turkey) and Sweden (from Finland, Yugoslavia, Greece, and Turkey).[100] Migrants who had arrived through the temporary foreign worker programs of the 1950s and 1960s were changing the demographic composition of these countries into cosmopolitan and multiethnic societies.

The 1960s and 1970s also marked a broader shift in the immigration policies of Western countries, which began moving away from national origin policies. Canada abolished its preference for western European migrants in 1962, and the United States amended the U.S. Immigration and Nationality Act in 1965 to break the link between allocated quotas and historical immigration patterns. In 1973, the White Australia policy was officially abandoned.[101] Western destination countries began adopting policies that were less discriminatory and more skill selective, moving away from recruiting temporary low-skilled guest-workers and toward bringing in high-skilled permanent residents.[102]

Since World War II, Europe has taken progressive steps toward establishing a common market of goods and people in the interest of creating regional interdependence that will prevent the recurrence of war between member states.[103] Cross-border mobility was a central issue during the movement toward a European Union, and the issue of migration has been on the agenda since the Treaty of Paris in 1951, which established the European Coal and Steel Community. The 1985 Schengen Agreement between France, Germany, Belgium, Luxembourg, and the Netherlands committed its signatories toward establishing a border-free Europe. When the Schengen Agreement came into effect in 1995, it removed systematic border controls for people—including third-party nationals—moving between Germany, Belgium, Spain, France, Portugal, Luxembourg, and the Netherlands. The Amsterdam Treaty of 1997 incorporated the Agreement into European Union law.

Rising Refugee Flows: Persecution and Expulsion

Since World War II, the world has witnessed a dramatic increase in the number of refugees and asylum seekers. The majority of these refugees were hosted by developing countries, but many were offered permanent residence in the West, and Cold War politics created special migration channels for movement from communist countries.[104]

Cold War politics and the political turmoil following decolonization drove the massive involuntary movement of people in Asia, the Middle East, and Latin America. The process of decolonization in the Indian subcontinent involved the 1947 partition of the British Indian Empire into the Dominion of Pakistan and the Union of India. Between 14.5 million and 17.9 million people moved between the countries during four years, resulting in "one of the largest and most rapid migrations in human history."[105] The creation of Bangladesh in 1971 sent an estimated 10 million Bengalis and Hindus into India.[106] Elsewhere in Asia, refugees flowed out of Tibet due to Chinese occupation, and many Chinese fled to Hong

Kong and Taiwan. Despite efforts by their respective governments to stop emigration, many ethnic and religious minorities escaped civil conflicts in Burma and Sri Lanka.[107]

Conflicts in Vietnam, Cambodia, and Afghanistan produced massive outflows of involuntary migrants in the 1970s. After the fall of Saigon in 1975, the socialist government of Vietnam abolished all "bourgeois trade" in the former capital, closing down about 30,000 businesses (most of which were owned by Chinese). The creation of a new currency bankrupted Chinese traders who were not already destitute, by eliminating their savings. A border war between Vietnam and China led to increased pressure on the Chinese to leave the country, and more than two million fled in the decade after 1975.[108] In neighboring Cambodia, the Maoist Khmer Rouge captured Phnom Penh in 1975 and remained in power until 1979. Their brutal and violent ideological campaign drove hundreds of thousands of refugees into Thailand and Vietnam. In Afghanistan, the 1978 revolution was quickly followed with invasion by the Soviet Red Army. About two million Afghanis were internally displaced by the conflict, and about a quarter of the population (as many as five million people) left the country as refugees, most settling in bordering Pakistan and Iran.[109]

Following the creation of the state of Israel, the country became both a source of Palestinian refugees and a destination for Jews persecuted abroad. Following the 1948 Arab–Israeli war, between 600,000 and 700,000 Palestinians fled Israel, and 4.6 million people are now registered as Palestinian refugees.[110] Hundreds of thousands of Jews were also displaced from Arab states in the late 1940s, and Israel took in about 600,000 of these refugees. Israel also hosted hundreds of thousands of Soviet Jews who fled persecution in the Soviet Union between 1960 and 1989.

Refugees also flowed out of countries that tried to close their borders. The Berlin Wall, separating East and West Germany, was the most famous of the barriers erected to prevent emigration from communist states to the west. Nevertheless, about 840,000 people fled the USSR between 1961 and 1989. They were accommodated by western countries, which used refugee policy as a tool of Cold War foreign policy.[111] Charles Keeley notes that refugee policy was used "to embarrass communist states, and in some cases was used with the intent of frustrating the consolidation of communist revolutions and hopefully destabilizing nascent communist governments."[112] Following the Vietnam War, the United States gave refuge to half a million Vietnamese, 182,000 Laotians, and 126,000 Cambodians.[113]

In Africa, states placed few restrictions on emigration (with the notable exception of apartheid South Africa), but during the 1960s and 1970s, there were several waves of expulsions on the continent. Ghana and Equatorial Guinea expelled Nigerians, Uganda forced out Kenyans, and Zaïre rejected various nationalities. In 1983, Nigeria expelled about two million foreigners, of whom about half were identified as being from Ghana. Cold War–era proxy wars and South Africa's policy of destabilization in southern Africa fueled African civil conflicts in the 1970s and 1980s, adding to continent's rising numbers of refugess.

The number of refugees increased dramatically over the second half of the century. In 1975, the UNHCR recognized 2.4 million refugees in the world. This number increased to 10.5 million in 1985 and to 14.9 million in 1990, finally peaking at 18.2 million in 1993. While the number of refugees dropped to 12.1 million in 2000, it has risen again to 15.1 million in 2009. Most of the world's refugees originate from areas of civil conflict, such as the Balkans, Afghanistan, Iraq, Burundi, Sierra Leone, Rwanda, Democratic Republic of Congo, Somalia, and Eritrea.

Despite the existence of an international refugee regime—which makes global refugee governance more comprehensive than for other types of migration—the management of asylum applications by governments is highly inconsistent. Each state applies its own procedures to asylum applications, and acceptance rates are characterized by variation between countries and from one year to the next within a single country. The refugee system has "shifted from a system designed to welcome Cold War refugees from the East and to resettle them as permanent exiles in new homes, to a 'non-entrée regime,' designed to exclude and control asylum seekers from the South."[114]

FINDING REASONS TO REGULATE

Migration since World War I has been characterized by increasing state efforts to manage and regulate migration. "The First World War marks a decisive break in the history of migration," notes Carl Strikwerda. "The war destroyed the international regime of the nineteenth century while the nationalism and ideological conflict resulting from the war prevented any new international regime from emerging."[115] Whereas in the nineteenth century, seismic economic forces propelled millions of people to new destinations, in the twentieth century, states increasingly tried to regulate flows of international migrants. Economic forces did not decline in importance, but states became more ambitious in their initiatives to control cross-border movement.

Migrants have been at the center of an evolving world order and an emerging global society. As the state system has grown more rigid, new approaches to governance have developed to accommodate peoples' unrelenting pressure to migrate. The early glimmerings of global governance and the development of a common market within Europe have both responded to migration pressures. The movement of people continually expands the frontier of what it means to be a foreigner, and multiculturalism and cosmopolitanism are now celebrated features of many societies. States still try to control and manage migration, however, and during periods of economic decline, we see political forces mobilize around the apparent threat migrants pose to wages, jobs, and social welfare in host countries.[116]

In a world where the physical and informational barriers to migration are lower than ever before, government policies still restrain what would otherwise be much larger flows of international migrants.

While the global economic gains from free migration would be tremendous,[117] concerns about national or local economic losses and the social impacts of migration are obstacles to more open migration policies. In part II, we will examine the contemporary features of international migration: its dynamics, regulations, and impacts.

PART II

❧

PRESENT

4

ఇ❧ఄ

Leaving Home: Migration Decisions and Processes

Having reviewed 60,000 years of human migration in the part I, part II covers the period from the early 1970s to today. This has been a period of unprecedented globalization. Accelerating cross-border movements of goods, services, ideas, and capital are drawing the regions of the world into an interdependent and interconnected community. Political changes associated with the fall of the Berlin Wall and collapse of the Soviet Union, the opening up of China, and democratization in much of Africa and Latin America have been both a cause and an effect of this accelerating integration. Rapid technological progress and the development of containerization, fiber optics, and mass computing have facilitated more rapid integration, as the increasing transfer of skills and ideas has prompted further innovation.[1]

The rise of cross-border flows resembles the "first wave" of early globalization between 1840 and 1914 that was accompanied by mass migrations. In the contemporary period (the "second wave"), however, the primary destination countries of migrants have imposed new controls and limits on the movement of people—a notable departure from the period before 1914, when controls were minimal and often ineffective.[2] Nevertheless, globalization sets in motion economic and social forces that are shaping the structures and networks that impact upon the migration decision. Convergence, deregulation, the growth of transnational corporations, the competition for skilled labor, growing income inequality, and the opening of emerging economies are introducing new risks, opportunities, and networks, as well as political and social change. Together, these transformations have helped to turn this period into another "age of migration."[3]

Economic transformations are not the only manifestations of globalization. As Steven Vertovec notes, globalization has involved "the increasing extent, intensity, velocity and impact of global interconnections across a broad range of human domains."[4] Changes in transportation and communications facilitate global networks through which ideas, goods, and finance move, and they also connect people around the world. Transnational networks serve as conduits for the movement of people back and forth across borders. While migration is a social phenomenon that stretches back to the first appearance of humans, globalization has made modern migration fundamentally different in its geographic scope, frequency, and intensity.[5]

People generally move in the context of unusual circumstances—rapid social and economic change, economic or political distress, or the availability of new opportunities—that make the prospects of migration attractive, despite its inherent costs and risks.[6] The migration decision is nested within a broader set of family considerations, social networks, and political and economic conditions. Migration does not usually begin and end with one choice, however—it involves a sequence of decisions that are influenced by the changing values and goals of the migrant in response to his or her conditions. Social networks, timing, context, history, risk, and opportunity all influence the migration decision.[7]

Migration processes are shaped by a range of interacting factors at the micro-, meso-, and macro-levels. By examining the complex decision to move from several different angles, we can make some broad generalizations about the variables that influence migration processes. At the micro-level, migration is a choice, albeit a constrained one. To the extent that potential migrants are free to choose, their decision is a cost/benefit calculation that takes stock of both the promises of migration and its psychological and financial risks.[8] At the meso-level, networks and social capital inform the decision to migrate, lower barriers, and facilitate cross-border mobility for certain individuals and groups. Individual choices and social networks are created within the context of macro-level structures—demographic, economic, and political conditions that exert "push" and "pull" forces.

MICRO-LEVEL: INDIVIDUALS AND FAMILIES

The decision to move is made at the individual or household level, when the risk and uncertainty of migration is weighed against the opportunities and benefits it promises. The earliest economic theories of migration proposed that the decision to move could be modeled according to wage differentials between countries. However, migrants often move to be closer to their families, pursue education, widen their prospects, or escape political or social constraints—factors that are not directly related to wages. Furthermore, the migration decision is not always made at an individual level. A potential migrant consults and coordinates with a group of nonmigrants—typically, a family—and shares the costs and benefits with them.[9] Migration can be part of a "livelihood strategy" for families to diversify sources of income, and not just the pursuit of personal gain.[10]

Individuals: Cost/Benefit Calculation

At the individual level, a neoclassical approach explains the migration decision through basic utility maximization. It assumes that, all else remaining unchanged (economists' heroic "ceteris paribus" assumption), individuals want to seek their highest utility, or well-being, and typically this involves pursuing higher wages.[11] Migration is a way to invest one's "human capital": people will assume the financial and psychological costs of migration in order to achieve the greatest return on their skills.[12] According to this approach, migration flows between two countries are the product of aggregated individual moves undertaken in response to individual cost/benefit calculations of this sort.[13]

On the surface, the neoclassical approach is appealing. After all, most migration is from developing countries to developed countries, where wages are much higher. The current wage differential between Organisation for Economic Cooperation and Development (OECD) countries and nearby low-wage countries creates pressure for migration that mirrors historical movement from low-wage to high-wage areas.[14] Unadjusted for purchasing power parity (PPP), wages in Japan are about $13.32 an hour, whereas in Vietnam, they are 13 cents an hour.[15] A low-skilled construction laborer in the United States will work less than 4 minutes to make enough to buy a kilogram (2.2 pounds) of flour, whereas a Mexican laborer at home will have to work for more than an hour.[16] A worker moving to the United States could increase his or her earnings (adjusted for PPP) from $17,000 per year to $37,989 per year through migration—with no extra training.[17] Wage differentials offer powerful incentives for cross-border migration to better-paying labor markets.

Historically, wage gaps between Asian and European countries and the New World were influential in driving the movement of migrants during the nineteenth century.[18] Migration rates to America fell sharply leading up to World War I as real wages in Europe began to catch up to those in the New World, keeping more migrants at home. A similar phenomenon has been identified in Morocco, Turkey, Malaysia, Taiwan, and South Korea—all have undergone a "migration transition" from source country to destination country as wages rise.[19] When wages are too low, however, chronic poverty can inhibit potential migrants from investing in migration.

At a general level, then, the migration transition—from sending country to receiving country—takes on the form of a "migration hump" that follows rising wage levels.[20] As real wages increase, more people can assume the costs and risks of migration, but as the wage gap closes, migration rates proceed to fall again. The phenomenon of the migration hump is supported by other demographic and social changes related to socio-economic development, but changes in wage ratios remain central to explaining why developing countries gradually transform from labor exporters to labor importers over time (see figure 4.1).[21]

While the neoclassical approach is appealing in its simplicity, it does not offer a comprehensive explanation for why people migrate. Sometimes people stop emigrating in large numbers long before wages equalize. Puerto Ricans are free to migrate to the United States—which has over three times the average income and a quarter of the unemployment rate of Puerto Rico—yet only one in four people born on the island elects to migrate.[22] Mass migration from Puerto Rico effectively ended in 1970s, and a similar pattern can be seen in falling migration patterns from Spain to Germany, where migration slowed down long before wages equalized.[23]

The concept of utility maximization can also encompass the pursuit of subjective well-being beyond higher wages. People choose to move

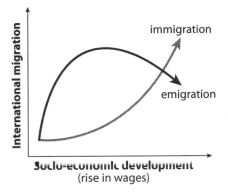

Figure 4.1. The relationship between socio-economic development and migration. Adapted from Hein de Haas. 2010. *Migration Transitions: A Theoretical and Empirical Inquiry into the Developmental Drivers of International Migration.* IMI Working Paper Series. Oxford: International Migration Institute, University of Oxford, p. 19, figure 2.

(or not) to fulfill additional goals, values, or desires: status, comfort, autonomy, and being close to family, their community, and friends.[24] While migrants often move in response to economic incentives, many will have a "target accumulation" motivation: moving to a high-wage labor market just long enough to save enough money to invest back home—to pay for a dowry, a house, or a business, for example.[25]

The factors influencing a migration decision can also depend on the history of migration within one's family or community. The first people to migrate are often single and young, have fewer family obligations at home, and are thus more prone to take risks in response to wage differentials between countries. After members of a family or community have become established abroad, the successive movement of people may be motivated by a desire to be close to family, friends, or a community.

The goals and values influencing individual decision-making depend on factors aside from wage differentials. In fact, for many it is difficult to know with any degree of certainty whether migration will improve their lives.[26] Migration often takes place in the context of social and economic change in which the potential migrant's values, status, and goals are augmented.[27] Douglas Massey and his colleagues note that people are likely to have "a propensity to stay at home that is overcome only during certain exceptional periods when usual circumstances coincide to alter the socio-economic context for decision-making in ways that make migration appear to be a good and reasonable investment of time and resources."[28]

A strict focus on individual decision-making also fails to account for why some people choose to migrate while others in similar circumstances do not. Particular communities or nation-states are more prone to migration, while others that have similar or lower levels of economic development experience lower levels of migration. Also, within the same community or country, not all individuals with the same socio-economic status will decide to migrate.[29] Understanding the variation between the migratory patterns of groups and even individuals requires us to look at other determinants of migration.

Families: Balancing Risk

The new economics of labor migration (NELM) approach proposes that the family—not the individual—is the primary unit of migration decision-making. Migration is still treated as rational response to wage disparities, but this approach accounts for relationships and duties—such as sending remittances—that characterize many migrant experiences.

The migration of one family member is a group response to risk in the absence of a welfare state. "Migration decisions are often made jointly by the migrant and by some group of nonmigrants," write Oded Stark and David Bloom. "Costs and returns are shared, with the rule governing the distribution of both spelled out in an implicit contractual arrangement between the two parties."[30] Some members of a family may work in the local economy, while others are sent to work overseas, often with higher wages, with the agreement that they will share their earnings.

Rates of migration tend to be highest from lower-income developing countries undergoing rapid economic growth.[31] When people are displaced from their traditional livelihoods, they are economically vulnerable, and the migration of family members to work abroad and send money home can help to keep the family out of poverty during periods of unemployment. This family-centered approach helps to explain the relatively high numbers of young female Asian expatriates. Women are generally regarded as a more reliable source of remittances than men, so their migration is often encouraged and financially supported to draw more income into the family or community.[32]

While migration may be risky for an individual, it can be an effective strategy for a family to diversify its sources of income. A family can collectively save to finance the migration of one member and support him or her during the initial search for work in the destination country. In the future, if one source of the family's income (such as local farming) should fail, another remains available. Regular remittances from overseas can allow a family to finance capitalist production: shifting from subsistence to commercial farming offers families the prospect of greater yields, but it also comes with the risk of using new production methods involving untested technologies, crops, and inputs.[33] Participating in a market economy exposes households to risk, and a stable source of income from overseas can allow families to self-insure again this risk in the absence of private insurance markets or government programs.[34]

Families may also send members overseas to finance production or consumption at home. In emerging economies, capital and consumer credit is usually not readily available. Even temporary migration by a family member can allow them to accumulate enough savings while overseas to invest in new enterprises at home. It can also allow families to purchase increasingly available items, such as cars and appliances.[35]

The family-centered model of migration decision-making takes account of migration as a social process. Migration may be a part of a group response to rapid economic change, when livelihoods are made more precarious by wage labor. Factors that push people into migration, however, still require a link between the source country and the destination country. The factors described earlier alter the decision-making calculus only at the micro-level. The translation of *potential* migration into *actual* migration requires networks and systems, which transmit information, finance, accommodation, and job prospects from the destination country to the source country.

MESO-LEVEL: NETWORKS AND SYSTEMS

Meso-level analysis draws attention to the social capital, relationships, and intermediaries that connect potential migrants with opportunities in destination countries. Networks serve to transmit knowledge, information, and social norms from migrants to family and friends at home, and they can be channels for cross-border mobility. Migration both relies on networks and creates and reinforces them.[36] "By and large," remarks Charles Tilly, "the effective units of migration were (and are) neither individuals nor households but sets of people linked by acquaintance, kinship and work experience."[37] While wage differences and individual cost/benefit analyses may create conditions for migration, it is the insertion of people into migration networks that explains why some migrate and others do not, and why migration flows endure over time between particular countries (or even particular communities).[38]

Social networks that facilitate migration develop over time, alongside the process of socio-economic development. As developing countries increasingly adopt market-based economic systems and integrate into the global economy, the migration process accelerates—first from rural to urban areas, and then overseas. Traditional and agrarian societies are destabilized by the development of a market economy, and people displaced from their livelihoods seek out wage labor, often in cities. They take on dirty and dangerous jobs that local workers disdain. After entering the modern economy, people's perceptions, lifestyles, and worldviews change. They can be exposed to cosmopolitan values, consumer habits, and transnational networks. Their economic situation may become more precarious, leading some individuals to assume the costs and risks of migration.[39]

In the first phase in the migration process, micro-level determinants may be particularly important; those willing to shoulder more risk ("pioneer" or "bridgehead" migrants) will seek out opportunities to migrate overseas.[40] The movement of the first groups of migrants produces a "herd effect": a stream of migrants emerges between a source country, undergoing economic development, and a destination country with higher wages. This migration stream eventually becomes self-sustaining, and as migrants maintain contact with family and friends at home, they create a "network effect" that increases the rate of migration even further. Networks relay information and resources that lower the risks for others to migrate, and a migration channel is opened up between source and destination locations through these networks. The continued movement of people through this channel strengthens the network and expands the number of people and locations it connects together. Over time and as migrant communities grow, networks can diminish in their

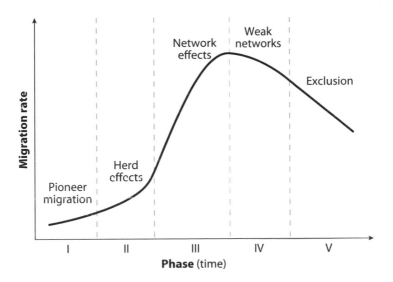

Figure 4.2. Network effects of migration to a particular country. Adapted from Hein de Haas. 2009. *Migration System Formation and Decline: A Theoretical Inquiry into the Self-Perpetuating and Self-Undermining Dynamics of Migration Processes*. IMI Working Paper Series. Oxford: International Migration Institute, University of Oxford, p. 24, figure 3.

significance as the connection between settled migrants and new arrivals from "home" weakens. Networks may eventually be used to discourage further migration if competition for migrant jobs in the destination country becomes more severe (see figure 4.2).[41]

Within this stylized description of the migration process, networks play critical roles at two stages. The first stage involves institutional networks, which assist migration in areas where social networks are not sufficiently well developed to facilitate cross-border movement.[42] State-supported or private labor recruiters help to initiate migrant flows by spreading (often limited) information about the destination country and offering jobs, accommodation, and support for potential migrants. Private intermediaries are prominent in Asian countries.[43] China grants licenses to state-owned contractors and local cooperatives to recruit and place workers overseas.[44] In Mexico, Morocco, the Philippines, and Turkey, the state cooperated with authorities in receiving states to promote early migration flows.[45] Cross-border job brokering creates labor flows between states that have few prior political or economic linkages.

At the second stage, social networks connect family and friends between source and destination countries. They continue to channel the
movement of people long after the economic justification for migration
has diminished[46]:

> Once begun, migrant flows often become self-sustaining, reflect-
> ing the establishment of networks of information, assistance and
> obligations which develop between migrants in the host society
> and friends and relatives in the sending area. These networks
> link populations in origin and receiving countries and ensure that
> movements are not necessarily limited in time, unidirectional or
> permanent.[47]

Networks turn cross-border family and friendship ties into social capital
for potential migrants at home to use to access a higher-wage economy.
Social networks provide information that lowers the risks and uncertainty of migrating, resources that diminish the financial burden of
moving, and contacts that provide job opportunities. Furthermore, many
destination countries have family reunification policies that provide
legal channels for the social migration of relatives.[48]

The availability of social networks in a destination country can also
influence the migration decision. Moving to an area with a high density of migrants lowers the costs associated with leaving home, such as
financial uncertainty and feelings of alienation and loneliness. The relationship between past and future migration from particular regions is
characterized by "chain migration": for every migrant who moves for
economic reasons, others (such as family members) are "pulled" along
for other reasons.[49] Chain migration is a result of the lowered risks associated with moving, the creation of new incentives for moving (to be
close to family and friends), and policy channels that facilitate family
migration.

Areas with high populations of migrants are also more likely to have
specialized services that help new arrivals find accommodation and employment. Home Town Associations based in destination countries help
migrants to get together, celebrate festivities, and mark cultural events,
as well as to raise funds for projects or social services back in their hometown. A "sense of solidarity with their place of origin (local nationalism
or regionalism), reciprocity with the homeland, and often an eagerness

to gain status and recognition in the place of origin" encourages migrants to develop civic transnational ties and activities.[50] A 1990 study of Brazilian migrants to Canada found that 30 percent stayed with friends when they first arrived, while another 20 percent stayed with relatives.[51] Another study showed that one-third of employed Koreans in the early 1990s found jobs with fellow Koreans.[52] Migrant enclaves—where members share a common source country or community of origin—can ease the financial costs and psychological adjustment associated with migrating to a new country.[53]

The type of networks used by migrants can depend on their skills and education. Those of higher educational background tend to rely more on such expatriate or hometown networks than on kin networks to initiate migration.[54] A study of migrants in Hong Kong found that lower-skilled workers rely heavily on kin networks when they move. Higher-skilled migrants, on the other hand, use networks of colleagues and alumni (as well as family).[55] Other (typically low-skilled) migrants and refugees use illicit networks and smugglers to cross tightly regulated borders into high-wage economies. Globalization and the international migration of criminals have facilitated the growth of transnational criminal organizations that profit from smuggling people. As borders become tighter, smuggling operations become more expensive—but they continue to provide a network of last resort for desperate migrants. Others end up as unwitting migrants, as they are deceived and entrapped by criminal networks that illicitly move people around the world to work as sex workers or cheap laborers.

A migrant may also use more than one network throughout the process of moving. Students who leave their home country to pursue higher degrees overseas often use networks and channels provided by universities to learn about opportunities, arrange accommodation, and navigate regulations. In the process of studying for a graduate degree, they may develop extensive contacts and networks—as well as a set of expectations and values—that lead them to settle overseas.[56]

The development of migrant networks around the world has generated well-connected diasporas and transnational communities. Expanding connectivity allows social networks to support transnational relationships and enterprises based on ties of family, kin, or village.[57] Recognition of the experience of migrant transnationalism now appears in statements by policy-makers. In a 2006 Report to the General Assembly, UN Secretary-General Kofi Annan remarked:

> Owing to the communications and transportation revolution, today's international migrants are, more than ever before, a dynamic human link between cultures, economies and societies. . . . The Internet and satellite technology allow a constant exchange of news and information between migrants and their home countries. Affordable airfares permit more frequent trips home, easing the way for a more fluid back-and-forth pattern of mobility.[58]

Annan's remarks highlight how new technologies and social practices are contributing to transformations in the lives of migrants.

The phenomenon of transnationalism extends beyond the private lives of migrants. It has supported small- and large-scale enterprises and also shaped government policies toward migrants. Alejandro Portes comments that transnational ties equip some migrants with knowledge, resources, and a cosmopolitan sensibility that can be harnessed for broader goals and activities: "Participants are often bilingual, move easily between different cultures, frequently maintain homes in two countries, and pursue economic, political and cultural interests that require their presence in both."[59] A large portion of the self-employed in a migrant community is composed of "transnational entrepreneurs"—moving back and forth between home and host countries.[60] This mobile class of migrants, which is not necessarily confined to the upper classes, also benefits from enabling government policies. The recognition of "dual citizenship" is now relatively common, and some governments have ministries set up devoted to overseas nationals, special investment opportunities, and voting arrangements for emigrants.[61] Migrant networks are more than one-way channels—they are dynamic conduits through which people, information, capital, and goods flow across borders.

Highly evolved cross-border networks give rise to "migration systems," which are supported by an industry of institutions that promote the continual flow (and circulation) of people between two or more countries.[62] Migration systems often develop within regions, such as the South Pacific, West Africa, Southern Africa, or the Southern Cone of Latin America, and between countries with political and economic ties, such as North Africa and France and the Caribbean and North America.[63] Flows within a system "occur within national contexts whose policy, economic, technological, and social dimensions are constantly changing, partly in response to feedbacks and adjustments that stem from the migration flow itself."[64] A migration industry of corporations, recruiters, lawyers, travel agents, development agencies, and even smugglers springs up to support the movement of people within the system. Linkages between countries in terms of economic policy and diplomatic relations are also shaped by and respond to the migration flows. It is to these macro-level determinants of migration that we now turn.

MACRO-LEVEL: DEMOGRAPHIC, POLITICAL, AND ECONOMIC CONDITIONS

The determinants of international migration at the macro-level exert "push" (supply) and "pull" (demand) effects on the movement of people. At the individual level, we already discussed the role of wage gaps between countries, but other factors shape the size of migration flows. Demographic, political, and economic conditions in sending and receiving countries function like battery poles, receiving their charge from a variety of sources.[65] Networks serve to link these poles together, but the power of attraction and repulsion generates the propensities for people to move. Macro-level factors, notes Thomas Faist, "have caused, prohibited, directed, and accelerated migration and refugee flows at key historical junctures."[66] Certain conditions, such as immigration policy, provide opportunities or constraints to the choices available to potential migrants.[67]

Demography

A country's distribution of age groups in the population—its demographic profile—can influence both its supply and its demand of migrants. Many developed countries have demographic profiles in which the number of working-age people is gradually being exceeded by the elderly and retired. This is a result of several decades of falling fertility rates—which is correlated with levels of economic development, urbanization, and female education and employment—and population aging as a result of healthier lifestyles and medical innovations. The least developed countries, on the other hand, typically have lower life expectancies and higher fertility, giving their demographic profile a "pyramid" shape.

The example of South Korea in 1960 and in 2000 illustrates the changing demographic structure of a country as it undergoes transformation into an industrial modern economy (see figure 4.3). In 1960, it has a pyramid shape, with most of its population concentrated among the younger age groups, and by 2000, it has a rugby-ball shape. Projections for 2040 are that it will look more like a coffin, with a larger elderly population. The demographic transition correlated with economic development mirrors the migration transition discussed earlier, where a country undergoing rapid economic transformation evolves from a migrant source country to a destination country.

Often it is those who are young and without children of their own that bear the uncertainty of migration. When a large share of the population is concentrated in the 18–35 age group, emigration rates tend to be higher.[68] As fertility levels decline, rates of emigration fall.[69] Population growth does not in and of itself fuel emigration, but when combined with other economic and political conditions, it can reinforce a tendency toward emigration.[70]

Today, European countries are concerned about population decline because of falling fertility rates. Most countries' fertility rates are below 2.1 children per woman, which is the "replacement fertility rate" for population levels to stay constant in developed countries. Declining fertility rates require governments to raise taxes, cut social benefits, keep more native-born people in the labor force (women, unemployed, older people), and/or attract migrant workers. The need to sustain the size of the workforce is leading authorities to argue for more liberal immigration policies to fill short-term labor gaps. In a recent report, the European Commission wrote:

> In the short to mid-term, labour immigration can ... positively contribute to tackling the effects of this demographic evolution and will prove crucial to satisfying current and future labor market needs and thus ensure economic sustainability and growth.[71]

The demographic differences between rich countries and their neighbors create incentives for both migrants and policy-makers to increase labor flows.[72]

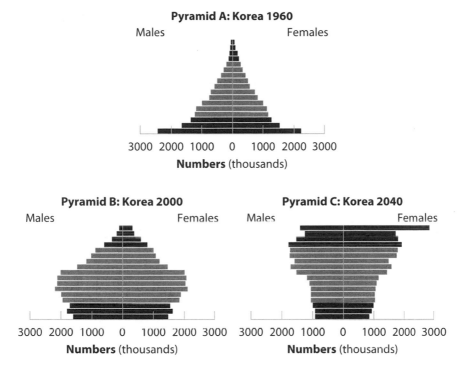

Figure 4.3. Age structure in Republic of Korea in 1960, 2000, and 2040 (projected). Every horizontal bar represents a 5-year age group. The lighter bars represent economically productive age groups (age 15–64 years). John Cleland, Stan Bernstein, Alex Ezeh, Anibal Faundes, Anna Glasier, and Jolene Innis. 2006. "Family Planning: The Unfinished Agenda," *The Lancet* 368(9549): 1810–1827, p. 1811. © Elsevier.

Economic Conditions

Generally speaking, people move away from areas of economic contraction toward areas of growth.[73] The centers of innovation and growth in a dynamic economy are always changing, and new industries develop as old ones fall away, creating the need for labor to be reallocated. The movement of people is expected to follow the movement of capital. This equilibrium model of migration relies on assumptions that are not consistently displayed in practice: rational behavior, perfect information, complete markets, little risk, and open borders are theoretical constructs that seldom exist in reality.[74] As we have discussed, migration processes are more complex and dynamic than the perfect mobility that equilibrium theory might suggest.

Nevertheless, it is instructive to consider how internal migration patterns illustrate some aspects of perfect mobility equilibrium. Lant Pritchett uses demographic changes in the United States to demonstrate how equilibrium models apply to population distribution in response to economic change and shocks. He proposes that structural changes or shocks to the economy will alter the "desired" or "optimal" population of a region. A classic example is that of a gold rush: first, people do not want to live in an area; then, gold is discovered and migrants flow in; and finally, when the gold has finished being mined, people leave again. Because there are no borders between states in the United States, people move with relative freedom in response to economic opportunity, and population distribution has changed dramatically during the past two centuries. Where certain industries have become less profitable—farming in the Great Plains, cotton farming in the South, and coal mining in Pennsylvania—many people have moved to cities. In the process, wages have stayed relatively stable, as people have moved in response to economic change. Pritchett proposes that a fully "globalized" world would see similar movements of people if they could cross borders freely.[75]

While open borders may be an unlikely prospect in the foreseeable future, Pritchett's example illustrates the role of economic growth and change in promoting mobility. The creation of new industries and markets displaces people from their old jobs and generates opportunities elsewhere. As has been mentioned already, in low- and middle-income countries, economic development typically promotes migration.[76] The process of economic transformation into an industrial economy displaces traditional livelihoods in favor of large-scale production through the process Joseph Schumpeter called "creative destruction":

> The fundamental impulse that sets and keeps the capitalist engine in motion comes from the new consumers, goods, the new methods of production or transportation, the new markets, the new forms of industrial organization that capitalist enterprise creates.[77]

The incorporation of developing countries into the global economy, rather than halting migration, can stimulate movement through the disruptive process of social and economic reorganization.

Increased international capital flows, notably in the form of foreign direct investment, have been associated with the expansion of export manufacturing and export agriculture.[78] As shown in part I, the development of industrial agriculture leads to the displacement of subsistence farmers, who often enter into wage labor either on the larger farms or in the urban sector. As more people enter into wage labor and the economy opens to global markets, the impact of shocks is transmitted more rapidly to workers, and global shocks can produce large-scale unemployment. With the return to subsistence farming no longer a viable option for unemployed workers, the prospect of migration becomes more appealing. While several years earlier, these same people would have scarcely conceived of moving overseas, changing expectations, values, preferences, and broadened horizons expand their ambitions.[79]

When they move to developed countries, notes Massey, "international migrants are generally responding to a strong and persistent demand that is built into the structure of post-industrial economies."[80] The structure of these economies is segmented into two sectors of work: a primary sector that offers well-paid and safe jobs that are often taken by natives, and a secondary sector composed of "dirty, dangerous, and difficult" jobs, which are poorly paid and undesirable for natives—thus requiring migrants to be filled. Agriculture in certain countries has proved particularly dependent on migrants. In the early 1990s, the U.S. Department of Labor found that around 85 percent of the 670,000 farm workers in the United States were migrants, many of whom were undocumented.[81]

The French car and building industries serve as a case study of labor market segmentation in the postwar period.[82] The labor shortage following World War II was fed by a foreign worker recruitment program, through which migrants' residence was made contingent on their working in particular industries. By the 1970s, 500,000 foreigners worked in the building industry, while 125,000 were in the car industry. Managers in both industries gained from hiring migrants, whose poorer levels of education made exploitation common—especially for undocumented migrants—and unionization more difficult to achieve. In the process, these lines of work declined in status for French workers, creating a dependency on foreign labor until economic restructuring in the mid-1980s.[83] The process of labor market segmentation results from the combination of immigration policies, employers' strategies, and institutional and attitudinal racism.[84]

During times of recession, migrants working in the secondary sector—in which unionization and job security are lower—often face higher levels of unemployment. In 2008, 623,000 migrant workers lost their jobs in Spain as a result of the economic downturn.[85] Changing economic conditions in Ireland led about a third of Polish migrants (around 70,000) to return home, where the economy was growing and the currency appreciating.[86] In the United States, the unemployment rate among Hispanics (8.8 percent) rose higher than the national rate (6.5 percent) by October 2008.[87] As the immigrant unemployment rate rises during a recession, the number of new migrants tends to be restricted.

Despite economic downturns, people continue to move (or stay), and government policies adapt to try to slow or reverse immigration. In Spain, the government devised a plan to promote the voluntary return of non-EU migrants by offering as much as $40,000 per migrant for handing in their residence permits and agreeing not to seek entry again for three years. While 87,000 were expected to return under the program, less than 1,000 initially accepted the offer.[88] The United States increased its number of deportations and introduced restrictive clauses into its stimulus and bailout packages to exclude the hiring of immigrants.[89] In the UK, the Home Office uses a points-based immigration system to "raise or lower the bar" to immigration according to economic conditions. Former Labor minister Frank Field commented that "[w]hen we're moving into a recession, the length of which we do not yet know, the immigration policy suitable for a boom is totally unsuitable for a recession."[90] The next section will examine the role of policy and other political conditions as determinants of migration.

Political Conditions

Macro-level political forces also influence migration decisions and flows. Political conflict destroys livelihoods, threatens lives, spreads disease, and leads to refugee flows. During times of peace, government policies on visas and methods of border control shape flows of voluntary migrants.

Conflict and Displacement

Since the end of the Cold War, civil wars have increased in frequency as interstate conflict has declined.[91] These internal conflicts have been connected to ethnic divisions, problems of state formation, and competition for natural resources. Unlike the national liberation struggles of the past, warring parties have pursued sectarian economic or ethnic interests rather than universalistic political goals. Government forces and insurgents have used extraordinary violence including torture and rape as a means of civilian control and mass population expulsion as a strategic goal.[92]

The scale of the problem is borne out by figures from the UNHCR, which identifies seven categories of "people of concern" as a result of political distress: asylum seekers; internally displaced persons (IDPs) assisted by the UNHCR; stateless persons; returned refugees; returned IDPs; and a broad category of "others of concern." By 2009, the total population of concern was estimated at 42 million persons, including 15.2 million refugees.[93] The political, economic, and social elements of instability and conflict are closely interrelated. Repressive totalitarian regimes frequently divert resources away from economic development and toward the military. During times of war, land, labor, and capital are not used to foster economic growth and development, which in turn gives rise to poverty, which becomes part of the conflict itself.

The root causes of civil conflict need not in themselves cause population displacement. They include historical events and conditions that have existed over many years, such as long-standing territorial disputes or important historic events. Proximate causes are the more immediate sources of conflict that arise from political mobilization around a long-standing root cause.[94] For example, while a border dispute may lie at the heart of a conflict, a series of escalating struggles to resolve the issue may eventually produce civil conflict. A large population of IDPs can act as a proximate cause in that it provides a reservoir of people seeking to escape misery at home. Eight of the top ten source countries of asylum seekers going to the EU also have large populations of IDPs.[95]

Existing migration routes and migration networks abroad facilitate the flow of refugees. The majority of refugees, however, remain within their region of origin. The UNHCR estimates that more than a third of recognized refugees originate from Africa, virtually all of whom are hosted within the continent.[96] Asylum seekers looking for third-country settlement are attracted to particular countries based on historical ties between origin and destination countries (colonial linkages, political and economic relations, preexisting migration networks); perceptions of a country's economy, society, and asylum policies; physical and legal accessibility; and chance events during the journey.[97] The most important factor in the decision-making process—to the extent that the asylum seeker can exercise choice—is to relocate to a country where there are family and friends. If that is not possible, or if the migrant has a choice between different countries where a familiar community exists, the second primary consideration is language, in addition to cultural affinity.[98] Geographical proximity is also important for refugees fleeing to Europe (although less so for those in North America): asylum seekers from Eastern and Southern Europe sought refuge in Austria and Germany, while North Africans have gone to France, Italy, or Spain.[99]

Government Policies

How states control their borders is influenced by various macro-level factors such as domestic politics, economic conditions, and demography. Massey et al. call these government policies the "intervening factors" between other macro-level influences: "In the world of the late twentieth century, distances are small but the barriers erected by governments are large, and the latter have become the principal factor determining the size and character of contemporary labor flows."[100] Policy shapes the context within which potential migrants make their decisions about whether to move, where to go, and for how long.

The role of government policy in creating an "opportunity structure" for migration is illustrated by the influx of ethnic Japanese from Brazil to Japan between 1989 and 1992. In 1989, Japan began to offer a special visa to overseas ethnic Japanese (called *Nikkeijin*) that gave them access to de facto permanent residence. The visa was instituted to ease severe labor shortages afflicting the manufacturing sector—caused by declining fertility rates and population aging—without challenging Japan's ethnic homogeneity by recruiting other foreign nationals (such as Filipinos, Koreans, or Chinese).

When the Nikkeijin visa was created, the largest Japanese diaspora of 1.2 million Nikkeijin lived in Brazil, a country in severe financial crisis. Working in a Japanese factory, Nikkeijin stood to earn five to ten times that earned by middle-class Brazilians, and they could save up to $20,000 per year. Labor recruitment agencies financed travel expenses, completed administrative paperwork, and finalized employment and accommodation arrangements, services that were later deducted from migrants' salaries. The number of Brazilian Nikkeijin living in Japan jumped from 14,528 in 1989 to 147,803 in 1992, and the migration of South American Nikkeijin to Japan continued through migrant networks. As of 2004, 286,557 Brazilian nationals and 56,000 Peruvian nationals were resident in Japan.[101] The economic crisis by 2008 had led the Japanese Government to not only end but also seek to reverse its policy, offering incentives for the Nikkeijin to return to Latin America.

Most government policies tend to view the migration process as a static and one-time decision that influences an individual's decision to cross a border. They are directed toward either increasing or decreasing barriers to entry, with a view to managing the number of people entering the country. This short-term and narrow view of migration often leads migration policy to fail, however, in terms of the effects that it produces.[102] Wayne Cornelius notes that "the gap between the *goals* of national immigration policy . . . and the actual results of the policies in this area (policy *outcomes*) is wide and growing wider in all major industrialized countries."[103] Because migration is a dynamic social process, often encompassing multiple moves, for many different reasons, due to a variety of factors, immigration policy cannot be viewed as a gate that opens and closes. It is simply another factor, albeit an important one, that influences migrant decisions and processes.[104]

Attempts by destination country governments to tightly control immigration and halt movement by particular classes of migrants frequently fail. Russia's Ministry of the Interior estimated in 2003 that there were five million foreigners of unclear legal status present in the country.[105] The total number of undocumented migrants in continental Europe is estimated to be between four and eight million.[106] In 2005, about a third of foreign workers in Japan and two-thirds in South Korea were undocumented.[107] In Singapore, despite heavy employer sanctions for hiring undocumented workers, a 1998 study found that more than 80 percent of the total foreign workforce did not have visas.[108]

Levels of undocumented migration are high even in the Gulf States, where it is usually necessary to fly across the border (a significant barrier to entry), temporary work visas are relatively easy to obtain, and harsh jail sentences are often meted out to overstayers.[109] To address this problem, the United Arab Emirates initiated a set of amnesties within the Gulf States between 1996 and 1998, during which undocumented migrants would leave or acquire a visa without facing jail or fines.[110] More than a million people participated in the amnesty process, most of whom were returned to their home countries.[111]

Immigration policies can also have unintended or unforeseen consequences. American immigration policy, for example, restricts migration in many respects but it favors family reunification. Studies have shown that family connections between potential Filipino migrants and relatives in the United States are closely associated with their intentions to migrate.[112] New migrants to the United States bring their relatives with them over a period of time through chain migration, but the rate of sponsorship slows down over time as the stock of eligible relatives remaining abroad gradually diminishes (as they enter into the United States).[113] Similarly, more than three-quarters of all migrants entering into France during the 1990s were family members of residents who had previous arrived as "temporary" labor migrants.[114] The phenomenon of chain migration has been discussed earlier, but in this case, it illustrates how immigration policies can frame decisions and propensities to move.

In Japan and Korea, official immigration policies do not permit the entrance of low-skilled labor, but visa pathways for "trainees" to enter the country have paved the way for a rapid increase in foreign workers. In 1993, Japan launched the Technical Internship Trainee Program, and by 2000, there were 54,000 "trainees" in the country.[115] In 2006, there were almost 93,000.[116] Most of the workers who enter under this program find work in agriculture, fishery, construction, food manufacturing, textile, machinery and metal, and other industries.[117] Korea introduced its Industrial Trainee Scheme the same year as Japan, and it was subsequently terminated in 2007 because of similar problems that have arisen in Japan with the Scheme being used as a "side-door" into the Korean labor market.

Government policies that try to shut down channels for labor migration can lead to an explosion in undocumented migration, through visa overstaying, smuggling, or migrants taking perilous journeys. The pressure to enter the EU has increased enormously, especially along the eastern land borders and southern sea boundary, where most of the

undocumented border crossings are made.[118] The International Organization for Migration (IOM) suggests that more than 25 percent of non-
EU nationals residing in the EU arrived through such channels—a 50
percent expansion of IOM estimates in the 1990s.[119]

In the United States, border enforcement has escalated throughout
the 1990s, leading to an increasing number of apprehensions of undocumented migrants arriving from Mexico. As the government has
strengthened border enforcement, it has diverted resources away from
investigating and deporting undocumented migrants within the country.
Undocumented migrants have only a 1 to 2 percent chance of being apprehended after arriving in the United States.[120] An estimated 12 million
undocumented migrants live in the United States.[121] The incentives to
migrate, therefore, remain high, since even those who are apprehended
at the border do not usually face detention or prosecution. The effects of
redirecting resources to border enforcement has been a dramatic increase
in the fees charged by smugglers, an increase in the number of border-
crossing deaths, and a greater propensity of undocumented migrants to
stay permanently in the United States (and bring their families) rather
than cross back and forth across the border.[122] During the period that
border enforcement increased, the percentage of undocumented migrants working on U.S. farms and in low-level service occupations and
construction also rose continually.[123] Migration pressure remains high:
the wage gap between Mexico and the United States is roughly 8:1, and
the economic slowdown in Mexico will enhance the likelihood of migrants taking the risky journey across the border.[124]

In summary, government policies shape the opportunity structure
within which migration decisions are taken and social networks develop,
but they face limits in their ability to fully control cross-border movement. The presence of social networks and other structural factors, such
as economic and demographic conditions, exert pressure on the borders
of receiving countries that cannot be entirely managed by raising and
lowering the barriers to migration. Restrictive immigration policies are
accompanied by the entry of undocumented migrants who find their
way into the country despite or because of the restrictions, often through
illicit means. These restrictive policies also have unintended humanitarian and economic consequences.

INDIVIDUAL, SOCIETY, AND NATIONAL INFLUENCES

The characteristics of migration can be summed up with three principles: the individual agency of a migrant, the social dynamics of migration processes, and political and economic structures.[125] To the extent that the decision to migrate is a choice, it is one that is influenced and constrained by a variety of factors. The desire to move because of wage differences between countries is not sufficient to turn a potential migrant into an actual migrant. Migration assumes different levels of cost and risk for each individual, depending on their level of education, financial resources, social capital, access to information, social networks, and other endowments. Furthermore, the "push" and "pull" factors associated with migration are products of the local or national context in both the home and destination countries. The dynamic interaction between individual goals and desires, networks, and macro-level factors helps to explain why some people migrate and others do not, but it does not amount to a general model or theory of migration. While the migration decision itself is complex, contemporary globalization is generally leading to increasing pressures on the borders of developed countries.[126] In the next chapter, we will take a closer look at the shared characteristics of national regulations that seek to manage migration in a globalizing world.

5

⌖

Immigration and Border Control

As the previous chapter illustrated, global integration and the falling costs of travel and communication are making migration attractive for more people. Our current period of globalization is also shaping the migration policies and priorities of states.[1] Since the 1970s, the flow of migrants has increased in scale and diversity, prompting a new phase of international migration that is defined by the state's "quest for control."[2] States employ more rigorous regulations and border control techniques to manage the movement of people.[3] They seek to keep out "undesirable" people, often for economic or security reasons, based on perceptions of the impacts of immigration. In this chapter, we look at the way governments exert control over migrants and borders. In the next chapter, we will examine current research about the impacts of migration on sending countries, on receiving countries, and on migrants themselves.

States manage immigration through policy categories and criteria that are used to select migrants: those who are useful to the economy, have relevant ancestral or family relations, or are fleeing persecution. As states become more "selective," their borders are also more heavily policed. The widening net of border surveillance is primarily aimed at keeping undocumented migrants from entering into or residing in destination countries. While the high levels of undocumented migration suggest that states are unable to fully control movement across their borders, regulation remains a major priority and concern of governments.

The similar policy categories used by states to manage migration provide a framework for the documentation of migration flows. These "channels" of migration can be grouped into a broad typology, which

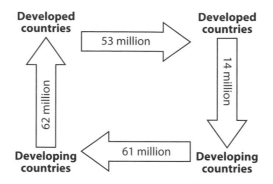

Figure 5.1. Patterns of global migration. The numbers reflect UN calculations of total migrant stocks. United Nations. 2006. "Report of the Secretary-General, International Migration and Development, UN General Assembly, 60th Session," *UN Doc. A/60/871*, 18 May 2006, p. 12. © United Nations. Reproduced with permission.

is meant to be indicative rather than exhaustive: economic migration (high-skilled, low-skilled, student, visa-free); social migration (family, ancestral); and refugee migration (refugee, asylum seeker). This typology will guide the first part of this chapter, where we review the policies used by states to control migration and present illustrative data about the magnitude of flows through these channels.

CHANNELS AND FLOWS OF MIGRATION

There are now more than 200 million migrants in the world, making up almost 3 percent of the world's population. Migration between developing countries is almost equal to migration from these countries to developed countries.[4] About a third of the world's international migrants have moved from one developing country to another. Migration is not a phenomenon experienced exclusively by richer countries (see figure 5.1). Nevertheless, the increasing scale of migration over the past two decades has led to a relative concentration of migrants living in the developed regions of the world. Seventy-five percent of all international migrants live in 12 percent of all countries, and one in five migrants live in the United States.[5] While the number of migrants in developing countries grew by only 2.8 million between 1990 and 2005, those living in the more developed regions increased by 33 million (see table 5.1).

TABLE 5.1

ESTIMATED NUMBER OF INTERNATIONAL MIGRANTS, 1990–2005.

World region	Number of international migrants (millions)		Increment (millions)
	1990	2005	
More developed regions	82.4	115.4	33.0
Less developed regions	72.5	75.2	2.8
Least developed regions	11.0	10.5	–0.5

Source: United Nations, 2006: 29.

The increasing number of migrants living in developed countries is not simply a consequence of movement *out* of developing regions. Citizens of wealthy countries are also more mobile than ever before, especially within the European Union (EU). Governments in recipient states have responded to these accelerating flows of people by structuring legal channels to regulate their entry and access to labor markets. Some of these channels—such as those for refugees and asylum seekers—are defined by international law. Others—such as high-skill, low-skill, student, and family classes—are the result of national policies that reflect emerging international norms in immigration law. The emergence of visa-free migration, most notably within the EU, is the product of international agreements designed to promote mobility, and it represents a major experiment in open borders and labor markets. The typology shown in table 5.2 introduces the framework that will guide this chapter, and it provides a summary overview of the magnitude and direction of modern international migration flows.

Because of the limitations of migration data—in terms of its availability, accuracy, and comparability—this table should be read as simply indicative of current migration trends. Migrants may move from one channel to another and be double-counted—for example, a student may graduate and be admitted as a high-skilled worker in the same country without ever leaving. In some categories, the estimated annual flows are based on crude estimates, especially in the case of undocumented workers, where the Global Commission on International Migration estimated the annual flow between 2.5 and 4 million. The conceptual distinction

TABLE 5.2

MAJOR CHANNELS OF INTERNATIONAL MIGRATION.

Regulatory channel	Leading source countries	Leading recipient countries	Estimated annual flow (millions)
Economic			
High-skilled[a]	India U.S. China Philippines UK	U.S. UK Canada Australia Germany	0.6
Low-skilled[b]	Philippines India Poland Indonesia Bangladesh	Saudi Arabia Thailand UAE Malaysia Kuwait	3.5
Visa-free[c]	Poland Romania Germany Italy UK	Germany Spain UK Ireland Italy	1
Students[d]	China South Korea India Japan Greece	U.S. UK Germany France Australia	2.9
Social			
Family[e]	Mexico Philippines China India Vietnam	U.S. Canada UK Australia France	1.7
Refugee			
Asylum seekers[f]	Iraq Somalia Russia Afghanistan China	U.S. Canada France Italy UK	0.4
Refugees[g]	Afghanistan Iraq Colombia Sudan Somalia	Pakistan Syria Iran Germany Jordan	1.5

Undocumented[h]	Mexico	U.S.	2.5
	El Salvador	Germany	
	Guatemala	Spain	
	Philippines	Italy	
	Honduras	UK	
TOTAL[i]	Mexico	U.S.	14.1
	India	Germany	
	Bangladesh	France	
	China	India	
	UK	Canada	

The leading rank-ordered source and recipient countries are primarily presented in terms of recent annual flows, but where this data has been difficult to identify or verify, we use measures of recent migrant stocks. Sources for the table are listed corresponding to each category.

[a] Source countries based on flows from Goldin and Reinert, 2007: 258, table 6.3. Recipient countries based on the stock of migrants with tertiary education in OECD countries in 2000. Frederic Docquier and Abdeslam Marfouk. 2006. "International Migration by Education Attainment, 1990–2000," in Caglar Ozden and Maurice Schiff, eds., *International Migration, Remittances and Brain Drain*, London: World Bank and Palgrave MacMillan. Annual flow based on calculations in Goldin and Reinert, 2007: 258, table 6.3.

[b] Source countries calculated based on flows from Goldin and Reinert, 2007: 258, table 6.3. Recipient countries based on the stock estimates of temporary foreign workers in 2008. Philip Martin. 2008. "Low and Semi-Skilled Workers Abroad," in *World Migration 2008: Managing Labour Mobility in the Evolving Global Economy*. Geneva: International Organization for Migration. Annual flow based on calculations in Goldin and Reinert, 2007: 258, table 6.3.

[c] Source countries, recipient countries, and annual flows all derived from 2006 flows in part VI (country notes) of OECD, 2008: 226–289.

[d] Source countries based on 2004 flows available through the *Institute for International Education Atlas of Student Mobility* at http://www.atlas.iienetwork.org/?p=48028. Recipient countries drawn from the number of foreign students in OECD countries in 2005. See OECD, 2008: 52, table I.6. Annual flow based on calculations from *Project Atlas 2007*, which draws data from partner organizations, UNESCO/OECD. See http://www.atlas.iienetwork.org/?p=48027.

[e] Source countries are derived from 2001 U.S. flows because the U.S. accepts several times more family migrants than any other country. In 2005, the U.S. accepted 782,100 family migrants, more than the next nine highest recipient countries combined. See Eleonore Kofman and Veena Meetoo. 2008. "Family Migration," in *World Migration 2008: Managing Labour Mobility in the Evolving Global Economy*. Geneva: IOM, p. 165. Recipient countries and annual flows are derived from 2006 flows in part VI (country notes) of OECD, 2008: 226–289.

[f] Source countries are determined based on asylum applications lodged in 2008 in 44 industrialized countries. UNHCR. 2008. *Asylum Levels and Trends in Industrialized Countries*. 24 March 2009. Geneva: UNHCR, p. 15, appendix table 2. Receiving countries are determined based on the total number of accepted asylum seekers in 2007. UNHCR. 2008. *Asylum Levels and Trends in Industrialized Countries*. 24 March 2009. Geneva: UNHCR, p. 7, table 2. Annual flow is rounded up from total numbers provided in the same report, p. 15, appendix table 2.

[g] Source countries and receiving countries reflect refugee stocks at the end of 2007. UNHCR. 2008a. *2007 Global Trends: Refugees, Asylum-Seekers, Returnees, Internally Displaced and*

Stateless Persons. Geneva: UNHCR, p. 8. Annual flow calculated based on increase of 9.9 million refugees at the end of 2006 to 11.4 million refugees at the end of 2007. UNHCR, 2008a: 6.

[h] Source countries are based on U.S. estimated stocks because the U.S. attracts by far the highest number of undocumented migrants, and while undocumented migration is also high in Europe, the source countries differ widely from country to country. The American numbers are from the U.S. Department of Homeland Security. Michael Hoefer, Nancy Rytina, and Christopher Campbell. 2007. "Estimates of the Unauthorized Immigrant Population Residing in the United States: January 2006," *Population Estimates 2007*. Washington, DC: Office of Immigration Statistics Policy Directorate. Recipient countries are based on estimated stocks of undocumented migrants in the U.S. and in Europe, drawn from the Database on Irregular Migration developed by the Clandestino Project, based at the Hamburg Institute of International Economics. See http://irregular-migration.hwwi.net/Database_on_irregula.estimates.0.html?&no_cache=1. Annual flow is based on calculations made by the Global Commission on International Migration. Global Commission on International Migration. 2005. *Migration in an Interconnected World: New Directions for Action*. Geneva: GCIM, p. 85.

[i] Source countries and recipient countries are based on the total share of the migrant population in table 7 in Christopher R. Parsons, Ronald Skeldon, Terrie L. Walmsley, and L. Alan Winters. 2007. "Quantifying International Migration: A Database of Bilateral Migrant Stocks," *World Bank Policy Research Working Paper 4165, March 2007*. Annual flow is the total of the preceding values.

between channels can also be fuzzy, such as between asylum seekers and refugees, or between low-skilled and undocumented workers. Despite the hazards of presenting this table using imperfect migration data, it still serves as a helpful illustration and approximation of current trends.

Several patterns emerge from the overview of international migration flows in table 5.2. We look first at the economic and social channels. In the high-skilled category, the leading source countries include both more developed and less developed countries. The United States is both a leading source and recipient country, illustrating the fact that migration is both a cause and consequence of a dynamic economy. Low-skilled migration emerges as the single largest channel, with most migrants working in the Gulf Cooperation Council states—dominated by Saudi Arabia—and Southeast Asia, notably Thailand and Malaysia. The sources of labor are relatively nearby, and this proximity contributes toward the development of regional migration systems. Student migration is dominated by advanced or advancing Asian economies, which are sending increasing numbers of their young people to study in Western universities. In the visa-free channel, although Poland and Romania—two of poorer and most recent EU member states—are the leading source countries, Italy, Germany, and the UK are leading source *and* recipient countries.

As in the case of skilled migration flows, intra-EU mobility illustrates how migration (both outward and inward) fuels dynamism. Last, family migration emerges as a leading legal channel for permanent migration to developed countries. The leading recipient countries are the "traditional countries of immigration"—the United States, Canada, and Australia—and France and the UK, former colonial powers.

Public discourse around immigration in many developed countries is infused with fears of mass entry by refugees, asylum seekers, and undocumented migrants, but the fact is that these movements—while significant—constitute less than a third of total flows. The estimated annual flow of asylum seekers is the smallest of all channels. Far more people fall into the refugee category, and most of the leading hosts are low-income countries that absorb the outflows of people fleeing conflict in neighboring countries. Last, undocumented migrants constitute one of the largest flows—primarily because of movement into the United States. While unauthorized entry is a leading pathway for these migrants into the United States, most undocumented migrants in Europe simply overstay visitor visas.[6]

It is notable that African countries are neither the leading source nor leading destination countries in most categories. This reflects the fact that migration is not simply driven by poverty, contrary to public perceptions (particularly in Europe) that Africa is a leading source of migrants. It also reflects the paucity of reliable data on migration within and from Africa. As a continent, Africa receives only $9.3 billion in recorded remittances a year, compared with $53.3 billion in South America, $47.5 billion in East Asia, and $39.9 billion in South Asia.[7] Many of the leading source countries of migrants are emerging economies that are undergoing development and integration into the world economy. Increasing mobility is a corollary of national development and global interdependence.

ECONOMIC MIGRATION

The post-WWII boom in Western Europe and the United States led to the erosion of the highly restrictive regime of international migration that developed in the early twentieth century. Low-skilled migrant workers were needed to fill temporary labor shortages in wartime United

States and 1950s–1960s Western Europe, particularly in the agriculture, construction, and transport sectors.[8] Western states began to open economic channels for mobility. In the decades after the war, immigration policy in high-income countries shifted from strict quotas and "country of origin" requirements to selection criteria based on labor market demands and family reunification. These reforms not only allowed for a much greater volume of flows, but also opened the door to migration from nontraditional sources in Africa, Asia, and Latin America. While these temporary worker programs ended in the 1970s, economic migration channels are now established policy tools for receiving countries to promote "demand-led" migration.[9]

High-Skilled Migration

Globalization has helped to shape a consensus among leading receiving countries about the desirability of highly skilled economic migration.[10] In the early 1990s, traditional countries of immigration redoubled their efforts to attract high-skilled migrants to work and settle permanently.[11] McLaughlan and Salt note, "the mainspring for policy has been the perceived benefit to national economic growth derived from the permanent acquisition of high-level human expertise."[12] Global economic competitiveness has driven a contest for skilled migrants to work in growing service sectors and the "knowledge economy." European and certain Asian countries, however, have been slower to implement high-skilled migrant programs that lead to permanent settlement.

The basic definition of a highly skilled migrant is one who has completed a formal two-year college education or more.[13] Some authors also include members of the "creative class": artists, athletes, performers, and entrepreneurs who may not meet the preceding formal definition, but make niche contributions to the economy and society.[14] Highly skilled migrants, concludes the *World Migration Report*, "are mainly in high value-added and high productivity activities that are essential in the global knowledge society."[15]

In skilled migration programs, admission is often linked to employment conditions. In most countries, government agencies identify particular sectors with shortages of local workers through "labor market testing." Some countries measure talent by awarding "points" on the basis of education, experience, language ability, and past earnings. Permanent residence is usually extended to temporary migrants only after their potential value to the economy has been demonstrated.[16] Not all programs allow migrants to bring their spouses and dependent children or to switch between employers.

Skilled migrant programs initially proliferated among developed countries during the information technology (IT) boom of the 1990s, as countries sought to attract temporary workers to fill shortage occupations.[17] The 1990 U.S. Immigration Act significantly increased the number of temporary visas available to highly skilled workers, and many other countries soon followed suit.[18] By the mid-1990s, 30 percent of documented migrants to the United States were highly skilled.[19] In 1998, France created a special status for scientists and scholars and simplified entry procedures for computer professionals. Germany launched a "green card" program in 2000 to attract foreigners working in health care and IT. In the EU, the percentage of skilled migrants as a proportion of overall migrants grew from 15 percent in the early 1990s to 25 percent in 2002.[20]

Many of the workers moving through high-skilled migration channels have come from less-developed countries with respected higher education institutions. In 2004, the three countries with the highest number of entries through Canada's points-based system were China, India, and the Philippines.[21] India accounted for over 60 percent of migrants to the United States working in the computer industry.[22] The Philippines exported up to 85 percent of the nurses it trained.[23] In the UK, the majority of newly registered nurses in 2002 reported foreign qualifications.[24]

In the past decade, European countries have joined Canada, the United States, Australia, and New Zealand in creating high-skilled migration programs that often lead to permanent residency. In 2004, Germany passed legislation that extends the offer of permanent residence to senior academics and researchers, top-level industry and business managers, and entrepreneurs. In 2006, the United Kingdom announced a new "points-based management system," which reflects some selection characteristics of the established Australian General Skilled Migration points test. The UK system, like most high-skilled programs, initially grants temporary work permits but offers the possibility of gaining the right of permanent residence. As such, the extended nature of many high-skill migration programs distinguishes them from low-skill programs, which explicitly aim to prevent any adjustment to permanent status.

Low-Skilled Migration

As the workforces of developed countries have become more highly educated, the unmet demands of agricultural, manufacturing, and service sectors have led states to open migration channels for foreign low-skilled workers. Recruiting low-skilled workers on short-term or seasonal contracts carries the risk of unintentionally generating a stream of permanent migrants (such as that which resulted from post-WWII "temporary" guest-worker programs in Europe).[25] Managing temporary programs, therefore, involves extensive state intervention, cooperation with employers, and the use of incentives and penalties to induce the return of low-skilled migrants. As a result of new programs, temporary low-skilled migration is "significant and growing," according to the OECD.[26]

There is no standard definition of low- or semi-skilled migrants, aside from their exclusion from most work permit schemes or points systems designed to attract skilled labor.[27] Low-skilled migration can refer to the characteristics of either the worker or the job performed.[28] Many countries' low-skilled migrant programs focus on low-wage nontradable sectors: construction, services (such as home and garden care), and seasonal agricultural labor. Migrant workers in such jobs may have higher education—being high-skilled workers in low-skill jobs—which is often referred to as "brain waste," to which we will return in the following chapter. Low-skill migrants are diverse in origin, destination, and function, but they typically arrive under a short-term, low-cost service contract (or illegally) and are expected to return home at the end of it.[29]

In Middle Eastern oil exporting countries, low-skill migrants make up significant portions of the population and workforce (see figure 5.2). Labor markets have gradually segmented: top managers are resident nationals; other Arabs and nationals from other countries (not least the United Kingdom, Australia, South Africa, and Pakistan) fill the other professional positions; and low-wage jobs go to migrants from South and Southeast Asia. Generally speaking, Indians and Pakistanis serve as

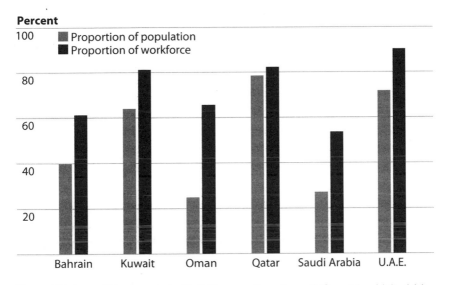

Figure 5.2. Low-skill migrants in Gulf Cooperation Council Countries. United Nations Population Division. 2006. *Trends in Total Migrant Stock: The 2005 Revision.* New York: United Nations; International Organization for Migration. 2005. *World Migration 2005: Costs and Benefits of International Migration.* Geneva: IOM.

laborers and construction workers (although many are also engineers and managers). Maids, nurses, and other service workers primarily come from Sri Lanka, the Philippines, and Thailand. With high unemployment among young adults—about 35 percent of Saudi Arabian 20- to 24-year-olds are unemployed—some Gulf States are capping migrant labor in the public service and selected sectors.

East Asian economies have also grown rapidly in recent decades, and many have turned to neighboring countries to fill low-skill manufacturing and service positions. Hong Kong, Japan, Malaysia, Singapore, South Korea, and Thailand all receive low-skilled migrants from less-developed neighbors such as China, Indonesia, and the Philippines, sometimes through official programs. Korea and Japan have historically resisted implementing official programs; instead they have filled many low-skill jobs with part-time foreign trainees, students, or overstaying visitors.[30] Japan has also "repatriated" citizens of Latin American countries with ancestral connections to Japan (Nikkeijin). Middle-income countries of Southeast Asia often both receive and send low-skilled expatriate laborers: Thailand receives laborers from Cambodia, Laos, and Myanmar, and it sends Thais to Middle Eastern construction and home care industries. Malaysia has long served Singapore with inexpensive labor, while hosting some 1.4 million foreign workers (approximately 15 percent of its labor force).[31]

Countries in Europe and North America, as well as Australia and New Zealand, are also reintroducing temporary low-skill migration programs. In the 2008 *World Migration Report*, Philip Martin writes:

> In a world of persisting demographic and economic inequalities and better communication and transportation links, young people in particular want to cross national borders for higher wages and better opportunities. There is general agreement that the world is about to enter a new stage in international labour migration, with more labour migration sources and destinations and migrants employed in a wider range of industries and occupations.[32]

New temporary worker programs involve stringent admission procedures, employer incentives and sanctions, and high levels of government regulation. Entry is usually contingent on a job offer, and there are limits on access to public services.[33] The number of temporary low-skill workers admitted into OECD countries rose every year between 2000 and 2008.[34] In 2005–2006, Australia, Canada, the United States, and New Zealand accepted 1.24 million temporary migrant workers.[35] The 2008–2009 recession undercut the demand for low-skill workers and prompted discussion of new protectionist measures and limits on migration in many countries, including the United States, Italy, the United Kingdom, and Spain.

Seasonal workers on farms constitute the largest category of temporary workers in OECD countries.[36] Under the Commonwealth Caribbean and Mexican Seasonal Agricultural Workers Program, Canadian farmers hire foreign workers for up to eight months a year. About 80 percent of these migrants are employed on fruit, vegetable, and tobacco farms in Ontario, where the average stay is four months.[37] Farmers have to offer at least 240 hours of work over six weeks and provide free health insurance, housing and meals or cooking facilities, and a fair wage. Canada's seasonal worker scheme has been held up as a model for other countries, despite criticisms from organized labor and human rights groups for the restrictions it places on migrants.[38]

The implementation of programs designed to attract temporary low-skill workers has been slow in many developed countries because of the expectation that migrants arriving through other channels will take on less desirable jobs. For instance, in North America and France, many low-skill jobs are done by migrants who have arrived through refugee resettlement or family migration channels.[39] In Europe, high-income countries currently meet their demands for low-skill labor through visa-free migration from Eastern Europe. As a result, many European countries have been hesitant to introduce low-skilled migration programs.[40] Furthermore, in the post-2008 recession, countries that use temporary migration programs—like Spain and Italy—have curtailed them and encouraged visa-holders to return home.

In the long run, however, the demand for low-skilled workers in developed countries will increase. As we show in part III, we will see the proliferation of more highly managed programs involving employer–government collaboration to ensure labor market testing, ethical recruitment, monitoring, and compliance with return requirements. An alternative model to highly managed migration, however, is currently being testing in regions that have adopted visa-free migration.

Visa-Free Migration

Regions of visa-free migration are social and economic experiments in opening up labor market access to nonnationals. While some regional trading blocs have visa-free travel provisions, the European Union and Australia and New Zealand have each established unique systems that allow citizens of one member country to reside, work, and access social benefits in the other(s). Movement within the European Economic Area (EEA) now makes up a significant proportion of all permanent-type and temporary migration in many European countries.[41] The scale and patterns of migration within the EU and between Australia and New Zealand provide insight into how other countries may be affected by, and manage, greater mobility in the future.

The Trans-Tasman Travel Agreement was introduced in 1973 to open visa-free movement between Australia and New Zealand. It provides labor market access for citizens of either country, with restrictions only for certain jobs in public service or that concern national security. The migration flows are much greater from New Zealand to Australia. In 2008, 521,223 New Zealanders were resident in Australia, and around 50,000 Australians lived in New Zealand.[42] This imbalance provoked a public debate that led to an Australian amendment to the Agreement in 2001, requiring that New Zealanders be resident in Australia for two years before they can claim social benefits. In fact, New Zealand–born residents in Australia have much higher rates of labor market participation that the native-born (78.5 percent and 68.9 percent, respectively).[43]

The progressive establishment of free movement across the European Economic Area has involved the reciprocal opening of national labor markets. The free movement of workers was established as a cornerstone of the common market in the foundational 1957 Treaty of Rome. During the 1990s, the zone of free movement expanded to include Iceland, Norway, and Switzerland (although these countries are not part of the EU). On 1 May 2004, eight former communist countries in Central and Eastern Europe (called the "A8")—Czech Republic, Estonia, Hungary, Latvia, Lithuania, Poland, Slovakia, and Slovenia—and the islands of Malta and Cyprus acceded to the Union. On 1 January 2007, Romania and Bulgaria became the newest members of the EU, bringing the total number of member states to 27 (see figure 5.3).

All EU nationals have the right to free movement between countries, but there are certain restrictions on their right to permanently reside and work in other member states. EU citizens may move to other member states without a visa and live for more than six months if they fall into at least one of the following categories: employed, self-employed, of sufficient means to not require access to health or social benefits, student, or family member of an EU citizen who meets one of the criteria. Following the accession of the new A8 countries in 2004, states were permitted to introduce national regulations on labor market participation by their citizens for a transitional period of up to seven years. Most of the pre-2004 EU states have now opened their labor markets completely to A8 countries, but Austria, Belgium, Denmark, Germany, and Luxembourg continue to maintain limited restrictions on labor market access. Similar transitional restrictions are observed with workers from the newest EU states, Romania and Bulgaria.[44]

Before the 2004 expansion, fewer Europeans were taking advantage of their right to free movement than many predicted. Most intra-EU flow was a legacy of guest-worker programs and informal labor migration

Figure 5.3. The European Union, 2009. Foreign and Commonwealth Office, United Kingdom. Http://collections.europarchive.org/tna/20080205132101/www.fco.gov.uk/servlet/Front%3Fpagename=OpenMarket/Xcelerate/ShowPage&c=Page&cid=1138869388884. Reproduced under the terms of the Click-Use Licence.

during the 1950s and 1960s, when sizable income differentials were prevalent. Convergence in wage and unemployment rates and cultural and linguistic preferences decreased incentives for many Europeans to migrate.[45] In 2000, less than 0.1 percent of the EU's population moved to another EU country.[46] The incorporation of the relatively less affluent

TABLE 5.3

FOREIGN LABOR INFLOWS TO UK BY ROUTE OF ENTRY, 2005.

	Number	Percent
Worker registration scheme (for A8 countries)	194,953	48.6
Work permits[a]	86,191	21.5
EU and EFTA	35,200	8.8
Working holiday makers	20,135	5.0
Highly Skilled Migrant Programme	17,631	4.4
Seasonal Agricultural Workers Programme[b]	15,455	3.9
Domestic servants	10,100	2.5
UK ancestry	8,260	2.1
Sectors-based schemes	7,401	1.8
Au pairs	2,360	0.6
Science and Engineering Graduates Scheme	2,699	0.7
Ministers of Religion	530	0.1
Total	400,915	100

Source: John Salt and Jane Millar. 2006. *Foreign Labour in the United Kingdom: Current Patterns and Trends*. Office for National Statistics, Labour Market Trends.

[a] Mostly from Commonwealth countries, plus China, Philippines, and Japan.

[b] Mostly from non-A8 Eastern European and former USSR countries.

A8 states into the common market, however, has led to a significant increase in intra-EU migration.

The UK, for example, experienced an influx of Polish migrants in the first years following the accession of the A8 countries (see table 5.3). In 2005, the number of new Polish workers in the UK alone (162,495) constituted more than 40 percent of all foreign labor inflows. Between May 2004 and December 2008, almost one million citizens of A8 countries applied to work in the UK. However, these flows are highly variable and not necessarily permanent. In 2008, net migration to Britain (the number of people arriving minus those leaving) fell by more than a third.

Certain countries like Poland, which previously accounted for a surge in migration, also brought sharp reversals. In 2009, with Poland doing relatively better than the UK in the economic crisis, the pound weakening relative to the zloty, and the labor market tightening in many Polish cities due to a construction and the aging of its baby boomers, more Poles

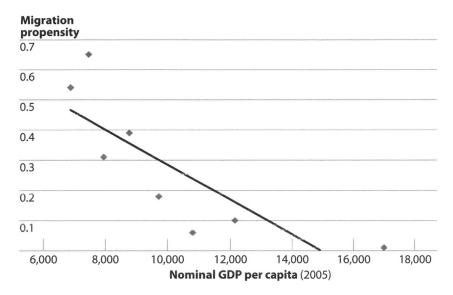

Figure 5.4. Propensity to migrate from A8 countries to the UK, 2005. Countries included are (from left to right): Lithuania, Latvia, Slovak Republic, Poland, Estonia, Hungary, Czech Republic, Slovenia. Propensity to migrate is the number registered to work in the UK as a percentage of the country's population. Nominal GDP per capita is based on IMF data. All numbers are based on 2005 data.

were expected to return to Poland than new arrivals.[47] The Migration Policy Institute estimated that up to half of the roughly 1.5 million Poles who had arrived in the UK since 2004 had left by the end of 2009.[48]

By looking at the relationship between a country's migration propensity to the UK and its GDP per capita, one can see that economic prosperity in the source country is a strong influence on intra-EU migration flows.[49] Citizens of Lithuania and Latvia—the poorest of the A8 countries—exhibit the highest propensity to move, whereas those from the Czech Republic and Slovenia—the wealthiest A8 countries—have markedly lower rates of migration to the UK (see figure 5.4).

Student Migration

Student migration has emerged as a significant migration channel since the 1990s, as economic considerations have increased the opportunities and incentives for student mobility.[50] Student migration has followed

TABLE 5.4

TOP HOST COUNTRIES OF FOREIGN STUDENTS, 2008.

United States	20%
United Kingdom	13%
France	8%
Germany	8%
Australia	7%
China	7%
Canada	5%
Japan	4%
Other	28%
Total	100%

Source: Institute for International Education. 2009. *Open Doors 2008: Report on International Education Exchange.* Washington, DC: Institute for International Education

advances in travel and communications, the growth of networks with previous student migrants, and university marketing campaigns. Policymakers recognize that in addition to providing much needed income for educational establishments and foreign exchange, foreign students are potentially useful as future skilled workers and thereby provide a flexible source to address skill backlogs in national labor markets. Students see overseas study as increasing their employability at home and/or their chances at future emigration. Foreign students tend to be concentrated in programs for graduate study or advanced research, where they can make up a quarter of the total student population at a university.[51] The leading destinations for foreign students are universities in the more developed countries (see table 5.4).

Almost three million students study overseas each year. EU countries provide around half the foreign students in France, Germany, and the United Kingdom.[52] Overall, however, about two-thirds of foreign students in OECD member countries are from developing countries, and Asia is the largest and fastest-growing source of foreign students.[53] China, India, and South Korea send large numbers, particularly to Australia, the United Kingdom, and the United States.[54] Between 2006–2007 and 2007–2008, all three countries increased their number of students in the United States by more than 10 percent.[55] China, which sent barely any students abroad under 30 years ago, is now the world's largest source of foreign students.[56] China's rising contribution has its origins in Deng Xiaoping's 1978 "Open Doors" policy, which sought to modernize the country by training scientists and technological professionals in Western institutions.

International Students at Oxford University

"More than a third (38 per cent) of academic staff, including 28 per cent of teaching and research staff and 43 per cent of research-only staff are citizens of foreign countries. Over a third (35 per cent) of the total student body—more than 6,800 students—are citizens of foreign countries, including 14 per cent of full-time undergraduates and 63 per cent of full-time graduate students. Students come to Oxford from 138 countries and territories and academic staff from 79. . . . The largest groups of international students come from the USA (1,394), China and Hong Kong (745), Germany (605), Canada (345), India (281) and Australia (253)" (as reported by University of Oxford, 2008–2009).

Foreign students who want to stay in their host country to work are not automatically granted work permits, but governments increasingly recognize the value of foreign graduates for their workforce. The U.S. Competitiveness in the Twenty-First Century Act of 2000 effectively exempted foreign graduate students from highly skilled H-1B visa quotas. In Australia, foreign graduates receive extra points in their work visa application for local qualifications, and the government has introduced a special visa category for IT students. New Zealand and Canada also grant extra points to those with locally conferred qualifications. In 2008, Canada passed the Post-Graduation Work Permit Program, which enables international students who have graduated from Canadian tertiary institutions to obtain work permits for up to three years.[57]

France and the UK have also streamlined the study-to-work transition. France has moved away from the so-called Pasqua Law in 1993, which barred foreign graduates from work and regular residence status, by introducing a new temporary work visa in 1998 for scientists, scholars, as well as certain highly skilled professional categories.[58] In line with its new points-based system, the UK has introduced a post-study category that enables all non-European students who have graduated from a UK university to remain in the country for two years with access to the labor market.[59]

In response to such policy reforms, foreign study is emerging as a major avenue by which eligible young people can obtain the right to work and permanently reside in high-income countries. Stay rates of foreign graduates are high, and a significant proportion of migrants admitted through high-skilled channels come from the ranks of the foreign student population. For example, 68 percent of foreign students who received doctorates from American universities in 2000 were still in the United States in 2005.[60] The high stay-rates of skilled workers from less developed countries gives rise to concerns that source countries are losing some of their most talented and well-resourced individuals to high-income countries through the student migration system. The debate around "brain drain" is one to which we will return in the next chapter, when we discuss the impact of migration on sending countries.

Although students are seen to be a desirable class of migrants, governments are also introducing greater scrutiny of student migration. They are becoming more selective in choosing which universities and colleges qualify to recruit foreign students. In the UK, the Home Office reported receiving 2,100 applications for registration in 2008, of which 460 were rejected.[61] Certification of legitimate institutions of higher education is accompanied by other measures to increase the surveillance on individual students whose legal status has become unclear. As concerns have risen regarding the use of student visas by potential terrorists, it may be expected that in those countries that consider themselves vulnerable, both the process of certification of education establishments as well as that of issuing student visas will become increasingly stringent.

SOCIAL MIGRATION

While immigration policy is primarily determined by economic priorities, most states provide channels for social migration. Social migration channels allow for movement to join members of the same family, household, or ancestral group. It is dominated by the family category, which allows established migrants to sponsor nonnational family members for permanent residence. Social channels of migration, therefore, produce unanticipated and variable flows of migrants, and they are the most well trodden route to establishing permanent residence.

Social migration often leads to permanent residency in the destination country, and flows typically follow upon past economic or refugee migration. One family member moves through an economic channel, establishes him- or herself, and then brings others through social channels. Ancestral migration flows usually occur in the opposite direction. Historical migrations out of a country (for refugee or economic reasons) may be followed years, decades, or even centuries later by "return" to an ancestor's country of origin.

Family Channels

Family migration is the largest single category for permanent entry into developed countries, and it is dominated by women.[62] Several types of migration are included within the family category. Family reunification is the process of an initial migrant moving alone to a destination country and later sponsoring other family members for entry. Family formation includes the marriage of a permanent resident or citizen to a foreign partner.[63]

While there is widespread support for family migration channels, the definition of "family" differs across legal contexts, shaping the character and volume of flows. There is limited consensus in policy across countries beyond the common practice of allowing spouses and unmarried dependent minors to obtain permanent residence.[64] In some countries, siblings, adult children, husbands, or parents of citizens are denied access to permanent residence. Policy-makers who want to apply restrictive definitions are sometimes constrained by human rights and other constitutional obligations.[65] In France and Germany, the judiciary blocked policy changes by governments to restrict family migration.[66] Belgium, Italy, the Netherlands, and Spain have also amended their legislation to recognize family reunification through migration as a human right.

The United States extends entry rights to "immediate relatives" of U.S. citizens, defined as spouses, parents, and unmarried children under the age of 21.[67] "Extended relatives" of U.S. citizens and the "immediate relatives" of permanent residents may still immigrate, subject to annual quotas. Quotas ensure that "extended relatives" wanting to migrate face long application processing periods: four years for unmarried adult sons and daughters of U.S. citizens, and 12 years for siblings of citizens. "Subquotas" restricting flows from specific high-demand source countries (China, India, Mexico, the Philippines) prolong the wait further. Filipino siblings face up to a 23-year wait for their application to be considered.[68]

European countries have more limited migration policies. In EU countries, only those who are dependent on the primary migrant are generally permitted to enter as family members. Adult children, siblings, and nondependent parents and grandparents are not recognized, however, under family migration categories in European countries.[69] The United Kingdom, for example, makes provision only for dependent parents and grandparents, and none at all for siblings. In 2003, EU members (excluding Denmark, Ireland, and the UK) established "minimum standards" for family migration, entailing the reunification of "nuclear families" where one member is an EU resident. Denmark's policies do not conform to these norms: spouses gain access only when both partners are over 24 years of age or the sponsor has long been resident in Denmark.[70] Spouses must demonstrate their "greater overall attachment to Denmark than to any other country."[71]

Family migration policies were initially designed with the assumption that future immigration would replicate previous patterns. However, some groups of migrants have been more likely than others to be followed by relatives through "chain migration." A chain initiated by a few thousand refugees from Vietnam to Australia over a generation ago now ranks as the third largest source of "family migrants" to Australia in 2002. Some 87 percent of family migrants to the United States and 74 percent of family migrants to Australia originate from low- and middle-income countries. Western European patterns are similar. More than a third of migrants to France originate from Turkey and North

Africa. Germany's leading sources are the former Yugoslavia, Poland, and Turkey.

Family channels mostly facilitate the flow of migrants from low- and middle-income countries to high-income countries. Two-thirds of migration to the United States and more than a quarter of migration to Canada and Australia is through family channels.[72] The majority of female migrants to Australia, New Zealand, Europe, and North America move for family reunification (although the proportion moving as primary migrants is increasing). In contrast, countries in the Middle East and Southeast and East Asia, which tend to discourage long-term settlement, have negligible flows of family migrants.

Ancestral Channels

While the volume of family migrants to a country tends to be determined by the strength of migrant networks and their ability to leverage opportunities in immigration policy, ancestral channels are a form of demand-led social migration. States use these channels to attract those who claim ancestral ties to the country to "return home."

Globally, ancestral channels for migration involve relatively smaller flows of migrants, although they are significant for particular countries. The most prominent forms arise from "ethnic reunification" policies that promote permanent settlement by nonresidents who have an ancestral connection to the primary national group. Underlying ancestral migration is the judicial norm of *jus sanguinis*, meaning "the right of blood": citizenship is determined by ancestry, not residence. Germany, Israel, and Russia are classic cases of providing legal avenues for coethnics to "return home," but many other states have adopted policies granting partial or full citizenship rights to foreigners with ancestral connections.

Whether such preferential treatment accords with liberal democratic norms or constitutes unfair discrimination is a subject of debate. Nationalists claim that such preferences are humanitarian, because they allow members of the same national group to overcome "accidental" geographical separation.[73] However, the humanitarian intentions of the policy extend only toward people with certain characteristics.[74] Often they aim to satisfy domestic political demands, or increase international influence or the power of the dominant ethnic group.

Israel's Law of Return is one of the largest ancestral migration programs. Individuals of Jewish ancestry, their families, and their grandchildren may enter Israel and take up citizenship, regardless of financial position, education, age, or health.[75] The policy reflects a key part of Israel's raison d'être—as a haven to Jews fleeing persecution.[76] Would-be "returnees" (olim) who lack the necessary funds to migrate have assistance available from the Israeli government and private foundations.

Since 1948, immigration has accounted for half of Israel's population growth.[77] The disintegration of the Soviet Union, conflict and famine in Ethiopia, and crisis in Argentina have prompted sudden and significant flows. Soviet disintegration led to a large increase in the number of Russian migrants: over one million Russian Jews migrated between 1985 and 2006.[78] Economic crisis and a synagogue bombing prompted a surge of over 6,000 Argentine Jews in 2002.[79] During the 1984 famine in Ethiopia, the Israeli Defense Force conducted Operation Moses to bring to Israel about 8,000 Ethiopian Jewish refugees who had fled to Sudan. In 1991, Operation Solomon brought 14,500 Ethiopian Jews to Israel in less than 36 hours during a period of political upheaval when Eritrean forces had destabilized Mengistu Haile Mariam's government.[80] Ethiopian Jews are considered one of the "lost tribes of Israel," and to have left Israel around the ninth century BCE. Israel's policy has extended the definition of ancestry to stretch back thousands of years, further than any other nation.

Germany's Aussiedler ("late repatriates") program dates from the 1950s, and targets those with German ancestry living in the former Soviet Union. Under the program, ancestral Germans and non-German family members from the former Soviet Union are entitled to German citizenship.[81] Ancestral Germans from other countries must demonstrate evidence of individual discrimination to access the program. Aussiedler inflows peaked during the late-1980s as Communist exit restrictions were lifted.[82] Between 1988 and 1997, 2.2 million ancestral Germans were admitted.[83]

The political sustainability of ancestral migration programs often depends on balancing nationalist sentiments with economic interests.

Under high domestic unemployment, such programs can be criticized for providing social welfare to newcomers who have not paid taxes, as happened in the case of Germany's *Aussiedler*. In response, the program introduced more stringent German language ability tests and the Government also capped the program, ruling that no *Aussiedler* born after 1992 will be eligible for immigration.[84]

A number of other countries in Europe operate programs similar to the *Aussiedler* in recognition of the legacies of postwar developments and emigration restrictions that accompanied communist regimes across Eastern Europe. During the 1990s, Greece's program targeted ancestral Pontian Greeks, attracting 300,000 migrants from Georgia, Armenia, and southern Russia.[85] Hungary operates similar programs, as does Russia for those living in former Soviet states. From 1992 to 1998, inflows of ancestral Russians from these states comprised nearly three million persons, similar to the number of Russian Jews and others who left for Israel and beyond.[86] Italy bestows citizenship on all descendants of Italian citizens born after 1861 if no person in the "chain of citizenship" has renounced it. Other European countries with "repatriation laws" include Armenia, Bulgaria, Croatia, Czech Republic, Finland, Hungary, Ireland, Poland, Slovakia, Slovenia, Turkey, and the Ukraine. Even the United States operates a type of "repatriation law" in providing for the immigration of "Amerasian" children fathered by a U.S. citizen and a Cambodian, Korean, Laotian, Thai, or Vietnamese mother after 1950 and before 1983.

Countries that saw past outflows of colonial emigrants have also maintained ancestral migration channels. France and the UK have long-standing policies admitting colonial settlers and their descendants, which have carried especially large volumes during crisis periods in former colonies. After the Algerian War in 1962, 900,000 *pied-noirs* (French colonists and their "white" descendants) fled Algeria for France, despite the fact that most had never previously set foot in France.[87] Similar flights of Portuguese settlers and *mestiços* accompanied independence in Angola and Mozambique. A number of acts during the 1960s, 1970s, and 1980s facilitated the "return" of British colonists' descendants, granting permanent residence to those with parents or grandparents born or naturalized in the UK.

Post-Colonial Immigration Policy in Britain

Britain's post-colonial immigration policy illustrates its shift toward defining citizenship according to ancestry, and the consequences for immigration. Prior to 1962, anyone resident in a British territory (including colonies) could legally claim citizenship and freely move to the UK. The 1962 Commonwealth Immigrants Act, however, imposed immigration controls on all those whose British passports were not directly issued by the British government, such as by the government of a British territory. Persons of Asian descent in Kenya and Uganda were given a two-year window to decide whether to assume citizenship in their newly independent country of residence or to become British citizens. The political instability in both countries led increasing numbers to move to the UK.

The sudden inflow of East African Asians provoked a backlash among some Parliamentarians. On 1 March 1968, emergency legislation was passed that restricted immigration to only those British citizens who had at least one parent or grandparent born, naturalized, adopted, or registered as a British citizen in the UK. Although the policy was defended as an innocuous application of the *jus sanguinis* principles common in the citizenship law of European countries, it nevertheless denied British citizens the right to immigrate to their sole country of citizenship merely on account of their ancestry.

The 1971 Immigration Act consolidated the policy, establishing the "right of abode" only for those born in Britain or with British ancestry. In August 1972, Idi Amin announced that Uganda's 72,000 Indians (two-thirds of whom held British citizenship) had three months to leave the country.[88] Although many were citizens, the 1968 and 1971 legislative acts barred them from entering the UK. In the ensuing refugee crisis, the British government considered resettlement options on British territories such as the Solomon Islands and the Falklands, before finally accepting 28,000 outright.[89] Canada accepted 6,000 Asians, most of British nationality, while the United States accepted about 1,500.[90]

The doctrine of *jus sanguinis* has been applied partially in other countries that extend limited citizenship rights to members of a national diaspora. India, for example, offers a "Person of Indian Origin" card to anyone with at least one Indian great-grandparent (so long as neither they nor any ancestor has been a citizen of a neighboring country). The card serves as a travel document, giving the holder the right to stay in India without a visa, but it does not extend any political rights to vote or hold office. The Slovak Republic, South Korea, and Lebanon have implemented similar policies.

While ancestral migration channels continue to be available in many countries—particularly in Europe—flows have been decreasing since the end of the Cold War. The number of *Aussiedler* migrants accepted by Germany dwindled to less than 8,000 in 2006.[91] Even in Israel, which is estimated to accept the highest number of ancestral migrants, the numbers have fallen from more than a million during the 1990s to less than 15,000 a year.[92] Ancestral migration channels may become less relevant. Meanwhile, many states are implementing "diaspora engagement policies" to retain contact with people who have ancestral connections to the nation.[93]

REFUGEE MIGRATION

While the channels thus far discussed have primarily been shaped by the immigration policies of states, the refugee migration channel has emerged through the development of international law. As was discussed in chapter 3, the international refugee regime grew in a piecemeal fashion in response to the humanitarian problems created by less porous borders and heightened nationalism in twentieth century Europe. People fleeing conflict and persecution in neighboring countries required documentation, protection, and even resettlement by other states. In the intervening years, the scale of refugee flows has grown dramatically, placing considerable strain on the refugee system.

A refugee is one who seeks protection in a nonnative country because of fear of persecution in his or her country of nationality.[94] The status of refugees is protected under the 1951 United Nations Convention Relating to the Status of Refugees, which has been signed by 147 UN member states. Countries that have signed the Convention or its 1967 Protocol agree to offer protection to refugees and not to return them to countries where they may face persecution.

The distinction between an asylum seeker and a refugee primarily relates to the procedures used to acquire formal recognition of refugee status. Refugees usually flee to neighboring countries from conflict or persecution at home, and in most cases do not go through a formal recognition process individually before they are acknowledged as refugees. Asylum seekers are more likely to apply—often individually or in small groups—for protection in more distant countries. The UNHCR clarifies the terminological distinction between an asylum seeker and a refugee:

> An asylum-seeker is an individual who has sought international protection and whose claim for refugee status has not yet been determined. It is important to note, however, that a person is a refugee from the moment he/she fulfils the criteria set out the *1951 Convention Relating to the Status of Refugees* (1951 Convention). The formal recognition of someone, for instance through individual refugee status determination, does not establish refugee status, but confirms it.[95]

An asylum seeker, therefore, is applying for humanitarian protection, which often brings access to assistance, benefits, and permanent residence in a host country. Asylum seekers are in the minority of refugees; most refugees live temporarily in countries close to the one they have fled with the intention of returning home.

In the 1980s and early 1990s, the number of refugees increased sharply as a result of conflicts in Latin America, Africa, and Asia, and later the collapse of the Soviet bloc and civil war in former Yugoslavia (see figure 5.5). The Cold War dominated asylum policies, effectively creating two parallel systems for recognizing refugees: one dictated by foreign policy and the other influenced by the UN Convention.[96] "Defectors" from the Soviet bloc won near-automatic asylum in the West, yet those fleeing civil war in allied countries received routine denials. Following the end of the Cold War, the number of refugees seeking asylum in Europe and North America increased, and many destination countries introduced new policies to manage and restrict their entry.[97] Consultations on a common asylum policy for Europe continue to emphasize

Number of refugees (millions)

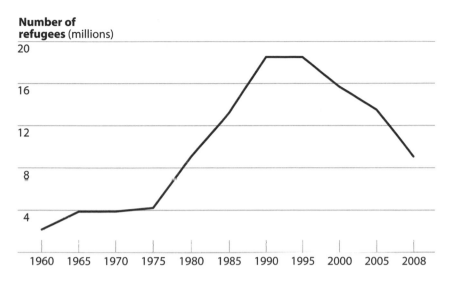

Figure 5.5. Estimated number of world refugees (millions), 1960–2008. Note: 1960–2005 values are taken from midyear totals. The 2008 number is taken from the end of the year. See Population Division of the Department of Economic and Social Affairs of the United Nations Secretariat. 2005. *Trends in Total Migrant Stock: The 2005 Revision*. New York: United Nations; UNHCR. 2009. 2008 *Global Trends: Refugees, Asylum-Seekers, Returnees, Internally Displaced and Stateless Persons* (published 16 June 2009). Geneva: UNHCR.

migration management and border control over broader humanitarian issues.[98] These increasingly restrictive policies are partially responsible for the decline in the number of refugees over the past decade.

In 2008, the UNHCR counted about 9 million refugees in the world.[99] The greatest share of refugees moves from one developing country to another, seeking safety or protection. While developed countries provide most of the funding to support refugee agencies, developing countries host the majority of the world's refugees (see table 5.5).[100] Asia and Africa host 75 percent of refugees of the world's refugees. The West Bank/Gaza, Jordan, Syria, Lebanon, Chad, and Ecuador host the largest number of refugees in proportion to the size of their national populations, and all six of these countries have annual per capita incomes below $10,000.[101] Of the six countries that host the largest numbers of refugees, five are developing countries: Pakistan, Syria, Iran, Jordan, and Tanzania.[102]

Perhaps the most protracted contemporary refugee case is that of the Palestinians. The creation of the state of Israel and the 1947 Arab–Israeli

TABLE 5.5

TOTAL REFUGEES BY COUNTRIES OF ORIGIN AND DESTINATION, END-2008.

Source country	Refugees	Destination country	Refugees
Iraq	1,873,519	Pakistan[a]	1,780,900
Afghanistan	1,817,913	Syria	1,105,698
Somalia	559,153	Islamic Republic of Iran	980,109
Sudan	397,013	Germany	582,735
Democratic Republic of the Congo	367,995	Jordan	500,413
Occupied Palestinian Territories [b]	333,990	Tanzania	321,909
Vietnam	328,183	Kenya	320,605
Burundi	281,592	Chad	302,687
Turkey	214,376	China	300,967
Serbia	185,432	United Kingdom	292,097

Source: UNHCR. 2009. *2008 Global Trends: Refugees, Asylum-Seekers, Returnees, Internally Displaced and Stateless Persons.* Geneva: UNHCR, appendix.

[a] Includes Afghans in refugee-like situations.

[b] Refers to Palestinian refugees under the UNHCR mandate only. Most Palestinian refugees fall under the mandate of the UNWRA.

War produced large outflows of Palestinian refugees. By 1948, between 600,000 and 700,000 Palestinians had fled Israel. The United Nations Works and Relief Agency for Palestine Refugees in the Near East (UNWRA) estimates the current number to be as high as 4.3 million, although many no longer meet the definition of the refugee convention because they hold citizenship in other countries.[103] The UNWRA supports refugees who live more or less permanently in 59 camps based in Jordan, Lebanon, Syria, the West Bank, and the Gaza Strip. Having been for sixty years a simmering cause of resentment, the status of refugees and the issues of repatriation, compensation, reparations, and residency are among the most fraught aspects of peace negotiations with Israel.

During 2008, 604,000 refugees returned voluntarily to their country of origin, a fall of more than 40 percent from 2005 (1.1 million).[104] Approximately 11.6 million refugees have returned home over the last decade, and the majority (7.4 million, or 63 percent) had UNHCR support. Repatriations and a declining number of violent conflicts worldwide have contributed to falling worldwide refugees stocks since 2000. However, some conflicts drag on, leaving large numbers of refugees unable to return home. The UNHCR estimates that the average duration of major refugee situations in developing countries increased from 9 years in 1993 to 17 years in 2003.[105]

To manage the dilemma between prematurely repatriating refugees and maintaining long-term border refugee camps, resettlement in a third country may be preferable. In 2008, the UNHCR submitted about 121,000 refugees to member states for resettlement.[106] This number is, however, greatly exceeded by the number of refugees that have been trapped in "protracted situations"—living semipermanently in refugee camps.[107] Accordingly, a process of rationing resettlement slots has evolved, under the guidance of the UNHCR. Priority cases include those at immediate risk of persecution, *refoulement*,[108] or violence; those who are injured or traumatized; as well as those who have other compelling reasons for resettlement due to legal, humanitarian, or medical concerns. Nevertheless, political concerns in receiving countries frequently influence resettlement priorities. Furthermore, political interest groups may arise to exert pressure on governments to accept or reject particular flows.

The UNHCR resettlement program focuses on "group resettlement." The approach has been systematized by the adoption of a framework among countries of resettlement to identify particularly vulnerable "sections" of the refugee population. The leading countries of origin in 2008 for UNHCR-facilitated resettlement programs were Burma (23,300), Iraq (17,800), Bhutan (8,100), Somalia (3,500), Burundi (3,100), and the Democratic Republic of the Congo (2,500).[109] In 2008, the United States, Canada, Australia, Sweden, and Norway hosted more than two-thirds of the resettled refugees, with the vast majority going to the United States.[110]

Refugees may also apply directly for protection as asylum seekers, in which case they may obtain recognition through asylum channels that differ from one country to the next. Some refugees apply for permanent resettlement by applying through UNHCR offices in, for example, Kenya, Malaysia, or Turkey. Others cross borders illegally and make applications for protection upon arrival. A favorable asylum decision usually carries with it the right of permanent residence in the country of application. If an appeal for asylum is unsuccessful, the migrant may be repatriated, may be moved to another country, may be allowed to remain

Total recognition rate (percent)

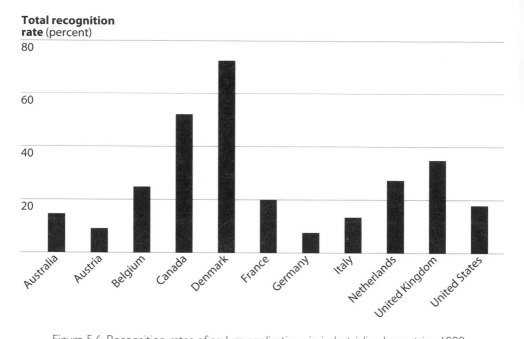

Figure 5.6. Recognition rates of asylum applications in industrialized countries, 1990–1999. UNHCR. 2005. *State of the World's Refugees*. Oxford, UK: Oxford University Press.

on humanitarian grounds (without refugee status), or may assume un-documented status.

The vast majority of asylum applicants are turned down. While refugee migration channels are derived from international law, asylum processes are still heavily determined by the policies adopted by governments to determine the validity of claims. These policies may be influenced by popular pressure to "crack down" on asylum claims or define the criteria for refugee status very narrowly, at the expense of humanitarian considerations. As a result of different asylum policies, destination countries show wide discrepancies in the rates at which asylum applications are accepted (see figure 5.6). While some people who apply for asylum do not really need protection—they would be "economic migrants" by another name—the determination procedures used by states vary to such an extent that UNHCR has pointed to "different standards for the treatment of asylum seekers."[111] While only 15 percent of Iraqi asylum seekers in the UK were granted refugee status, more than two-thirds were recognized in Germany, and none were recognized in Greece.[112]

Asylum policy intersects directly with the theme of the next section: border control. Some asylum seekers and economic migrants enter a destination country through unauthorized means, and the response of many states to undocumented migration has been to enhance border control and enforcement.[113] The threat of terrorism has reinforced this trend. As countries become more selective about the types of migrants they are willing to admit, the regulations used to assert control are evolving and becoming more stringent.

BORDER CONTROL

In the past twenty years, two developments have shaped the way that many receiving countries control their borders. The first is accelerating globalization, which has been accompanied by intensifying global competitiveness and a "war for talent" to attract migrants that can feed innovation and economic growth. At the same time, in the age of globalization, governments seek to use migrants to externalize the effects of economic downturns, by adjusting their policies on migration. The second development is the spectre of terrorism and growing security concerns. Concerns regarding globalization and security have combined to put migration high on the many countries' political agendas.[114] Receiving countries have sought to maintain mobility for some migrants and visitors—such as tourists and business people—while making their borders less permeable to those who are perceived to displace local workers or to present security risks. In pursuit of greater precision in border control, states have adopted new technologies, shifted liabilities to nonstate actors, and developed multilateral and bilateral agreements.

Technology and Surveillance

Technologies used for border control have sought to take advantage of breakthroughs in medicine and electronics. While there is a move to increase accuracy through the use of biometric and other data, there is also a greater reliance on imprecise methods, such as statistical risk analysis. Biometric data is carried on machine-readable passports or identity documents that can be scanned to compare the individual's identity with electronic databases of "watch lists" (often developed through international collaboration).[115] The degree of scrutiny applied to potential migrants often relies on generalized "risk" factors based primarily on statistics and sociology. In the United States, for example, nationality is a risk category, and special attention is directed toward men from a subset of (predominantly Muslim) countries.[116] Other risk categories include age, family, previous income, and assets. What these two trends have in common is the increasingly sophisticated level of surveillance applied to potential migrants hoping to enter certain destination countries.

A recent description of "robo-guards" and the borders of the future identifies the extent to which new technologies are already being deployed. In the United States, this includes the $8 billion Secure Border Initiative network, established by the U.S. Department of Homeland Security with Boeing Intelligence and Security Systems. The network will introduce acoustic and vibration sensors designed to trigger automatic cameras and surveillance drones along the border with Mexico. It will eventually include ground surveillance radar made by Israel Aerospace Industries. In the European Union, the TALOS detection system draws on a ten-country technological consortium and is developing prototypes for a mobile network of ground robots, drones, and command centers.[117]

The development of more reliable identification of individuals is considered a high priority. Biometric identification has been defined as "automated methods of recognizing a person based on a physiological or behavioural characteristic."[118] For the purpose of border control, the main biometric identifiers are fingerprint data, facial scanning, and iris recognition. One or more of these is increasingly required on passports and/or visas for potential migrants to European and North American countries.

Following the events of 11 September 2001, the United States introduced the Visitor and Immigrant Status Indicator Technology (US-VISIT) program to use digital photos, machine-readable passports, and electronic monitoring systems at its borders. A digital photograph and inkless fingerprints are taken at the points of arrival and departure to track the entry and exit of visitors and migrants to the United States. Initially, the program was applied only to visitors who require a visa to enter the United States, but in 2004, it was extended to the 27 countries included in the U.S. visa-waiver program (most of Europe, Japan, New Zealand, Australia, and Singapore).

On 8 June 2004, the Ministers of Interior of all 25 EU member states agreed to incorporate biometrics in travel documents. All newly issued EU passports must now contain digital facial images and biometric fingerprints.[119] These biometric data and personal details are stored on a chip in the relevant passport, in national databases and also in the Schengen Information System (SIS) II database. During the ten-year introduction phase for these passports, all border controls are gradually being equipped with new biometric verification systems. The UK immigration authorities have recently introduced the Iris Recognition Immigration System (IRIS), whereby an individual's iris pattern and passport details are stored in a database, which enables that person to pass through immigration electronically without a face-to-face encounter with an immigration official.

While these technologies will no doubt make it harder to produce counterfeit travel documents, they are by no means perfect. A report to the Council of Europe concluded the following:

> An absolutely certain match or non-match between the enrolled data and the data subsequently submitted to the system is technically unfeasible. The use of a system based on biometric data relies inevitably on a mere statistical certainty. There is no zero default system. . . . Biometric systems are thus inherently fallible.[120]

The "false rejection rate" of biometric identifiers is estimated to be 0.5 to 1 percent, which means that of the 20 million visa applicants in the EU during the year 2007, 100,000 to 200,000 would wrongly be refused a visa or entry into the EU.

The effectiveness of biometric identification as a form of border control and method of limiting undocumented migration is also questionable. In the United States, 14 million visitors have been tracked through the US-VISIT program since January 2004, and only 370 people have been prevented from entering the United States.[121] Furthermore, in the United States, the OECD estimates that 45 percent of undocumented migrants entered the country legally and proceeded to overstay their visas; the rates in other countries are even higher.[122] While the entry of such migrants is documented, they can become relatively "invisible" to regulations once inside the country and working in a shadow economy.

To combat this trend, many developed countries are sharing databases to make it more difficult for migrants who overstay their visas in one country to gain legal entry to another. This practice is part of a larger trend of coordinating border controls, discussed next.

Border Coordination

Coordination primarily involves sharing databases and security resources, aligning migration-related policy, and collaborating on border enforcement. The European Union has developed the most sophisticated system of multilateral coordination, and other forms of collaboration feature in bilateral agreements and regional trading blocs.

The European Union has developed an extensive set of multilateral border controls through the intergovernmental agency Frontex.[123] Frontex was established by EU member countries in October 2005 to integrate the national border security systems of member states.[124] Around the same time, the Prum Treaty was signed by Austria, Belgium, France, Germany, Luxembourg, the Netherlands, and Spain, with the intention of combating terrorism, cross-border crime, and undocumented migration. The Treaty provides for networking national databases and closer cross-border cooperation between police and immigration services.

Cooperation on external migration control in Europe has also developed outside the EU framework through bilateral arrangements. Spain and Morocco carry out joint naval patrols in the Mediterranean aimed at intercepting migrant-laden boats. The EU has also sent attachés from the Interior Ministry to West African countries to collaborate with source country governments in preventing undocumented migration.[125] Italy, Libya, and Tunisia in mid-2004 concluded an agreement for joint patrols, modern border control equipment, and the establishment of reception centers to intercept migrants prior to crossing the sea. As many as 1.5 million would-be migrants are estimated by the United Nations to be waiting for passage to Europe in Libya, and Libya has begun to police its southern borders with Chad, Niger, and Sudan, with the aim of pushing the immigration "front-line" farther south into Africa.[126]

The United States and Canada also coordinate certain border control activities. The September 11 attacks led to a rapid tightening of security at the Canada–U.S. border and a higher level of cooperation on border issues. These areas include developing common biometrics standards; sharing information and management of refugee and asylum claims; locating customs and immigration officers of both countries at selected major airports to cooperate in identifying high-risk travelers; automating existing exchanges of information databases; and cooperating on the removal of deportees.[127] Passports are also now required by U.S. and Canadian citizens to cross the border.

Coordination extends beyond interstate collaboration. Governments increasingly enlist the support of "third-party actors"—nonstate institutions that interact with migrants. In the process, the concept of "border control" becomes more abstract, as entry to a country is controlled by institutions that regulate mobility both within the country and far outside its actual borders.

Third-Party Actors

States are increasingly enlisting other agencies, such as airlines, employers, and local authorities, to collect data, provide services, or administer programs.[128] Gallya Lahav notes the growing reliance of states on such third-party actors:

> Policy implementation has relied on the enlistment or collaboration of non-State actors, who have the economic, social and/or political resources to facilitate or curtail immigration and return. They represent the efforts of States to extend the burden of implementation *away* from central governments and national borders, and *to the source* of control, thereby increasing national efficacy and reducing the costs to central government.[129]

State use of third-party actors involves outsourcing both regulatory functions as well as whole areas of policy-making around processing and enforcing migration rules. While consular offices and border controls serve as the official ports through which people pass, airlines are effectively the gatekeepers of cross-border movement. The unique position of airlines and airport authorities has led states to shift liability onto them for regulating the flow of people.[130]

Employers and local authorities are also liable for upholding immigration policy. In 2007, the European Commission called for heavier sanctions for noncompliance with laws against hiring undocumented workers. These could include fines, repayment of wages, unpaid taxes and social security, and assuming the deportation costs of removing an un-documented worker.[131] The United States has sought to strengthen the enforcement of these sanctions in the past decade. Government agencies can be reluctant, however, to dedicate sufficient resources and personnel to enforce the legal measures in place.[132] Where enforcement is successful, some governments are increasingly turning toward the use of detention centers to hold undocumented migrants while their cases are investigated.

Detention Centers

Migrants entering into major countries of immigration without adequate documentation may find themselves incarcerated, sometimes indefinitely. The use of detention centers has emerged most prominently as a way in which some states confine asylum seekers while their applications are processed, but other undocumented migrants have also been detained while authorities seek deportation orders. Detention of undocumented migrants is often subject to very little judicial scrutiny, and some detainees languish for years without recourse or appeal.

In the UK, asylum applications can be made at the port of entry, and an immigration officer may decide to detain an applicant pending a decision on the case. Officers are not obliged to give specific reasons for the detention of an applicant, and there is very little oversight of the decision to detain.[133] Moreover, asylum seekers can be detained at any stage of their application, and there is no maximum period of detention stipulated.[134] Amnesty International, in a comprehensive study of the conditions of detained asylum seekers in the UK, criticized the system as resulting in the arbitrary detention and wrongful and unnecessary incarceration of particularly vulnerable persons. They reported that the average length of detention had increased to over 8 months and was frequently for a period of 12 months.[135] Over 800 persons are detained at any time in Immigration Removal Centres and prisons throughout the UK.[136]

The United States has increasingly used immigration-related detention, and since 1996, the number of detainees has multiplied almost fivefold (see figure 5.7). The law requires mandatory detention for any

Detainees
(thousands)

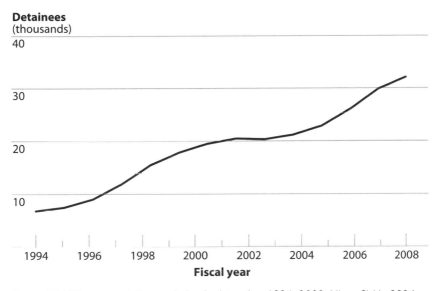

Figure 5.7. U.S. average daily population in detention, 1994–2008. Alison Siskin. 2004. "Immigration-Related Detention: Current Legislative Issues," CRS *Report for Congress*, 28 April 2004; U.S. Immigration and Customs Enforcement. 2007. *Fiscal Year 2007 Annual Report: Protecting National Security and Upholding Public Safety*, available at http://www.ice.gov/doclib/about/ice07ar_final.pdf; Associated Press. 2009. "Immigrants Face Lengthy Review with Few Rights," available at http://www.timesrecordnews.com/news/2009/mar/16/immigrants-face-lengthy-detention-few-rights/.

alien who is suspected of criminal or terrorist activity, and many asylum seekers awaiting decisions on their applications are also detained. While the primary reason for detaining migrants is meant to be because of their threat to public safety, more than half of detainees (18,690) have no criminal conviction—not even for illegal entry or low-level crimes.[137] Several thousand migrants continue to face "indefinite detention" because they are scheduled for deportation but are from countries that refuse to accept their return or that lack normal diplomatic relations with the United States (e.g., Cuba, Iran, and North Korea).[138]

In Australia, the 1992 Migration Reform Act makes detention mandatory for any unauthorized arrivals until their cases are assessed, and children are not exempt from this policy.[139] While the policy has been to deport or "remove" undocumented migrants as soon as possible, in practice decisions cannot always be made speedily, and there have been cases where undocumented migrants have been held in detention for periods up to five years. At the end of 2003, the average detention period for a child was 1 year, 8 months, and 11 days.[140] Australia's asylum review procedure is managed according to a governmental administrative system rather than the courts.[141]

The prevalence of detention centers in many destination countries reflects and reinforces the criminalization of asylum seekers and migrants. It is the blunt edge and last resort of border control.

BEYOND BORDER CONTROLS

The migration policies of states reflect their dual desire to manage borders that are both more permeable and more highly regulated than ever before. While developed countries increasingly align the objectives of their immigration policies, if not their admissions procedures, they continue to face the challenge of undocumented migration. Despite the existence of immigration policies that are based on similar economic imperatives, borders are not impervious. The high numbers of undocumented migrants—an estimated 12 million in the United States alone[142]—indicate that conventional border control strategies are unsuccessful at limiting the entry of migrants who work outside the legal system. Labor demand and market pressures conflict with the inclinations of state control.

The challenge of undocumented migration illustrates the limits of state capacity to fully control movement across borders.[143] While states justify strengthened border enforcement as a deterrent to undocumented migration and as a "security" measure, many undocumented migrants enter legally under temporary categories and then proceed to work in shadow economies for low wages—without the protections of legal status. The precarious position of undocumented workers indicates that despite efforts to control migrants and borders, the factors driving international population movements are ultimately autonomous from the intentions of states. Cross-border mobility is a timeless social process, and its current acceleration is a cause and consequence of globalization and economic growth. Addressing the problem of undocumented migration will require governments to redirect their focus away from a preoccupation with border control. This is a subject to which we will return in chapter 8.

At the dawn of the twenty-first century, the public view of migration is influenced by the imperatives of globalization, the insecurity symbolized by 11 September 2001, and cultural differences that challenge national identities. No matter how we may see it, however, migration is a natural and irrepressible force that will only intensify in the coming decades. Our knowledge of the real impacts of migration will inform the policies that states create to harness the opportunities presented by mobility. The next chapter examines what we know about how migrants are shaping the societies and economies of their new homes, and those they have left behind.

6

 oYo

The Impacts of Migration

The impact of international migration is perhaps the most widely researched topic in the field of migration studies, but it is also the most commonly misunderstood in public discourse. News broadcasts refer to an "invasion of illegal aliens,"[1] fear of a "flood of migrants,"[2] and the "threat" of "brain drain."[3] Around 50 percent of respondents in both Europe and the United States perceive immigration as more of a problem than an opportunity, citing concerns about immigration leading to a rise in crime, increasing tax rates, and taking jobs away from natives.[4] Although the views of politicians at times may be more favorable to immigration, governments respond to negative public perceptions by introducing populist regulations and policies intended to restrict the flow of migrants.[5] To the extent that they are effective, such policies could suffocate national economies, deepen poverty, and starve societies of diversity. This chapter reviews the evidence (and some of the theory) about the impacts of migration—not only on receiving countries, but on sending countries and individual migrants themselves.

Even modest increases in the rate of migration would produce significant gains for the global economy. Both rich and poor countries would benefit from increased migration, with developing countries benefiting the most. As increased migration has a more dramatic impact on the incomes of the poor countries, it serves to reduce inequality between countries. The World Bank estimates that increasing migration equal to 3 percent of the workforce in developed countries between 2005 and 2025 would generate global gains of $356 billion.[6] Other models suggest that with a 5 percent increase in migration, 80 percent of the gains would accrue to developing countries.[7] Completely opening borders, some economists predict, would produce gains as high as $39 trillion for the world economy over 25 years.[8] These numbers compare with the $70 billion that is currently spent every year in overseas development assistance and the estimated gains of $104 billion from fully liberalizing international trade.[9] A small increase in migration would produce a much greater boon to the global economy and developing countries than free trade and development assistance combined.

While most of the benefits of migration are dispersed and generalized, the burden of bearing the costs falls narrowly and unevenly on particular people, sectors, and localities. The costs of migration are often short-run, while the full benefits of increased mobility appear only in the medium or long run. In this respect, the issues raised by increasing migration resemble the long-standing debate over free trade: the economic benefits are distributed and not necessarily tangible, whereas the costs are highly visible and localized.[10] This pattern is evident in both developed and developing countries. Reaping the full benefits of migration requires governments to relieve its short-run costs and mitigate negative impacts on localities and groups that are shouldering a heavier share of the costs.

Particular countries or localities at certain times may bear a disproportionate share of the costs of migration without anticipating that these will bring medium-term benefits. This is particularly the case where large numbers of migrants, in relation to the native population, arrive with no intention of long-term settlement. The island of Malta is small in terms of its size and population (about 400,000 natives), but due to its location off the toe of Italy, it is a relatively close entry point from Africa into the European Union. With tens of thousands of migrants from North Africa arriving on its shores or stranded by smugglers in its territorial waters, it requires assistance from the European Union and others to meet the challenges of migration.

The impacts of migration are felt by receiving countries, sending countries, and individual migrants. Rather than provide a comprehensive overview of the volumes of research on these topics, we will instead seek to clarify areas that are frequent subjects of debate, a great deal of which generate more heat than light. In receiving countries, we examine how migration affects the economy through growth, wages, and innovation.

We also review the fiscal impacts of migration and how increasing diversity impacts societies. For sending countries—particularly developing countries—debate over the benefits of migration often revolves around remittances, the "brain drain," and the role of diasporas in development. When it comes to migrants themselves, the impacts of moving can be seen in terms of education, health, and employment, as well as vulnerability and the experience of isolation and xenophobia. Examined from these different perspectives, it becomes clear that international migration does not offer unmitigated blessings, as promising as they may be. There are tremendous gains to be reaped by promoting mobility, but governments also need to manage and compensate for the unevenly distributed costs.

IMPACTS ON RECEIVING COUNTRIES

During the 2008–2009 economic crisis, several developed countries heard calls for their governments to crack down on immigration, and especially immigrant access to jobs. In the UK, Prime Minister Gordon Brown advocated "British jobs for British workers," and in the 2010 general election, all three major parties advocated reduced levels of migration, with this featuring as a key area of public debate. In the United States, bailout packages included provisions that firms had to accept limits on immigrant hires. Spain offered cash payments to migrant workers if they would leave the country and forfeit rights to return for no less than three years. These indicative responses to a recession illustrate the widespread perception that migrants are a drag on the economy. The logic driving this perception is that migrant workers present additional competition for scarce jobs. This logic, however, is false.

Economic Impacts

Growth

At an aggregate level, immigration stimulates economic growth in receiving countries. Low-skilled foreign workers often take jobs that are considered less desirable by natives, or they provide services—such as home care or child care—that release skilled workers into the labor market. Highly skilled migrants typically work in growing sectors of the economy, or in areas such as health care, education, and information technology that are short of native workers.[11] In short, migration creates more opportunities for people to specialize in their work, which produces a net economic stimulus.

Macroeconomic studies of developed countries with significant foreign-born populations have consistently found that migration boosts and sustains growth. A recent longitudinal study of OECD countries found that increased immigration is accompanied by commensurate increases in total employment and GDP growth.[12] A government-sponsored study in the UK found that migrants contributed about £6 billion to the national economy in 2006.[13] George J. Borjas estimates that migrants make a modest net contribution of $10 billion a year to the U.S. economy, a figure that other economists have suggested is at the low end of the range.[14] Between 1995 and 2005, 16 million jobs were created in the United States, and 9 million of them were filled by foreigners.[15] During the same period, migrants made up as many as two-thirds of new employees in Western and Southern European countries.[16]

While economists agree that immigration produces net benefits for the economy, they debate how to measure these effects. For example, Borjas finds that immigration boosts growth overall, but he cautions that the benefits are unevenly distributed and that those workers who are competing for jobs with migrants will lose from immigration through lower wages or crowding out. Others argue that the direct impacts on native workers are actually marginal and that migrants are meeting crucial gaps in the workforce.[17] Although foreigners make up around 10 to 15 percent of the workforce in the UK, about half of all new jobs are filled by migrants, either because they are in areas requiring particular skills (like plumbing or banking) or because natives do not want them (such as jobs like fruit picking or elder care).[18] Other countries rely more heavily on migrants, without whom their economies would collapse. In some Gulf Cooperation Council countries, migrants constitute more than 90 percent of the labor force.

Migrants also tend to be more mobile than native workers, and their flexibility and willingness to move in response to labor market demands can help to stabilize economies. The authors of an OECD study found that higher levels of migration within the EU can "speed up adjustment to changing conditions" and "help soften the cost of structural change on the native population."[19] As old jobs and industries disappear and new ones are created, perhaps thousands of miles away, migrants move more quickly to new dynamic centers than a rooted native population.[20]

The aggregate contribution of migrants to economic growth is now widely recognized, but there is still debate over the full range of the costs and benefits. For example, when a low-skilled migrant from Mexico moves to California and offers affordable child care, a mother staying at home is released to join the workforce. Through the movement of one person, two people enter the workforce, and they will both earn wages that are spent on goods and services. Migration produces its own multiplier effects. Such indirect and second-order effects of migration are still underspecified, and the overall contribution of migrants to economic growth is therefore underestimated. So too are the dynamic effects of migration associated with innovation and technological change. While the benefits are diffuse, the costs of migration are felt through wage pressures in certain low-skilled sectors and potential local fiscal burdens and social pressures in communities experiencing a sudden influx of migrant labor. We now turn to this first issue, wages—one that animates so much of the immigration debate in developed countries.

Wages

The overwhelming conclusion of research on wages is that the impacts of immigration on native workers are very small at most, and may be irrelevant. Most work on the subject has focused on the United States, where relatively high numbers of undocumented workers exert greater downward pressure on overall wages because they often have to accept pay below minimum wage. In Europe and Australia, where levels of undocumented migration are lower, there is very little evidence that native wages are affected at all by immigration.[21] Following the 2004 EU Accession of Eastern European countries, the massive inflows of migrants to the UK and Ireland did not displace local workers or increase unemployment.[22] Borjas, who has been cited as a pessimist on the impact of immigration on wages, now concludes: "the measured impact of immigration on the wage of native workers fluctuates widely from study to study (and sometimes even within the same study) but seems to cluster around zero."[23]

Even if wages are slightly lower for the small share of the population competing directly with migrants for jobs (typically high school dropouts and other immigrants), these affected workers gain through lower prices for goods and services.[24] In the late 1980s and 1990s, U.S. cities that had higher levels of immigration saw reductions in the costs of housekeeping, gardening, child care, dry cleaning, and other labor-intensive services.[25] Lower prices benefit all consumers, with poor people benefiting the most, since a higher share of their consumption is affected by the prices of local goods and services. When U.S. cities that have received larger numbers of migrants are compared with those experiencing lower migration rates, it is found that immigration produces no negative effects for U.S. workers.[26]

The impact of migrants on wages is influenced by whether or not they are complementary to native workers.[27] This means that when migrants specialize in jobs that would not otherwise have been created or filled, their work is beneficial for everyone. This could involve jobs that require longer hours and more physical work. Or, when they open restaurants and offer lawn care or elderly care they create new jobs or release more highly skilled workers into the economy. These are small changes at the individual level but they can aggregate into a general economic benefit. Migrants also make large and singularly notable contributions to the economy through innovation—creating new products, concepts, and businesses that are at the cutting edge of our global economy.

Innovation

Knowledge, entrepreneurship, and technology are the driving force of a dynamic economy. Two reliable ways to generate ideas and innovation in an economy are to increase the number of highly educated workers and to introduce diversity into the workplace. Both of these objectives are advanced through immigration, and the experience of countries like the United States bears out the bold propositions of "new growth theory." While economic growth in the United States has been sluggish compared to other countries, its most dynamic industries have high concentrations of migrants.

Fareed Zakaria argues that the global "edge" of the United States and its "ability to invent the future" rest on high levels of immigration."[28] In his acclaimed book, *The Post-American World*, he writes:

> America has found a way to keep itself constantly revitalized by streams of people who are looking to make a new life in a new world.... America has been able to tap this energy, manage diversity, assimilate newcomers, and move ahead economically. Ultimately, this is what sets the country apart from the experience of Britain and all other historical examples of the great economic powers.[29]

The United States has long benefited from the creative and intellectual contributions of its migrants. According to some sources, immigrants have made up more than three times as many Nobel Laureates, National Academy of Science members, and Academy Award film directors as have native-born Americans.[30] Migrants have been founders of firms like Google, Intel, PayPal, eBay, and Yahoo. More than a quarter of all global patent applications from the United States are filed by migrants, although they are only about 12 percent of the population.[31]

Harvard researchers William Kerr and William Lincoln make a direct connection between U.S. immigration policy that is open to skilled workers and information technology innovation. They find that higher rates of temporary high-skilled admissions "substantially increased" rates of invention.[32] By 2000, migrants accounted for 47 percent of the U.S. workforce with a science or an engineering doctorate, and they constituted 67 percent of the growth in the U.S. science and engineering workforce between 1995 and 2006.[33] In 2005, a migrant was at the helm of 52 percent of Silicon Valley start-ups, and a quarter of all U.S. technology and engineering firms founded between 1995 and 2005 had a migrant founder. In 2006, foreign nationals living in the United States were inventors or coinventors in 40 percent of all international patent applications filed by the U.S. government.[34] Migrants file the majority of patents by leading science firms: 72 percent of the total at Qualcomm, 65 percent at Merck, 64 percent at General Electric, and 60 percent at Cisco.[35]

Higher rates of immigration also have second-order effects on innovation. Ethnic diversity plays a key role in attracting and retaining creative and talented people to cities. Economic geographer Richard Florida argues that diversity increases a region or city's ability to compete for talent:

> To support high-technology industries or a wide range of economic activity in general, regions compete for a variety of talent across a variety of fields and disciplines. Regions that are open to diversity are thus able to attract a wider range of talent by nationality, race, ethnicity, and sexual orientation than are those that are relatively closed.[36]

Diversity becomes a stimulant to further innovation and growth. Using complex modeling, Scott E. Page shows that diverse perspectives can support innovation by enabling people to find novel solutions to problems.[37] His theoretical observations are borne out empirically by Kerr and Lincoln. They find that migrant innovation "crowds in" invention by residents—growth in a region's migrant population on an H-1B visa (for the high skilled) stimulates patent filings by natives.[38] Another study finds that in the long-run, a one percentage point increase in U.S. migrant university graduates increases patents per capita by 15 percent.[39]

While most of the empirical research on migrant innovation has been based on U.S. cases, the adoption of policies to facilitate the immigration of high-skilled workers in other countries indicates that similar effects are experienced or anticipated elsewhere. As high-skilled migration becomes more widely accepted and desirable for developed countries, public opposition to opening borders to larger flows of low-skill migrants is driven in part by concerns over their burden on public spending. We review evidence of the fiscal impacts of immigration in the following section.

Fiscal Impacts

To the extent that immigrants produce fiscal costs, they tend to be small, short-run, and local. In the United States and Europe, the fiscal impacts of migrants are between +/– 1 percent of the GDP. According to one economist, there is a "striking . . . degree of consensus" among scholars that high-skilled migrants make a substantial fiscal contribution to their host economies and that low-skilled migrants who settle permanently impose a minor cost on taxpayers.[40] The costs are greater for states that have more progressive taxation systems, such as the Nordic countries. Overall, however, these impacts are not significant and are likely to be compensated for by the overall and dynamic contributions migrants make to national income.

Studies show a notable degree of variation between countries in terms of migrant use of social services. In Canada, nonrefugee immigrants use less unemployment benefits, social security, and housing support than domestic residents.[41] In many European countries, on the other hand, immigrants use more social security and unemployment benefits than in Canada or the United States.[42] In Sweden, 25 percent of immigrants are below the poverty line (compared with 15 percent of natives),[43] and in Denmark, immigrants draw 18 percent of social benefits, while their population share is less than 3 percent.[44] These numbers may reflect the needs of refugees and asylum seekers in countries where admission rates are relatively high. In Germany, Greece, Portugal, Spain, and the UK, migrants are less or equally dependent on social services as local citizens. An ILO study showed that the foreign-born population contributed about 10 percent more to the UK government revenue than they received through benefits. The study concluded: "Were it not for the immigrant population either public services would have to be cut or the government would need to increase the basic rate of income tax by one penny in the pound."[45]

Research based on data from 2004 to 2008 on the net fiscal impact of the immigration of Polish, Czech, and other migrants to the UK from the ten countries that joined the European Union in 2004 showed that the migrants contributed "significantly" more in taxes than they received in benefits and services. The 2008–2009 migrants from the accession countries paid 37 percent more in direct and indirect taxes than they received in benefits and from public services such as education, the National Health Service, or social housing. The research found that the longer the migrants stay in the UK and are able to occupy jobs in line with their educational qualifications, the more they contribute. The study concluded that "from the fiscal point of view, the immigration has not been at all a burden on the welfare system. Rather it has contributed to strengthen the fiscal position." [46]

The migrants most likely to generate fiscal burdens are those who are unemployed (i.e., not paying taxes) and drawing on social benefits. In general, labor force participation among foreign-born men actually exceeds that of the native born.[47] Those who are more likely to be outside the workforce are women who have migrated through family channels or asylum seekers whose participation in the labor market is limited by law or due to trauma or language barriers. In the UK, levels of inactivity and unemployment vary dramatically from one expatriate group to the next, even if the overall fiscal impacts of migration are "minimal, or at least equal to the contributions made by migrants."[48] Eighty-five percent of Poles and Canadians are employed, whereas around 50 percent of migrants from Pakistan, Iran, and Bangladesh are employed—reflecting the cultural constraints on many female migrants from these countries.[49] Furthermore, while about 1 percent of Poles and Filipinos in Britain claim income support, about 39 percent of Somali migrants (many of whom are refugees) do.[50] Although their conclusion has been contested as reflecting a static view of migration, a UK House of Lords report noted that "the positive contribution of some immigrants is largely or wholly offset by negative contributions of others."[51]

Paradoxically—given public concerns about the potential social burdens they bring—undocumented workers make significant contributions to the public purse. In the United States, they have a higher rate of labor market participation than native workers or other migrants.[52] Many of these workers use fake social security cards to obtain work, and employers pay social security into "suspense files" that cannot be matched with a recorded name. Between 1990 and 1998, the U.S. government accumulated more than $20 billion in unmatched social security contributions that will never be claimed as benefits.[53] About two-thirds of undocumented migrants in the United States also pay income taxes through automatic deductions, and they pay sales and property taxes like everyone else.[54] Afraid to reveal their status, these workers rarely claim welfare benefits and therefore make a substantial net contribution to public finance.

While the overall national fiscal burden of migrants is marginal, the concentration of migrants in localities or regions can strain local government resources. In some UK localities, the concentration of migrants is as high as 24 percent, which is far above the national migrant stock of 9.3 percent of the total population (see table 6.1).[55] While localities can expect to reap long-term wage benefits from immigration, in the short term, many will experience increased congestion and infrastructure

TABLE 6.1

BRITISH LOCAL AUTHORITIES OUTSIDE LONDON WITH
LARGE MIGRANT POPULATIONS, 2008.

Local authority	Foreign-born population share (%)
Slough	24.0
Leicester	23.0
Luton	19.6
Oxford	19.3
Birmingham	16.5
Manchester	14.8
Coventry	13.0
Bradford	11.8
Wolverhampton	11.2
Brighton and Hove	10.8

Source: Max Nathan. 2008. *Your Place or Mine? The Local Economics of Migration.* London: Institute for Public Policy Research, p. 13, table 4.1.

Note: Data are for local authority districts and unitary areas (UAs)

overload.[56] An influential study of migration in the United States found that while the fiscal impact of migration is "strongly positive at the national level," it can be "substantially negative at state and local levels."[57]

The costs imposed by migrants are usually borne by local authorities—who provide public services, health care, education, etc.—while their tax contributions go the national government. Managing the fiscal costs of migration may require redistributing tax benefits to address the excess burden placed on particular local and regional authorities.

Some migrants can be a burden on public services in the short run, but in the long run, most will make a net contribution. For migrants from Asia and the Pacific Islands to New Zealand, it is estimated that they take five years to become net positive contributors to the economy. In fact, migrants actually pay more money through taxes to the government than native-born citizens. The United Nations notes that each migrant makes a net annual fiscal contribution of about $2,000, compared with $1,800 for a New Zealand born.[58] Research on Germany has shown that a migrant who arrives at age 30 would make a net contribution (taxes minus services consumed) of $150,000 during his or her lifetime.[59]

Overall, the economic impacts of migration are positive for receiving countries. Growth is stimulated through both low-skill and high-skill migration, wages are only marginally affected (if at all), nonrefugee migrants produce modest fiscal gains, and they have been shown to foster significant levels of innovation. While governments increasingly appreciate the economic benefits of migration, the social effect of growing diversity is a recurrent policy challenge in receiving countries. We discuss the social impacts of migration on receiving countries in the next section.

Social Impacts

As the previous chapter illustrated, international migration is increasing in scale and diversity, which produces greater ethnic, religious, and cultural difference in receiving countries (see table 6.2). The social impacts of migration reflect a similar pattern to that identified earlier: there are at times short-run and local costs, which are outweighed by the long-run and dispersed benefits promised by increasingly diverse societies. The social costs are felt in localities experiencing rapid and concentrated immigration, which can be accompanied by deteriorating trust and sense of community. The benefits of immigration, on the other hand, are also well documented. Diverse societies are more creative and dynamic, open, and cosmopolitan. Toronto is one of the most diverse cities in the world—47 percent of its residents are foreign born—and the Economist Intelligence Unit has ranked it as the fifth-most-livable city in the world.[60]

T. H. Marshall, a British social scientist writing in the mid-twentieth century, argued that the political, civil, and social rights that the state extends to its citizens are rooted in national consciousness and feelings of mutual trust and reciprocity. "Citizenship," he wrote, "requires a bond of a different kind, a direct sense of community membership based on loyalty to a civilization that is a common possession."[61] Such ideas about citizenship are challenged within countries welcoming higher numbers of foreign-born residents. Migrants may initially be excluded from certain citizenship rights, but most developed countries offer paths to permanent residency or naturalization. As countries become more diverse, the social basis of citizenship is tested and evolves.

TABLE 6.2

PERCENTAGE OF FOREIGN-BORN RESIDENTS IN THE TOTAL POPULATION
OF OECD COUNTRIES, 2005.

Country	Foreign-born (%)
Luxembourg	32.6
Australia	23
Switzerland	22.4
New Zealand	19.5
Canada	19.3
Germany	12.5
Austria	12.5
United States	12.3
Sweden	12
Belgium	10.7
Ireland	10.4
Greece	10.3
Netherlands	10.1
France	10

Source: Graeme Hugo. 2005. "Migrants in Society: Diversity and Cohesion," *Global Commission on Migration*, p. 9, table 2.

In 2007, influential social scientist Robert Putnam published survey results that show that in the short to medium run, immigration challenges social solidarity and inhibits social capital.[62] In localities in the United States, Australia, Sweden, Canada, and Britain, ethnic diversity is connected to lower trust and sometimes lower investment in public goods. In the short run, Putnam concludes, "there is a tradeoff between diversity and community."[63] Ultimately, this trend can become a medium-term challenge if it leads to the social marginalization of migrants, which is correlated with poverty, crime, and low achievement among migrants and their children.[64]

The idea that diversity undermines social solidarity has also been featured in research comparing public spending on social services in Europe and the United States. One noted study by Alesino and Glaeser concludes that because European society is more homogenous than the

United States, people are more trusting and inclined to be generous to strangers through welfare spending.[65] Interpersonal trust is seen to be central to sustaining support for a system of redistribution. The foundations of citizenship—what Marshall called "a direct sense of community membership"[66]—are corroded as the racial composition of society is altered through immigration. The public perceives the welfare state to be a system for transferring resources to minorities, and they withdraw their support for the system over time.

When Alesino and Glaeser's provocative findings are tested with larger data sets, however, the results are not convincing. Looking at twenty-one OECD countries between 1970 and 1998, Soroko, Banting, and Johnston find that there is no evidence that countries with large migrant populations are unable to maintain generous welfare states.[67] What mattered more than *absolute* sizes of migrant populations was the *pace* at which they grew. Countries that experienced rapid immigration and sudden growth in minority populations saw social spending increase more slowly.

Research by Banting and Kymlicka finds that multiculturalism policies appear to ease the tensions between having large minority populations and redistributive policies.[68] Countries that have adopted the most comprehensive multiculturalism policies—including celebration of multiculturalism, reducing legal constraints on diversity, and active support for minority groups—have been more successful at maintaining elements of a welfare state than those countries that have resisted such policies.

Diversity appears to weaken social trust at the neighborhood level when it is accompanied by diminishing interaction between residents. The authors of one study conclude that "if you have social ties to others in your diverse neighborhood, the diversity of that neighborhood may not be as threatening to your level of interpersonal trust as for someone who lives in a diverse neighborhood without such social interactions."[69] Using a sixteen-country European sample, Herreros and Criado show that societies with higher levels of social trust are better at integrating migrants than those with lower levels of trust. "Those with high social capital," they conclude, "exhibit more positive attitudes toward immigration than the rest of the population."[70] Migration does not make societies less trusting; they may have been like that before the influx of migrants.

The short-run impact of migrants on receiving country societies depends on how they are treated by native residents, their opportunities for social mobility, and access to social and political rights. Settlers who face social marginalization will often form defined ethnic minorities. In addition to living in particular neighborhoods, these groups "may have a disadvantaged socioeconomic position and be partially excluded from the wider society by one or more of such factors as weak legal status, refusal of citizenship, denial of political and social rights, ethnic and racial discrimination, and racial violence and harassment."[71] Ethnic minorities can persist over time and develop into a socio-economic underclass through exclusion and racialization.[72] Migrants rarely introduce antisocial behavior to their receiving country. Where these patterns develop, they are often the result of social exclusion or lack of access to jobs and opportunities because of discrimination.[73]

In the short run, therefore, increasing ethnic diversity tests the adaptive capacity of receiving countries and localities. Popular criticisms of multiculturalism policies have focused on their failure to "integrate" and "assimilate" migrants, but they have paid far less attention to the role of the receiving society in expanding its social and cultural accommodation of migrants.[74] As Putnam concludes in his research, "the central challenge for modern, diversifying societies is to create a new, broader sense of 'we.'"[75] In practical terms, this means that migrant groups need their own associations, networks, languages, and cultures. Integration requires policies that extend settlement services, assistance with labor market access, language training, and the removal of barriers that prevent the involvement of migrants in society.[76]

Expanding opportunities for migrants to fully participate in their host societies in the short run is a valuable investment, given the long-run benefits of social diversity. Citing a study by Pascal Zachary, Richard Florida notes that "the United States' economic competitiveness in high-technology fields is directly linked to its openness to outsiders, while the relative stagnation of Japan and Germany is tied to "closedness" and relative homogeneity."[77] Openness to migrants pays dividends in the long run.

At a local or group level, Scott E. Page argues that the cognitive diversity brought by immigration assists with problem solving and productivity:

> Interacting with a large number of diverse people should be more cognitively taxing than hanging out with your closest friends who look, think and act just like you. Situated in a diverse polyglot, people . . . cannot avoid having their worldview a bit more exposed to new ways of seeing and thinking, and as a result they cannot help but become a bit more productive.[78]

Exposure to disagreement from a minority stimulates thinking about problems from multiple perspectives—what social psychologists call "divergent thinking."[79] Groups composed of similar people are more likely to engage in "convergent thinking," which reinforces the status quo. The different life experiences, social norms, and personal values of migrants contribute to more effective and creative decision-making than consultation among similar people.

Cultural diversity is not only useful for decision-making and production, it also adds value to cities and boosts their economies. Migrant-run businesses may sell goods and services that introduce novel cultural amenities—such as new foods or art forms—into local economies, which are valued by natives of a receiving country.[80] The development of cultural diversity, studied in U.S. cities between 1970 and 1990, has been shown to boost local wages and the rental prices of housing.[81] While most of the benefits of diversity accrue at a national level, there are also local gains to be reaped in the long run.

The evidence reviewed here underlines the contention of a recent book on the subject, *Immigrants: Your Country Needs Them.*[82] For all of the public agonizing in developed countries over how immigration will affect their way of life, the most desirable future is one with higher levels of immigration. The challenge is to manage the local and short-run economic and social strain that any concentrated and rapid influx of different people brings. The substantial local, national, and long-run benefits make it worthwhile. However, by simply looking at the impacts of migration on receiving countries, we are limiting ourselves to only part of the picture. Emigration has effects on sending countries as well, and the real and potential contributions of migration to development should be considerations in any assessment of international migration.

IMPACTS ON SENDING COUNTRIES

While most political and media attention on migration—and as a result, funding for research—remains focused on receiving countries, the impacts on sending countries are as deserving of inquiry. While this imbalance remains, in recent years, increasing attention from researchers and multilateral organizations has been given to questions of migration that concern developing countries and migrants themselves.

In 2006, UN Secretary General Kofi Annan issued a report on "International Migration and Development," which drew on the Global Commission on Migration, the first global initiative on migration of its kind. The same year, the World Bank formalized its "international migration agenda," which has since focused on the role of remittances in development and the risks of brain drain. In 2007, over 150 states came together in the first Global Forum on Migration and Development (GFMD), and they continue to meet in a different country every year at the GFMD. In 2009, the United Nations Development Programme issued its Human Development Report on "Overcoming Barriers: Human Mobility and Development." These initiatives at an international and multilateral level are the fruits of an encouraging increase in research and advocacy by a number of countries and civil society organizations.

In Annan's opening comments to his 2006 report, he noted that globalization is opening new possibilities for developing countries that send migrants to benefit from mobility:

> This new era has created challenges and opportunities for societies throughout the world. It also has served to underscore the clear linkage between migration and development, as well as the opportunities it provides for co-development, that is, the concerted improvement of economic and social conditions at both origin and destination.[83]

Much of the optimism about "co-development" has been driven by the growing volume of international remittances flowing from migrants working in developed countries to their families living in developing countries. Annual remittances now exceed the value of official development assistance or portfolio investment for most developing countries, and they rival flows of foreign direct investment.[84] The risks of migration for developing countries, on the other hand, are expressed in the question asked by the World Bank's 1995 *World Development Report*: "Can something be done to stop the exodus of trained workers from poorer countries?"[85] The spectre of brain drain, it was proposed, threatens to depopulate struggling countries of their valuable human capital.

This section looks at how sending countries are affected by the two issues of remittances and "brain drain." The initial unguarded optimism around remittances has since been tempered by more realistic assessments of who they help and how they contribute to development. And long-held concerns about brain drain are now diminished by new research on human capital formation, "brain circulation," and the role of diasporas in development. In reviewing the evidence and debate over brain drain and remittances, we see that both produce costs that in certain respects are corrected in the long run.

Brain Drain and Brain Circulation

Examined on the surface, brain drain statistics paint a devastating picture of the impact of skilled emigration on some developing countries. More than 70 percent of university graduates from Guyana and Jamaica move to developed countries, and other countries have similarly high percentages of their graduates leaving: Morocco (65 percent), Tunisia (64 percent), Gambia (60 percent), Ghana (26 percent), Sierra Leone (25 percent), Iran (25 percent), Korea (15 percent), Mexico (13 percent), and the Philippines (10 percent).[86]

High-skilled emigration is depicted as the principal risk of mobility for developing countries.[87] While Europe and East Asia actually send the highest *number* of educated migrants, Africa, the Caribbean and Central America send the largest *proportions* of their educated population overseas—around 20 percent from sub-Saharan Africa[88] and more than 50 percent from most Caribbean and Central American countries.[89] For sub-Saharan African countries, this loss is particularly significant because only 4 percent of the population possess university degrees.[90] Caribbean

TABLE 6.3

SUB-SAHARAN AFRICAN INTERNATIONAL MEDICAL GRADUATES IN THE U.S. AND CANADA.

Country of training	Number of African-trained medical graduates in U.S.	Number of African-trained medical graduates in Canada	Number of physicians remaining in home country	% of total African-trained, now in U.S. or Canada
Nigeria	2158	123	22,894	9
South Africa	1943	1845	23,844	14
Ghana	478	37	1210	30
Ethiopia	257	9	1564	15
Uganda	133	42	722	20
Kenya	93	19	4001	3
Zimbabwe	75	26	1694	6
Zambia	67	7	676	10
Liberia	47	8	72	43
Other 12 Countries[a]	83	35	12,912	1
Total/average	5334	2151	65,589	10

Source: Stephen Bach. 2006. "International Mobility of Health Professionals: Brain Drain or Brain Exchange?" *UN-WIDER Research Paper No. 2006/82*, p. 8.

[a] Other 12 countries with at least one graduate in the U.S.

and Central American countries have such small populations that the mass departure of graduates can hollow out the skill base of both the public and private sectors. In Asia, on the other hand, skilled migration rates are low enough and populations generally large enough that the impacts of human capital depletion are not as great.

In addition to the general depletion of human capital, particular concerns are raised by the cost of emigrating health care professionals from developing countries (see table 6.3). For many less-developed countries, the outflow of medical professionals has imperiled already weak public health systems. Malawi, for instance, lost more than half of its nursing staff to emigration over a recent period of just four years, leaving only 336 nurses to serve a population of 12 million. Meanwhile, vacancy rates stand at 85 percent for surgeons and 92 percent for pediatricians. In the face of the HIV/AIDS pandemic, health services have been hard to come by. Rates of perinatal mortality doubled from 1992 to 2000, a rise that is in part attributed to falling standards of medical care.[91]

The risks of brain drain are real for a subset of countries, but a closer look at why and how brain drain happens recasts it as a problem to be managed through migration policy rather than stopped altogether. As Hein de Haas et al. note, it is not clear that many of those migrating would have been as productive at home:

> In the Maghreb, Egypt, Jordan and Yemen there is high unemployment among university graduates. Mass unemployment and frustration among a new generation of relatively well-educated youngsters has become a general social problem. . . . Decades of government job guarantees for graduates have induced students to seek any degree, regardless of its utility in production, since a degree, by itself, has long been a guarantee of a government job. Governments can no longer provide the necessary jobs, while statist policies impede private sector job creation.[92]

Most brain drain originates in developing countries with high rates of unemployment, and the evidence suggests that many graduates leave because they would otherwise be unproductive at home. Organized or xenophobic attacks on particular groups have also played a role in the departure of skilled workers, as have acute concerns regarding kidnapping (particularly in parts of Latin America) and crime (the high murder rate is a common explanation for the emigration of many skilled South Africans). Many doctors migrate out of frustration with inadequate resources and crumbling public health systems.[93]

While the mass emigration of graduates may have short-term collective costs for some countries, research on the "new economics of brain drain" suggests that it may have medium- and long-term benefits. Oded Stark observes that the problem of brain drain is rooted in the "leakage" of human capital from a country, but seen within a broader context, this concern is exaggerated. Without the prospect of migration, people generally underinvest in their education because the opportunities for putting it to use and the relative competition for jobs may not require much schooling. However, knowledge of the opportunity to migrate to a developed economy where wages are higher for skilled labor leads people to

pursue more advanced education. While the country still loses a proportion of its human capital to emigration, it is left with a higher number of
graduates within the country than it would have without "brain drain."[94]
Migration, Stark notes, is "a harbinger of human capital gain" and not
"the culprit of human capital drain."[95]

The phenomenon of "brain gain" has been seen in Fiji and the Philippines, two countries from which large numbers of skilled migrants
leave. The Philippines has become a veritable exporter of human capital in terms of the nurses that it trains to send overseas to the United
States and elsewhere. The emigration opportunities associated with
nursing have stimulated the development of a sophisticated system of
high-quality private education that helps to educate low-income women.
Large numbers of nurses stay after their education, and today the Philippines has more trained nurses per capita *at home* than wealthier countries such as Thailand, Malaysia, or Great Britain.[96] Similarly, a study of
more general skilled emigration from Fiji showed that these departures
had the effect of raising the net stock of domestic human capital. In other
words, Fiji ended up with *more* skilled workers at home than they would
have if emigration rates had been lower.[97]

The incentives for brain gain in sending countries may also be supported by skilled migrants who have worked abroad and return home
to foster new industries. The point is illustrated by the story of Luis
Miyashiro, an entrepreneur in Peru. Miyashiro is a Peruvian national
who moved to Japan for several years under the Nikkeijin visa program,
designed to attract those with ancestral connections to work in Japan.[98]
After several years in Japan, he returned to Lima and founded Norkys,
a chain of chicken restaurants. The new chain renovated the food-stand
concept that is popular in Lima by adding Japanese standards of cleanli-
ness and efficiency. The new fast food chain was launched with ideas and
capital from Japan, and it was the first of its type in an Andean country.

The example of Norkys exemplifies how return migration can stimulate local development, and it also illustrates the transmission of "social
remittances"—"ideas, behaviours, identities and social capital that flow
from receiving- to sending-country communities."[99] When migrants
lost to "brain drain" return home, they bring with them social and cultural resources that sometimes influence entrepreneurship as well as
family, social, and political life. Return migration rarely happens in large

numbers, however, without the presence of other factors conducive to development. The return of skilled migrants is a significant phenomenon in China, for example, but it has yet to take hold in countries like Guyana.

The phenomena of "brain circulation" and return migration suggests that some migrants move overseas for education or early career development and later return home either permanently or episodically. Yevgeny Kuznetsov remarks that historical patterns of brain drain, which drew promising students from developing countries to challenging careers in developed countries, are now showing signs of "turning into a back and forth movement, or diaspora network":

> Talented students still go abroad to continue their studies and work in the developed economies, but then use their own global networks, and especially those of the diasporas, to help build new establishments in their home countries.[100]

The development of dynamic information technology industries in Taiwan and Israel has been a result of migrants returning home in the early 1980s from the United States and Silicon Valley. Return migrants brought capital, technical and operating experience, knowledge of business models, and networks of contacts in the United States.[101] The two countries now boast leading firms in software, security, PC production, and integrated circuits. A similar process of return migration is now occurring in India, with skilled workers from Silicon Valley bringing expertise and capital from abroad to develop the Bangalore IT industry.[102]

Members of a country's diaspora can play a "bridging" role in connecting their home countries with foreign expertise, finance, and contacts—overcoming what can be volatile political negotiations with foreign companies. "Network diasporas," Kuznetsov argues, "are but the latest bridge institutions connecting developing economy insiders, with their risk mitigating knowledge and connections, to outsiders in command of technical know-how and investment capital."[103] For countries to successfully tap into their overseas expertise, there need to be conditions at home that are attractive for expatriates to return to or invest in. Migrants in a diaspora are unlikely to spontaneously fire up a flailing national economy; they are a resource that can reinforce or accelerate existing positive trends.[104]

India's Dynamic Diaspora Network

The development of global supply chains, decentralized systems of production, and modern information technologies have facilitated the transformation of brain drain from India into "diaspora networks" that are supporting the IT sector at home. India's universities are thriving, and many of its best graduates seek out jobs in Silicon Valley, where they are supported by established professional networks for Indian nationals. It is easier to start a business in the United States, but software engineers are more plentiful and inexpensive in India, so handfuls of Indian entrepreneurs have started cross-regional companies that link Silicon Valley capital with workers living in Mumbai and Bangalore. The entrepreneurs and engineers that moved to Silicon Valley years or decades ago are also increasingly moving home, a phenomenon that is related to new visa restrictions on the entry of skilled workers to the United States.[105] While such restrictions are introduced to ostensibly defend the jobs of native workers, they are having the inadvertent effect of promoting the development of competitive industries overseas.

Even when skilled expatriates do not return home, they may remain connected through diaspora networks that support development in the sending country. Between 1985 and 2000, for example, overseas Chinese contributed about 70 percent of China's total foreign direct investment.[106] Taiwan has relied on diaspora networks for decades to promote the flow of ideas, goods, capital, skills, and technology. It serves as an intermediary between Chinese and Southeast Asian markets and American capital, skills, and ideas.[107] This "symbiotic relationship" has developed over 40 to 50 years through close relations between the United States and Taiwan.[108] The relationship will likely grow stronger as China's strategic role increases and Taiwan provides U.S. firms with access to mainland China.[109]

To capture the benefits of diasporas for national development, some countries are developing ad hoc "diaspora engagement policies." Ireland and New Zealand, following upon the example set by India and China, are attempting to harness the expertise and finance of their diasporas for national development. Ireland drew upon Irish-American business connections and its skilled expatriate workers to attract Intel to Ireland.[110]

New Zealand has introduced a "World Class New Zealander Network" to attract expatriates to invest in their home country.[111]

The political significance of diasporas should also be considered. In the short run, the loss of local and national leaders to migration can deprive a country of key visionaries and community builders, but their later return can ultimately help them chart a new path for their home countries. Consider, for example, the cases of Mohandas Gandhi, Kwame Nkrumah, Ho Chi Minh, or Ellen Johnson-Sirleaf—leaders who spent their young adult years overseas, where they assimilated new ideas that allowed them to later play crucial roles in nation building at home. Viewed collectively, the South African diaspora—in the form of people forced into exile and their children—made important contributions to the anti-apartheid struggle, and many went back in 1994 to support Nelson Mandela's government. Diasporas from many Latin American countries, who initially fled dictatorial regimes, went back following early democratic reform to provide leadership. Through their actions in their adoptive homes, the Jewish and Taiwanese diasporas have helped to sustain Israel and Taiwan politically and in terms of innovation and finance. The Lebanese diaspora has also played a key role in ensuring that despite successive political and other crises the country has managed to stay solvent.

The influence of diaspora communities is not necessarily benign. Exile groups at times seek to return to power, even at the cost of undermining democratic process. For example, a recent United Nations investigation found that extremist networks in Europe provided financial and operational support to Rwandan Hutu militias responsible for alleged war crimes in the Democratic Republic of Congo. Leadership of the diaspora included individuals involved in the Rwanda 1994 genocide. [112]

Some countries extend political rights to their diaspora populations to maintain their support for the country. Colombia, for example, defines its expatriates as one of five minorities that are granted reserved seats in Parliament. France, Italy, and Portugal also have parliamentary seats set aside for expatriate representation, and many other countries (e.g., Argentina, Brazil, United States, Canada, Germany) permit expatriates to cast absentee ballots.[113] Eritrea's constitution guarantees the right of emigrants abroad to vote in national elections, and over 90 percent of Eritreans abroad participated in the 1993 Referendum for Independence.[114]

Skilled migrants are also taking a spontaneous interest in their home countries, and many seek out ways of "giving something back." Research among Turkish and South African migrants has found a pervasive sense of moral obligation or duty to contribute skills and expertise to their home countries, even if they are unable to return permanently.[115] In a similar vein, a group of Ugandan women in the UK began Mifumi in 1994 as a nongovernmental organization (NGO) to support the education of women and children in the Tororo district of Uganda. The organization now has offices in Uganda and a grant to expand their programming to twenty regions throughout the country.[116] Many migrants find ways to remain connected with their home country throughout their lives, and this may involve simply sending money home. As the next section discusses, the volume of remittances flowing to developing countries has increased rapidly in the past twenty years.

Remittances

As the number of migrants from developing to developed countries has grown in the past thirty years, they have contributed to the remarkable growth in the volume of recorded remittances to developing countries (see figure 6.1). From about $31.1 billion in 1990, they are estimated to have reached about $316 billion in 2009.[117] Whereas the share of remittances flowing to developing countries was 57 percent in 1995, it had risen to 72 percent by 2005.[118] Kofi Annan called remittances "the most immediate and tangible benefit of international migration."[119]

Dilip Ratha, a lead economist at the World Bank, speculates that remittances received from migrants abroad are the largest source of external finance for developing countries. If informal and unrecorded channels of remittances to developing countries were included, they would show that remittances are "larger than foreign direct investment and more than twice as large as official aid received by developing countries."[120] The dramatic increase in recorded remittances in the past twenty years can be explained by a number of factors: better measurements of remittance flows; closer scrutiny of money transfers since the 11 September 2001 attacks; a reduction in remittances costs; the depreciation of the U.S. dollar and relative rise in value of other currencies; and growth in the stock of migrants and their incomes.[121]

U.S. dollars
(billions)

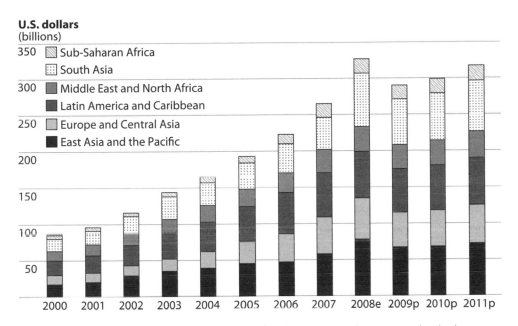

Figure 6.1. Flow and forecast of international migrant remittances to developing countries (2000–2011). Note: Numbers are World Bank staff calculations based on IMF balance of payments statistics. Data for 2008 are estimated, and data for 2009–2011 are from the World Bank baseline projection. Data for 2000–2006 are from Dilip Ratha. 2007. "Leveraging Remittances for Development," *Migration Policy Institute Policy Brief, June 2007,* p. 2, table 1. Data for 2006–2007 from Dilip Ratha, Sanket Mohapatra, and Zhimei Xu. 2008 "Outlook for Remittance Flows 2008–2010: Growth Expected to Moderate Significantly, but Flows to Remain Resilient," *Migration and Development Brief No. 8.* Washington, DC: World Bank, p. 2, table 1. Data for 2008 (estimated), and 2009–2011 (projected) from Dilip Ratha and Sanket Mohapatral. 2009. "Revised Outlook for Remittance Flows 2009–2011: Remittances Expected to Fall by 5 to 8 Percent in 2009," *Migration and Development Brief No. 9.* Washington, DC: World Bank, p. 2, table 1.

The World Bank reported a slight decline in the volume of remittances due to the 2008–2009 global recession. The drop in remittances was less severe than falling portfolio debt and equity flows and the sharp contraction in foreign direct investment because remittances are generally less volatile and less procyclical.[122] The relative resilience of remittances is related to various factors that ensure their persistence over time: they flow from the accumulated stock of migrants so they withstand short-run changes in mobility; they constitute a relatively small part of the income of migrants, so they are expected to continue even in the face of hardship; fiscal stimulus packages in developed countries will likely create jobs for migrant workers; and migrants work longer hours or reduce their own consumption to send more when their dependents are most in need.[123] Nevertheless, recent evidence from the United States suggests that only a quarter of the Hispanic migrants who lost their jobs managed to keep sending remittances and that remittance flows from the United States to Latin America dropped 11 percent in 2009.[124]

The economic impact of remittances on migrants' countries of origin can be significant. Remittances make of a large share of the GDP in small developing countries, and in larger countries, the annual flow can reach into the tens of billions (see figure 6.2). The primary, and perhaps most important, impact of remittances is that they directly reduce poverty in the countries to which the remittances are sent. A study of 71 developing countries finds that "international migration and remittances significantly reduce the level, depth and severity of poverty in the developing world."[125] A 10 percent increase in per capita remittances can lead to a 3.5 percent decline in the proportion of people living on under $1 per day in the source country.[126] Surveys in developing countries show that fewer remittance-receiving households are below the poverty line than nonreceiving households.[127] Most remittances are used for basic subsistence needs and for improving housing conditions. In Pakistan, Turkey, and Somalia, remittances help households to overcome short-term income fluctuations.[128] Recipients in Bangladesh count remittances as half of their household income, and in Senegal, the share is as high as 90 percent.[129] In Turkey, 80 percent of receiving households spend remittances on daily expenses.[130] In Latin America and the Caribbean, more than 50 million people are supported by remittances.[131]

Remittances sent home by asylum seekers can be vital to the survival of communities decimated by conflict in the source country. Remittances were sustaining so many communities in Somalia that the November 2001 closure of the al-Barakat *hawilad* money transfer network (due to alleged ties with al-Qaeda) led to a food crisis affecting about 300,000 people.[132] In El Salvador, remittances sent by refugees living in the United States are estimated to sustain 15 percent of domestic households. To sustain these flows, the Salvadoran government has gone so far as to offer legal assistance to Salvadorans in the United States to prolong

a.

Total receipts
(US$ billions).

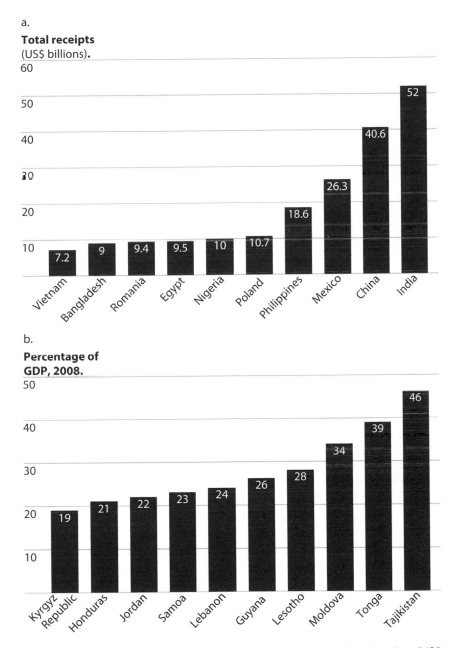

b.

**Percentage of
GDP, 2008.**

Figure 6.2. International remittances: top ten countries in terms of total receipts (US$ billions) and as percentage of GDP, 2008. Dilip Ratha, Sanket Mohapatra, and Zhimei Xu. 2008. "Outlook for Remittance Flows 2008–2010: Growth Expected to Moderate Significantly, but Flows to Remain Resilient," *Migration and Development Brief No. 8.* Washington, DC: World Bank, box figure 1.

"temporary protected status," a refugee-like status that allows them to remain legally in the United States.[133]

Country studies also show that remittances improve the health and education of children, and they have a positive influence on infant health and in reducing child mortality.[134] School dropout rates are lower among households receiving remittances in Sri Lanka and El Salvador, and in Sri Lanka, children in remittance-receiving households have higher birth weights (indicating access to better health care).[135] Children from Mexican families in which one or several members had migrated completed between 0.7 and 1.6 more years of schooling than children who did not have family members who had migrated.[136] Remittances have also raised the levels of children's education in Jordan, Thailand, and the Philippines. While these higher levels of education could be due to the selectivity of migration (families with a member overseas may be likely to spend more on education, regardless of remittances), a study of the Philippines during and after the 1997–1998 financial crisis saw unanticipated increases in remittances spent on enhancing children's schooling. These results show a direct link between remittances and education spending.[137]

As private transfers, remittances can also stimulate local development. In Pakistan and Thailand, families receiving remittances use them to hire farm labor and purchase equipment, which in the long run leads to farm modernization and output growth. In China and South Africa, farming households that received remittances increased crop production over time because of the availability of extra capital for investment.[138] Remittances can also promote access to self-employment and provide financing for small business.[139] In Mexico, a fifth of the capital invested in small-scale enterprises comes from remittances.[140] Remittance receipts of $2 billion are estimated to have created additional economic worth of $5.8 billion.[141]

Remittances may also take the form of collective transfers. In 2005, "collective" contributions of about $20 million were sent through Mexican Home Town Associations (HTAs), committees established by migrants to support development at home.[142] Migrant associations established by New York's Jewish communities during World War I helped to finance reconstruction in Europe. Today, migrant associations are directly involved in socio-economic development in home communities all over the world. They helped to organize disaster relief after Hurricane Mitch in Central America in 1998, and after earthquakes in Turkey (1999) and Gujarat, India (2001).[143] Others have helped to build and fund clinics, schools, universities, and infrastructure development in their communities of origin.

HTAs have become especially prominent and influential in Mexico. Portes notes that these HTAs "have acquired such power and visibility as to become interlocutors of the Mexican state and federal authorities and to acquire a frequently decisive significance in the development prospects of their hometowns."[144] One example of their influence is the creation of the Mexican Government's *Tres por Uno* (three for one) program in response to HTA activity. Every dollar sent through collective remittances is matched with a dollar each from local, regional, and national authorities to fund philanthropic causes and infrastructure development. Between 1999 and 2001, migrants contributed $2.7 million to such programs.[145]

Even when households in source countries spend remittances on consumption, the expenditures can have multiplier effects that boost local and national economies. Remittances used to fund a lavish wedding or build a new home will support local employment and stimulate demand for products that increase the incomes of households without migrants.[146] Every dollar in remittance spending creates two or three dollars of income in the source country, depending on whether remittances are spent on buying imported or locally produced goods.[147] Through their multiplier effects, remittances have increased the average per capita income in many Central American countries by around 7 to 14 percent.[148] The multiplier effects of remittances are generally higher at a national level (because the production and distribution of goods is spread out), but local expenditures can have a significant and more immediate impact by supporting service providers and retailers.[149]

The benefits remittances create for households and some communities indicate their unique potential for relieving poverty and promoting local development. There are a very small number of countries, however, for which remittance flows are substantial relative to the GDP, and in only eleven countries are remittances larger than merchandise exports.[150] The distribution of remittances is also uneven at an international level—the poorest countries (particularly in sub-Saharan Africa) tend to receive much lower flows than South Asian and Latin American countries. Even though for some African countries, such as Lesotho, remittances can be a very significant share of their total income, foreign aid to Africa is still three times the total volume of recorded remittances.[151] Those countries for which remittances are a significant source of external capital are the exception and not the rule.

Even in areas receiving large transfers, remittances do not constitute an adequate independent stimulus to development. As Bimal Ghosh notes:

> Although remittances to Kerala, a leading remittance-receiving state in India, have helped to improve the welfare of the migrants' households and raise levels of economic activity in construction, trade, transport and personal services, their contribution to the state's economic growth in terms of agriculture and industry have been extremely small.[152]

The primary benefit of remittances is that they reduce the burden of poverty for recipient households in the short run. They provide a modest boost to the economy in the medium run and build up the human capital base of a country in the long run. These significant benefits should be harnessed by receiving countries, but the potential effects on the economies of developing countries should not be unduly exaggerated.

Last, it is worth acknowledging that remittances represent the bright side of an imperfect system, where members of a household often have to spend long periods of time away from their families in order to provide for them. The effects of migration on those left behind can be traumatic for families, particularly when a head of household is away for extended periods. In Bangladesh, for example, when an adult male (husband and father) moves for work, the wife is typically left to move in with her in-laws. While remittances from migrant husbands increase the standard of living among the family, the women left behind assume more household responsibilities and may lose some independence when remittances are received and distributed through in-laws. Extended absences are the norm, and typically the migrant returns home only for a few weeks or a month a year. Many women report feelings of heightened insecurity when their husbands are absent. In the case of a wife and mother migrating, leaving a male-headed household, the effects on some children include lower school attendance and earlier marriage of adolescent girls.[153]

The impacts of migration on those left behind are still not well understood, but when families are divided, there is an inevitable social cost that may not be simply compared with, or offset by, the economic benefits of remittances. In general, however, migration has significant household and national benefits for sending countries, and it also provides net benefits to the migrants themselves. The central question of the impact on the migrants themselves is often neglected and is the subject of the next section.

IMPACTS ON MIGRANTS

As we discussed in chapter 4, migrants generally move to improve their welfare, well-being, and livelihoods. Studies of migrants show that these expectations are at least partially fulfilled. People who move are better paid, better educated, and healthier than those left behind. The experience of migration is not without its downsides, however. Migrants are often vulnerable to abuse and illness—particularly forced migrants, such as those who are trafficked or asylum seekers who travel through perilous journeys to reach their destination. Once they arrive at their destination, many face xenophobia and social exclusion and, in extreme cases, even death. The discrimination and marginalization experienced by migrants and their communities can even limit the opportunities available to second and third generations. We begin this section by discussing the benefits that moving brings to international migrants, before turning to negative considerations.

Employment and Wages

The majority of migrants are economically better off for moving, especially those who move from developing to developed countries. Workers from developing countries who move to the United States earn four times as much as they would have at home.[154] Clemens, Montenegro, and Pritchett note:

A Peruvian-born, Peruvian-educated, 35 year-old urban male formal sector wage-worker with 9 years of schooling earns an average of $1,714 per month working in the United States but the average person with these observable traits earns $452[155] working in Peru.[156]

Studies of other countries have confirmed similar results, even when migrants do not move to OECD countries. Thai workers in Taiwan and Hong Kong earn at least four times more than they would make as low-skilled workers in Thailand.[157] In Tajikistan, the income of a seasonal out-migrant could easily cover the household expenses of a family for an entire year.[158]

Research for the UN Human Development Report shows that high-skilled workers experience significant wage benefits from moving as well (see figure 6.3).[159] A doctor from the Ivory Coast will make six times as much working in France. A junior lecturer from China will earn more than five times more in Australia than at home. Moving from Malawi to South Africa will more than double the wages of a nurse. And software engineers get paid at least three or four times more in the United States than in India.

The wage benefits to migrants are in stark contrast to their peers at home, even if they may not be equal to the wages and employment opportunities of native workers in destination countries. Migrants to the United States typically have higher rates of employment than natives (although this is a trend that reversed in 2008–2009), but foreign-born employees—at all levels of education—earn less per week than native-born colleagues.[160] Migrants earned about 23 percent less than native-born workers in the United States in 2007.[161]

Female migrants occupy a particularly disadvantaged or precarious position in the labor markets of receiving countries. The OECD reports that "immigrant women are generally the group with the least favorable outcomes in the labor market . . . both in absolute terms and relative to children of natives of the same gender."[162] They also tend to be disproportionately represented in low-paid and casual work, such as care activities, cleaning, or domestic work.[163]

Migrant workers, in general, are more heavily concentrated in casual, temporary, and high-risk work. In Spain, for example, 56 percent of the foreign-born work in temporary jobs, compared with less than 30 percent of locals.[164] This trend applies to every European country except

Annual salary
(thousands of U.S. Dollars)

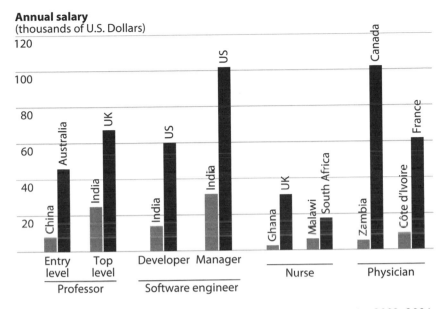

Figure 6.3. Gaps in average professional salaries, selected country pairs, 2002–2006. Michael A. Clemens. 2009. "Skill Flow: A Fundamental Reconsideration of Skilled-Worker Mobility and Development," *UNDP Human Development Report 2009 Background Paper 8*, p. 63, figure 2. Reproduced with permission.

for Austria and Switzerland (see figure 6.4).[165] It is symptomatic of the barriers migrants face when looking for paid work in receiving countries—they may encounter discrimination, language difficulties, and a lack of official recognition of their skills and credentials. In Canada, Jeffrey G. Reitz estimates that foreign-educated migrants earn $2.4 billion less than native-born Canadians with comparable skills because they accept work that is below their skill and qualification level.[166] He concludes that "the real problem is not so much their skill levels, important as they may be, but rather the extent to which these skills are accepted and effectively utilized in the Canadian workplace."[167] This phenomenon of "brain waste" may also be a product of skilled migrants moving to countries where their qualifications are not as relevant to labor market needs.[168] In either case, university-educated migrants are more likely than natives to be employed in low-skilled jobs.

Low-skilled migrants are particularly vulnerable in times of economic crisis. Although in many European countries, rates of unemployment among migrants are lower than those of the indigenous population (in

Share of temporary employment (percent)

■ Native-born
◆ Foreign-born

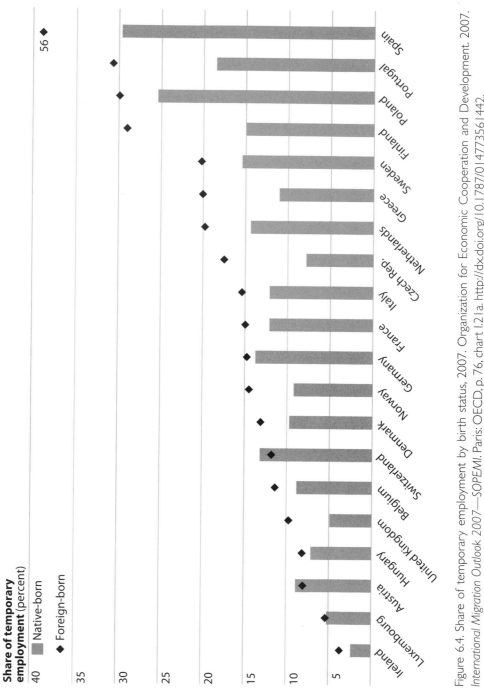

Figure 6.4. Share of temporary employment by birth status, 2007. Organization for Economic Cooperation and Development. 2007. *International Migration Outlook 2007—SOPEMI*. Paris: OECD, p. 76, chart I.21a. http://dx.doi.org/10.1787/014773561442.

the UK for example, close to 5 percent at the end of 2009, when the rate was closer to 10 percent for UK-born workers), this masks the fact that many of the unemployed migrants return home, with emigration accelerating sharply during the downturn.[169] The ease of movement of European nationals has made it more likely that they return home in times of economic downturn. In the United States, in contrast, the extent of border controls makes migrants less confident about reentry, and accordingly, unemployment among migrants rose more rapidly (to 12 percent among Hispanics compared to about 9 percent for U.S.-born workers).[170] The economic collapse in Dubai had a dramatic impact on a significant proportion of the 4.5 million Indian workers in the Gulf, with employment in the construction industry in 2009 estimated to be under half of the previous year's levels.[171]

The relative gains in wage earnings experienced by most migrants are qualified by the obstacles they face in destination country labor markets. In terms of educational attainment and health care, however, the results are more categorically positive. We look at these impacts in the next section.

Welfare

Because most migrants move to relatively more developed countries, access to higher incomes, better infrastructure, and public services contribute to relative improvements in their health and education and that of their children. Still, migrants may suffer more from particular conditions such as stress, depression, and anxiety, which can be traced to the circumstances or experiences of migration. In terms of education, the children of migrants show relatively high rates of achievement in destination countries. They acquire more education than they would have at home, but members of some groups have lower levels of achievement (compared to native students) because of factors related to social exclusion, language, and urban poverty.

Health

The health outcomes of migrants to developed countries improve most directly because of their higher levels of income, relative to pay at home.[172] A study using U.S. data finds that the health of immigrants improves notably in their first year after moving.[173] Other studies point to a "healthy migrant" phenomenon, where migrants show better health outcomes than native-born citizens. Incidents of infant mortality, breast and cervical cancer, sexually transmitted infections, heart disease, diabetes, teen pregnancy, suicide, tobacco use, and alcohol use were all found to be generally lower among immigrants than native-born U.S. citizens.[174] A study by the Canadian government finds that recent immigrants, particularly from non-European countries, are in better health than their Canadian-born counterparts.[175] These effects are achieved through a combination of selection bias (people healthier than the norm are more likely to migrate) and recent migrants taking advantage of the higher incomes and health facilities that accompany moving to a more developed country.

The longer migrants stay in destination countries, however, the more their "health advantage" appears to dissipate. These short-lived dramatic health gains for migrants are explained by the adoption of unhealthy lifestyles and eating habits, the conditions of precarious and risky work, and the mental strains of being far from home. Public health researchers from the University of Toronto conclude:

> The more "they" become like "us," immigrants and immigrant children fail to maintain their initial health advantages ... The process is poorly understood, but may be the result of the adoption of our poor health behaviors and life styles, leaving behind resources (social networks, cultural practices, employment in their field of training, etc.), and ways in which the settlement process wears down hardiness and resilience.[176]

The health of migrants relative to the native-born may tend to converge over the long term, but the relative health benefit of moving over staying is generally retained.

People who move under conditions of distress or political insecurity and end up living in precarious situations, however, will almost certainly not reap the same health benefits as most migrants. Those fleeing civil wars or humanitarian disasters are usually leaving countries with weakened health systems, and the conditions of warfare often increase vulnerability to the outbreak of infectious diseases. Migrants' health is most at risk when they are exposed to hazardous journeys, are "warehoused" in refugee camps, or assume undocumented status and hesitate to seek medical assistance (or are excluded from access). On arrival in a destination country, undocumented migrants may live in crowded and unsanitary conditions that increase their vulnerability to other health risks.[177] Refugees have a high risk of contracting diseases due to separation of families, breakdown of social structures, and poor access to health care.[178] The World Health Organization (WHO) has found that undocumented migrants and asylum seekers suffer from mental illness and are often excluded from treatment and therapy.[179] Many migrants have little or no access to mental health care because they are excluded from existing service arrangements or because such services do not exist or do not address the specific needs of migrants.

The welfare outcomes experienced by migrants are, to a certain extent, conditional upon their circumstances and background. Those who move for economic reasons to societies with accessible public services are likely to benefit the most. The circumstances and conditions of migration are no less important when it comes to educational achievement.

Education

Migration improves educational attainment relative to those left behind, even if migrants do not always perform as well as the native-born. As with health care, the educational achievements of migrants are explained by their relatively higher incomes and greater access to facilities. The educational benefit of moving is vividly depicted in figure 6.5, which shows that school enrolment is consistently higher for children of families that migrate to a country with a higher Human Development Index (HDI) rating.[180] As expected, the gains are the largest for children moving from countries that score poorly on this development index.

At a national level, the educational gains from migration vary with the age of the migrant. Those who migrate to the United States as children (before 13) or as young adults (25–29) reap the greatest educational benefits from moving.[181] Immigration between ages 13 and 19 confers a relative disadvantage on migrants, however, because of obstacles with language and integration in schools—which are no easier to overcome in teenage years.

Second-generation students acquire more education than both native-born and most first-generation migrants.[182] Studies on first- and second-generation migrants in Europe have been less conclusive than in the

Gross enrollment ratio (percent)

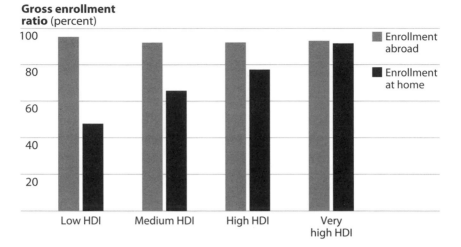

Figure 6.5. Gains in schooling: comparing gross enrollments at origin and abroad. United Nations Development Programme. 2009. *Human Development Report 2009 Overcoming Barriers: Human Mobility and Development.* New York: UNDP, p. 73. © United Nations. Reproduced with permission.

United States, in part because most countries do not have the depth of time-series data and research on large-scale immigration that is available for the United States.[183] First-generation migrants from Turkey and Pakistan generally exhibit lower educational attainment than the native-born population, but there is evidence that the second generation is experiencing upward mobility.[184] Government policy aimed at the education of new migrants—particularly those who arrive as teenagers—can make a significant impact on their welfare and social integration. Such policy measures include language training, social assistance, school selection processes, classroom settings, and early childhood education.[185]

Educational attainment among first- and second-generation migrants also varies widely by region of origin. Migrants to the United States from Africa, Asia, Philippines, and north and western Europe stay in school, on average, for more than one year longer than native-born counterparts or migrants from Mexico and southern Europe.[186] In Canada, the children of migrants generally attain higher levels of education than their fathers, but differences in attainment indicate that social, economic, and cultural factors affect achievement among the second generation (see figure 6.6).[187] More than 40 percent of Filipino fathers have some university

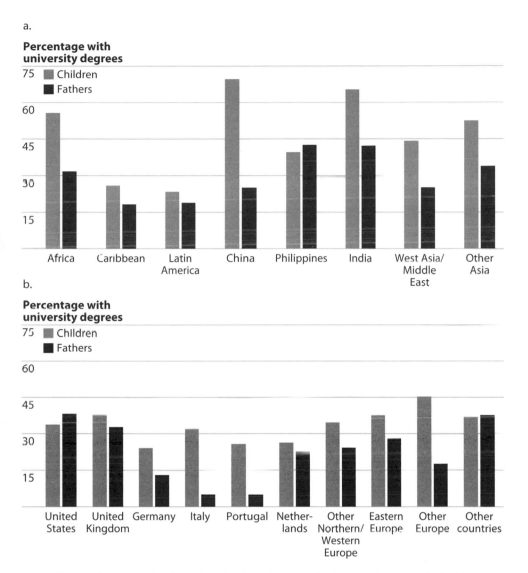

a.

**Percentage with
university degrees**

Figure 6.6. Comparing the educational attainment of migrant fathers and their children in Canada, by source region, 2008. Teresa Abada, Feng Hou, and Bali Ram. 2008. Chart 1-1: "Comparing children and fathers' educational attainment — Non-U.S./European source regions/countries" in "Group Differences in Educational Attainment among the Children of Immigrants," *Analytical Studies Branch Research Paper Series*. Ottawa: Statistics Canada, p. 18. *Catalogue* 11F0019MIE2008308, no. 308, http://www.statcan.gc.ca/bsolc/olc-cel/olc-cel?lang=eng&catno=11F0019M2008308.

education, and a slightly lower percentage of their children earn a degree. In contrast, around 20 percent of Chinese fathers have a degree and about 70 percent of their children go on to complete university.

Not all countries provide equal access to education for migrant children and youth. Developed countries almost universally provide access to schooling for all types of migrants (permanent, temporary, undocumented, or asylum seekers). In most OECD countries, migrant students attend schools with similar standards to native students. If they do not, it is often related to local income levels or residential segregation rather than their migration status. Many developing countries, however, officially restrict access for certain types of migrants or present obstacles to attendance because of xenophobia and discrimination in schools. For example, more than one-third of school-aged children of migrants in South Africa face obstacles attending school because of income restrictions and/or exclusion by school administrators.[188] While the South African constitution does not permit discrimination against foreigners, migrants encounter systemic problems with accessing public services from low-level gatekeepers and bureaucrats.[189]

In general, migrants improve their health and education by moving. Most are better off than if they had stayed put. Where social mobility is restrained, however, disadvantage and poverty can perpetuate itself into the second and third generations. We now examine how xenophobia and social exclusion influence the well-being and welfare of migrants.

Xenophobia and Social Exclusion

While many countries have responded to growing diversity by embracing multiculturalism policies and antiracism campaigns, migrants still experience xenophobia, hostility, and discrimination, particularly during times of economic crisis or insecurity. In its extreme form, xenophobia can lead to violence and direct attacks on migrants. It can also promote systemic discrimination against foreigners and migrants. Xenophobia tends to dissipate over time as migrants become integrated into society and contact between migrants and nationals increases, but discrimination against migrant groups can also impact their earnings and participation in social life. For some groups in the United States, most particularly Latinos, this has produced a long-term process of "downward assimilation," where poverty and social exclusion become systemic among successive generations.

Xenophobia is an attitude of intolerance and hostility toward nonnatives that can erupt into violence when it plays upon popular insecurities and fears. The effects of xenophobia have been recently visible in South Africa, where despite a progressive Constitution, high unemployment has helped to stimulate widespread anti-immigration sentiment. A 2000 survey showed that the majority of the population felt that too many foreigners were being let in and that undocumented migrants should have no legal protection.[190] In May 2008, this hostility exploded into violence, which was halted only with the deployment of the military. The International Organization for Migration summed up the outcome of the attacks in Alexandra: "62 people, including 21 South Africans, were dead; at least 670 wounded; dozens of women raped; at least 100,000 persons displaced and property worth millions of Rand looted, destroyed or seized by local residents and leaders."[191] The attacks were primarily instigated by local leaders and groups, who faced limited opposition from police and other authorities.

In Europe, the continued prejudice and attacks endured by the Roma people and the genocide and mass expulsions associated with the Bosnian and Serbian conflict are testimony to the continued role of xenophobia and antimigrant mobilization. More recently in Italy, attacks on Roma and on Africans have intensified. In January 2010 in Calabria, at least five migrant African farmworkers were shot and 66 injured by local vigilantes.

The endorsement of xenophobia by officials can lead to state-sponsored discrimination against migrants. In Russia, a prejudiced attitude toward ethnic groups from the Caucasus—Georgians, Armenians, Azerbaijanis, Chechens, and Dagestanis—is perpetuated through depictions in the media and public statements by high officials. Newspapers describe them as "inconvenient guests," and Moscow Mayor Yuri Luzhkov has said that the authorities do not welcome people "of Caucasian nationality."[192] In the days following the September 2004 Beslan siege, Moscow police launched "Operation Migrant," raiding hostels, hotels, and markets frequented by migrant workers and ultimately detaining some 11,316 foreigners for "violating the passport regime."[193]

Intolerance toward migrants also manifests itself in the less overt, but no less insidious, practice of workplace discrimination. The ILO ascribes the unusually high unemployment rates of Pakistanis and Turks in Denmark (which are almost double those experienced by other migrants) to systemic discrimination.[194] More than 40 percent of migrants from these countries are unemployed. A cross-national study comparing Belgium, the Netherlands, Spain, and Germany found that migrants faced discrimination in one out of three employment applications.[195] Rates were highest in the Netherlands (37 percent) and lowest in Germany (19 percent). Men with Arabic-sounding surnames receive fewer call-backs for jobs in Sweden, despite having more experience than other applicants.[196] Field experiments in Canada have produced similar results using Chinese, Indian, and Pakistani names.[197]

While xenophobia and discrimination may lessen over time as migrant groups become more integrated into society, it can also set the stage for generations of poverty. Portes describes the circumstances faced by many Mexican families in the United States (especially those who are undocumented), where poverty, discrimination, and racism disadvantage the second generation of migrants:

> Poorly educated migrants who come to fill menial positions at the bottom of the labour market and who lack legal status have greater difficulty supporting their youths. Because of poverty, these migrants often move into central city areas where their children are served by poor schools and are daily exposed to gangs and deviant lifestyles . . . . Because of their condition of vulnerability, children of unauthorized migrants are among the most likely to confront the challenges posed by the host society unaided and, hence, to be at risk of downward assimilation.[198]

"Downward assimilation" is the process of migrants' successive generations moving *down* in socio-economic status because of racism and social exclusion. In table 6.4, comparative social indicators of ethnic groups in the United States illustrate the long-term effects of exclusion and marginalization. While the process of downward assimilation has been well documented in the United States, it has not been observed to the same degree among migrants to Europe.[199]

Migrants' experience of xenophobia and discrimination is not confined to only European and North American countries, as the Russian

TABLE 6.4

INDICATORS OF DOWNWARD ASSIMILATION AMONG SECOND-GENERATION
YOUNG ADULTS IN THE U.S.

Group	School dropouts[a] (%)	Early child-bearing[b] (%)	Young males incarcerated for a crime[c] (%)
Mexican	24.1	25.2	5.8
Guatemalan, Salvadoran	22.3	16.5	3.0
Chinese	3.6	0.9	0.6
Indian	5.9	1.6	1.0
Korean	3.2	2.8	0.9
Filipino	5.9	7.3	1.2

Source: Alejandro Portes. 2008. "Migration and Development: A Conceptual Review of the Evidence," in Stephen Castles and Raul Delgado Wise (eds.), *Migration and Development: Perspectives of the South*. Geneva: IOM, table 3.

[a] Among males and females aged 25–39.
[b] Among females aged 20–24.
[c] Among males aged 18–39.

and South African examples illustrate. While history suggests that societies' sustained exposure to difference tends to promote tolerance and acceptance in the long run, the costs of social exclusion can be severe. The persistent prejudices faced by many Africans, Turks, and Pakistanis in Europe; Latin Americans in the United States; and African foreigners in South Africa illustrate the need for a proactive state to promote integration, accommodation, and social mobility at local levels. The types of migrants who face xenophobia are often those who are most vulnerable: the low-skilled, undocumented, and refugees. In the next section, we discuss the vulnerability of these migrants.

Vulnerability

While for many people, migration evokes the promise of opportunity, adventure, and new horizons, for others, it can involve perilous journeys and a lack of control of their destinies.

For too many, the decision to migrate ends in tragedy. A scan of the media each week reveals the death toll associated with migration: those who have drowned in their attempt to cross into Europe, suffocated in compartments of goods vehicles trying to enter the UK, or dehydrated as they cross expanses of the U.S.–Mexican frontier. While it is impossible to get an accurate count of these deaths, there is on average more than one death per day recorded on the U.S.–Mexico border alone.[200] The number of people who have died crossing the U.S. border has increased steadily over the past decades, more than doubling since 1995. It has been suggested that of the many thousands who annually take treacherous ocean routes from Africa to the Spanish Canary Islands or across the Mediterranean, as many as one in eight do not complete the crossing, with many of these missing persons presumed to have drowned.[201]

More stringent border controls make it more likely that people are forced to take greater risks. The combination of increasing pressures to migrate and more sophisticated controls at traditional frontier crossings may be expected to lead to increased diversion of migrants to more dangerous crossings.

The statistics and literature underestimate the deaths and do not reflect the bravery and tragedy that remains associated with migration. For those who survive the journey, the process of migration can still be traumatizing, and the circumstances of moving to a new country—often with limited legal rights—can make migrants vulnerable to exploitation and abuse. The most vulnerable tend to be those who are forced to migrate, either as refugees or as trafficked persons. In this section, we look at several cases of migrants for whom moving is characterized by high risk and limited choices.

Low-Skilled Migrants

Low-skilled migrants often move to countries where they have limited legal rights (in the case of seasonal labor) or almost none at all, if they are undocumented. The nature of the work they undertake and the lack of adequate workplace protection generates particular risks. The United Nations reports that in Europe, the occupational accident rate for migrants is twice as high as for native workers, which is related to the "dirty, dangerous and difficult" jobs often reserved for migrants.[202]

Migrant agricultural workers in both developed and developing countries suffer disproportionately from illnesses related to exposure to toxic pesticides.[203] Most of these migrants do not have access to health care because they lack insurance or are unaware or unable to access health facilities.

Low-skilled migrants and undocumented workers are also particularly vulnerable to exploitation by employers and recruiting agents. Migrants from South Asia often borrow heavily to pay the substantial fees charge by recruitment agencies to secure a job abroad.[204] When they arrive in Saudi Arabia, the contracts they signed with recruiters are at times replaced by Arabic documents offering far below the agreed wage. Unaware of their rights or fearful of being sent home without earning any money, migrants are forced by their circumstances to endure such exploitation. Female migrant workers may also suffer degrading abuses. In the words of *Human Rights Watch*, "Some women workers [were so] traumatized from rape and sexual abuse at the hands of employers [that they] could not narrate their accounts without anger or tears. Living in forced confinement and extreme isolation, [it was] difficult or impossible for these women to call for help, escape situations of exploitation and abuse, and seek legal redress."[205] Without adequate legal protections or opportunities to unionize, low-skilled migrants in foreign countries too frequently become victims of deception and abuse.

The investigation into the death of 23 cockleshell pickers trapped by a rising tide in England's Morecambe Bay in February 2004 revealed that they were undocumented migrants who could not speak English and were working for an organized gang.[206] Public reaction to the tragedy led to the regulation of the UK shellfishing industry by a Gangmaster Licensing Authority. However, as Oxfam notes in considering the lessons five years after the tragedy, "abuse of migrant workers continues."[207]

Human Trafficking

Human trafficking, or "modern slavery," is proliferating as transnational economic networks expand across increasingly open borders. The UN estimates that 2.5 million people are in forced labor (including sexual exploitation) at any time, as a result of trafficking.[208] The total trade in people (including trafficking and human smuggling) is worth $7 to $10 billion a year.[209] Trafficking often involves deception and coercion of aspiring migrants by brokers who profit from the cross-border trade in people. As Moisés Naím, editor of *Foreign Policy* magazine, writes:

> Migrants can be driven by opportunity, hope, despair, or simply the need to survive. Human traffickers prey on these impulses and, thanks to their ability to elude government-imposed obstacles, they can turn human impulses into profits.[210]

The most publicized aspect of human trafficking is the sex trade, which is global in scope. The sex trade disproportionately involves women, who are often either kidnapped or lured under false promises of clerical work or jobs in the entertainment industry.[211]

Trafficking also emerges as a response to a growing demand for children or wives. In China, for example, the long-term effects of a one-child policy and patterns of sex-selective abortion have produced a population with more men than women. Chinese men living near the Vietnamese border are known to pay for brides from China's populous southern neighbor. A report by *The Economist* describes the rise in kidnappings from the Vietnamese Hmong minority:

> The abductions follow a pattern: a Hmong girl is wooed by an out-of-towner—whether from Vietnam or China is not clear—who speaks her language. She is lured to a rendezvous to be drugged and smuggled into China, probably near Lao Cai, about an hour's drive from Sapa. Tall, pretty girls are said to be particular targets.[212]

Other Vietnamese brides in China indicate their resignation to their fate and a willingness to accept their circumstances. One Vietnamese woman from Hanoi was deceived by a friend of her aunt's into a marriage, which cost her Chinese husband $48.[213] Her parents reported the trafficker to the police in Vietnam and had him arrested, but she since decided to stay in China—even returning after visiting family in Hanoi. The "bride trade" across the Vietnam–China border shares characteristics with other cases of human trafficking, where migration involves a complex combination of deception, coercion, economics, and constrained choice.[214]

Children are also trafficked for economic and sexual exploitation. Many large European cities host informal labor markets where young children, mainly boys, are used for peddling and begging and older children as cheap construction labor.[215] UNICEF estimates that about 1.2 million children are channeled into the sex trade every year, but much of the trade is underground and difficult to study.[216] The impact of the trade on the mental and physical health of children is a matter of great concern. Children involved in prostitution are 6 to 16 times more likely to be infected with a sexually transmitted disease than adolescents worldwide.[217]

Refugees

Refugees often go through protracted situations of uncertainty and insecurity, unable to return home, settle permanently in their country of first asylum, or gain resettlement in a third country. They may be confined indefinitely in camps or holding areas near volatile border areas, where they are exposed to renewed violence.[218] Even where refugees do not face immediate threats to their security, they are vulnerable to arbitrary policy changes that place them at risk of destitution, arrest, or involuntary and premature repatriation.

In some countries, refugees remain confined to camps in remote locations, entirely dependent on the assistance of the international community for basic needs of sustenance, shelter, and other services. Denied freedom of movement, given little or no opportunity to develop economic self-sufficiency, and with scant information as to when or if they will ever be able to return, life is characterized by insecurity. Health and education indicators among encamped refugees are often poor due to limited opportunities and services. There are also high rates of suicide, alcoholism, abuse, and drug smuggling, and the trafficking of women and children occurs with alarming frequency.[219]

The experiences of refugees, trafficked persons, and low-skilled workers highlight the need for adequate legal and political protection for migrants. Other categories of migrants are exposed to similar risks and vulnerabilities when they move to new countries, often relying on strangers to assist their passage, unfamiliar with language and culture, and lacking information or access to legal systems. Without the protection of states, the impact of migration on people can be traumatic.

IMPACTS ON SOCIETIES AND MIGRANTS

Migration promises tremendous benefits for sending and receiving societies as well as for migrants themselves. Some of these gains—higher wages for migrants and increased productivity for receiving societies, for example—are generated simply by opening borders to larger flows of people. More migration makes good economic sense. However, there are also costs and risks associated with migration, and these are typically felt in localities that experience a rapid and large increase in the foreign-born population. Recognizing that enabling more migration is in our collective longer-term interest, the orientation of governments toward "management" should shift away from the quest to control borders and toward harnessing the social and economic potential of migrants and offsetting short-run and local costs.

In part II, we have scanned the contemporary terrain of migration. We have seen that while the proportion of migrants is smaller than that of the late nineteenth and early twentieth century, the numbers and sources of migrants have been steadily increasing. The costs and risks associated with moving are reduced by cheaper transport, communication, and financial systems, and the spread of transnational networks around the world makes migration more feasible than ever before. Growing wage disparities between rich and poor countries offer enticing incentives for many people to move, but developed countries are introducing ever-more complex systems for controlling entry. State resources are focused on trying to manage the flow of people across borders, even though there is little evidence that governments are successful at achieving this objective. When one considers the long-term benefits promised by increasing migration to receiving countries, the project of trying to ascertain who to keep out and who to let in appears as cumbersome as old Soviet models of state planning.

In part III, we peer into the future of international migration. The forces shaping our world presage a future in which migration and migrants will be even more widespread. The next chapter considers the economic, social, and environmental factors that will propel increasing numbers of people across borders.

PART III

⚜

FUTURE

7

⚜

The Future of Migration

*The future will probably be as messy as the past, and all
predictions are likely to be wrong, but one thing is clear:
there is no return to the neat idea of closed-off nation states
with homogenous national communities.*
—*Stephen Castles[1]*

While it may be impossible to predict the future, all the evidence
tells us that the first half of the twenty-first century will be characterized by more migration. Over the last twenty-five years, the total
number of international migrants doubled, and we can confidently say
that this strong growth trend will be amplified over the next fifty years.
History teaches that rapid economic and political change—and, increasingly, environmental change—dislodges people from their traditional
routines, compelling them to seek opportunity and security in unfamiliar new homes. Against a backdrop of rapid globalization, the individual
risks and costs of moving internationally will continue to fall with lower
transport costs, better connectivity, and growing transnational social and
economic networks. By the middle of the twenty-first century, our societies will be more diverse than ever before. The global community will
be connected in a manner not experienced since our evolutionary origins
in Africa.

In this chapter, we will trace the contours of future migration by examining factors that will increase both the supply of and demand for
migrants. This approach mirrors a mainstream tendency to think of
migration in terms of "push" from source countries and "pull" from

destination countries, but we aim to avoid some of the pitfalls of this perspective. Reducing international migration to "push" and "pull" neglects the role of local and national context, networks, and social capital in determining who moves and where they go. Many factors will make people (particularly from developing countries) inclined and equipped to migrate in the future, and structural changes in developed countries will generate pressure on states to accept more migrants. As globalization deepens, institutions develop to facilitate increasing cross-border flows, and transnational networks are encircling the globe, facilitated by new technologies. The direction of flows will be predominantly from developing to developed countries, although movement between developing countries and between the richest countries will continue to be significant.

On the supply side, persistent intercountry inequality maintains large wage gaps that offer incentives for individuals to move. As economic growth in low-income countries provides more people with the resources and capabilities to migrate, they will do so in larger numbers. Current high levels of fertility in developing countries will lead to large cohorts of young, working-age adults who are more inclined to seek their fortunes abroad. Last, most projections of the future include increasing environmental stress due to climate change, and as people's livelihoods are threatened, they will look for opportunities to move. The growing supply of potential migrants will include both low-skilled and high-skilled migrants.

In most of the developed countries, shortages of labor will intensify pressure on policy-makers to bring in more migrants to meet growing labor and demographic gaps. Persistently low fertility rates in developed countries mean that sustaining current levels of economic growth and public services will require large influxes of migrants just to keep workforces at a stable size. Already, many developed countries rely on undocumented workers to fill low-skilled jobs. High-skilled labor will also be in greater demand in the future, as footloose companies continue to pressure governments to relieve mobility restrictions. Developed countries will also have to compete with emerging destination countries, such as a China, for increasingly scarce labor. The sharp decline in fertility in many developing countries, coupled with rapid economic growth, means that by the middle of the twenty-first century, we may face a situation where there are too *few* migrants moving to developed countries to meet the demand for workers.

With more people on the move than ever before, new approaches to managing migration are needed in order to maximize its benefits. The twentieth century assumption that migration is strictly a national problem to be handled independently by nation-states is no longer valid. A twenty-first-century approach to international migration demands that we come to terms with the social and economic forces propelling people across borders and that the instruments of governance equip countries to reap the full benefits of global mobility.

THE BACKDROP OF GLOBALIZATION

Globalization is a complex process of expanding cross-border relationships and flows, and two particular features will accelerate migration in the future: the progressive reduction of barriers to global economic flows and growing transnationalism (where people's interactions and identities are less contained by national boundaries). It is foolhardy to confidently judge the future based on the past, but the broad strokes of history suggest a long-term movement toward increasing integration, greater exchange, deepening cross-cultural contact, and higher levels of cooperation across borders.[2] The pace of globalization may be erratic, but the movement and interaction of people across borders is part of a feedback process that sustains and is sustained by global integration in other spheres.

Globalization is rooted in social and economic relationships that have been building in complexity for centuries, and it has been supported by the more recent creation of international organizations. The establishment of the World Bank and International Monetary Fund in the wake of World War II and the more recent transformation of the General Agreement on Trade and Tariffs (GATT) into the World Trade Organization (WTO) have been steps toward a rule-based international economic order. While these institutions have flaws and the international order remains fragmented, they are hallmarks of an age defined by global interdependence. As transnational activity expands in scope and volume, we require more effective institutions to govern the space across and

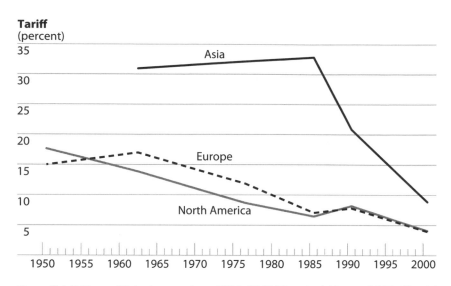

Tariff
(percent)

Figure 7.1. Falling tariffs in three regions, 1950–2000. Timothy J. Hatton. 2007. "Should We Have a WTO for International Migration?" *Economic Policy* 22(50): 339–383, p. 343, figure 1. © John Wiley and Sons. (Citing Findlay and O'Rourke, 2007: "North America is Canada and the US; Europe is the EU-15 excluding Ireland and Luxembourg but including Norway and Switzerland; Asia is represented by Indonesia, Philippines, Taiwan, Thailand, China, Korea and Japan. Not all countries are represented in all years" [p. 343].)

between nation-states. This is particularly the case for labor and migration, which have not benefited from the global cooperation that has evolved over the past fifty years in other areas of economic globalization. In the case of trade in goods and services and finance, a succession of global negotiations had led to the formation of institutions and been associated with lower barriers and establishing minimum standards and global laws to govern international trade and capital flows.

The successive rounds of the GATT negotiations, for example, progressively reduced barriers to cross-border flows (in this case, trade) over the second half of the twentieth century (see figure 7.1). Average tariffs on industrial goods dropped from 40 percent of their market value in 1947 to about 3 percent in 1994. Rules and norms governing international trade have since been embodied in the World Trade Organization. While trade relations remain unequal and rules around tariff escalation and agricultural subsidies privilege developed countries, the flow of goods between countries is gradually channeled within the framework of a liberal international economic order.[3] The result has been an overall (albeit uneven) increase in the total volume of international trade—one estimate is that the WTO facilitated an additional $8 trillion in world trade in 2000 alone.[4]

The WTO, IMF, and World Bank provide frameworks through which cross-border flows of goods and capital have intensified—particularly in the past 30 years—and new items are added to their agenda by states and interest groups. In the mid-1990s, the issue of copyright enforcement in developing countries was added to the agenda of WTO negotiations. Although the Agreement on Trade Related Aspects of Intellectual Property Rights (TRIPS) has not been as successful as its advocates had hoped, it illustrates how the framework of global economic governance can be exploited to challenge the validity of national regulations in new areas.[5] As cross-border flows of goods and capital have grown, the exclusion of labor from the global agenda of openness has been increasingly challenged in multilateral institutions. Advocates of more migration have tried to use the General Agreement on Trade in Services (GATS), a treaty of the WTO, to lower national barriers to migration. The examples of copyright and labor mobility indicate that the process of globalization generates its own momentum. As states see cross-border exchange as a mutually beneficial ("win-win") process, rather than a competitive one, they are more inclined to expand interdependence and cooperation.[6]

Migratory flows are the orphan of the international system, with powerful countries arguing against a global migration organization and a rules-based system. Fair rules protect the weakest against the strongest players, and the absence of such rules means that the richest and most powerful nations are able to make up their own rules regarding migration.

Lant Pritchett, a former senior economist at the World Bank, writes what many others are thinking: "If everything else is globalized then why not labor?"[7] People are working in countries that are increasingly globalized, but labor mobility is still highly restricted. Whereas in 1975, two-thirds of the world's labor force were in economies that were insulated from global markets by protectionism and central planning, at the turn of the century more than 90 percent of workers were in countries linked into international markets.[8] Pritchett is not the only one asking why labor has been excluded from falling barriers to economic flows. The Organization for Economic Cooperation and Development (OECD), the United Nations Development Programme, the World Bank, and the United Nations Secretary-General have all recently called for more "economically rational" governance to facilitate international labor mobility.[9] In 2005, the Global Commission on International Migration (GCIM) delivered its final report to UN Secretary-General Kofi Annan, in which it called for a new international regime to govern cross-border flows of migrants.[10] The processes of globalization and the growing number of international migrants are provoking policy-makers to ask why people should be confined to nation-states when barriers to the movement of capital and goods have progressively fallen. The fact that citizens of the richer countries do not suffer as many restrictions on movement as those of poorer countries adds to the sense of injustice.

Globalization is not only influencing how policy-makers think about migration, it is also leading more and more people to move. In the words of Jan Aart Scholte, globalization is characterized by the "deterritorial-ization" of exchanges and relationships—an observation that is just as true for social relations as economic ones.[11] The growth of communications technologies has collapsed social distance between people separated by thousands of miles. In early 2009, an estimated 1.5 billion people were regular users of the Internet, and the UN estimates that more than 60 percent of the people in the world have a mobile phone subscription (up from less than 20 percent in 2002).[12] Air transport costs also fell rapidly between the 1960s and 1990s, enabling people to more easily travel to see loved ones, do business, or move their families.[13] Whereas in the mid-nineteenth century, a family fleeing Russia for the United States would have left their home without being certain that they would ever speak to or see their relatives and friends again, today those social ties would remain intact. It is now cheaper than ever for people to keep in touch across vast distances, and for even those on modest salaries to afford periodic airline tickets to visit home. The result is a significant reduction of the social and psychological costs and risks of migrating.

Greater connectivity not only makes it easier to keep in touch with friends and family *after* leaving, it also facilitates sprawling transnational social networks that link people around the world. As the scale and sources of migration have grown in the latter half of the twentieth century, even second-generation migrants maintain close connections to their ancestral homes. Peggy Levitt refers to this phenomenon as a growing "transnational social field": "Simultaneity, or living incorporated into daily activities, routine, and institutions located both in a destination country and transnationally is the reality for increasing numbers of migrants and their descendants."[14] While borders maintain physical distance between people, the lives of migrants and nonmigrants can be connected in a myriad ways through e-mail, phone calls, Skype calls, and family visits. Transnational networks serve as conduits of culture, information, ideas, beliefs, and money between migrants and nonmigrants. Transnational ties can "test the nature and reach of nation-states."[15] As Steven Vertovec concludes, "Migrant transnational practices are stimulated and fostered by many of these globalization processes. In turn, transnational migrant practices themselves accumulate to augment and perhaps even amplify transformative global processes."[16]

Globalization and migration are intertwined processes that are leading humanity to the same cosmopolitan future, where people, goods, ideas, and finance are able to flow more freely across national borders. As trade has been increasingly liberalized, some economists have turned to labor mobility as the next frontier where more openness can produce global economic benefits.[17] And as more people's everyday lives and relationships transcend borders, the way in which we conceive of national homogeneity and citizenship is transformed. The process of globalization advances in fits and starts. It is creating the institutions, relationships, and ideas that are laying the groundwork for a twenty-first century characterized by more openness to migration. Within this enabling environment, growing supply and demand for migrants will produce larger cross-border flows of people. We turn first to the factors that will support a growing supply of migrants.

SUPPLY OF MIGRANTS

A growing supply of migrants will result from greater pressure and propensity for people to move. The *pressure* to migrate arises from the push and pull factors (whether economic, social, or political) that make migration attractive, whereas the *propensity* to migrate is related to individuals' ability and willingness to bear the costs of moving.[18] Historical trends help to identify areas that produce migration pressure, and future forecasts illustrate how these areas will evolve in the coming half-century. We highlight six interrelated factors that can be expected to foster a growing supply of potential migrants: persistent intercountry inequality and wage disparities; economic growth in the poorest countries; rural displacement and urbanization; rising education standards in developing countries; growing working-age populations in developing countries; and environmental stress. These factors, in themselves, will not launch people over borders to seek their fortune in distant lands, primarily because migration is still heavily influenced by national regulatory regimes. Given the opportunity, however, more and more people will be prepared to assume the risks and costs of migration.

While we expect the future to be characterized by a growing supply of people looking to move, we do not subscribe to fear-mongering approaches that depict overwhelming poverty in developing countries leading to a "flood" of poor people moving to rich countries. As we discussed earlier, the decision to migrate is complex and impossible to narrow down to a single determinant such as poverty. The poorest people usually lack the resources, education, and networks to be able to migrate internationally. Poverty is not an adequate explanation for why people will look to move in the future, although migrants will continue to pursue higher wages, better opportunities, and greater security. As in the past, migrants will look to move to proximate countries or to where their social networks will carry them. This, as we show later, is also true for climate change, which according to some accounts is also expected to lead to an exodus of individuals to seek refuge elsewhere.

Persistent Intercountry Inequality and Wage Disparities

Wage disparities create migration pressure. Most historians agree that the large-scale migrations of the nineteenth and twentieth century were influenced by significant wage disparities between source and destination countries. Comparing sending and receiving countries in the nineteenth century, the ratio of average wages century were between two-to-one (Unites States/Ireland) and four-to-one (United States/Italy, United States/Sweden).[19] Individuals have an economic incentive to migrate when wages for the same job are higher elsewhere. Pritchett makes the correlation between pressures in the past and future:

> If a wage gap of 4 to 1 between the United States and Italy in 1870 was sufficient to create a migration that reduced population by 30 percent over a forty-year period—even when transport costs were higher, travel was more dangerous, and communication with loved ones left behind was much more expensive and less reliable—then it is at least plausible that the existing wage differences indicate potential forces for substantially larger labour movements than those currently observed.[20]

Today, the wage disparities between countries are larger than ever before, and the processes of globalization appear to be exacerbating intercountry inequality. While it is impossible to accurately forecast wage disparity, even a substantial reduction in inequality will not relieve this migration pressure in the future.

Since the mid-nineteenth century, many of the current developed countries have experienced long-run growth that has transformed them into high-income industrialized economies. Among these countries, there has been a significant degree of convergence in per capita incomes; however, the experience of remarkable economic growth has been far from universal. A much larger set of countries has experienced lower rates of growth since 1870. Pritchett estimates that between 1870 and 1990, "the ratio of per capita incomes between the richest and poorest countries increased by roughly a factor of five."[21] This divergence in growth and incomes has led to rising rates of intercountry inequality.

The popular claim that globalization leads to the convergence of incomes between poor and rich countries has been shown to be demonstrably false, thus far.[22] This is not to say that developing countries do not grow through their participation in the global economy or that people in developing countries do not make more than they would have otherwise. It means that when we compare *whole countries*, income inequality appears to grow wider through the process of globalization—primarily because growth among a subset of the poorest countries (including the failed states) stagnates compared to the rest. The income gap between the richest country and poorest country in the world about 250 years ago was about 5 to 1, whereas today it is around 400 to 1. Although

Gini coefficient

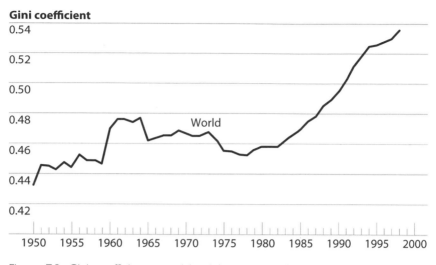

Figure 7.2. Gini coefficient: unweighted intercountry inequality, 1950–1998. Each country is one observation. Branko Milanovic. 2003. "The Two Faces of Globalization: Against Globalization as We Know It," *World Development* 31(4): 667–683, p. 675, figure 3. © Elsevier.

incomes in all countries have risen over the long term, economists have found that "virtually all of the observed rise in world inequality has been driven by widening gaps between nations."[23]

Branko Milanovic, a World Bank economist, illustrates this phenomenon by applying the Gini coefficient measure of inequality to the GDP per capita for 144 countries between 1950 and 1998 (see figure 7.2). Each country is treated as one unit, so China is given equal weighting to Fiji. This approach illustrates how economic conditions and opportunities differ dramatically from one country to another. While inequality remained relatively stable between 1960 and the mid-1970s, it has risen by about 20 percent since 1978. Whereas for much of history, inequality was greatest *within* countries, today inequality *between* countries is far more significant.

As a corollary of rising intercountry inequality, wages are higher in rich countries than in poor ones. Millions of Europeans left for the Americas in the late nineteenth century to seek, among other things, wages that were two to four times higher than those at home. Today, migrants stand to earn as much as *fifteen* times more by moving to another country to work. In a study comparing the wages for migrant

TABLE 7.1

ESTIMATES OF WAGE RATIOS FOR MIGRANT WORKERS IN THE U.S.

(COMPARING HOME WAGES WITH U.S. WAGES).

Source country	Wage ratio
Yemen	15.45
Nigeria	14.85
Egypt	11.92
Haiti	10.31
Sierra Leone	7.43
Ghana	7.12
Pakistan	6.57
Vietnam	6.49
India	6.25
Jordan	5.65
Bolivia	5.03
Guyana	3.87
Philippines	3.82
Jamaica	3.63
Nicaragua	3.52
Guatemala	2.94
Mexico	2.53
Thailand	2.17
Dominican Republic	1.99

Source: Michael A. Clemens, Claudio E. Montenegro, and Lant Pritchett. 2009. "The Place Premium: Wage Differences for Identical Workers across the U.S. Border," *Harvard Kennedy School Faculty Research Working Paper Series, RWP 09-004.* This table presents model 6 in table 1. In the authors' calculations, the numerator represents workers born in each country of origin and (likely) educated there, having arrived in the U.S. at or after age 20.

workers in the United States to what they could have earned at home, the average migrant worker (the mean across forty-two countries) would make more than five times as much in the United States than at home.[24] Some of the individual country wage ratios are presented in table 7.1. Even the most *conservative* estimate of the welfare gain to a moderately skilled worker in the median country of their sampling who moves to the United States is $10,000 (PPP adjusted) per worker, per year—which is double the average income per capita in the developing world.[25]

Wage differences alone do not produce outflows of migrants, but they generate pressure for migration. The growing disparities will make it more tempting for families either to move together or to send individual members abroad to supplement their collective income. Migration is never without its costs and risks, but as incomes rise in lower income countries and networks and migration chains are established, more people will be able to afford to migrate and will be willing to do so. We discuss the role of the economic factors in the next section.

Economic Growth in the Least Developed Countries

Developing countries have historically gone through a "migration transition" as their economies grow and societies modernize. Southern European and East Asian countries saw emigration initially rise with per capita incomes and then gradually fall as rising wages reduced migration incentives. These countries transitioned from being primarily source countries to become migration destinations. In this section, we are concerned with the first part of this process, or what Timothy J. Hatton and Jeffrey G. Williamson call the "emigration life cycle":

> Country-specific emigration life cycles across the long nineteenth century make it clear that real wage or income per capita gaps will not by themselves explain emigration: during the course of modern economic growth in Europe, country emigration rates rose steeply at first from very low levels, after which the rise began to slow down as the emigration rates climbed to a peak, and subsequently they fell. This life cycle stylized fact has emerged from study after study, both for aggregate time series as country emigration rates and for regional emigration rates within countries.[26]

People in poor, agrarian countries generally do not move in large numbers, so the rising rate of emigration follows their emergence from what Hatton and Williamson call "the poverty trap" of low wages and low mobility.

In the next fifty years, we will see a significant shift in the composition of international migrants as the least developed countries experience rising incomes that allow more people to afford migration. Hatton and Williamson anticipate that rates of emigration from Latin America and the Caribbean will slow down; flows from the Middle East, Asia, and North Africa will remain steady; and migration out of sub-Saharan Africa will increase substantially.[27] These projections are based on the logic that many middle-income countries have already reached the peak of their emigration life cycle, and rising wages are decreasing pressure for people to leave. The most dramatic increases in emigration occur as economic growth in low-income countries leads to rising incomes, demographic changes, and better education, which together will help propel more people over borders. The World Bank's 2009 medium-term economic growth projections anticipate the fastest rates of real GDP growth in sub-Saharan Africa and in South and East Asian countries.[28]

While some policy analysts have proposed to boost trade, foreign direct investment, and aid to the least developed countries in order to *slow* migration, such policies are more likely to *increase* migration in the short to medium term. As Hein de Haas notes, "migration and development are functionally and reciprocally connected processes."[29] Absolute poverty and wage gaps alone do not produce outflows of migrants, and the development process itself has historically stimulated migration. Although the introduction of the North American Free Trade Agreement (NAFTA) in 1994 was expected to decrease the flow of Mexican migrants to the United States, economic integration was actually accompanied by a steady rise in Mexican emigration over the following decade.[30] Based on historical trends, as the least developed countries experience economic growth, they will produce a rising supply of migrants for at least several decades.[31]

Social and economic development involves more than just rising wages, it is also accompanied by urbanization, rising education standards, demographic changes, and environmental stress, including climate change. Rapid change in these areas will also help to produce a growing supply of potential migrants. These pressures will be experienced most dramatically in the least developed countries, but their effects will also

TABLE 7.2

LARGEST CITIES IN THE WORLD BY 2025, POPULATION ESTIMATES (MILLIONS).

City (country)	1975	2007	2015	2025
Tokyo (Japan)	26.6	35.7	36.3	36.4
Mumbai (India)	7.1	19.0	22.0	26.4
Delhi (India)	4.4	15.9	18.7	22.5
Dhaka (Bangladesh)	2.2	13.5	17.0	22.0
Sao Paolo (Brazil)	9.6	18.8	20.5	21.4
Mexico City (Mexico)	10.7	19.0	20.2	21.0
New York–Newark (U.S.)	15.9	19.0	20.0	20.6
Kolkata (India)	7.9	14.8	17.0	20.6
Shanghai (China)	7.3	15.0	17.2	19.4
Karachi (Pakistan)	4.0	12.1	14.9	19.1
Kinshasa (DR Congo)	1.5	7.8	11.3	16.8
Lagos (Nigeria)	1.9	9.5	12.4	15.8
Cairo (Egypt)	6.5	11.9	13.5	15.6
Manila (Philippines)	5.0	11.1	12.8	14.8
Beijing (China)	6.0	11.1	12.8	14.5

Source: United Nations Department of Economic and Social Affairs. 2008. *World Urbanization Prospects: The 2007 Revision.* New York: United Nations.

be felt in other developing countries as well. In the next section, we look at the first of these factors, urbanization.

Urbanization

For the first time in history, more than 50 percent of humankind lives in cities. All signs point to a future with even more urbanization, a process that will be especially dramatic in developing countries. By 2050, a quarter of all urban residents will be in Africa or the Middle East, and half will be in Asia. The largest cities in the world will be in developing countries (see table 7.2).

One reason for the rapid growth of cities in developing countries is a growing "population bulge" (an issue to be discussed further later in this chapter) that leads to a natural increase in urban populations. The other reason is rural–urban migration. The mass movement toward cities has historically accompanied industrialization and economic development as more people were displaced from rural areas and sought their fortune in growing industries based in urban areas. These "Great Migrations" off the land are now being mirrored in major source countries of international migrants, like China, Mexico, and Turkey. About 1.3 billion people are still employed in agriculture, and over the next half-century, 500 million farmers are expected to abandon the countryside for cities.[32] New urban residents may not intend to migrate overseas when they first move to the city, but the process of urbanization brings them closer to the networks, resources, income, and education that enable international mobility. Moving to a city, or living in one, markedly increases the propensity for people to migrate abroad.

The example of mobility in China helps to illustrate how urbanization and international migration help to reinforce each other. Millions of peasants are moving to cities looking for work, and millions more city-dwellers are relocating overseas. The leading origins of internal migrants are Sichuan, Hunan, Jiangxi, Hunan, and Gansu, and these areas have produced negligible flows of international migrants. The primary sources of emigrants, instead, are some of the main destinations for peasants seeking their fortune in the city: Zhejiang, Fujian, and Guangdong province. In other words, the same cities that are rapidly growing are also sending a growing supply of international migrants. The two streams of movement are separate, and they are likely to stay that way. But as urbanites leave the city for other countries, they create labor deficits that are filled by internal migrants from the countryside, who themselves later become candidates for emigration as they tap into urban migration networks.[33] In the next twenty years, 300 million Chinese are expected to move from the countryside to cities.[34] A similar process is expected to take hold around the world, particularly in developing countries (see figure 7.3).

In many African countries, urbanization is taking place in the absence of industrialization and rapid economic growth. Between 1950 and 2000, the number of city-dwellers in Africa more than doubled, and the numbers will continue growing in the twenty-first century.

Where cities grow in the absence of an industrial base and job creation, a different type of emigration pressure emerges from the frustrating experience of high rates of youth unemployment. By 2030, about 60

Percentage

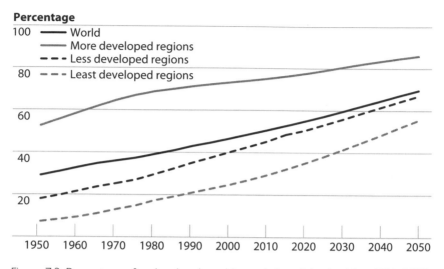

Figure 7.3. Percentage of regional and world populations living in cities, 1950–2050. United Nations Department of Economic and Social Affairs. 2008. *World Urbanization Prospects: The 2007 Revision.* New York: United Nations.

percent of all urban residents will be under the age of 18. In sub-Saharan Africa, the economically active population is expected to grow steadily until 2040—more and more young people will be living in cities and looking for work.[35] School enrollment tends to be higher in cities, and young people are more exposed to global media, which together tend to elevate expectations about lifestyle and earnings.[36] Without sufficient employment opportunities, this particular demographic group has historically been the most willing to take on the costs of moving to seek their fortune elsewhere. Whereas the pressure to move is derived from wage gaps and inequality, urbanization contributes to a greater propensity for migration. The same can be said of educational attainment, which we discuss next.

Rising Educational Attainment

Educational attainment and the propensity to migrate are closely correlated. It has long been observed that young people leave the countryside for the city either because they have acquired an education for which there are few relevant jobs in rural areas or because they want to pursue an education available only in the city.[37] Urbanization and rising educational attainment are mutually reinforcing trends, and a similar logic applies to the pursuit of higher education and international migration. In the next half-century, millions more students from developing countries will finish postsecondary education at home or will study internationally. In either case, this trend will augment the supply of potential migrants.

Current trends and future forecasts presage rapid growth in the number of skilled workers from developing countries. There are several influences behind these trends: rising completion rates at the primary and secondary levels, the internationalization of higher education, and new investments in tertiary education for developing countries. As we discussed in the previous chapter, opportunities for skilled migrants overseas are leading higher numbers of young people in developing countries to pursue tertiary education. All of these trends are reinforced by the global competition for skills and visa regimes in developed countries that welcome skilled workers. As more students in developing countries finish university, their expectations for future employment and earnings rise, leading a growing number to look for opportunities to emigrate.

Current investments in primary and secondary education in developing countries will continue producing higher completion rates over the next fifty years. The Millennium Development Goals (MDGs) have focused attention on primary education in particular, with the objective of achieving universal primary schooling by 2015. While the primary education MDG will almost certainly not be reached by 2015, remarkable gains have been made nonetheless. Furthermore, by 2050, more than 70 percent of children in all regions are likely to have completed primary school and the trend for secondary school is similar, if not as dramatic in overall gains.[38]

As more students in developing countries complete primary and secondary education, the demand for tertiary education has also increased. A World Bank study notes that students in developing countries look to foreign schools because of "excess demand for domestic higher education and the need for internationally recognized qualifications in emerging regional and global markets for highly skilled labor."[39] Global enrollments in higher education have increased from 69 million in 1990 to 114 million in 2004.[40] Between 1999 and 2004, enrollments in countries outside of Europe and North America increased by 90 percent—driven

Population
(millions)

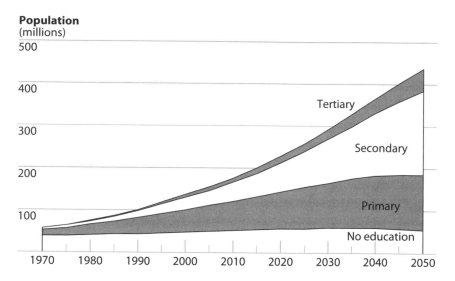

Figure 7.4. Long-term trend in size of the working-age population in sub-Saharan Africa by level of educational attainment, 1970–2050. Migration Policy Institute, ed. 2009. *Talent, Competitiveness and Migration.* Gütersloh, Germany: Verlag Bertelsmann Stiftung. Source: Wolfgang Lutz, Warren Sanderson, Sergei Scherbov, and K. C. Samir. 2008. *Demographic and Human Capital Trends in Eastern Europe and Sub-Saharan Africa.* Washington, DC: Migration Policy Institute, p. 22.

in part by a doubling of foreign aid dedicated to postsecondary education over this period.[41] Latin America, China, and India expect to have their skilled labor supply increase by 2 to 3 percent a year between 2005 and 2020.[42] Sub-Saharan Africa will see its number of university graduates more than double by 2050 (see figure 7.4).[43]

As the demand for higher education in developing countries increases, more youth are studying overseas. Between 1999 and 2004, the number of young adults from sub-Saharan Africa studying abroad increased by 78 percent.[44] In 2009, almost three million students attended a foreign university, and experts project the numbers to rise to between eight and fifteen million by 2025.[45] Most of this flow is driven by rising demand from developing countries, where current opportunities are inadequate, exclusionary, or simply lack the prestige or quality of a foreign education. The availability of quality graduate programs is limited in most developing countries, and many students have their studies disrupted by social or political obstacles—factors that push them overseas.[46] Of course, many are "pulled" abroad as well by the prospect of employment opportunities. About 25 percent of skilled migrants to the United States had previously been enrolled in a U.S. university, and about half of skilled migrants to Australia have an Australian degree.[47] The internationalization of tertiary education has proven to be a key driver of mobility, and it could amplify current projections about future educational attainment in developing countries.

Cross-border education is also diversifying as foreign universities set up branch campuses in developing countries and offer a widening array of distance education programs. Vietnam, for example, has been actively embracing this new trend: Royal Melbourne Institute of Technology University (RMIT; Australia) operates branch campuses in Hanoi and Ho Chi Minh City, Troy State University (United States) runs the International College of IT and Management, and the University of Hue has recently established a joint-degree program with the University of Hawaii (United States). In Thailand, branch campuses of Al-Azhar University (Egypt), Jinan University (China), and Swinburne University of Technology (Australia) have either been established or have plans to open. The Aga Khan University (Pakistan) has opened a branch campus in Kenya focusing on nursing, and Alliant International University (United States) offers education in social sciences and the humanities.[48] While some may expect that the availability of a foreign education closer to home may decrease migration pressure, the IOM notes that it is more likely that these new forms of cross-border education will facilitate, not diminish, skilled migration in the future.[49] What makes many of them appealing to students is their English-language instruction, recognized foreign credentials, international curricula, and networks—all of which enable international mobility.

While students in developing countries are increasingly pursuing higher education, many of them are receiving degrees recognized by developed countries. It may still be too early to judge the full implications of this growing phenomenon, but higher educational attainment and the availability of employment prospects overseas give this population of university-educated young adults a greater propensity for migration. Many developing countries will be experiencing a "youth bulge" in the coming decades, and the growth in working-age populations will contribute to greater migration pressure.

Growing Working-Age Populations in Developing Countries

In forecasting future population trends, the concept of the "demographic transition" can explain why the age distribution within nations and regions changes over time. The demographic transition is the movement of a country—over several decades—from a pattern of high mortality and high fertility to one of low mortality and low fertility. Death rates typically drop faster than birth rates (which may actually increase due to better maternal health),[50] and as a result, countries beginning the transition experience a population bulge. The age distribution becomes younger at this first stage of the demographic transition, and the working-age population increases annually—with more people entering the workforce than are leaving it.[51]

These population changes are linked to broader socio-economic processes of development and urbanization—which improve incomes and access to health care and education—that lead mortality rates to fall. The reason that cities have grown so fast in developing countries—aside from rural–urban migration—is because they were typically the first part of the country to experience the demographic transition. Health care services are more easily available and information is transmitted more quickly in urban areas, which leads mortality to decline before the trend takes hold in rural areas.[52] Most highly populated countries in the developing world have recently passed this stage of accelerated population growth, which is currently contributing to growing numbers of working-age people.

Historically, countries experiencing the first phase of the demographic transition have experienced high rates of emigration. This was certainly true of Europe in the nineteenth century, when a boom in the number of "migration-sensitive" young adults led to greater migration pressure. Emigration from Sweden in the nineteenth and twentieth centuries, for example, peaked when population growth was fastest and declined as pressures decreased and the large adult cohort entered into old age.[53] Similarly, emigration from Germany was much greater than from France, where population increased at a relatively slower rate.[54] Similar migration pressures are expected to accompany demographic transitions in developing countries.[55] Hatton and Williamson argue that the growth in emigration from developing countries after the 1960s was related to

Millions

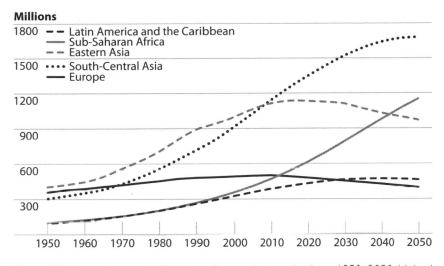

Figure 7.5. Population aged 15–64, medium variant projections, 1950–2050. United Nations. 2009. *Population Prospects: The 2008 Revision.* Available at http://esa.un.org/unpp; accessed 29 May 2009.

the appearance of "fat" young adult cohorts—particularly in East Asia—just as the United States and other countries introduced less discriminatory immigration policies.[56] The population bulge increases migration pressure, but whether this turns into actual migration depends on other factors at the receiving end.

What we can say for certain is that working-age populations are already growing rapidly in some developing countries due to late demographic transitions. While many countries in East Asia are beyond the phase of their demographic transition when population growth peaks, other developing countries are still expecting significant population growth over the next forty years (see figure 7.5). Even after fertility declines, the total population continues to increase because the big cohorts born due to earlier higher fertility enter child-bearing age. The most dramatic effects will appear in sub-Saharan Africa, where the population will grow by a billion people between 2005 and 2050. Despite the devastation of HIV/AIDS, the working population will continue to grow overall in African countries (see figure 7.6). The economically active population between ages 15 and 64 will also grow steadily among developing countries in South-Central Asia[57]—which include countries from Iran across to India and Nepal—in the next half-century. Countries in the

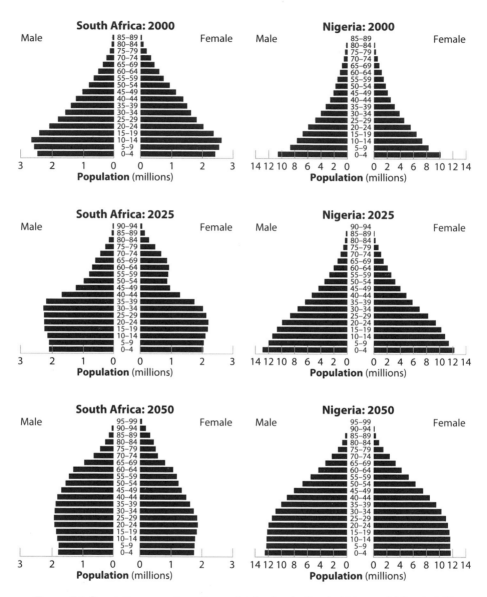

Figure 7.6. Population growth and age distribution in South Africa and Nigeria. U.S. Census Bureau Data.

Middle East and North Africa will also grow at a similar rate, although not reaching the magnitude of these regions.

Analyzing these trends, Bruno Losch notes that population growth in many developing countries (but particularly in Africa) will present unprecedented political and economic challenges:

> [The growth in the economically active population] is a huge pressure which offers opportunities in terms of growing domestic markets but in a context of very low diversified economies with few alternatives. . . . This situation is absolutely new and original in world history. It will drive a big push for migration which will strongly challenge the continental political order. . . . It will also present a strong international [migration] pressure.[58]

Population growth in countries where unemployment is high will generate migration pressures that can be managed by providing access to international labor markets. Losch notes that without migration opportunities, this scenario raises the possibility of "trapped populations who have no alternatives to sustain their livelihood . . . [and increasing] all the associated social and political risks of such situations."[59]

It should be clear that population growth *by itself* does not drive migration, and population increase is not an indefinite process. Developed countries that underwent their early demographic transition in the nineteenth century benefited from out-migration because it helped to stabilize wages in the face of population growth.[60] These countries have since seen population growth level out and begin to shrink because of low fertility. As we show later, the extraordinarily rapid decline in fertility in a wide range of developing countries means that it is now anticipated that only Africa will be above replacement fertility levels (of just over 2 children per woman) by 2050. Most countries are aging demographically, and in the longer term, many developing countries may be expected to experience labor shortages, especially in the younger cohorts. Nevertheless, for the foreseeable future, developing countries will be populated by an unprecedented number of young people who exhibit a greater propensity to migrate.

These growing populations will also face dramatic environmental changes associated with global warming.

Climate Change and Environmental Stress

Projections of climate and environmental change in the twenty-first century include scenarios of extreme weather, deforestation, declining fish stocks, pollution of water supplies, and degradation of agricultural land. These scenarios are based on uncertain emissions estimates and uncertain projections of the physical effects of climate change from a range of models. The 2006 *Stern Review on the Economics of Climate Change*, sponsored by the British government, noted that without a reduction in carbon emissions, the livelihoods of people could be affected by changes in access to water, food production, health, and use of land and the environment.[61] Climate change would have the most severe consequences for developing countries because of geography and the relative lack of economic and political resources to respond to severe environmental stress. The Intergovernmental Panel on Climate Change (IPCC) has noted that shoreline erosion, coastal flooding, and agricultural disruption can promote human migration as an adaptive response. The debate around the implications of climate change for migration revolves around the magnitude and permanence of displacement by environmental factors.

In the coming century, climate change would make many parts of the world less viable places to live, threatening the security and livelihoods of millions of people. Constant and extreme drought would become more frequent and severe. Extreme weather would intensify storms and floods, with more rain falling in South Asia and less falling in interior sub-Saharan Africa. Agricultural yields in sub-Saharan Africa and Central and South Asia could, as a consequence, fall dramatically. As a result of melting glaciers in South Asia, China, and the Andes, flooding would increase during the wet season and water supplies would diminish during the dry season—potentially affecting more than a billion people. Sea-level rise could lead to the significant loss of coastal lowlands.[62]

As with the other factors influencing the supply of migrants in the future, it is impossible to arrive at a reliable estimate of the number of people who will migrate in response to environmental changes. In the words of William B. Wood, official geographer of the U.S. Department of State, "there is usually no simple relationship between environmental causes and societal effects."[63] While there is widespread agreement that humanity will face unprecedented and systemic environmental disruption over the coming century, how people respond to these challenges will be heavily influenced by local conditions and the political response of states.[64]

The term "environmental refugees" was first coined by Lester Brown in the 1970s and has been used with increasing frequency in recent years, even though it has no agreed definition in international law and is not part of the United Nations framework for refugees. The UNHCR avoids the term—which risks undermining its well-established refugee regimes—preferring instead to refer to "environmentally displaced persons," a term that does not carry the misleading reference to cross-border movements. The IOM refers to "environmental migrants" as "persons or groups of persons who, for reasons of sudden or progressive changes in the environment that adversely affect their lives or living conditions, are obliged to have to leave their habitual homes, or choose to do so, either temporarily or permanently, and who move either within their territory or abroad." This debate may evolve as individuals who are clearly forced to flee their country (such as may be the case for Maldives citizens) at some future date perhaps win the right to relocate as "environmental refugees."[65]

The dramatic forecasts of as many as 200 million "environmental refugees" by 2050 have been widely cited in official reports, but they have not held up to wider scrutiny.[66] We believe it is unlikely that climate change alone will lead to a tenfold increase in the number of refugees and displaced persons, and doubling of the total number of migrants, as implied by these guesstimates. Nevertheless, few analysts would expect drastic environmental changes to have no significant effect on mobility. Environmental stress in the twenty-first century will have unpredictable impacts on international migration but will certainly intensify migration pressure in developing countries—where changes are expected to be most dramatic and the adaptive capacity is the weakest.

Environmental change will shape migration patterns based on how such damage affects peoples' livelihoods and the capacity of local communities and households to adapt. A United Nations University report found that "the principal pathway through which environmental change affects migration is through livelihoods. . . . The more direct the link between environmental quality and livelihoods, the stronger the role of environmental push factors in migration choices."[67]

In the case of sudden environmental catastrophes, people typically migrate to nearby areas and often return to their homes. Dramatic floods in central and southern Mozambique in March 2000 displaced about one million people from their homes, but within a few months, most had been able to return.[68] The 2004 Asian tsunami caused the deaths of about 200,000 people and displaced around half a million. Most of this movement was within the local region, and very few actually crossed borders to seek refuge.[69] A year later in 2005, Hurricane Katrina caused the largest movement of people in the history of the United States. In a period of two weeks, as many as 1.5 million people fled the Gulf Coast (three times more than moved in the Dust Bowl migration of the 1930s). With up to a third of the New Orleans residents yet to return, those scattered by the disaster have remained in the United States, and the impact on international migration has been negligible.[70] In part, this reflects the size of the United States and the potential for domestic migrants to escape the disaster.

International migration is contemplated when the socio-economic basis of peoples' livelihoods is severely and permanently threatened and domestic alternatives are exhausted. Families may send a member overseas to diversify their sources of income if farming is less productive or if traditional sources of employment are less lucrative. However, historical examples suggest that people prefer to move only short distances (often not crossing borders) in response to slow-onset environmental change. In the case of encroaching desertification in the Sahel, for example, the response of many residents appears to be temporary internal movement and/or the diversification of income opportunities.[71] A survey of 204 families in the Nandom arid region of Northern Ghana, suffering from desertification, indicated that while migration within Ghana was a common response to environmental stress, none of the families had members who had left Ghana. In part, this reflects the employment and other opportunities elsewhere in Ghana, with over 700,000 North–South migrants counted in Ghana's 2000 census.[72]

Insofar as peoples' basis for earning a living is compromised, pressure for international migration may mount—but this will depend on the extent to which there may be other closer alternatives and on government and other adaptive measures to support the increasingly precarious existence of people under threat from environmental change. Scenarios of large swatches of land affected by climate change would limit local adaptive strategies and promote more varied and radical responses. As many have identified in Sudan and elsewhere in the Sahel, environmental stress may also lead to tensions and conflict over land and resource use, and political refugees may cross over borders.[73]

Studies by the Dutch government and the U.S. Geological Survey warned in 2009 that sea levels could rise by 55 centimeters to 1.5 meters during the twenty-first century.[74] The implications of a dramatic rise in sea level would be particularly serious for the inhabitants of the Maldives, where 80 percent of the land area is less than one meter above sea level and 47 percent of houses are within 100 meters of the coast. Storm surges in 2007 inundated 55 of its islands, and rising sea levels are projected to make these surges more regular and severe.

In 2008, Maldives President Mohamed Nasheed publicly discussed investing funds from tourism to buy land for relocation in nearby India, Sri Lanka, or Australia. In the meantime, inhabitants of the lower lying islands will likely continue moving to Male, the most populated island and the capital, which has a seawall and uses desalination plants. Population pressures, however, are already being felt on the islands and especially in Male, which is the second most densely populated island in the world. As sea levels rise in the Indian Ocean and the islands in the Maldives become less habitable, the population will become more concentrated in Male, and the number of people looking to emigrate could increase.

Climate change also poses a major threat to Bangladesh, where many of the country's people live in densely populated coastal areas. Rising sea levels will exacerbate coastal flooding, and tropical cyclones and storm surges would be more severe. Fluctuating rainfall patterns and melting glaciers in the Himalayas would lead to higher flows during the monsoon season. A lead author of the IPCC report, Dr. Atiq Rahman, speculates that 35 million people could be displaced from the coastal regions of Bangladesh by 2050.[75] It is still unclear precisely how these climate threats would influence out-migration from Bangladesh, and overseas development assistance has already begun to focus on building infrastructure and systems that will facilitate internal migration and diminish the human impact of floods and storms.[76]

The way in which environmental change impacts peoples' livelihoods and generates migration pressure will be heavily determined by states' social policies and their capacity to respond to immediate crises. As Oli Brown notes:

> It is clear that many natural disasters are, at least in part, "man-made." A natural hazard (such as an approaching storm) only becomes a "natural disaster" if a community is particularly *vulnerable* to its impacts. A tropical typhoon, for example, becomes a disaster if there is no early-warning system, the houses are poorly built and people are unaware of what to do in the event of a storm.[77]

This observation is also reflected in current thinking about how famines occur, influenced by Amartya Sen's widely cited work comparing the 1943 Bengal famine with the 1968–1973 Ethiopia famine.[78] The proximate cause of falling food production may be (partially) environmental, but the systemic cause of food shortages, scarcity, and starvation is actually a country's socio-economic structure and political response.

We can also look at the very different impacts of comparable extreme weather events on Bangladesh and the United States. The 1991 Tropical Cyclone Gorky killed 138,000 people and left as many as 10 million homeless in Bangladesh. The following year, a relatively stronger storm (Hurricane Andrew) hit Florida and Louisiana, killing only 65 people and leading to very little permanent displacement.[79] The human impact of future extreme weather patterns will be shaped by the quality of housing, early warning systems, state capacity, and disaster resilience, among other factors. Furthermore, the poorest people are often the most affected by such disasters because so many live in marginal and vulnerable areas. The contrasting impact of the devastation caused by the 2010 earthquake in Haiti that killed over 200,000 people with the death toll of around 500 people associated with the much stronger quake in Chile a few months later highlights the need to focus on both the nature of the extreme events as well as local vulnerabilities.

Climate change scenarios depict an unpredictable future that is still, to a certain extent, contingent on what governments do today to reduce carbon emissions and mitigate the worst of its effects. The environmental effects of climate change will also be accompanied and compounded by population growth and urbanization over the coming half-century.

While climate change will influence the lives of millions, if not billions, of people, it will impact migration in the same way as other factors. As peoples' livelihoods are compromised and they face social and economic distress and possible famine, they will search for greater security and better opportunities. While many will move locally, others will draw on social and family networks to move internationally. Rather than think of "environmental migrants" as a separate class, we should consider the changing environmental landscape to be another factor that adds to pressure for migration from developing countries to their wealthier neighbors or even farther afield.

To summarize this section, in the future, an increasing number of people—primarily from developing countries—will be looking to migrate. People will have more reasons to migrate, and more people will have the social and economic resources to do so. The "pressure points" include intercountry inequality and wage disparities, growing working-age populations in many developing countries, and environmental stress. More people will have the capacity and propensity to move because of economic growth in poor countries, urbanization, and rising education standards.

The supply of migrants will not grow at an equal rate from all countries, however. We expect to see the most significant growth in migrants from poor countries as their populations grow rapidly and more people are equipped with the financial resources to move. International migration will be less East Asian and more African in the future. As more people are willing and able to move, most will still need host countries to open their doors. In the next section, we discuss some of the reasons that developed countries will accept increasing numbers of migrants in the coming decades.

DEMAND FOR MIGRANTS

Potential migrants will often be discouraged from attempting to move in the first place without the pull of demand from destination countries. As Jeffrey S. Passel, a demographer at the U.S. Pew Hispanic Center, remarks: "If jobs are available, people come. . . . If jobs are not available, people don't come."[80] National data from key destination countries like the United States and the UK show that migration flows slowed down dramatically several months before a recession was widely acknowledged in 2008. In the year ending in August 2008, for example, the flow of Mexican migrants to the United States (one of the largest bilateral flows in the world) dropped by about 25 percent, and the net flow of migrants from Mexico (those leaving minus those returning) fell by 50 percent—both compared to the previous year.[81] In the UK, net immigration from all countries also fell by about 25 percent in 2008, compared to the year before.[82]

The demand for migrants in many developed countries may have experienced a temporary reversal during the recession, but during the next fifty years, it will dramatically expand. Opening the doors to more immigration will be an appealing policy option for many developed countries as they face shrinking workforces and aging populations, both of which will contribute to a growing economic demand for more low-skilled workers. Large companies will also step up their current lobbying efforts to increase mobility for high-skilled workers, particularly in academic, business, and technology areas. Recent research on the relationship between immigration and innovation in the United States is bolstering the evidence they need to argue for more open borders on the basis of promoting global competitiveness.

Population Decline and Population Aging

Over the next fifty years, demographic changes in many developed countries will make expanding migration an increasingly attractive policy option. Medical and public health advances mean that people are living longer, while persistently low fertility levels and the end of the post-WWII baby boom mean that the number of native-born workers in developed countries will fall in the coming years. In most wealthy countries, but also in many developing countries, populations are getting older and smaller, creating demand for migrant workers.

Earlier in this chapter, we outlined the demographic transition developing countries are facing in the coming century, with falling child mortality rates leading to a population boom. In the second stage of a demographic transition—which has been well under way in developed countries for more than a century—fertility falls, and the short-term

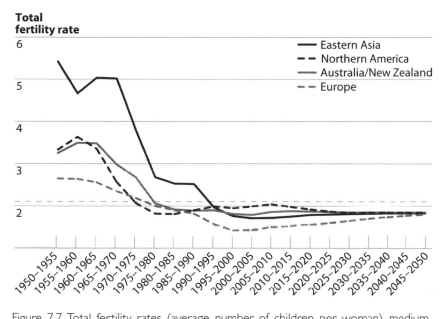

Figure 7.7. Total fertility rates (average number of children per woman), medium variant projections, 1950–2050. United Nations. 2009. *Population Prospects: The 2008 Revision.* Available at http://esa.un.org/unpp; accessed 29 May 2009.

result is a growing ratio of adults to children. The population growth of the first stage of the transition is eventually reversed as this smaller cohort of children joins the workforce, causing a net contraction in the working population as their parents and grandparents retire. Eventually, the population as a whole begins to shrink.

In most developed countries, the fall in fertility has been extremely rapid (see figure 7.7). "Replacement-level fertility" is 2.1, the average number of children per woman required to sustain the size of a population into the future. In Europe, the current fertility rate is below 1.5, and Japan, Korea, and many countries in Eastern Europe have fertility rates below 1.3. These numbers indicate a medium-term trend of population decline in these countries, even if fertility rates begin to increase (as they have in the past few years in France, Australia, and New Zealand). The United Nations projects that the populations of Japan and Russia will each shrink by about 25 million people between 2010 and 2050.[83] Population decline will not be uniform across developed countries. Major destination countries such as Canada, the United States, and the UK will

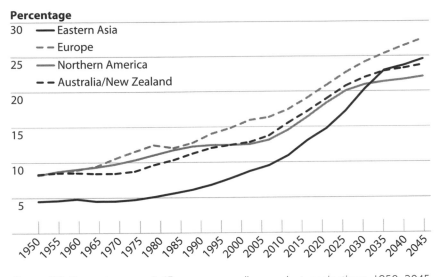

Figure 7.8. Percentage aged 65 or over, medium variant projections, 1950–2045. United Nations. 2009. *Population Prospects: The 2008 Revision.* Available at http://esa.un.org/unpp; accessed 29 May 2009.

continue to grow at modest rates, in part because of migration policies and higher fertility rates among particular (including recent migrant) populations.

As fertility is falling in many developed countries, populations are also aging. Advances in medical techniques, public health, and general diet and nutrition mean that people are now living longer than ever before. Southern Africa is the exception, due to the ravages of HIV/AIDS, but virtually all other regions are seeing significant increases in life expectancy. Life expectancy at birth in developed countries has increased from 66 years in 1950 to 77 years in 2005, and it is expected to continue increasing to about 83 years by 2050.[84]

Not only are people living longer, those who are entering into old age are the large post-WWII birth cohort—better known as the "baby boomers." The result is a dramatic rise in the percentage of people over the age of 65, particularly in developed countries (see figure 7.8). In 1950, about 8 percent of people in developed countries were over 65, while by 2050, more than 26 percent will be elderly. As population projections for the European Union and Russia illustrate, charts of the age structure of developed countries will resemble a coffin shape—where the population

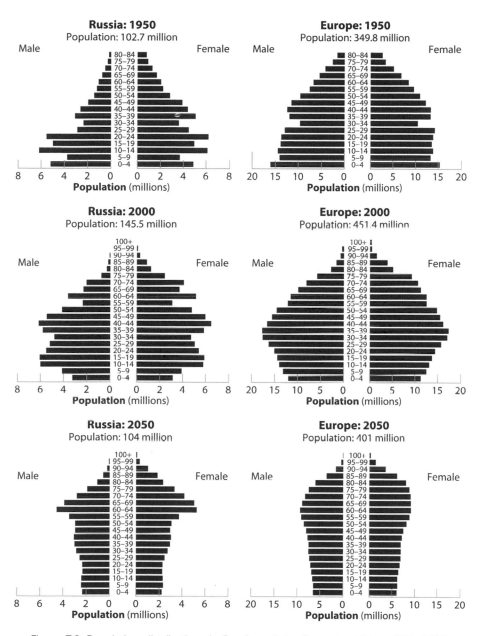

Figure 7.9. Population distributions in Russia and the European Union, 1950–2050. The horizontal scale is millions of persons by sex. The charts are drawn with United Nations data and appear in Paul Demeny. 2004. "Population Policy Dilemmas in Europe at the Dawn of the Twenty-First Century," *Population and Development Review* 29(1): 1–28, p. 6, figure 1, and p. 10, figure 3. © John Wiley and Sons.

**Total
dependency ratio**

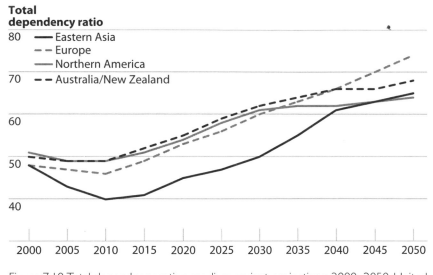

Figure 7.10. Total dependency ratios, medium variant projections, 2000–2050. United Nations. 2009. *Population Prospects: The 2008 Revision.* Available at http://esa.un.org/unpp; accessed 29 May 2009.

distribution is more concentrated among the older age groups (see figure 7.9). Those who are over 65 are, by and large, no longer in the workforce, and they draw disproportionately on public finances because of pension and health care costs. The fiscal burden of this aging population will be borne by an ever-smaller number of workers.

The economic impact of changes in age structure is reflected by a country's changing "dependency ratio." The dependency ratio is a simple equation that shows the relationship between the working population and the nonworking (dependent) population.[85] A higher dependency ratio indicates a greater cost to the working population of caring for children and the elderly. The average dependency ratio for developed countries at the beginning of the century was about 49, while by the middle of the century, it will have grown to 71 (see figure 7.10). Rising dependency ratios actually *underestimate* the relative cost of population aging because they do not take into account the rising costs of health care in many countries, and particularly the higher costs incurred by the elderly. While progress in medicine is likely to continue to lead to life extension, there is less optimism about arresting neurodegeneration. As a result of living longer, the share of people living with Parkinson's, Alzheimer's, and dementia is likely to increase dramatically, compounding the costs and need for elderly care.

The growing burden placed on a shrinking workforce of a rapidly aging population is almost without historical precedent. It presents several difficult policy problems for governments. How do they sustain growth with a contracting active population? Maintain pensions for more retired people? Pay for the expensive health care required by an aging population? Keep public finances stable with a smaller workforce? The problems of aging and falling fertility are mutually reinforcing. At a time when the strain on public services is greatest, there will be less in the public purse to pay for pensions and health care and fewer people available in the workforce to contribute to taxes and to take care of the elderly.

To address these challenges, the OECD and UN have proposed several solutions that do not involve increasing migration. Governments could raise taxes, postpone retirement, induce more women to work (with child care, part-time work, and other incentives), and roll back public services. Few of these are expected to be popular or easy policies for democratic governments to enact.[86] Even if developed countries *could* implement comprehensive policy reforms, they may still not be sufficient to counteract the economic consequences of tectonic demographic shifts.

Current United Nations projections paint a scenario of population decline in developed countries over the next half-century, and current rates of migration will only partially compensate for a shrinking labor force (see Figure 7.11). Many developed countries, particularly in Europe and East Asia, are already debating the prospects of "replacement migration." In 2000, the United Nations produced a report outlining the scale of international migration that would be needed to "offset" the effects of the coming demographic transformation.[87] The report found that in Europe and Japan, "only international migration could be instrumental in addressing population decline and population aging in the short to medium term."[88] In a similar vein, the vice president of the European Commission, Jacques Barrot, was quoted in 2008 saying: "The demographic situation of Europe means a need for focused migration. . . . Immigration is both an economic and moral obligation."[89] When later asked to clarify his comments, the Commissioner noted that higher levels of immigration could help to address population aging. He noted that the

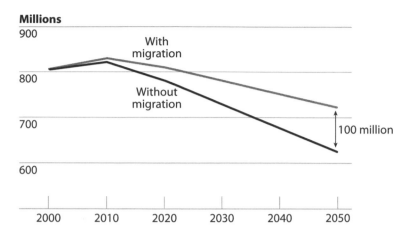

Figure 7.11. Labor force (aged 15–64) projection for developed countries with and without migration, medium variant, 2000–2050. International Migration Institute. 2008. "Global Migration Futures: Towards a Comprehensive Perspective," presentation at James Martin 21st Century School, 22 April 2008 (mimeo). The chart is "Projected population aged 15-64 with and without migration (medium variant)" in Opening Statement at *High-Level Dialogue on International Migration and Development*, United National General Assembly, © United Nations, 2006. Reproduced with permission.

EU Commission "proposes to respond through bilateral agreements and a partnership for mobility" with developing countries.[90]

Replacement migration scenarios appear to most observers to be politically impractical at the level of implementation, but they illustrate the magnitude of the policy challenge facing developed countries. To keep dependency ratios constant between 2000 and 2050, Europe would have to admit more than 1.3 *billion* migrants by 2050 (see table 7.3).[91] Such a radical change to immigration policy would significantly alter the composition of the countries affected, and perhaps for this reason, it will almost certainly not be implemented. However, some degree of replacement migration will almost certainly be necessary to accompany a wider range of public policy reforms to address changing demographics.

The phenomenon of population aging and rising dependency ratios is not restricted to developed countries. Many developing countries will echo these demographic trends. The number of elderly (60+) exceeded the number of children (0–14) in Europe around the turn of the century, and East Asia is expected to experience a similar transition before

TABLE 7.3

TOTAL IMMIGRATION NECESSARY TO MAINTAIN CONSTANT 2000 OLD-AGE
DEPENDENCY RATIOS INTO 2050.

Country/region	Total number (millions)	Average annual number (millions)
France	89.6	1.8
Germany	181.5	3.6
Japan	523.5	10.5
United Kingdom	59.7	1.2
United States	592.6	11.9
Europe	1,356.9	27.1

Source: United Nations. 2000. *Replacement Migration: Is It a Solution to Declining and Aging Populations?* New York: United Nations.

2050. China is forecasted to see a 250 percent increase in its old-age dependency ratios between 2005 and 2050.[92] Population aging and falling fertility in rapidly growing countries like China could lay the foundation for a global competition for scarce labor.

Absolute changes in labor demand will depend on the extent to which new technologies substitute for workers, but low-skilled work in the service sector and high-skilled work in knowledge-based sectors will resist such change. The fastest growing areas of employment—in health care and IT, for example—already draw disproportionately on migrant labor. Technological change creates *new* types of jobs for high-skilled workers, and there are limits to the low-skilled jobs it can replace. Machines and automation may reduce the labor inputs at a manufacturing plant, but they cannot staff a pharmacy, provide child care, or attend to an elderly patient.

Industries that are particularly starved for labor will lobby for opening borders to low-skilled and high-skilled migrants alike. While the decision to expand immigration quotas is a political one, history shows that migration often occurs in spite of official policy and not always because of it. With an expanding supply of potential migrants and countries in need of more workers, the pressure for movement may overwhelm the explicit intentions of government management. Nevertheless, growing labor demands and fiscal pressures will necessarily make the argument for relaxing restrictions to entering developed countries. This economy-wide argument will be increasingly echoed by particular industries that rely heavily on migrants to maintain their competitive edge.

Growing Demand for Low-Skilled Labor

Developed countries are already witnessing a contraction in the supply of native low-skilled labor, a trend that will continue into the future. The causes are twofold: aging and shrinking populations, and rising educational attainment. As we discussed earlier, the labor forces of developed countries are becoming smaller as a result of large-scale demographic changes. This leaves fewer low-skilled workers for industries like agriculture, construction, and hospitality, where there are limits to the substitutability of new technologies for labor. Without increased migration, these labor shortages will generate a long-term drag on the economies of developed countries.

Growing aging populations will also generate an unprecedented demand for low-skilled health and home care services. Projections of future job growth now routinely include low-paid service occupations in areas related to aging populations. The occupations with the fastest predicted growth over the coming decade include home health aides; nursing aids, orderlies, and attendants; personal and home care aides; medical assistants; and maids and housekeepers.[93] These are all jobs that require short-term on-the-job training or a vocational certificate. These are also the kinds of jobs that native workers in developed countries are less likely to accept, and ones that are already staffed disproportionately by migrants. As elderly populations grow larger, demand for workers in low-paid service industries will also expand and generate a need for more low-skilled migrants.

The effects of a shrinking labor force will be compounded by the fact that as educational attainment rises in developed countries, fewer people will be interested in taking on low-skilled service jobs or in working in the trades and construction. The proportion of the workforce with tertiary education in developed countries is already at a historic high, and this trend is projected to extend into the future. Between 2005 and 2025, OECD countries are expected to see a 35 percent increase in the percentage of their workforces with tertiary education (see figure 7.12).[94] As education levels rise, so do expectations about work.

Tertiary educational attainment (percent)

■ 2005
◆ 2025

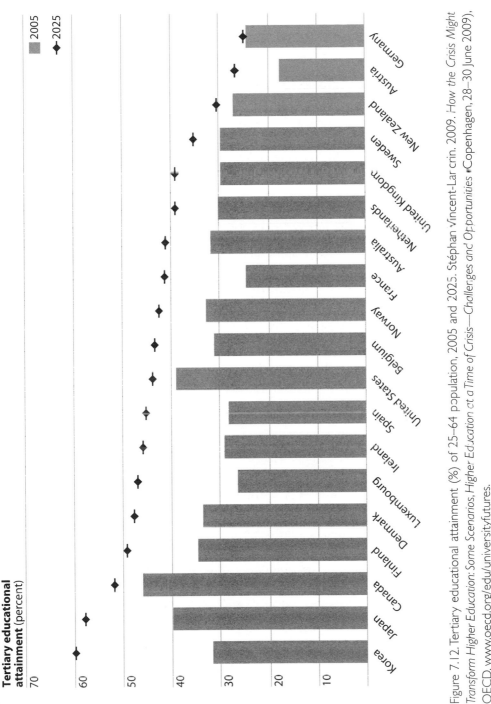

Figure 7.12. Tertiary educational attainment (%) of 25–64 population, 2005 and 2025. Stéphan Vincent-Larcrin. 2009. *How the Crisis Might Transform Higher Education: Some Scenarios, Higher Education at a Time of Crisis—Challenges and Opportunities* (Copenhagen, 28–30 June 2009), OECD, www.oecd.org/edu/universityfutures.

Highly educated workers are less willing to work in manual trades, even if compensation rises. This is already a problem in Canada, which has a chronic shortage of plumbers, carpenters, and electricians. These jobs do not fit the definition of low-skilled work, but they require practical training through apprenticeships rather than advanced academic learning. The demand for certified tradespeople has meant rising incomes and plentiful work for some, but shortages remain because Canadian youth increasingly pursue higher education instead of apprenticeships. More than half of the tradespeople in Ontario will retire in the next five years, leaving businesses that depend on them starved for labor. It is estimated that one million jobs in the trades will need to be filled by 2020.[95]

In the European Union, the accession of Eastern European countries has created a pool of young and mobile low-skilled workers to meet demands in services and construction. It became common after 2004 to see Poles and Czechs serving tourists in the UK and feeding a construction boom in London. Twenty-one percent of the migrants to the UK from these countries between 2004 and 2007 took jobs in hotels and the catering sector, and 26 percent went into trade and craft occupations in the manufacturing sector.[96] Gaps may be reappearing, however, with the trend of return migration that accompanied the 2008 financial crisis and subsequent recession.

In general, however, developed countries have tried to restrict the movement of low-skilled workers, primarily because of concerns that they and their children do not adapt as quickly as high-skilled workers.[97] Employment rates are lower for low-skilled workers, often because the language barriers are higher. Nevertheless, they have continued to move through family migration programs or as asylum seekers. Many others try to enter without authorization. The hiring regulations around high-skilled jobs are more consistently enforced than those around low-skilled workers, so undocumented migrants may work undetected for years. Working outside of the law exposes them to exploitation and abuse. The regulation/enforcement gap in low-skilled sectors represents a political compromise for governments that face pressure to be "tough on illegal immigration," when key sectors of the economy depend heavily on the low-skilled labor that they provide. Undocumented migration is quietly tolerated because such migrants are feeding critical demands in the workforce.

The current situation will be increasingly untenable in the coming decades. Developed countries cannot continue to meet the growing gaps in their workforces through growth in undocumented migration. Their governments are under pressure by businesses to expand programs for temporary low-skilled migration. These would mimic aspects of the guest-worker programs developed in the post-WWII economic boom to meet labor demands in the United States and Western Europe. Such programs, however, led to the permanent settlement of many guest-workers and their families. Furthermore, if the demand for low-skilled workers is likely to persist for several decades, circulating workers in and out of the country to do the same jobs defies economic logic. Workers will be tempted to revert to undocumented status, and employers may be more inclined to risk minor penalties in order to hire them permanently.

Just as the old industrial countries in Europe and North America are attracting high numbers of low-skilled migrants, China, Malaysia, Thailand, and Indonesia may also be recruiting from other developing countries. China has already started to attract African migrants. As China–Africa trade increased around 2003, the number of Africans moving to Guangzhou has grown by 30 to 40 percent a year, according to Chinese official statistics. Many of them buy Chinese manufactured goods to resell at home. City newspapers have put the number of Africans at 100,000, most of whom are from Nigeria, Guinea, Cameroon, Liberia, and Mali.[98] These new settlements will develop into networks to facilitate movement in higher numbers as demand for workers grows.

While the current status quo in developed countries is to discourage low-skilled migration, as world population levels stabilize in the next fifty years, a global labor shortage could prompt fierce competition for migrants. We are already witnessing the intensification of global competition for high-skilled workers.

National Competitiveness and Mobile Skilled Labor

International economic forces are pushing countries toward more openness, and demographics and technological changes are expanding the demand for skilled workers in growing sectors such as health care and information technology.[99] Within this context, influential ideas about fostering national competitiveness by promoting knowledge-intensive industries (especially in science and technology) are informing immigration policies. While business interests have long been a constituency pushing for fewer restrictions on cross-border movement, their arguments have become increasingly influential. The result has been a progressive (and selective) dismantling of barriers to skilled migration, a trend that will continue in the coming decades.

Leading corporations and businesses are increasingly competing for talent at a global level. They testify that it is more difficult to attract employees in a knowledge economy, especially when jobs involve working across borders and cultures. A report by KPMG, a management consulting group, notes:

> As corporations expand and join the globalized economy, the demand for talent has never been greater. This factor, combined with declining fertility rates and an increasing demand for talent within developing countries, has led to the so-called "labour crunch" where competition for skilled labour is intense.[100]

The "war for talent" means that businesses are often looking for people with cross-cultural skills and perspectives and the education to thrive in an information-driven environment. This desirable skill set often means that corporations want a mobile workforce to work where they want. Borders are seen as obstacles to the commercial ideal of a "flat world." Throughout recent history, business has lobbied for more open borders, while labor unions have sought to restrict migration. The momentum of globalization, however, is reinforcing the efforts of large companies to acquire exceptions to immigration restrictions. As one commentator writes: "Immigration policy today is driven by businesses that need more workers—skilled and unskilled, legal and illegal."[101]

The lobbying efforts of large companies, supported by a growing body of research on innovation and endogenous growth, have prompted a widespread shift in thinking among developed country governments about the desirability of skilled migration. Most developed countries have implemented or are implementing channels to attract university-educated migrants, enabling their companies to participate in the "international competition for talent."[102] The European Commission has announced that it will need 20 million skilled migrants by 2020 and has issued a directive for the creation of a "blue card" that would allow the

EU to compete for talent with the United States, Australia, and Canada. In December 2001, the UK immigration minister, Lord Rooker, introduced a new program to attract highly skilled migrants with the following words:

> The program represents a further step in developing our immigration system to maximize the benefits to the UK of highly skilled workers who have the qualifications and skills required by UK businesses to compete in the global marketplace   It will allow eminent scientists to base their research projects [in the UK], should encourage the movement of business and financial experts to the City of London and give those at the top of their chosen profession the choice of making the United Kingdom their home.[103]

The past decade has seen official policy discussion of skilled immigration influenced by concerns about global competitiveness, where migration is seen to be crucial for sustaining knowledge-intensive industries.[104]

In the United States, the issue of H-1B temporary visa quotas for skilled workers has been a flashpoint for debate about the relationship between U.S. global competitiveness and protecting employment for native workers. Technology industries, in particular, have openly challenged restrictions. A survey released by the Computing Technology Industry Association in October 2008 found that about 10 percent of jobs in IT were left unfilled because of visa restrictions, which amounted to a $100 billion shortfall for the U.S. economy.[105] Microsoft founder Bill Gates has testified before Congress and made pointed public comments about the government policy: "The theory behind the H-1B (visa)—that too many smart people are coming—that's what's questionable . . . . It's almost an issue of a centrally controlled economy." When asked about what he would do as a lawmaker, Gates replied: "I'd certainly get rid of the H-1B visa caps. That's one of the easiest decisions . . . . It doesn't make any sense."[106]

The high-tech industry is spending millions of dollars lobbying Congress and the White House to revise H-1B quotas. In 2008, the industry spent $120 million in federal lobbying.[107] This amount is triple what the industry spent in 1998 and has increased every year since then (it includes, but is not limited to, immigration-related lobbying).[108] Foreign businesses have recently started their own lobbying for higher H-1B quotas in the United States. In March 2009, a delegation from the Indian National Association of Software and Service Companies met with top White House officials over H-1B restrictions, calling them an "extreme concern" (the Indian IT industry received 11 percent of the visas issued in 2008).[109]

There is evidence that such lobbying is already working. A systematic study of business lobbying efforts in the United States found that "barriers to migration are lower in sectors in which business interest groups incur larger lobby expenditures and higher in sectors where labor unions are more important."[110] Business interests are inherently aligned with more liberal immigration policy, but the global economy is placing more pressure than ever on businesses to compete for talent and move their workforce around easily. In all likelihood, they will continue stepping up their lobbying efforts to dismantle obstacles to migration.

The pressures of national competitiveness in a global economy will increase in the next fifty years, and developed countries will intensify their contest for skilled labor. This trend will also be driven by the expansion of large emerging economies, like India and China, which will compete for high-skilled workers. Restrictions on skilled migration to the United States has already led large Indian technology firms, such as Wipro and Satyam, to expand their operations at home because of blocked access to U.S. markets.[111] This explains, at least in part, an eightfold expansion of the Indian IT industry between 1994 and 2001.[112] In the future, concerns about promoting national innovation and growth may outweigh domestic pressures to "safeguard" jobs for natives.

Debates over the global movement of skilled labor are already tending toward the industry position. As a report on skilled migration noted, "Much of what appears to be governments' changing the way they compete for the world's skilled workers is really the selective removal of their own barriers in the international labor market."[113] The competition for skilled migrants is not only national, it is also becoming local in areas that have been economically devastated by the movement of manufacturing industries overseas and subsequent population decline. A grassroots effort for economic revitalization in Cleveland, Ohio, has focused on attracting migrants. "I think that's the future of Cleveland," one local activist said. "If we don't get some good, talented, capable people here, we're in trouble."[114] Philadelphia also started a similar campaign and brought in more than 100,000 new migrants between 2000 and 2006.[115] Their campaign to boost the regional economy by attracting skilled international migrants featured new coalitions between civic leaders, migrant groups, chambers of commerce, and city halls.

In the foreseeable future, the management of migration at a national level should involve progressively lowering barriers to skilled migration. Research on innovation, entrepreneurship, and endogenous growth highlights the potential benefits of increasing a country's volume and diversity of human capital. Restrictive immigration policies have been shown to have a direct impact on the rates of innovation in the United States (and presumably other countries as well).[116] Developed countries that maintain obstacles to skilled migration will lose out to emerging economies as they become more open to mobility. Armed with a growing volume of evidence, multinational corporations are exerting considerable pressure on governments to permit mobility for their workers and recruits. Even local communities are finding that as manufacturing industries are shipped overseas, they are also competing for talent to revitalize their economies. While nationalist backlashes and the recessionary impulse toward scaling back on globalization may reverse the trend toward more skilled migration, such an effect is likely to be temporary. In the medium term, it will be overwhelmed by the economic demand for more migration.

The future, it is said, is made of the same stuff as the present.[117] Most people will move for the same reasons in the future as they do today: to pursue welfare, prosperity, peace, security, fulfillment, and opportunity—for themselves and their families. However, the social and economic transformations at hand presage a twenty-first century that will give more people the means and reasons to move. How *many* people make the journey to another country will depend on the pace of development in emerging economies, immigration policies in destination countries, and the design of effective mechanisms to manage and integrate foreigners into their new homes. Migration controls will remain relevant in the coming decades, but they will be limited in their ability to radically curtail migration.[118]

Developed countries will face difficult choices between a future of economic prosperity, security, and health in old age, and one of greater cultural uniformity generated by long-settled populations. If we agree that prosperity and social welfare are primary goals of government policy, then governments and electorates may well prefer to accept more social, linguistic, and cultural diversity that higher rates of migration will produce in the interests of a more dynamic and secure future.[119] The global governance of migration is still relatively underdeveloped and immature in the context of the increasingly transnational character of international migration and relative to trade and financial flows. In the concluding chapter, we will examine global migration governance and proposals for reform.

8

⚛

A Global Migration Agenda

In the preceding chapters, we have contended that migration is a defining characteristic of human societies and a driving force of global history. The audacious movement of our common ancestors out of Africa launched the settlement of diverse ecologies, forcing adaptation, innovation, and learning. Before the advent of modern communications technologies, migrants and travelers served as the broadcast medium connecting settlements and civilizations. They carried knowledge and know-how across cultural and geographic boundaries, transmitting the ideas that animate human progress. Information traveled at the pace of steady steps advancing forward.

Over tens of thousands of years, societies were organized around the mastery of basic arts of survival. Human communities gradually innovated and discovered ways in which to feed, clothe, and shelter their members. The appearance of agriculture, cities, and civilizations marked a new period where the generation and application of knowledge assumed new importance. The goal of mere survival gave way to learning about superior techniques of production, social organization, and spiritual matters, which were more relevant to advancing civilization. Global infrastructure and technologies afford us greater collective capacity for learning and innovation now than ever before, but the borders of states generate unprecedented friction on the movement and mixing of people. The world has never been more integrated or connected, and yet the movement of people and migration is now more regulated than ever before in history.

The movement of people has never been entirely peaceful, and the history of migration is narrated by tragedy and warfare as much as by commerce and education. But migrants—free, forced, or constrained—have always been a powerful stimulant to innovation and progress. They bring new ways of doing, thinking, and understanding, and their integration into society challenges ingrained racial or parochial attitudes, pushing back cultural frontiers. Migration is not a problem to be solved; it is an intrinsic element of international society and inextricably bound up with globalization itself.

In our contemporary age, the net impacts of migration continue to be positive for both sending and receiving countries, and especially for the migrants themselves. Migration is not without its risks and costs, and it is important to identify these as well as the benefits. It is a key twenty-first-century challenge to craft a more humane and more open migration system that harnesses the tremendous benefits of increased migration while minimizing and mitigating its costs. This chapter will outline a normative framework for meeting this challenge.

Migration policy should be reoriented away from an obsession with border control and toward a progressive embrace of international mobility as an integral and welcome feature of globalization. We see the ideal long-run outcome as one of freer cross-border movement, as we believe this is both ethically and economically desirable. The benefits to human development are considerable, as noted by John Kenneth Galbraith when he famously proclaimed migration to be "the oldest action against poverty."[1] There are, however, major political and social obstacles to creating a system of freer movement. Among these are the concerns of nation-states, which claim sovereign responsibility for governing their borders to prevent security threats, restrict social benefits to nationals, and regulate labor market access. The steps toward greater freedom of movement will necessarily have to be incremental, given legitimate security concerns and powerful nationalist reflexes, which promote strict border controls.

Advancing a global migration agenda requires a widespread acceptance—among stakeholders in government, business, and civil society—of the desirability of greater cross-border movement, and an understanding of its causes and consequences. Global coordination should ideally be embodied in an international agreement and advanced and defended by an international organization. However, to wait until a legitimate, effective organization is established to advance this agenda would be to delay it indefinitely. The progressive realization of freer movement can and should be negotiated and agreed bilaterally and regionally, as indeed has been the case within the European Union, in West Africa, and in a number of other regions. The pace of reform may be slow, but steps should be taken along an ordered path toward facilitating greater movement across borders.

THOUGHT EXPERIMENTS

In the absence of global rules for international migration, how might states respond to the growing pressures for greater mobility? It is worth embarking on a thought experiment to consider whether open borders or the other extreme, national isolation and ending migration, are viable options. These may seem to be extreme or unrealistic examples, but both have been attempted by modern states, and vocal social groups have agitated for variations of these models. Let us imagine what might happen and look to the experiences of countries that have tried them.

End All Migration

Under what circumstances would a country consider sealing its borders and ending migration? A government may cite reasons of national security, to prevent the entry of subversive or dangerous people. The reappearance of strict border controls and passport documents during World War I reflected European governments' concerns about admitting foreign agents, for example. Concerns about population could also figure into a decision to close borders. In the early nineteenth century, Britain banned the emigration of skilled workers as it was industrializing, but many left anyway—recruited by employers in France, Germany, Russia, and America.[2] More recently, some academics have argued for severe limitations on immigration to avoid unsustainable population growth (although most have stopped short of advocating zero immigration).[3] In the UK, David Cameron, the Conservative Party prime minister, has indicated his support for limiting the population to below 70 million to contain the "very great pressures on public services."[4]

There is also a growing chorus calling for limits on immigration for environmental reasons.[5] Stephen Nickell highlights the need for more research into how the environmental and other costs associated with more migration may be offset by the longer term benefits and suggests that a case may be made for limiting migration on environmental grounds particularly where space is limited.[6] A country may close its borders temporarily to prevent the spread of disease, as some analysts have speculated would occur in the case of a global pandemic.[7]

In our globalized world, it would be unusual for border closure to be more than a short-term response to particular threats or political pressures. Globalization has knit countries together in a dynamic network of cross-border exchange, of which migration is a constituent element. Most countries rely on global networks for a significant share of their GDP. Furthermore, even with the availability of information over the Internet and satellite networks, without people crossing borders, the dynamic processes of fertilization, invention, and imitation would simply atrophy. Preventing migration would lead to economies becoming anemic through the social and cultural isolation brought on by closed borders. In the short term, it would lead to social and economic disruption, and in the long term, to the weakening of endogenous growth.

To imagine how closed borders lead to economic stagnation and cultural ossification, we have only to look at the twentieth-century examples of post-Revolutionary Cuba or North Korea (other examples include the Soviet Union, which was the most significant attempt to prevent emigration in the twentieth century, as well as apartheid South Africa and the Israeli isolation of the Palestinian Territories).[8] In these cases, however, even strong and repressive states have been unable to fully enforce closed borders. The social pressure for cross-border mobility ultimately makes the policy unsustainable, despite the willingness of governments to use violence against their own people to prevent migration. In Cuba, between 1959 and 1980, emigration was strictly limited and not permitted to nonallied countries. As Cuba's economy worsened, people became so desperate to leave that some resorted to crashing buses into the Venezuelan and Peruvian embassy compounds to claim refugee status. Despite the government's initial display of force in response to the situation, it eventually caved in to public discontent and temporarily opened its borders for emigration.

In the case of North Korea, the government continues to treat emigration as an act of treason, and visitors to the country are generally allowed to stay only temporarily as tourists or guests. Small numbers of North Koreans, primarily from groups considered loyal to the regime, are sent to work as temporary "guest-workers" in other countries—such as the Czech Republic, Russia, Poland, Qatar, and Kuwait. Those caught trying to leave without authorization are sent to labor camps for two to seven years.[9] Despite these risks, however, tens of thousands of North Koreans have fled across the border to China, and a portion has eventually sought refugee status in South Korea, Thailand, and Vietnam.[10] Most of those who successfully leave the country pay for brokers (human smugglers) to assist their passage to China.[11]

In the twentieth century, closed borders have been attempted outside of wartime only by authoritarian states. Countries that tried to halt migration also isolated themselves internationally, becoming pariah states. Furthermore, the consequences of isolation have been disastrous. The world moves on without them, and they become increasingly disconnected from the social and scientific progress that travels through closer integration and exchange. Halting migration entirely would be economically and politically untenable for a country that has globalized and liberalized parts of its economy. Furthermore, as many developed countries are facing shrinking workforces and aging populations, they are increasingly unable to afford closing their borders.

Open Borders

Alternatively, what if a country unilaterally opened its borders to the free flow of people? What if anyone from anywhere could move to, say, the United Kingdom to live and work? Such a scenario may seem to be unrealistic, but it was the status quo (albeit with notable exceptions) during much of the nineteenth-century period of globalization, as we discussed in chapter 2. The free movement of people was seen to be a logical corollary of liberalizing trade and finance and of throwing off the shackles of feudalism. The prevailing rationales for free movement and open borders were ethical—that people had the right to move—and economic—that the movement of people responded to similar economic forces (namely, supply and demand) as the movement of goods and capital.

At times of major economic or social upheaval—such as the Irish famine, the anti-Jewish pogroms in Russia, or rapid industrialization—the result of open borders was mass migration. Two significant aspects of the nineteenth-century migration to the New World are less recognized than the fact of mass migration itself. First, a large number of migrants returned to their home countries after several years—half of those leaving Spain and Italy, for example. Second, sending countries went through life cycles of emigration. The volume of migrants remained high during the nineteenth century and early twentieth century, but the sources of emigrants shifted over time.[12] The flow of people rose to a peak as the demographic push factors and economic pull factors increased, and descended into a valley as they diminished.

As we discussed in chapter 2, the effects of open borders during the nineteenth and early twentieth century were generally positive for the economies of both sending and receiving countries, not to mention most migrants themselves. International mobility was fuel for unprecedented economic growth in industrializing nations, and migrants from this period are credited with the creation of notable technologies and businesses. While open borders created social problems for receiving countries, migrant populations eventually thrived. Eighteenth-century Irish migrants to New York City initially assimilated into slums and a thriving gang culture. Within a generation, however the men went from being criminals to filling out the ranks of the police and law profession, and the women redeemed an early reputation for prostitution by making up two-thirds of the city's teachers at the turn of the century.[13]

More recently, the enlargement of the European Union eliminated certain border controls for new accession states in Eastern Europe. When the "A8" states[14] joined the EU in 2004, the United Kingdom unilaterally offered full access to its labor market, even though most other member states (except Ireland and Sweden) temporarily restricted immigration. Economic analysis before the enlargement predicted that immigration from all A8 states (combined) to the UK would be between 5,000 to 13,000 per year from 2004 to 2010.[15] Between 2004 and 2008, however, about one million workers from A8 countries arrived in the UK.[16] While the actual influx of A8 migrants far exceeded projections, new migrants helped to fill gaps in the UK labor market—particularly in construction, the trades, and services—and they made net contributions to the public purse.[17] About half of those who arrived stayed only temporarily, working for a few months or a couple of years and then returning home.[18] Migration has proven remarkably responsive to economic conditions. The number of new arrivals from Poland dropped by 47 percent between late 2007 and late 2008, primarily because of a weakening of labor markets and of the British pound and a surge in the Polish economy.[19]

The UK experience of opening borders to A8 countries provides evidence of the economic gains promised by theorists: it has reduced inflationary pressures, lowered unemployment, and boosted the economy.[20] It also shows that in the absence of border controls, migration to high-wage countries can be rapid and larger than expected. However, low-cost transportation and close proximity can also facilitate dynamic patterns of return and circular migration and the phenomenon of transnationalism.[21] If free movement within the European Union has been so successful, should border controls be dismantled elsewhere?

A LONG-TERM VISION OF FREER MOVEMENT

In 1774, Thomas Jefferson addressed the Virginia delegation to the Continental Congress with the following appeal:

> Nature has given to all men [a right] of departing from the country in which chance, not choice, has placed them, [and] of going in quest of new habitations, and of there establishing new societies, under such laws and regulations as, to them, shall seem most likely to promote public happiness.[22]

As a philosopher, Jefferson considered the right of free movement to be universal and timeless, but as a politician, he warned that too-rapid immigration could threaten the social foundations of liberal democracy. While he objected to any obstacles to immigration, Jefferson also argued that government should be active in promoting the integration of migrants into society so that they can share their skills and creative energies.

Jefferson struggled with the same tensions between individual rights and national solidarity that characterize our contemporary debates around immigration. Within liberal societies, people adhere to the principle that one's social position or circumstances of birth should not inhibit the flourishing of the individual in society. And yet, a collectivist interpretation of national sovereignty is upheld, which prevents us from extending these same values to those beyond our borders. When it comes to immigration policy, our ideals of human rights and equality prove to be exclusive and limited in practice.

Most people implicitly accept that national sovereignty ought to trump the desire of individuals to pursue their destiny where they choose. Perhaps the best-known defender of the conventional view is philosopher Michael Walzer, who argues that liberal values are in fact culturally relative. They are a product of "the particularism of history, culture and membership," he says.[23] Accordingly, Walzer argues, states have a right to control immigration to protect the cultural integrity of these values: "The distribution of membership is not pervasively subject to the constraints of justice. Across a considerable range of the decisions that are made, states are simply free to take in strangers (or not)."[24] Communities have a right to collective self-determination, he asserts, and they can reject the claims of nonmembers to individual self-determination. We give our national communities the right to arbitrarily exclude strangers.

This conventional approach to national sovereignty and individual rights, however, is increasingly inconsistent with emerging international principles and norms. In the twentieth century, sovereignty was invoked as the absolute and inviolable right of states to decide the fates of their citizens. Institutions of global governance are built on the foundations of this model of sovereignty, as are most countries' immigration policies. Within the United Nations, however, the doctrine of the "responsibility to protect" (R2P) has been advanced to recast the ideal of state sovereignty for an interconnected world. Simply put, R2P means that states have duties of protection toward their citizens, and this makes the recognition of their sovereignty conditional, not absolute. Sovereignty implies responsibility, for one's own citizens and for others. The doctrine reflects how global integration and the diffusion of liberal values are challenging the legitimacy of actions by states that restrict the liberty and security of their citizens. An orthodox interpretation of R2P focuses on the extremes of genocide, war crimes, ethnic cleansing, and crimes against humanity as cases when state sovereignty may be limited. But the wider implication of this emerging norm is that individuals have legitimate ethical claims on humanity, beyond their national community.

A norm of delimited state sovereignty is also reflected in certain elements of the immigration policies of receiving states. First, states accept that they have moral and legal obligations to extend aid, assistance, and even political membership to outsiders who arrive at their borders because of persecution.[25] Second, many governments periodically offer a route to citizenship for migrants who have joined their society as undocumented migrants. States recognize that the moral basis for deporting undocumented migrants becomes weaker as those people integrate themselves into society over time, as de facto members.[26] Third, most governments grant citizenship to the spouses of their members, even if they are born outside of the country. Governments accept that collective self-determination—and by implication, state sovereignty—has limits when it comes up against the moral and ethical claims of individuals for personal self-determination. However, the dilemma between national sovereignty and universal human rights is still managed with clumsy and inconsistent government policies.

"We are like travelers," writes Seyla Benhabib, "navigating an unknown terrain with the help of old maps, drawn at a different time and in response to different needs."[27] The world is partitioned into nation-states, which with some notable exceptions are raising the bars to entry. However, an exclusionary interpretation of sovereignty conflicts with our aspirations to apply universal and humanity-embracing standards when it comes to refugees, development assistance, climate change, and global health. *Within* national boundaries, we consider the right of citizens to choose their home to be of greater relevance than the claims of a community to maintain a unique local culture. Few would question whether an individual should be allowed to migrate from Oxford to Manchester, or from Halifax to Vancouver. At a global level, then, on what grounds do we defend rigid restrictions on *international* mobility?[28]

This question is especially confounding in light of the clear relationship between migration and human development. In the 2009 *Human Development Report*, the authors note: "The ability to move is a dimension of freedom that is constitutive of development—with both intrinsic as well as instrumental value."[29] For centuries, humans have moved to seek opportunity, prosperity, and security, and these decisions have been elemental expressions of the basic desire to choose a better life. There is also consistent evidence that when people can freely choose to move, the benefits in terms of welfare and development reverberate beyond the limited circles of their families. Migration, writes Galbraith, "selects those who most want help. It is good for the country to which they go; it helps break the equilibrium of poverty in the country from which they come." From the perspective of human development, he asks: "What is the perversity in the human soul that causes people to resist so obvious a good?"[30]

The majority of people who want to migrate pose no threat to the stability of the countries to which they want to move. They want only to pursue greater opportunity and security. The liberal values that form the civic core of most developed countries provide few coherent reasons to prevent the entry of such people. We maintain rigid (and unevenly applied) border controls for fear of being overwhelmed by an influx of those we perceive to be different in culture and race, imagining that they pose a threat. Whether these threats are real or perceived is rarely considered. Often irrational fears feed popular support for contradictory government policies that aspire toward universalism in some areas, while circumscribing it in others. A coherent application of liberal values leads to the conclusion reached by philosopher Joseph Carens:

> Free migration may not be immediately achievable, but it is a goal toward which we should strive. And we have an obligation to open our borders much more fully than we do now. The current restrictions on immigration in Western democracies—even in the most open ones like Canada and the United States—are not justifiable. Like feudal barriers to mobility, they protect unjust privilege.[31]

From an ethical position, the desirable long-run outcome is for people to be freer to move and work where they choose.

The research on the economic impacts of international migration, discussed in chapter 6, adds to a compelling case for freer movement because of promised welfare gains. Open borders would produce economic gains as high as $39 trillion over 25 years, shared by sending countries, receiving countries, and migrants themselves.[32] These economic benefits are a product of people being able to move freely to where higher paying jobs are available, filling gaps and relieving labor market pressure. If the workforces of developed countries were augmented by only a 3 percent increase through immigration, the welfare gains of $156 billion would be shared relatively equally between developed and developing countries.[33] The evidence is increasingly clear that the economic and welfare benefits of higher levels of international migration far outweigh the short-term costs and risks. These net benefits are conservatively estimated, as they do not take account of the dynamic gains that migration brings, not the least of which is in providing a vibrant basis for economic and social advancement.

Aside from the collective benefits anticipated by these projections, there is a more fundamental relationship between migration and poverty. Without border controls, people can migrate to escape poverty and destitution. Borders enclose many people within a poverty trap.[34] The extreme example is in the countries of the Sahel, where colonial borders have been drawn around countries that have little economic, ethnic, or historical cohesion. In the past, there would have been mass emigration; now citizens of these countries are trapped in poverty and a cycle of conflict.

This is a global phenomenon, as Kerry Howley explains:

> Say you're a Bangladeshi taxi driver struggling to survive on your daily wage in Dhaka. . . . Microcredit loans might net you an extra $700 over the course of a lifetime. Working [in the United States], you're likely to make the same amount in a month. Nothing rich countries can send the global poor—not loans, not textbooks, not fair-wage campaign materials—will boost the income of the average worker nearly so much as letting him walk among the wealthy. Transported from Haiti or Nigeria to the United States or Canada, a low-skilled worker will watch the value of his labor jump more than 700 percent—instantly.[35]

When we consider that wealthy countries spend $70 billion in overseas development assistance a year, liberalizing movement offers unparalleled benefits to the world's poor. Migration in early history, as in the nineteenth century, was the principal means by which many of our ancestors escaped dire poverty and were able to construct better lives. This option has now been closed for citizens of the poorest and most fragile states, often with devastating consequences.

There are, of course, practical limits to immediately dismantling border controls: national and local institutions lack the capacity to administer and provide public goods for a sudden and rapid influx of migrants; significant numbers of people in receiving countries would respond with (possibly violent) xenophobia; countries with welfare states would experience short-term fiscal pressure; and most of all, in most countries, public opinion remains strongly opposed to open-border scenarios, so this could be precarious for politicians and may require visionary leadership. The presence of these immediate obstacles should not limit our vision of a desirable future, however. Border controls are a relatively recent historical phenomenon, and their ethical and economic justification is increasingly under assault by the forces of globalization and a growing awareness of the need for a progressive realization of human rights.

Security is a real and pressing concern. However, the idea that it can be addressed by focusing on threats carried by migrants has not been borne out by the evidence of homegrown crime and terrorism. The threat to societies may come from all citizens, and the priority is to have a shared sense of community as well as to ensure that the threats posed by all people are identified. Ensuring that all citizens have a stake in the system and are legal, in terms of immigration as well as tax and other identities, is vital to advance the security identity.

It may be impractical to immediately resurrect open borders, but intermediate steps can be taken to improve the management of migration. If migration is seen by the public as more of an opportunity than a threat, and if local and national governments develop their capacity to harness the benefits (and minimize the costs) generated by higher levels of migration, it will be more practical and widely acceptable to gradually reduce barriers to mobility. A global migration agenda requires both a long-term objective of freer movement and a framework for practical steps that can take us in that direction. It is not our purpose to prescribe specific policy directions, but we will outline an agenda that should guide the necessary political discussions about revising national migration regimes.

PRINCIPLES FOR GLOBAL MIGRATION

The idea of a global migration agenda has been proposed, revised, and repeated numerous times at international forums during the past two decades. Because the primary participants in these forums have been states, the perspective on migration and what is to be done has often been colored by a bias against mobility. At the 1994 Cairo Population Conference, rather than active promotion of migrants' rights, participants agreed that the international community ought to "seek to make the option of remaining in one's country viable for all people." Similar—albeit more nuanced—sentiments were present in the 2005 report of the Global Commission on International Migration (GCIM). Greater efforts should be made in developing countries, the Commission recommended, "so that the citizens of such states do not feel compelled to migrate." While we recognize that this is desirable, it is only a partial solution.

Over the past decade, proposals to expand global governance of international migration have been more frequent. Like other areas of transboundary activity—such as climate change, international trade, and communicable diseases—migration has commanded international attention by virtue of its connection with globalization. While a single institution does not govern migration, an increasing number of international efforts have focused on how to bring it within a multilateral framework. These include the GCIM in 2005, the High Level Dialogue on Migration and Development in 2006, and the launch of the Global Forum on Migration and Development in 2007. Scholars have debated the merits of a World Migration Organization,[36] General Agreement on the Movements of People,[37] New International Regime for Orderly Movements of People,[38] or a Global Mobility Regime.[39] Despite this flurry of activity since the turn of the century, the focus of most proposals has been on reducing the inefficiencies and abuses of the current system, rather than on progressively dismantling barriers to an ideal of freer movement.

In our view, the global migration agenda should be centered on a clear long-term objective of progressive movement toward open borders. Recall that the General Agreement on Trade and Tariffs was a result of the gradual acceptance of the idea that global prosperity would be better served by open markets and free trade, even though it was recognized that radical reform would produce significant costs and losses. Careful study and shared data meant that some of the costs and dislocations associated with trade reform were anticipated with compensatory measures. While the reduction of tariffs, quotas, and subsidies has been gradual and incomplete, the international momentum toward open markets is carried forward by widespread adherence to the idea that free trade is desirable.

In the case of migration, a similar commitment to the ideal of openness should be reflected in a coherent policy agenda that sees migration as an integral element of a more inclusive globalization, aiming to benefit all countries and people.

We propose five key principles that should guide engagement with migrants and migration by governments and international organizations: extend transnational rights; promote social and economic advancement for migrants; widen the umbrella of legal migration; combat xenophobia and migrant abuse; and improve data collection. A global migration agenda need not be advanced only by official agencies. It should also include businesses, labor unions, diaspora groups, religious communities, and civil society groups. These objectives reiterate recommendations made elsewhere, and there is particular resonance with some of the proposals made by the GCIM. Together, they touch on policy areas that require reform in the medium term if the ideal of freer movement will be achievable and sustainable in the long term.

I. Extend Transnational Rights

Migrants increasingly sustain multiple ties across borders that link them with friends and family around the world. Migration more often than not involves successive movements, and the phenomenon of circular migration has become increasingly common. Migrants can acquire dual citizenship and split their time between two or more countries. Cultural ties to a homeland are now sustained even into the third and subsequent generations of migrants, and hometown associations maintain social connections between migrants and those left behind. Small and medium-sized enterprises run by migrants have multinational supply chains, and billions of dollars in finance flows between friends and family in the form of remittances. Transnationalism is a social and economic reality, "a key manifestation of globalization."[40] Embracing transnationalism through migration policy involves addressing several key areas: portability of pensions and benefits, remittances, and political rights.

Portability refers to "the migrant worker's ability to preserve, maintain and transfer acquired social security rights independent of nationality and country of residence."[41] Currently, portability is guaranteed only through certain multilateral and bilateral treaties—most notably within the European Union. Gaps and inconsistencies in treaties can leave some workers facing arbitrary deductions or the loss of entire pensions or benefits. For example, a Moroccan working in Germany can return to Morocco and receive a full pension entitlement, whereas an Algerian in the same circumstances will receive a 30 percent pension reduction.[42] Obstacles are even greater for accessing health care benefits overseas, even though doing so could allow national insurance schemes to lower costs.[43] Only 25 percent of migrants work in countries where they are covered by bilateral pension agreements, and 75 percent of migrants working abroad and paying taxes at home do not receive any benefits.[44] A harmonized and aggregating multilateral agreement on the portability of pensions and particular benefits would enable more people to move without facing arbitrary penalties.

Remittances are often a lifeline and source of investment capital for families in developing countries. The official channels for remitting funds can be expensive and difficult to access, particularly for undocumented workers. The World Bank estimates that a drop in the average costs of wiring money home from 13 percent (in 2000) to 3 percent would save migrants and their dependents $10 billion a year.[45] Expanding banking services and regulating transaction costs would help more money flow toward poor families and entrepreneurs in developing countries. Government banks can also step in, as has the State Bank of India. It has opened overseas branches where there are large expatriate communities, it offers higher interest rates than local bank accounts and tax exemptions on a proportion of the interest earned, and it allows account holders to have beneficiaries in India. The Mexican and Philippines governments have also created collective remittance channels that channel capital to local infrastructure and development projects. These examples are exceptions rather than the rule, however, and barriers to remittances need to be lowered further. In addition, attempts by sending states to class remittance flows as aid or by receiving states to divert remittances to state coffers should be outlawed by international agreement, as these are private not state transfers.

Third, states ought to design migrant engagement policies that extend political rights to citizens residing abroad and to certain noncitizen residents. A Canadian national residing long-term in the United States without receiving U.S. citizenship could find herself disenfranchised by both countries. Other migrants find themselves in similar situations, where splitting their residence means that they lose voting rights or access to political representation. Some countries, like France, Italy, Portugal, and Colombia, grant expatriates (citizen nonresidents) parliamentary representation, and others like the UK grant voting rights to resident members of the Commonwealth (noncitizen residents). Citizens of former colonies have at times been able to reactivate rights derived from allegiance to former empires. The French, Portuguese, Dutch, Spanish, and British governments apply different policies toward their former colonies. These mixed approaches to extending political rights represent the efforts of states to retain connections with their citizens overseas, or to incorporate aliens who are integrating into their societies. Such engagement policies remain ad hoc, however, and they require new thinking for how democratic principles apply in the context of transnationalism.[46]

2. Promote Social and Economic Advancement for Migrants

Migrants—even temporary ones—have particular needs that include access to language training, quality education, and recognition of foreign qualifications (or access to upgrading). Those that are able to fully participate in society and compete for jobs commensurate with their skills and training will reinforce social trust and create better opportunities for their children. Making such services available is a sound investment for governments and community groups that see migrants for what most of them are: capable and hard-working people aspiring to social mobility.

The scale of contemporary migration has contributed to settlement in ethnic enclaves. Historically, this is not a new phenomenon. Centuries ago, merchants in the Malacca Straits (Malaysia) or Alexandria (Egypt) would cluster and organize by country of origin, sometimes by force of the law. However, when new migrants become integrated into an urban underclass that is afflicted with social pathologies (poverty, violence, and criminal activity), aspirations for social mobility are undermined. Second-generation children may end up with worse life prospects than their parents. A primary obstacle to integration and social mobility for migrant parents and children is language acquisition. Migrants who do not speak the language of their host country tend to become more socially and geographically isolated. A vicious cycle results, where migrant enclaves form and become increasingly inward-looking. The formation of enclaves is also catalyzed by the experience of racism and xenophobia, which leads to what some sociologists call "reactive ethnicity."[47] Providing the education and skills to participate fully in mainstream society is key to breaking out of this cycle.

The children of migrants—especially the low-skilled—require particular attention to ensure that they receive adequate health care and education to succeed in their host country. In Germany and the Netherlands, more than 40 percent of the children of migrants have mothers who possess a primary-level education or lower. As OECD Secretary-General Angel Gurría commented, "[This] is not the kind of population which our institutions are used to dealing with."[48] Extra resources and special efforts are needed to ensure that the children of parents with little education are able to achieve at the same level as their peers.

Migrants also face barriers to accessing host country labor markets, especially when their professional qualifications are unrecognized. They may acquire skills and training at home and be unable to apply them in their host country because of inefficient or unfair protocols for recognizing foreign certification. In some cases, this reflects problems with equivalence, and in others, it relates to language proficiency. Host countries that attract skilled migrants would be better served by efficiently recognizing equivalent foreign qualifications and by providing bridging programs that allow skilled migrants to upgrade their training and credentials. Where developed countries are attracting significant numbers of health professionals to work in national health systems, means of compensating the sending countries for the cost of human capital formation should be explored.

Another matter to be addressed is the systems for processing asylum claims. The number of asylum claims lodged in developed countries has risen dramatically from 50,000 a year in the 1970s to about 500,000 a year. They have begun to drop off again in recent years, but only because of more restrictive measures adopted by destination countries. The procedures for processing asylum claims in most developed countries continue to be inconsistent, unpredictable, and slow. In the UK, the target for reaching a decision on asylum claims is around four months, and in the United States, it is 180 days; however, these guidelines are regularly exceeded. While claims are being processed, refugees may be held in detention centers or forced to live on meager allowances without access to the labor market. Of particular concern are child asylum seekers, who often lack access to adequate health care, education, and a stable environment for their emotional development.[49] Such is the level of increased claims that it may be sensible for states to adopt group determination schemes that recognize "manifestly well-founded claims."[50] Denials, however, require case-by-case determinations.

Migrants face innumerable obstacles to social and economic advancement in host societies, and even though most are self-selected to be hard working and entrepreneurial, they often need additional help to succeed. This is especially true for refugees and low-skilled migrants, but it also applies to skilled migrants, who may face challenges in obtaining work within their professions. Providing extra resources to help migrants acquire the knowledge and skills to thrive is not a drain on the public purse. It is an investment in their future, the future of their children, and the future prosperity and cohesion of the host society.

3. Widen the Umbrella of Legal Migration

Levels of undocumented migration have reached highly significant levels in many countries. The Global Commission on International Migration estimated that 2.5 to 4 million people move across borders every year without authorization.[51] People migrating outside of the legal framework may be moving freely for economic reasons, or they may be trafficked for more sinister purposes. Migrants moving without the protection of the law or full access to the labor market and social services in the destination country suffer from considerable disadvantages.

While many developed countries (most notably the United States) have fought undocumented migration by channeling more resources to border control, the results of this approach have been predictably unsatisfactory. Instead of resisting economic demands for low-skilled labor, host countries should widen the umbrella of legal migration through regularization processes and temporary guest-worker programs. At the same time, higher penalties and more comprehensive enforcement could reduce exploitation by smugglers and limit employers' use of underpaid undocumented labor.

One approach to bringing more undocumented migrants into the legal system is through regularization programs—also referred to as "amnesty," "legalization," or "normalization." Migrants who have lived and worked in a country for several years without legal documents are given the option of receiving residency, either temporarily or permanently. The UK offers indefinite leave to remain to undocumented migrants who have been in the country continuously for fourteen years. Other countries offer periodic "one-shot" options of regularization for people who have lived in the country for a certain number of years. The United States and eight EU countries have enacted twenty-two such programs since 1980. These programs not only have different conditions (in terms of residency and work requirements), they also grant different types of residency—from six months to permanent residence. When viewed comparatively, the practice requires greater consistency to reflect a shared standard of fairness and justice.

There is little evidence on the costs and benefits of amnesty programs. However, a recent report undertaken on behalf of the London Mayor concluded that an amnesty for the estimated 618,000 undocumented migrants in Britain would provide a net boost of £3 billion to the economy. Of this, an estimated £846 million would be in the form of taxes. The study dismissed fears that an amnesty would lead to further large-scale illegal migration. It found that a regularization program would be likely to raise an individual's earnings by 25 percent and the employment rates of the migrants by 6 percent.[52]

Despite the recurrence of undocumented migration and repeated domestic debates over regularization, few norms govern such programs, and they are often viewed as exceptional government actions. Destination countries should establish thresholds in terms of the *length of time* an undocumented migrant has settled and the *total estimated number* of undocumented migrants as triggers for automatic regularization processes. The former would recognize the moral claims that long-term residents have on their host society, and the latter would enable states to minimize the systemic social problems created by an underclass of people living and working without the protection of the law.[53] The importance of bringing all people under the law is especially significant given rising security concerns.

Policies to encourage migration to sectors or parts of the country that would particularly benefit have long been part of the Canadian framework for migration. Such incentives may be adopted more widely in future. For example, in the United Kingdom, the government's new policy of "earned citizenship" identifies a range of skills that are in short supply and also indicates that migrants will get bonus points if they go to live and work in Scotland, where the population is aging. [54]

A second way to bring more migrants under the law is to expand temporary migration programs (TMPs), a solution that has been advocated by the World Bank, the World Trade Organization, the GCIM, and the OECD. Alan Winters has estimated the economic gains from modestly sized TMPs to be in the billions of dollars.[55] Proposed TMPs would regulate the movement of workers, ensure that they receive adequate pay and health care, and ensure that they return home when their labor is no longer required. An essential part of an improved migration program has to be sanctions against employers who exploit undocumented migrants. U.S. law includes such sanctions, but they have seldom been implemented.[56] While many imagine TMPs to be an ideal arrangement, we should recall that similar programs in Germany and the United States have led large numbers of workers to settle permanently.[57] In anticipation of this outcome, the resurrection of TMPs should include pathways for workers to establish permanent residency and even citizenship. They should also involve language and skills training that will enable those workers who stay to integrate into society.

4. Combat Xenophobia, Discrimination, and Abuse

To ensure the full participation of migrants in their societies, host countries have a duty to prevent migrant abuse and to combat xenophobia. While the former may simply be a matter of passing relevant legislation and dedicating resources to law enforcement, the latter is more complex. It involves media developing the will to communicate the positive contributions of migrants to public life and to include minorities in the symbolic representation of the nation. It also means regulating the outcomes of xenophobia, such as stereotyping and discrimination, in the workplace.

The fear of outsiders is a deeply rooted psychological reflex, and combating xenophobia requires an active reorientation of public discussion to reflect the valuable contributions of migrants. Xenophobia is perpetuated through popular discourse and media representation, which can be fueled by statements of public officials who look to capitalize on people's insecurities. Media outlets highlight social divisions and superficial controversies, and news stories stoke public fears by focusing attention on the involvement of minorities in crime, poverty, social deviance, or cultural difference. These feed into widespread suspicion and even fear of foreigners.

Attitudes to migration vary a great deal between and within countries and over time. Opinion surveys in a wide range of countries reveal that attitudes are at best loosely related to the reality on the ground. Britons are currently the most skeptical of migration, perhaps reflecting concerns regarding the number of new arrivals from Eastern Europe in recent years, even though the proportion of migrants in its population is less than many of the others surveyed.[58]

Xenophobic views are often held by disadvantaged members of destination-country populations, who fear competition from migrants for less-skilled jobs. Such people also typically share neighborhoods with less-privileged recent migrants. Hostility to migrants can be linked to a decline in social protection of vulnerable natives. Combating xenophobia, therefore, may also require governments to design measures that relieve economic pressures on the poor and that guard against inflaming social tensions through the appearance of giving favorable treatment to recent arrivals.[59]

Government, the media, and civil society groups all share responsibility for reorienting public discourse toward a favorable and balanced representation of migrant groups. As multiculturalism policies have come under fire in Europe, arguments for more proactive integration of migrants into mainstream society acquire popular support. However, these calls for "social cohesion" and "assimilation" often reflect the underlying belief that migrants need to "fit in" to their new society, even though they encounter discrimination and inequality along the way.[60] While there is an element of truth in the idea that migrants have a responsibility for cultural adaptation, reciprocity is also required. Host societies need to accommodate new migrants by openly valuing racial and cultural diversity and promoting equal access to jobs, housing, and public services. Religious, cultural, and ethnic pluralism are empirical facts of modern societies, wrought out of decades and centuries of migration. Combating xenophobia requires movement toward a public discourse that is self-conscious about the merits of pluralism, the value of equality, and the hazards of prejudice.

5. Improve Data Collection

As cross-border flows are greater in volume than ever before, governments rely heavily on data to calibrate domestic policies with their effects. We carefully monitor the movement of capital and goods—from toys to Toyotas—across borders, but the availability of similar data on the movement of *people* remains inconsistent from one country to the next, making comparative analysis difficult or impossible. The deficiencies of migration data have been highlighted since the 1980s, but little progress has been made since. A scorecard of countries' collection of migration data, produced by the Center for Global Development (CGD) in 2009, found that only six countries (four of them small island-states) gathered the data that are required to conduct comprehensive analysis of international migration.[61] A blue-ribbon commission convened by the CGD called the lack of migration data "the biggest blind spot in our view of the world economy."[62] Insofar as reliable data is needed to systematically analyze the causes, dynamics, and impacts of international migration, as well as the role of government policies, we still lack an adequate picture of cross-border movement around the world. As a result, we know less than we should about how to maximize the benefits of migration and minimize its risks and costs.

Improving data collection on international migration would be relatively simple and inexpensive in the short term. The CGD commission recommended that countries simply add three basic questions to every population census: country of citizenship, country of birth, and country of last residence. Making such data publicly available with cross-tabulations by age and sex would enable analysts to answer major policy questions that are currently out of reach with existing data. These questions include the total volume of temporary and return migration, the impacts of guest-worker programs, how diasporas affect trade and investment in their country of origin, and which policies encourage permanent migration and which promote temporary migration.[63] In the long run, however, the CGD commission notes that these changes will need to be complemented by building statistical and research capacity in developing countries.

THE NEED FOR GLOBAL LEADERSHIP

Embracing more migration is in our collective interest. The coming century will witness unprecedented demographic changes in societies around the world, especially in the developed countries facing shrinking populations. And as information technology proliferates and cross-border social networks expand day by day, people will continue to move—many temporarily and some permanently. The same inclination that led small groups to populate the earth with diverse communities is also bringing us closer to a cosmopolitan future. While we are able to anticipate this future, our governments and institutions remain wedded to ad hoc and incoherent approaches to managing international migration, rooted in an antiquated doctrine of national primacy. We need leadership that can effectively advance a global migration agenda.

Advocating on behalf of a global migration agenda requires the type of leadership and multilateral coordination that is best provided by an international organization with a clear mandate and the necessary resources at its disposal. Currently, international migration is governed by a patchwork of bilateral, regional, and multilateral agreements, a handful of international laws, and several international organizations. In response to recommendations by the GCIM in 2005, the Global Migration Group (GMG) formed as an interagency group to work on a common agenda for international migration. The Group comprises fourteen agencies from across the UN system, as well as the International Organization for Migration, that have migration-related mandates.[64] While the GMG is intended to be a step toward establishing a global agency for economic migration, it currently serves as a reminder of the tensions between key players and their inability to forge a coherent approach to international migration. What is needed is an international organization with a mandate to promote the progressive realization of free movement.

The issue of global migration governance has been widely discussed and analyzed, particularly during the research phase of the GCIM. Compromise solutions—of which the GMG is one—have been deemed the most realistic because they work with the existing institutional architecture and avoid convincing states to cede part of their sovereignty in order to liberalize migration. However, it is unclear what these compromise arrangements are expected to achieve, aside from maintaining the status quo with greater efficiency.[65] There is currently no shortage of international organizations with mandates relating to migration. If we are to have an international organization dealing with migration at all, its objective should be to promote the sustainable expansion of migration through standard setting, advocacy, and pushing forward multilateral negotiations.

The institutional architecture already exists, in large part, for the emergence of a multilateral organization to govern migration. It took 80 years for the World Health Organization to be established in 1948, and almost 50 years for the World Trade Organization to be fully realized in 1994.[66] But in the case of migration, the International Organization for Migration (IOM) already exists with a high level of capacity and expertise, and the UNHCR serves the role of advocating on behalf of refugees. The IOM, however, lacks formal inclusion within the UN system, and it possesses an ambiguous mandate, having been initially established as the Intergovernmental Committee for European Migration to help resettle displaced people after World War II. Since then, it has acquired a broader mission to promote "humane and orderly migration [that] benefits migrants and society," but without UN status, it remains unusually deferential to the sometimes-narrow interests and demands of its 127 member states. Most notably, the IOM lacks a specific mandate to protect the rights of voluntary migrants, a task that is left up to states—most of which have not signed the United Nations Convention on the Rights of Migrant Workers and Members of Their Families.

The IOM has the potential to provide independent and robust global leadership in the promotion of international migration. It should be brought within the UN system with a long-term mission to liberalize migration and a mandate to promote this goal by hosting negotiations, setting standards, monitoring government policies, compiling data, conducting research, and offering technical assistance to developing countries. The IOM already has some capacity to do these things, with 420 field offices in over 120 countries, a significant research program, and experience with capacity building and migration management. What it does not have is the necessary legitimacy, governance, or executive power to accomplish this transformation. Despite the recommendation from the GCIM that the IOM be brought within the UN system to become a global agency for economic migration, this has not advanced.

A common criticism of proposals to create an international organization with a central mission of expanding world migration is that neither receiving countries nor sending countries would see their national interests served by greater international mobility.[67] Receiving countries can already choose unilaterally to admit as many migrants as they appear to want. Sending countries may hesitate to encourage more of their educated population to depart. Those who reap the greatest gains from migration are migrants themselves.

While these conventional views may be true in the short run, in the medium and long term, we have shown that sending and receiving countries actually reap significant benefits from mobility. Even if the quantifiable economic benefits are presently modest, migration generates positive externalities even if these may be long term and difficult to measure. High-skilled migrants support endogenous economic growth by bringing valuable knowledge, skills, and networks, and low-skilled migrants fill growing labor gaps. The most significant obstacle to creating a global migration institution is that the mutual benefits of expanded migration are achieved beyond the political time horizons of decision-makers. What is in our collective long-term interest does not necessarily match the short-term domestic interests of politicians or all their constituencies.

Ironically, therefore, the very reason that a multilateral institution is needed is also the primary obstacle to its creation. However, as contemporary economists can testify, ideas pertaining to liberty, universalism, and cooperation have the capacity to outlast inwardness and nationalism. With typical perspicacity, economist Charles Kindleberger hinted at the remarkable shift toward a cosmopolitanism sensibility that has accompanied globalization:

> Man in his elemental state is a peasant with a possessive love of his own turf; a mercantilist who favours exports over imports; a Populist who distrusts banks, especially foreign banks; a monopolist who abhors competition; a xenophobe who feels threatened by strangers and foreigners.[68]

These reflexive tendencies are reinforced by prevailing "common sense," but they are not unassailable, as the past two centuries of economic history have demonstrated. International networks and flows have proliferated in spite of our ingrained prejudice toward outsiders. As Kindleberger added, the principles of economics ought to be employed "to extirpate these primitive instincts and teach cosmopolitanism."[69] Globalization may not have slain economic nationalism and parochialism, but the ideas that sustain them appear increasingly quaint and outdated.

In the context of extraordinary demographic, environmental, and economic changes in the coming century, we cannot simply wait for the emergence of an international organization to advance a global migration agenda. Bilateral and regional agreements should provide interim frameworks to free up cross-border mobility. Legislative reform at a national level is needed to craft more enlightened policies that safeguard the welfare of migrants and harness the opportunities presented by mobility. In pursuit of these goals, civil society organizations, religious communities, business associations, and opinion leaders should be at the vanguard of reforming our patchwork system of global migration governance.

So long as nationalism can legitimately trump the more universal claims of international cooperation, world development, poverty alleviation, and human freedom, the project to advance an agenda for the liberalization of migration will be stalled. However, our national myths are gradually deconstructed as historical revision lays bare the truth about the central role of cross-cultural contact in the creation of our societies. When we ask ourselves the perennial question "Who are we?" answering exclusively with nationalism is less and less convincing in the twenty-first century.

Genetic and other evidence has placed the old arguments for ethnic purity in the dustbin of history. The ethical justification for discriminating on the basis of nation-states is also becoming moribund. While the world may still hold tightly to its national categories, as an excuse for restricting human liberties, they are being eroded by the tides of history. We contend that the idea of freer movement and the need for a global institution to promote and protect it will end up like the other big ideas of history—democracy, free trade, global peace—that emerged from the margins of impossibility into the realm of the self-evident. As our distant ancestors would have told us, the earth is one country and all of humanity its citizens.

Notes

INTRODUCTION

1. Christiane Harzig, Dirk Hoerder, and Donna Gabaccia. 2009. *What Is Migration?* Cambridge, MA: Polity Press, p. 26.

CHAPTER 1. MIGRATION FROM PREHISTORY TO COLUMBUS

1. Patrick Manning. 2005. *Migration in World History.* London: Routledge; Jason Shogren, Richard Horan, and Erwin Bulte. 2005. "How Trade Saved Humanity from Biological Exclusion: An Economic Theory of Neanderthal Extinction," *Journal of Economic Behavior and Organization* 58: 1–29.

2. Manning, 2005.

3. William H. McNeill. 1984. "Human Migration in Historical Perspective," *Population and Development Review* 10(1): 1–18.

4. Like most events in prehistory, the date of Homo sapiens' departure from Africa is the subject of academic debate. At present, the most widely accepted range is 50,000–60,000 years ago. It is cited in recent research using linguistic and genetic analysis. See Manning, 2005; Spencer Wells. 2002. *The Journey of Man: A Genetic Odyssey.* Oxford, UK: Princeton University Press. Wells is also the director of the Genographic Project at National Geographic, and the project has adopted 50,000 years ago as the estimated date of human departure from Africa.

5. Manning, 2005.

6. Wells, 2002: 29, 33.

7. Christiane Harzig, Dirk Hoerder, and Donna Gabaccia. 2009. *What Is Migration History?* Cambridge, UK: Polity Press, pp. 10–11.

8. William H. McNeill. 1978. "Human Migration: A Historical Overview," in William H. McNeill and Ruth S. Adams (eds.), *Human Migration: Patterns and Policies.* Bloomington: Indiana University Press, p. 3.

9. David Christian. 2005. *Maps of Time: An Introduction to Big History.* London: University of California Press; Patrick Manning. 2006. "Homo sapiens Populates the Earth: A Provisional Synthesis, Privileging Linguistic Evidence," *Journal of World History* 17(2): 115–158.

288 NOTES TO CHAPTER 1

10. Manning, 2006.

11. Manning, 2005: 21.

12. Shogren, Horan, and Bulte, 2005.

13. Manning, 2005.

14. Brian Fagan. 2007. *People of the Earth: An Introduction to World Prehistory*. London: Prentice Hall.

15. Manning, 2006.

16. Christian, 2005: 233.

17. Manning puts the date of the first movement into North America around 30,000 years ago, whereas Wells suggests it was 10,000–15,000 years later. These two dates provide a fairly acceptable range of time within which the events likely took place.

18. Christian, 2005; Manning, 2006.

19. Ted Goebel, Michael R. Waters, Dennis H. O'Rourke. 2008. "The Late Pleistocene Dispersal of Modern Humans in the Americas," *Science* 319 (5869): 1497–1502.

20. Wells, 2002: 144.

21. Charles Pasternak. 2004. *Quest: The Essence of Humanity*. Chichester, UK: John Wiley and Sons, Ltd., p. 114.

22. Wells, 2002.

23. Fagan, 2007.

24. Ibid.

25. Christian, 2005: 234.

26. Pasternak, 2004: 139.

27. Harzig, Hoerder, and Gabaccia, 2009: 13.

28. New Scientist. 2009. "French Immigrants Founded British Farms," 5 December 2009, p. 17.

29. Christian, 2005.

30. Ibid.: 181.

31. Jared Diamond. 1998. *Guns, Germs and Steel*. Vintage: London, p. 106.

32. Manning, 2005: 74; Brian Sykes. 2001. *The Seven Daughters of Eve*. London: Corgi Books, p. 329.

33. Ornella Semino and Giuseppe Passarino et al. 2000. "The Genetic Legacy of Paleolithic Homo sapiens sapiens in Extant Europeans: A Y-Chromosome Perspective," *Science* 290: 1155–1159.

34. Diamond, 1998: 30.

35. Wells, 2002: 158.

36. Christian, 2005: 284.

37. Ibid.: 182.

38. This description is adapted from Harzig, Hoerder, and Gabaccia, 2009: 15–17.

39. McNeill, 1984: 3.

40. Christian, 2005.

41. Ibid.

42. McNeill, 1984: 2–3.

43. McNeill, 1978.

44. Ibid.

45. Philip D. Curtin. 1984. *Cross-Cultural Trade in World History*. Cambridge, UK: Cambridge University Press, p. 2.

46. Ibid.

47. Ibid.: 60.

48. Jerry H. Bentley. 1993. *Old World Encounters, Cross-Cultural Contacts and Exchange in Pre-Modern Times*. Oxford, UK: Oxford University Press.

49. McNeill, 1978: 12.

50. Ibid.: 12.

51. Bentley, 1993.

52. Pasternak, 2004.

53. Harzig, Hoerder, and Gabaccia, 2009: 19.

54. Rey Koslowski. 2002. "Human Migration and Pre-Modern World Politics," *International Studies Quarterly* 46(3): 375–399.

55. Koslowski, 2002.

56. Ibid.: 379.

57. Ibid.: 380.

58. Ibid.: 383.

59. Christian, 2005.

60. Bentley, 1993: 32.

61. Christian, 2005.

62. Manning, 2005.

63. Curtin, 1984.

64. Manning, 2005: 89.

65. McNeill, 1984: 9.

66. Manning, 2005: 89.

67. Karl Jaspers. 1951. *Way to Wisdom: An Introduction to Philosophy*. New Haven, CT: Yale University Press: 99–100.

68. Bentley, 1993.

69. Manning, 2005.

70. The Asian Age. 2001. "Professor Amartya Sen in India," 28 February 2001. Available at http://www.tata.com/company/Media/inside.aspx?artid =mWEoPvKEFew=.

71. Manning, 2005.

72. Ibid.

73. Curtin, 1984: 107.

74. Ibid.: 107.

75. Ibid.

76. Jerry H. Bentley. 1998. "Hemispheric Integration, 500–1500 CE," *Journal of World History* 9(2): 237–254, p. 247.

77. Andrew Watson. 1983. *Agricultural Innovation in the Early Islamic World: The Diffusion of Crops and Farming Techniques, 700–1100*. Cambridge, UK: Cambridge University Press.

78. William H. McNeill. 1998. "World History and the Rise and Fall of the West," *Journal of World History* 9(2): 215–236.

79. Curtin, 1984: 105.

80. Manning, 2005: 106.

81. Bentley, 1998.

82. Bentley, 1998; William H. McNeill. 1967. *A World History*. Oxford, UK: Oxford University Press.

83. Jack Weatherford. 2004. *Genghis Khan and the Making of the Modern World*. New York: Three Rivers Press.

84. Michael E. Smith. 1984. "The Aztlan Migrations of the Nuhuatl: Myth or History?" *Ethnohistory* 31(3): 153–186.

85. Smith, 1984.

86. David Eltis. 2002. "Introduction: Migration and Agency in Global History," in David Eltis (ed.), *Coerced and Free Migration: Global Perspectives*. Stanford, CA: Stanford University Press.

87. Bentley, 1993: 30.

88. Curtin, 1984: 114.

89. Ibid.

90. Ibid.: 116.

91. Robert Winder. 2004. *Bloody Foreigners: The Story of Immigration to Britain*. London: Abacus.

92. McNeill, 1984: 13.

93. Ibid.: 14.

94. Curtin, 1984: 116.

95. William H. McNeill. 1982. *The Pursuit of Power: Technology, Armed Force, and Society since AD 1000*. Oxford, UK: Blackwell: 55.

96. McNeill, 1967.

97. William H. McNeill. 1963 [1991]. *The Rise of the West: A History of the Human Community* [with a retrospective essay]. Chicago: University of Chicago Press.

98. Curtin, 1984.

99. Ibid.: 134.

100. Pasternak, 2004: 136.

101. Felipe Fernandez-Armesto. 2006. *Pathfinders: A Global History of Exploration*. Oxford, UK: Oxford University Press.

102. McNeill, 1982: 46.

103. Kenneth Pomerantz. 2000. *China, Europe, and the Making of the Modern Economy*. Princeton, NJ: Princeton Univesity Press; Diamond, 1998.

104. McNeill, 1963 [1991].

Chapter 2. Global Migrations: Toward a World Economy

1. Felipe Fernandez-Armesto. 2006. *Pathfinders: A Global History of Exploration*. Oxford: Oxford University Press: 165.

2. Fernandez-Armesto, 2006: 157.

3. Karl Marx. 1976. *Capital: A Critique of Political Economy*, vol. 1, trans. Ben Fowkes. Harmondsworth: Penguin: 247.

4. Fernandez-Armesto, 2006.

5. Ibid.: 226.

6. Dan O'Sullivan. 1984. *The Age of Discovery, 1400–1550*. London: Longman: 20.

7. O'Sullivan, 1984: 21.

8. Fernandez-Armesto, 2006: 181.

9. David Northrup. 1998. "Vasco da Gama and Africa: An Era of Mutual Discovery, 1497–1800," *Journal of World History* 9(2): 189–211.

10. Northrup, 1998.

11. Christiane Harzig, Dirk Hoerder, and Donna Gabaccia. 2009. *What Is Migration History?* Cambridge, UK: Polity Press, pp. 26–27.

12. William H. McNeill. 1963 [1991]. *The Rise of the West: A History of the Human Community* [with a retrospective essay]. Chicago: University of Chicago Press.

13. Ibid.

14. Ibid.

15. Jonathon W. Moses. 2006. *International Migration: Globalization's Last Frontier*. London: Zed Books.

16. David Christian. 2005. *Maps of Time: An Introduction to Big History*. London: University of California Press, p. 393.

17. Patrick Manning. 2005. *Migration in World History*. London: Routledge, p. 108.

18. Jared Diamond. 1998. *Guns, Germs and Steel*. Vintage: London, p. 210.

19. Ibid.: 77–78.

20. Colin Bundy. 1988. *The Rise and Fall of the South African Peasantry*. London: James Currey.

21. Cited in Steve Olson. 2002. *Mapping Human History*. Boston: Mariner, p. 224.

22. Diamond, 1998: 44.

23. Daron Acemoglu, Simon Johnson, and James Robinson. 2001. "The Colonial Origins of Comparative Development: An Empirical Investigation," *The American Economic Review* 91(5): 1369–1401.

24. Ibid..

25. Ibid.:1374.

26. Ibid., 2001.

27. Our thanks to Robin Cohen for this observation.

28. See McNeill, 2000.

29. Our thanks to Robin Cohen for this observation.

30. Harzig, Hoerder, and Gabaccia, 2009: 28.

31. John R. McNeill. 2000. "Biological Exchange and Biological Invasion in World History," unpublished paper prepared for the *19th International Congress of the Historical Sciences Oslo*, 6–13 August 2000.

32. McNeill, 2000: 9.

33. McNeill, 1963 [1991]: 584.

34. William H. McNeill. 1967. *A World History.* Oxford, UK: Oxford University Press.

35. Ibid.

36. Ibid.

37. Jonathan I. Israel, quoted in John F. Richards. 1997. "Early Modern India and World History," *Journal of World History* 8(2): 197–209.

38. Stephen Castles and Mark Miller. 2003. *The Age of Migration: International Population Movements in the Modern World*, 3rd ed. Basingstoke, UK: Palgrave MacMillan: 51.

39. David Northrup. 2003. "Free and Unfree Labour Migration, 1600–1900: An Introduction," *Journal of World History* 14(2): 125–130.

40. Herbert S. Klein. 1999. *The Atlantic Slave Trade.* Cambridge, UK: Cambridge University Press.

41. Ibid.: 140, table 6.2.

42. Manning, 2005: 135.

43. See Harzig, Hoerder, and Gabaccia, 2009: 35.

44. Jan S. Hogondorn. 1984. "Review Essay: The Economics of the African Slave Trade," *Journal of American History* 70(4): 854–861.

45. Hogondorn, 1984.

46. Barbara L. Solow. 2001. "The Transatlantic Slave Trade: A New Census," *The William and Mary Quarterly* 58(1): 9–16.

47. Scheidel, 1997, cited in Nathan Nunn. 2008. "The Long-Term Effects of Africa's Slave Trade," *The Quarterly Journal of Economics* 123(1): 139–176.

48. Nunn, 2008: 3.

49. Ibid.: 2.

50. Robert Winder. 2004. *Bloody Foreigners: The Story of Immigration to Britain.* London: Abacus, p. 126; Steve I. Martin. 1999. *Britain's Slave Trade.* London: Channel 4 Books.

51. Martin, 1999.

52. Quoted in David Northrup. 1995. *Indentured Labour in the Age of Imperialism: 1834–1922.* Cambridge, UK: Cambridge University Press, pp. 18–19.

53. Timothy J. Hatton and Jeffrey G. Williamson. 2005. *Global Migration and the World Economy: Two Centuries of Policy and Performance.* Boston: MIT Press, p. 10.

54. Our thanks to Stephen Castles for this clarification.

55. Klein, 1999: 183.

56. Ibid.: 185.

57. Hatton and Williamson, 2005.

58. The phrase "informal empire of financial and commercial networks" is from Northrup, 1995: 30.

59. Northrup, 1995: 30.

60. Ibid.

61. Robin Cohen. 2006. *Migration and Its Enemies: Global Capital, Migrant Labour and the Nation State*. London: Ashgate, p. 19.

62. Ibid.: 20.

63. Ibid.: 20.

64. M. Madhaven. 1987. "Indian Emigration," in Sidney Klein (ed), *The Economics of Mass Migration in the Twentieth Century*. New York: Dragon House, p. 74.

65. United Nations. 2004a. *World Economic and Social Survey 2004: International Migration*. New York: United Nations.

66. Hatton and Williamson, 2005.

67. Madhaven, 1987:106.

68. Northrup, 1995: 52.

69. Ibid.

70. Ibid.: 52.

71. Hatton and Williamson, 2005.

72. Potts, 1990, cited in Castles and Miller, 2003: 55.

73. Castles and Miller, 2003.

74. Hatton and Williamson 2005.

75. Ibid.

76. Quoted in Moses, 2006: 47

77. Hatton and Williamson, 1998.

78. Ibid.

79. Ibid.

80. Hatton and Williamson, 2005: 74.

81. Ibid.: 75.

82. Castles and Miller, 2003.

83. Adam McKeown. 2007. "Ritualization of Regulation: The Enforcement of Chinese Exclusion in the United States and China," *The American Historical Review* 108(2): 377–403.

84. Hatton and Williamson, 1998.

85. Harzig, Hoerder, and Gabaccia, 2009: 37.

86. Winder, 2004: 196.

87. Ibid.: 229.

88. Hatton and Williamson, 1998.

89. Timothy Hatton and Jeffrey Williamson. 1998. *The Age of Mass Migration: Causes and Economic Impact*. Oxford, UK: Oxford University Press.

90. Carl Solberg. 1978. "Mass Migrations in Argentina, 1870–1970," in William H. McNeill and Ruth Adams (eds.), *Human Migration: Patterns and Policies*. London: Indiana University Press, p. 148.

91. Solberg, 1978: 151.

92. Hatton and Williamson, 1998.

93. Herbert S. Klein. 1995. "European and Asian Migrations to Brazil," in Robin Cohen (ed.), *The Cambridge Survey of World Migration*. Cambridge, UK: Cambridge University Press, pp. 208–214.

94. Klein, 1995.

95. Hatton and Williamson, 2005: 51.

96. Hatton and Williamson, 1998: 9.

97. Castles and Miller, 2003.

98. Ibid.: 59.

99. Werner Bertelsmann, quoted in John Torpey. 2000b. *The Invention of the Passport: Surveillance, Citizenship and the State*. Cambridge, UK: Cambridge University Press, p. 111.

100. Castles and Miller, 2003: 61.

101. Ibid.: 61.

102. Winder, 2004: 156–177, 228–229.

103. Castles and Miller 2003: 61–62.

104. Adam McKeown. 2004. "Global Migration, 1846–1940," *Journal of World History* 15(2): 155–189, p. 166.

105. Ibid.

106. Ibid.

107. Ibid.

108. Ibid.

109. The largest recipients of Japanese migrants between 1868 and 1941 were: United States (338,459); Brazil (188,985); China (95,508); Siberia/USSR (56,821); Philippines/Guam (53,115); Canada (35,777); Peru (33,070); Mexico (14,667); Malay/Singapore (11,809); and Argentina (5,398). See http://www.discovernikkei.org/wiki/index.php/Japanese_Immigration_Statistics. Source: Wakatsuki Yasuo. 1995. *Sengo hikiage no kiroku*. Tokyo: Jiji Tsoshinsha, pp. 16–17, 85.

110. Harzig, Hoerder, and Gabaccia, 2009: 42.

111. McKeown, 2007.

CHAPTER 3. "Managed" Migration in the Twentieth Century (1914–1973)

1. Timothy Hatton and Jeffrey Williamson. 2005. *Global Migration and the World Economy*. Boston: MIT Press, p. 396.

2. Ibid.: 396.

3. Thanks to Stephen Castles for the observation about Russia.

4. John Torpey. 2000b. *The Invention of the Passport: Surveillance, Citizenship and the State*. Cambridge, UK: Cambridge University Press, p. 92.

5. Alan Dowty. 1989. *Closed Borders: The Contemporary Assault on Freedom of Movement.* London: Yale University Press.

6. Quoted in Torpey, 2000b: 92.

7. Quoted in Dowty, 1989: 43.

8. Quoted in Torpey, 2000a: 92.

9. Quoted in Dowty, 1989: 53.

10. Quoted in Torpey, 2000b: 91.

11. Thanks to Stephen Castles for this interesting point.

12. Torpey, 2000b: 111–112.

13. Ibid.: 121.

14. Dowty, 1989: 57.

15. B. Traven. 1934 [1991]. *Death Ship: The Story of an American Sailor.* Knopf: New York, republished by Lawrence Books: New York, p. 57.

16. Aristide R Zolberg. 1997. "Global Movements, Global Walls: Responses to Migration, 1885–1925," in Wang Gungwu (ed.), *Global History and Migrations.* Boulder, CO: Westview Press, pp. 279–303, p. 303.

17. Charles Pasternak. 2004. *Quest: The Essence of Humanity.* Chichester, UK: John Wiley and Sons, Ltd, p. 140.

18. Ian Goldin. 1987. *Making Race: The Politics and Economics of Coloured Identity in South Africa.* London: Longman, pp. 3–28.

19. Desmond King. 2000. *Making Americans: Immigration, Race, and the Origins of a Diverse Democracy.* London: Harvard University Press, p. 53.

20. King, 2000.

21. Zolberg, 1997: 296.

22. King, 2000: 171.

23. Ibid.: 296.

24. Stephen Castles and Mark Miller. 2003. *The Age of Migration: International Population Movements in the Modern World,* 3rd ed. Basingstoke, UK: Palgrave MacMillan, p. 58.

25. John Walker. 1987. "Migration to Australia and New Zealand," in Sidney Klein (ed.), *The Economics of Mass Migration in the Twentieth Century.* New York: Dragon House, p. 156

26. Ibid.: 161.

27. Randall Hansen. 2000. *Citizenship and Immigration in Post-War Britain: The Institutional Origins of a Multicultural Nation.* Oxford, UK: Oxford University Press.

28. Ian R. G. Spencer. 1997. *British Immigration Policy since 1939: The Making of Multi-Racial Britain.* London: Routledge.

29. Robert Winder. 2004. *Bloody Foreigners: The Story of Immigration to Britain.* London: Abacus, p. 278.

30. Dirk Hoerder. 2002. *Cultures in Contact: World Migrations in the Second Millennium.* London: Duke University Press, p. 492.

31. Ibid.: 493.

32. Ibid.: 503.

33. Dowty, 1989: 88.

34. Hoerder, 2002: 449.

35. Ibid.: 449.

36. Michael R. Marrus. 2002. *The Unwanted: European Refugees from the First World War through the Cold War*. Philadelphia: Temple University Press.

37. Saskia Sassen. 1999. *Guests and Aliens*. New York: The New Press.

38. Marrus, 2002: 61.

39. Ibid.: 63.

40. Ibid.: 63.

41. Spencer, 1997: 10.

42. Gershon Shafir. 1995. "Zionist Immigration and Colonization in Palestine in 1948," in Robin Cohen (ed.), *The Cambridge Survey of World Migration*. Cambridge, UK: Cambridge University Press, pp. 405–409, p. 406.

43. Shafir, 1995: 406.

44. Carl Strikwerda. 1999. "Tides of Migration, Currents of History: The State, Economy, and the Transatlantic Movement of Labour in the Nineteenth and Twentieth Centuries," *International Review of Social History* 44: 367–394.

45. Dowty, 1989: 82.

46. Strikwerda, 1999: 387.

47. Hatton and Williamson, 2005: 179.

48. Zolberg, 1997: 280.

49. Sarah Collinson. 1993. *Europe and International Migration*. London: Pinter Publishers, p. 40.

50. Strikwerda, 1999: 388.

51. Jeffrey Williamson. 2004. "The Political Economy of World Mass Migration: Comparing Two Global Centuries," *American Enterprise Institute*, 11 May 2004, pp. 20–22.

52. King, 2000.

53. Anthony M. Messina and Gallya Lahav, eds., *The Migration Reader: Exploring Politics and Policies*. London: Lynne Rienner Publishers, p. 134.

54. Torpey, 2000: 38.

55. Greg Burgess. 2008. *Refuge in the Land of Liberty. France and Its Refugees, from the Revolution to the End of Asylum, 1787–1939*. Basingstoke, UK: Palgrave MacMillan.

56. Castles and Miller, 2003: 64.

57. Ibid.: 65.

58. Ibid.: 65.

59. Hoerder, 2002: 468–471.

60. Colin Holmes. 1995. "Jewish Economic and Refugee Migrations, 1880–1950," in Robin Cohen (eds.), *The Cambridge Survey of World Migration*. Cambridge, UK: Cambridge University Press, pp. 148–153.

61. Hoerder, 2002: 481–483.

62. Lydia Potts. 1990. A World Labour Market: A History of Migration. London: Zed Books, p. 152; Hoerder, 2002: 495.

63. Hoerder, 2002: 483.

64. Ibid.: 483.

65. Ibid.: 484.

66. Ibid.: 484.

67. Aristide Zolberg. 2006. "Patterns of International Migration Policy," in Anthony M. Messina and Gallya Lahav (eds), *The Migration Reader: Exploring Politics and Policies*. London: Lynne Rienner Publishers, p. 119.

68. Sassen, 1999.

69. Ibid.: 78.

70. Laura Barnett. 2002. "Global Governance and the Evolution of the International Refugee Regime," *International Journal of Refugee Law* 14(2/3): 238–262.

71. Jan Lucassen and Leo Lucassen, eds. 1997. *Migration, Migration History, History: Old Paradigms and New Perspectives*. Bern: Peter Lang.

72. Barnett, 2002: 243.

73. Germany refused to allow Jews to leave with their assets.

74. Barnett, 2002.

75. See Goran Melander, quoted in Barnett, 2002: 244.

76. *United Nations Convention Relating to the Status of Refugees*, chapter 1, article A (A.2).

77. Barnett, 2002: 247.

78. Ibid.: 251.

79. Charles Tilly. 2006. "Migration in Modern European History," in Anthony M. Messina and Gallya Lahav (eds.), *The Migration Reader: Exploring Politics and Policies*. London: Lynne Rienner.

80. John Torpey. 2000b. "States and the Regulation of Migration in the Twentieth-Century North Atlantic World," in Peter Andreas and Timothy Snyder (eds.), *The Wall around the West: State Borders and Immigration Controls in North America and Europe*. Oxford: Rowan and Littlefield Publishers, Inc., pp. 31–54.

81. Castles and Miller, 2003: 65.

82. Diana Kay. 1995. "The Resettlement of Displaced Persons in Europe, 1946–1951," in Robin Cohen (ed.), *Cambridge World Survey of World Migration*. Cambridge, UK: Cambridge University Press, p. 154.

83. Norman Plotkin. 1987. "Latin America after World War II," in Sidney Klein (ed.), *The Economics of Mass Migration in the Twentieth Century*. New York: Paragon Books, p. 123.

84. Sassen, 1999: 96.

85. Hoerder, 2002: 501.

86. Ibid.: 502.

87. Castles and Miller, 2003: 72.

88. Torpey, 2000.

89. Castles and Miller, 2003.

90. Philip Martin. 2002. "Mexican Workers and U.S. Agriculture: The Revolving Door," *International Migration Review* 36(4): 1124–1142.

91. Kay, 1995: 154.

92. Castles and Miller, 2003: 69.

93. Ibid.: 72.

94. Ibid.: 72.

95. Ibid.: 71.

96. Stephen Castles and Godula Kosack. 1984. *Immigrant Workers and Class Structure in Western Europe,* 2nd ed. Oxford, UK: Oxford University Press.

97. Hoerder, 2002.

98. Ibid.: 548–9.

99. Robin Cohen. 2006. *Migration and Its Enemies: Global Capital, Migrant Labour, and the Nation-State.* Aldershot, UK: Ashgate, p. 46.

100. Cohen, 2006: 46.

101. Hatton and Williamson, 2005: 220.

102. Ibid.: 396.

103. Castles and Miller, 2003: 109.

104. Sassen, 1999.

105. Prashant Bharadwaj, Asim Ijaz Khwaja, and Atif R. Mian. 2008. "The Big March: Migratory Flows after the Partition of India." *HKS Working Paper No. RWP08-029.* Available at SSRN: http://ssrn.com/abstract=1124093

106. Dowty, 2000: 167.

107. Ibid.

108. Ibid.

109. Robert D. Kaplan. 2001. *Soldiers of God: With Islamic Warriors in Afghanistan and Pakistan.* New York: Vintage.

110. Dowty, 2000.

111. Cohen, 2005.

112. Charles Keeley. 2001. "The International Refugee Regime: The End of the Cold War Matters," *International Migration Review* 35(1): 303–314.

113. Torpey, 2000: 44.

114. Castles and Miller, 2003: 107.

115. Strikwerda, 1999: 385.

116. Hatton and Williamson, 2005: 396; Jeannette Money. 1999. *Fences and Neighbors: The Political Geography of Immigration Control.* Ithaca, NY: Cornell University Press, p. 214.

117. Dani Rodrik. 2002. "Final Remarks," in T. Boeri, G. Hanson, and B. McCormick (eds.), *Immigration Policy and the Welfare System.* Oxford, UK: Oxford University Press, p. 314.

Chapter 4. Leaving Home: Migration Decisions and Processes

1. See Ian Goldin and Kenneth Reinert. 2007. *Globalization for Development: Trade, Finance, Aid, Migration, and Policy,* 2nd ed. Basingstoke, UK: Palgrave MacMillan.

2. Douglas S. Massey and J. Edward Taylor. 2004. "Back to the Future: Immigration Research, Immigration Policy, and Globalization in the Twenty-First Century," in Douglas S. Massey and J. Edward Taylor (eds.), *International Migration: Prospects and Policies in a Global Market*. Oxford, UK: Oxford University Press, pp. 373–387, p. 377.

3. Stephen Castles and Mark J. Miller. 2009. *The Age of Migration: International Population Movements in the Modern World*, 4th ed. New York: Palgrave MacMillan.

4. Steven Vertovec. 2009. *Transnationalism*. London: Routledge, p. 2.

5. Hein de Haas. 2008b. "Migration and Development: A Theoretical Perspective," *Working Paper 9*, International Migration Institute, James Martin 21st Century School, University of Oxford, p. 15.

6. Douglas S. Massey et al. 2002. *Worlds in Motion: Understanding International Migration at the End of the Millennium*. Oxford, UK. Oxford University Press, p. 10.

7. Sarah Collison. 2009. "The Political Economy of Migration Processes: An Agenda for Migration Research and Analysis," *Working Paper 12*, International Migration Institute, James Martin 21st Century School, University of Oxford, p. 8.

8. Sonja Haug. 2008. "Migration Networks and Migration Decision-Making," *Journal of Ethnic and Migration Studies* 34(4): 585–605.

9. Oded Stark and David E. Bloom. 1985. "The New Economics of Labor Migration," *The American Economic Review* 75(2): 173–178.

10. Collinson, 2009.

11. John R. Harris and Michael P. Todaro. 1970. "Migration, Unemployment and Development: A Two-Sector Analysis," *American Economic Review* 60(1): 126–142.

12. George J. Borjas. 1999a. *Heaven's Door: Immigration Policy and the American Economy*. Princeton, NJ: Princeton University Press, p. 19.

13. Douglas S. Massey et al. 1993. "Theories of International Migration: A Review and Appraisal," *Population and Development Review* 19(3): 431–466, p. 435.

14. Timothy J. Hatton and Jeffrey G. Williamson. 1994. "What Drove the Mass Migrations from Europe in the Late Nineteenth Century," *Population and Development Review* 20(3): 533–557.

15. Lant Pritchett. 2006. *Let Their People Come: Breaking the Gridlock on Global Labor Mobility*. Washington, DC: Center for Global Development.

16. Ibid.

17. Guillermina Jasso, Mark R. Rosenzweig, and James P. Smith. 2003. "The Earnings of US Immigrants: World Skill Prices, Skill Transferability, and Selectivity." Available at http://econwpa.wustl.edu:80/eps/lab/papers/0312/0312007.pdf.

18. Hatton and Williamson, 1994.

19. Hein de Haas. 2007a. "North African Migration Systems: Evolutions, Transformations, and Development Linkages," *Working Paper 6*, International Migration Institute, James Martin 21st Century School, University of Oxford.

20. The "migration hump" concept was developed by Philip L. Martin. See Philip L. Martin. 1993. *Trade and Migration: NAFTA and Agriculture*. Washington, DC: Institute for International Economics.

21. de Haas, 2008: 16.

22. Peggy Levitt. 2001. *The Transnational Villagers*. Stanford: University of California Press.

23. Massey et al, 2002: 9.

24. Haug, 2008: 587.

25. Douglas S. Massey, Jorge Durand, and Nolan J. Malone. 2002. *Beyond Smoke and Mirrors: Mexican Immigration in an Era of Economic Integration*. New York: Russell Sage Foundation.

26. Philip L. Martin and J. Edward Taylor. 2001. "Managing Migration: The Role of Economic Policies," in Aristide R. Zolberg and Peter M. Benda (eds.), *Global Migrants Global Refugees: Problems and Solutions*. Oxford, UK: Berghahn Books, pp. 95–120.

27. Stephen Castles. 1989. "Migrant Workers and the Transformation of Western Societies," *Western Societies Program Occasional Paper No. 22*, Centre for International Studies, Cornell University.

28. Massey et al., 2002: 10.

29. Alejandro Portes and Jozsef Borocz. 1989. "Contemporary Immigration: Theoretical Perspectives on Its Determinants and Modes of Incorporation," *International Migration Review* 23(3): 606–630, p. 607.

30. Stark and Bloom, 1985: 174.

31. de Haas, 2008.

32. Janet Rodenberg. 1993. "Emancipation or Subordination? Consequences of Female Migration for Migrants and Their Families," in *Internal Migration of Women in Developing Countries*. New York: United Nations.

33. Massey et al., 2002: 278.

34. Massey et al., 1993: 436.

35. Martin and Taylor, 2001.

36. Steven Vertovec. 2003. "Migration and Other Modes of Transnationalism: Towards Conceptual Cross-Fertilization," *International Migration Review* 37(3): 641–665.

37. Charles Tilly. 1990. "Transplanted Networks," in Virginia Yans-McLaughlin (ed.), *Immigration Reconsidered: History, Sociology, and Politics*. Oxford, UK: Oxford University Press, pp. 79–95.

38. Portes and Borocz, 1989: 612.

39. This general narrative of the migration process is drawn from Massey et al., 1993.

40. Castles, 1989: 106; George J. Borjas and Stephen G. Bronars. 1991. "Immigration and the Family," *Journal of Labour Economics* 9(2): 123–148.

41. Gil S. Epstein. 2008. "Herd and Network Effects in Migration Decision-Making," *Journal of Ethnic and Migration Studies* 34: 567–583.

42. Manolo I. Abella. 2004. "The Role of Recruiters in Labour Migration," in Douglas S. Massey and J. Edward Taylor (eds.), *International Migration: Prospects and Policies in a Global Market*. Oxford, UK: Oxford University Press.

43. Ibid.: 201.

44. Ibid.: 201.

45. Stephen Castles. 2007. "Comparing the Experience of Five Major Emigration Countries," *Working Paper 7*, International Migration Institute, James Martin 21st Century School, University of Oxford.

46. Alejandro Portes and Josh DeWind. 2004. "A Cross-Atlantic Dialogue: The Progress of Research and Theory in the Study of International Migration," *International Migration Review* 38(3): 828–851, p. 831.

47. Monica Boyd. 1989. "Family and Personal Networks in International Migration: Recent Developments and New Agendas," *International Migration Review* 23(3): 638–670, p. 641.

48. Massey and Taylor, 2004.

49. Timothy Hatton and Jeffrey Williamson. 1998. *The Age of Mass Migration.* Oxford, UK: Oxford University Press.

50. Luis Eduardo Guarnizo. 2003. "The Economics of Transnational Living," *International Migration Review* 37(3): 666–699, p. 677.

51. Peter Stalker. 2000. *Workers without Frontiers.* New York: ILO/Lynne Rienner.

52. Ibid.

53. Levitt, 2001.

54. Nasra M. Shah and Indu Menon. 1999. "Chain Migration through the Social Network: Experience of Labour Migrants in Kuwait," *International Migration* 37(2): 361–382.

55. Jean-Baptiste Meyer. 2001. "Network Approach versus Brain Drain: Lessons from the Diaspora," *International Migration Quarterly Review* 39(5): 91–110.

56. Ibid.: 98.

57. Robin Cohen. 2008. *Global Diasporas: An Introduction.* London: Routledge, p. 143.

58. Quoted in Vertovec, 2009: 158–159.

59. Alejandro Portes. 1997. "Immigration Theory for a New Century: Some Problems and Opportunities," *International Migration Review* 31: 799–825, p. 812.

60. Vertovec, 2009: 102.

61. Ibid.: 97.

62. Mary M. Kritz and Hania Zlotnik. 1992. "Global Interactions: Migration Systems, Processes, and Policies," in Mary M. Kritz, Lin Lean Lim, and Hania Zlotnik (eds.), *International Migration Systems: A Global Approach.* Oxford, UK: Oxford University Press, pp. 1–16.

63. Castles and Miller, 2009: 27.

64. Kritz and Zlotnik, 1992: 4.

65. The metaphor of battery poles is taken from Martin and Taylor, 2001: 102.

66. Thomas Faist. 2000. *The Volume and Dynamics of International Migration and Transnational Social Spaces.* Oxford, UK: Oxford University Press, p. 296.

67. Faist, 2000.

68. Hatton and Williamson, 1998: 40.

69. Ibid.: 40.

70. Hania Zlotnik. 2004. "Population Growth and International Migration," in Douglas S. Massey and J. Edward Taylor (eds.), *International Migration: Prospects and Policies in a Global Market.* Oxford, UK: Oxford University Press, pp. 15–34, p. 33.

71. Quoted in Castles and Miller, 2009: 224.

72. Pritchett, 2006: 30.

73. Massey et al., 2002: 13.

74. Ibid., 2002: 15.

75. Pritchett, 2006: 43–62.

76. de Haas, 2008.

77. Joseph Schumpeter. 1942 [1975]. *Capitalism, Socialism and Democracy.* New York: Harper, pp. 82–85.

78. Saskia Sassen. 1988. *The Mobility of Labour and Capital: A Study of International Investment and Labor Flow.* Cambridge, UK: Cambridge University Press, p. 18.

79. Ibid.: 19.

80. Massey and Taylor, 2004: 385.

81. Susan Gabbard, Rick Mines, and Beatriz Boccalandro. 1994. "Migrant Farmworkers: Pursuing Security in an Unstable Labor Market," *Research Report No. 5,* U.S. Dept. of Labor, Office of the Assistant Secretary for Policy, Office of Program Economics.

82. Stephen Castles and Mark J. Miller. 2003. *The Age of Migration: International Population Movements in the Modern World,* 3rd ed. New York: Palgrave MacMillan, pp. 193–194.

83. Ibid.: 193–194.

84. Castles and Miller, 2009; Ian Gordon. 1995. "Migration in a Segmented Labour Market," *Transactions of the Institute of British Geographers* 20(2): 139–155.

85. Adeline Percept and Clément Perrouault. 2009. "Spain Offers Immigrants an Incentive to Leave," *France 24,* 22 January 2009. Available at http://www.france24.com/en/20090122-spain-immigration-zapatero-financial-crisis-unemployment.

86. *The Economist.* 2009d. "The People Crunch," 17 January 2009, pp. 56–57.

87. *The Economist.* 2008b. "Tough Times," 29 November 2009, p. 55.

88. *The Economist,* 2009d; Percept and Perrouault, 2009.

89. *The Economist,* 2009d; *The Economist,* 2009b. "Economics Focus: Give Me Your Scientists," 7 March 2009, p. 80.

90. BBC News. 2008. "Migrant Numbers 'Must Be Reduced,'" 18 October 2008. Available at http://news.bbc.co.uk/1/hi/uk_politics/7677419.stm.

91. Human Security Centre. 2005. *Human Security Report.* Oxford, UK: Oxford University Press, figure 1.1.

92. Mark Duffield. 2001. *Global Governance and the New Wars. The Merging of Development and Security.* London: Zed Books.

93. UNHCR. 2009. *2008 Global Trends: Refugees, Asylum-Seekers, Returnees, Internally Displaced and Stateless Persons*. UNHCR: Geneva.

94. Anna Lindley. 2008. "Conflict-Induced Migration and Remittances: Exploring Conceptual Frameworks," *Working Paper Series No. 47*, Refugee Studies Centre, University of Oxford.

95. Stephen Castles and Sean Loughna. 2003. "Trends in Asylum Migration to Industrialized Countries: 1990–2001," *UNU-WIDER Discussion Paper No. 2003/31*, p. 16.

96. Robert E. B. Lucas. 2005. *International Migration and Economic Development: Lessons from Low-Income Countries*. Cheltenham, UK: Edward Elgar, p. 67.

97. Vaughan Robinson and Jeremy Segrott. 2002. "Understanding the Decision-Making of Asylum-Seekers," *Home Office Research Study 243*, Home Office Research, Development and Statistics Directorate, July 2002.

98. Robinson and Segrott, 2002: 62.

99. Lucas, 2005: 72.

100. Massey et al., 2002: 14.

101. Chikako Kashiwazaki. 2006. "Japanese Immigration Policy: Responding to Conflicting Pressures," Migration Information Source, Migration Policy Institute. Available at http://www.migrationinformation.org/Profiles/display.cfm?ID=487.

102. Stephen Castles. 2004. "The Factors That Make and Unmake Migration Policies," *International Migration Review* 38(3): 852–884.

103. Wayne Cornelius, quoted in Castles, 2004: 870. Italics in the original.

104. Boyd, 1989: 647.

105. United Nations. 2004b. *World Population Prospects: 2004 Revision*. New York: United Nations, p. 47.

106. Michael Jandl. 2003. "Estimates of the Number of Illegal and Smuggled Immigrants in Europe," presented at 8th International Metropolis Conference, Vienna, Austria, 17 September 2003.

107. Lucas, 2005: 40.

108. Ibid.: 42.

109. Nasra M. Shah. 1998. "The Role of Social Networks among South Asian Male Migrants in Kuwait," in Reginald Appleyard (ed.), *Emigration Dynamics in Developing Countries. Vol. II: South Asia*. Aldershot, UK: Ashgate Publishing, pp. 30–70.

110. International Organization for Migration. 2000. *World Migration Report*. Geneva: IOM, p. 113.

111. Lucas, 2005: 39.

112. Boyd, 1989: 648.

113. Guillermina Jasso and Mark R. Rosenzweig. 1986. "Family Reunification and the Immigration Multiplier: US Immigration Law, Origin Country Conditions, and the Reproduction of Immigrants," *Demography* 23: 291–311.

114. Lucas, 2005: 34.

115. OECD, 2008: 255.

116. Ibid.: 255.

117. Kashiwazaki, 2006.

118. Lucas, 2005: 36.

119. Ibid.: 36.

120. Wayne Cornelius. 2001. "Death at the Border: The Efficacy and 'Unintended' Consequences of the US Immigration Control Policy 1993–2000," *Working Paper 27*, Center for Comparative Immigration Studies, University of California, San Diego.

121. Castles and Miller, 2009: 205.

122. Cornelius, 2001: 678.

123. Belinda T. Reyes and Hans Johnson. 2000. "Holding the Line? The Effect of Border Enforcement on Unauthorized Immigration," Public Policy Institute of California, San Francisco.

124. Cornelius, 2001: 680.

125. Castles, 2004: 870.

126. Francesc Ortega and Giovanni Peri. 2009. "The Causes and Effects of International Migrations: Evidence from OECD Countries 1980–2005," *NBER Working Paper 14833*. Cambridge, Mass: NBER.

CHAPTER 5. IMMIGRATION AND BORDER CONTROL

1. We have drawn for this chapter on the analysis and data first developed together with Andrew Beath.

2. Stephen Castles and Mark J. Miller. 2009. *The Age of Migration: International Population Movements in the Modern World*, 4th ed. New York: Palgrave MacMillan, p. 181.

3. Saskia Sassen. 1996. *Losing Control?* New York: Columbia University Press, p. 86.

4. United Nations. 2006. "Report of the Secretary-General, International Migration and Development, UN General Assembly, 60th Session," *UN Doc. A/60/871*, 18 May 2006, p. 12.

5. Ibid.: 12.

6. Frank Duvell. 2009. "Irregular Migration in Northern Europe: Overview and Comparison," presented at Clandestino Project Conference, London, 27 March 2009.

7. International Organization for Migration. 2008. *World Migration 2008: Managing Labour Mobility in the Evolving Global Economy*. Geneva: IOM, p. 515.

8. Stephen Castles and Godula Kosack. 1974. "How the Trade Unions Try to Control and Integrate Immigrant Workers in the German Federal Republic," *Race and Class* 15(4): 497–514.

9. Stephen Castles. 2006. "Guestworkers in Europe: A Resurrection?" *International Migration Review* 40(4): 741–766, p. 760.

10. Organization for Economic Cooperation and Development. 2008. *International Migration Outlook 2008—SOPEMI*. Paris: OECD, p. 54.

11. Hania Zlotnik. 2005. "International Migration Trends since 1980," presented at International Migration and the Millennium Development Goals: Selected Papers of the UNFPA Expert Group Meeting, Marrakech, Morocco, 11–12 May 2005, p. 24.

12. Gail McLaughlan and John Salt. 2002. "Migration Policies toward Highly Skilled Foreign Workers," *Report to the UK Home Office*, March 2002, p. 4.

13. Lindsay Lowell. 2008. "Highly Skilled Migration," in *World Migration 2008: Managing Labour Mobility in the Evolving Global Economy*. Geneva. International Organization for Migration, p. 52.

14. Richard Florida, Charlotta Mellander, and Kevin Stolarick. 2008. "Inside the Black Box of Regional Development—Human Capital, the Creative Class and Tolerance," *Journal of Economic Geography* 8(5): 615–649.

15. Lowell, 2008. 53.

16. Demetrios Papademetriou. 2003. "Managing Rapid and Deep Change in the Newest Age of Migration," *Political Quarterly* 74(1): 39–58.

17. Lowell, 2008: 54.

18. Ibid.: 54.

19. Ibid.: 54.

20. Ibid.: 54.

21. Castles and Miller, 2009: 121.

22. Ian Goldin and Kenneth Reinert. 2007. *Globalization for Development: Trade, Finance, Aid, Migration and Policy*, 2nd ed. Basingstoke, UK: Palgrave MacMillan, p. 161.

23. Linda H. Aiken, James Buchan, Julie Sochalski, Barbara Nichols, and Mary Powell. 2004. "Trends in International Nurse Migration," *Health Affairs* 23(3): 69–77. Common destinations for Filipino nurses include the United Kingdom, Saudi Arabia, Ireland, Singapore, and the United States. The British and Filipino governments recently signed an agreement to facilitate the recruitment of Filipino health care professionals by Britain's National Health Service.

24. The respective numbers were 16,155 (with foreign qualifications) versus 14,538 (with domestic qualifications). Aiken et al., 2004.

25. Castles, 2006.

26. OECD, 2008: 133.

27. Philip Martin. 2008. "Low and Semi-Skilled Workers Abroad," in *World Migration 2008: Managing Labour Mobility in the Evolving Global Economy*. Geneva: International Organization for Migration.

28. OECD, 2008: 126.

29. Martin, 2008: 91.

30. In 2001, Japan admitted approximately 100,000 people with restricted permission to work, although 75% of these are female "entertainers" working in the sex industry. Many other low-skill positions are filled by the 28,000 working students,

50,000 trainees, and 280,000 persons overstaying their visa. In an attempt to introduce some regularity to its foreign workforce, the South Korean government has introduced an "employment permit system" via which migrants from eight countries—China, Indonesia, Kazakhstan, Mongolia, the Philippines, Sri Lanka, Thailand, and Vietnam—may obtain one-year permits to work in industries such as manufacturing, construction, coastal fisheries, agriculture, livestock farming, and services. See Peter Stalker. 2000. *Workers without Frontiers*. New York: ILO/Lynne Rienner; International Organization for Migration. 2005. *World Migration 2005: Costs and Benefits of International Migration*. Geneva: IOM.

31. IOM, 2005.

32. Martin, 2008: 77.

33. OECD, 2008: 133.

34. Martin, 2008: 82.

35. Ibid.: 85.

36. OECD, 2008: 134; Philip Martin, Manolo Abella, and Christiane Kuptsch. 2006. *Managing Labour Migration in the Twenty-first Century*. London: Yale University Press, p. 109.

37. Martin, Abella, and Kuptsch, 2006: 110.

38. Ibid., 2006: 110.

39. OECD, 2008: 133.

40. Castles, 2006: 750.

41. OECD, 2008: 35.

42. Australia Department of Citizenship and Immigration. 2008. *Population Flows: Immigration Aspects, 2007–8*. Canberra: Australian Government.

43. Ibid., 2008.

44. As of 2009.

45. Ettore Recchi, Damian Tambini, Emiliana Baldoni, David Williams, Kristin Surak, and Adrian Favell. 2003. "Intra-EU Migration: A Socio-demographic Overview," *Working Paper 3*, Pioneur Project. Available at http://www.obets.ua.es/pioneur/documentos_public.php

46. Recchi et al., 2003: 17.

47. The Guardian. "Net Migration Falls by a Third as Departures from UK Soar," 27 November 2009, p. 6.

48. Madeleine Sumption and Will Somerville. 2009. *The UK's New Europeans: Progress and Challenges Five Years after Accession*. London: Equality and Human Rights Commission and Migration Policy Institute.

49. Laura Chappell, Dhananjayan Sriskandarajah, and Tracy K Swinburn. 2008. "Building a New Home: Migration in the UK Construction Sector," *Economics of Migration Project, Working Paper 2*. London: Institute for Public Policy Research, p. 14.

50. Stéphan Vincent-Lancrin. 2008. "Student Mobility, Internationalization of Higher Education and Skilled Migration," in *World Migration 2008: Managing Labour Mobility in the Evolving Global Economy*. Geneva: IOM, p. 105.

51. OECD, 2008: 117.

52. IOM, 2005: 483.

53. Vincent-Lancrin, 2008.

54. IOM, 2005: 120.

55. Institute for International Education. 2009. *Open Doors 2008: Report on International Education Exchange.* Washington, DC: Institute for International Education.

56. Karine Tremblay. 2005. "Academic Mobility and Immigration," *Journal of Studies in International Education* 9(3): 196–228.

57. OECD, 2008: 118.

58. Tremblay, 2005.

59. OECD, 2008: 117.

60. Michael Finn. 2005. "Stay Rates of Foreign Doctorate Recipients from U.S. Universities, 2005," Division of Science Resources Statistics of the National Science Foundation. Available at http://orise.orau.gov/sep/files/stayrate07.pdf.

61. *The Economist.* 2009c. "The Immigration Superhighway," 18 April 2009, p. 29.

62. Eleonore Kofman and Veena Meetoo. 2008. "Family Migration," in *World Migration 2008: Managing Labour Mobility in the Evolving Global Economy.* Geneva: IOM.

63. John Salt. 2005. "Types of Migration in Europe: Implications and Policy Concerns," presented at European Population Conference 2005: Demographic Challenges for Social Cohesion, 7–8 April 2005, Strasbourg.

64. United Nations, 2004.

65. Article 16 (3) of the Universal Declaration of Human Rights affirms that families are entitled to protection by society and the state.

66. Stalker, 2000.

67. This is conditional, however, on the capability of the "sponsoring citizen" to support his or her relatives once in the United States. As in many other countries, spouses of American citizens wanting to immigrate are initially granted a temporary residence permit, with permanent residence granted only if the citizen and immigrant remain married and resident in the United States for the next two years.

68. National Foundation for American Policy, 2006. "Nearly 40 Asian American and Pacific Island Organizations Unite to Demand Fair and Humane Integration Program," Press Release, 19 May 2006. Available at http://www.apalc.org/pdffiles/Immigration%20Reform%20Press%20Release%200506.pdf

69. Kofman and Meetoo, 2008: 157.

70. IOM, 2005.

71. Ibid.

72. Kofman and Meetoo, 2008: 151.

73. Christian Joppke and Zeev Roshenhek. 2001. "Ethnic-Priority Immigration in Israel and Germany: Resilience Versus Demise," *Center for Comparative Immigration Studies Working Paper 45.* San Diego: University of California.

74. Alexander Yakobson and Amnon Rubinstein. 2005. *Democratic Norms, Diasporas, and Israel's Law of Return*. New York: American Jewish Committee, p. 6.

75. Joppke and Roshenhek, 2001.

76. IOM, 2005.

77. Joppke and Roshenhek, 2001: 12.

78. United Nations. 2004a. *World Economic and Social Survey 2004: International Migration*. New York: United Nations, pp. 42, 63. See also Israel Central Bureau of Statistics 2007 data at: http://www.cbs.gov.il/shnaton58/download/st04_04.xls

79. IOM, 2005.

80. Joel Brinkley. 1991. "Ethiopian Jews and Israelis Exult as Airlift is Completed," *New York Times*, 26 May 1991. Available at http://www.nytimes.com/1991/05/26/world/ethiopian-jews-and-israelis-exult-as-airlift-is-completed.html?sec=&spon=&pagewanted=all.

81. Yakobson and Rubenstein 2005: 6.

82. United Natinos, 2004.

83. Joppke and Roshenhek, 2001: 13.

84. Ibid.

85. Yakobson and Rubenstein, 2005: 8.

86. United Nations, 2004.

87. Jennifer Hunt. 1992. "The Impact of the 1962 Repatriates from Algeria on the French Labor Market," *Industrial and Labor Relations Review* 45(3): 556–572.

88. Robert Winder. 2004. *Bloody Foreigners: The Story of Immigration to Britain*. London: Abacus, p. 380.

89. Winder, 2004: 382.

90. Vaughan Robinson. 1995. "The Migration of East African Asians to the UK," Robin Cohen (ed.), *The Cambridge Survey of World Migration*. Cambridge, UK: Cambridge University Press, pp. 331–336.

91. OECD, 2008: 244.

92. Israel Central Bureau of Statistics 2007 data at http://www.cbs.gov.il/shnaton58/download/st04_04.xls.

93. Alan Gamlen. 2006. "Diaspora Engagement Policies: What Are They, and What Kinds of States Use Them?" *COMPAS Working Paper No. 32*, Centre on Migration, Policy and Society, University of Oxford.

94. The United Nations Convention Relating to the Status of Refugees, chapter 1, article A (A.2) formally defines a refugee as "Any person . . . who owing to a well-founded fear of being persecuted for reasons of race, religion, nationality, membership of a particular social group or political opinion, is outside the country of his nationality and is unable or, owing to such fear, is unwilling to avail himself of the protection of that country; or who, not having a nationality and being outside the country of his former habitual residence as a result of such events, is unable or, owing to such fear, is unwilling to return to it."

95. UNHCR. 2008b. *2007 UNHCR Statistical Annex*. Geneva: UNHCR, p. 2.

96. C. B. Keeley. 2001. "The International Refugee Regime(s): The End of the Cold War Matters," *International Migration Review* 35(1): 303–314.

97. Castles and Miller, 2009: 193.

98. Ibid., 2009: 193.

99. UNHCR, 2009.

100. U.S. Committee for Refugees and Immigrants. 2008. *World Refugee Survey 2008*. Washington, DC: USCRI, p. 29.

101. Ibid.: 29.

102. UNHCR, 2009.

103. Castles and Miller, 2009: 167.

104. UNHCR, 2009: 2.

105. United Nations Population Division. 2004. *Seminar on the Relevance of Population Aspects for the Achievement of the Millennium Development Goals*, New York, 17–19 November 2004. Available at http://www.un.org/esa/population/publications/PopAspectsMDG/

106. UNHCR, 2008a: 38.

107. Protracted situations occur when populations of 25,000 or more have been in exile for five or more years in developing countries.

108. The 1951 Convention Relating to the Status of Refugees states in article 33(1): "No Contracting State shall expel or return ('refouler') a refugee in any manner whatsoever to the frontiers of territories where his life or freedom would be threatened on account of his race, religion, nationality, membership of a particular social group, or political opinion."

109. UNHCR, 2009: 12.

110. USCRI, 2008: 27.

111. UNHCR. 2008a. *2007 Global Trends: Refugees, Asylum-Seekers, Returnees, Internally Displaced and Stateless Persons*. Geneva: UNHCR, p. 17.

112. Ibid.: 17.

113. Wayne A. Cornelius. 2001. "Death at the Border: The Efficacy and "Unintended" Consequences of U.S. Immigration Control Policy 1993–2000," *Working Paper 27*. Center for Comparative Immigration Studies, University of California, San Diego.

114. Fiona B. Adamson. 2006. "Crossing Borders: International Migration and National Security," *International Security* 31(1): 165–199.

115. Rebekah Thomas. 2005. "Biometrics, International Migrants and Human Rights," *European Journal of Migration and Law* 7: 377–411.

116. Mark B. Salter. 2004. "Passports, Mobility, and Security: How Smart Can a Border Be?" *International Studies Perspectives* 5: 71–91, p. 78.

117. New Scientist. 2010. "Robo-guards and the Borders of the Future," 9 January 2010, pp. 201–221.

118. John R. Vacca. 2007. *Biometric Technologies and Verification System*. Oxford, UK: Butterworth-Heinemann, p. 3.

119. EC Council Regulation No. 2252/2004 on Standards for Security Features and Biometric Data in Passports and Travel Documents Issued by Member States."

120. "Progress Report on the Application of the Principles of Convention 108 to the Collection and Processing of Biometric Data: Council of Europe Consultative Committee on the Convention for the Protection of Individuals with Regard to Automatic Processing of Personal Data," February 2005.

121. Thomas, 2005: 398.

122. OECD, 2008.

123. The formal name of the agency is European Agency for the Management of Operational Cooperation at the External Borders of the Member States of the European Union.

124. Except the UK and Ireland, who opted out.

125. OECD, 2008: 100.

126. United Nations Office on Drugs and Crime. 2006. *Organized Crime and Irregular Migration from Africa to Europe*. Vienna: UNODC.

127. Available at http://www.publicsafety.gc.ca/prg/le/bs/sbdap-eng.aspx, http://www.dhs.gov/xnews/releases/press_release_0057.shtm.

128. Gallya Lahav. 2003a. "Migration and Security: The Role of Non-State Actors and Civil Liberties in Liberal Democracies," in *United Nations Department of Economic and Social Affairs, Population Division, Second Coordinating Meeting on International Migration, 15–16 October*, pp. 89–106, p. 92.

129. Lahav, 2003: 92.

130. Gallya Lahav. 2003b. "The Rise of Non-State Actors in Migration Regulation in the United States and Europe: Changing the Gatekeepers or 'Bringing the State Back In'?" in Nancy Foner, Rubén G. Rumbaut, Steven James Gold (eds.), *Immigration Research for a New Century: Multidisciplinary Perspectives*. London: Russell Sage Foundation.

131. Castles and Miller, 2009: 182.

132. Ibid.: 182.

133. Amnesty International. 1995. *Prisoners without a Voice. Asylum-Seekers Detained in the United Kingdom*. London: Amnesty International, pp. 53–69.

134. Peter Fell and Debra Hayes. 2007. What Are They Doing Here? A Critical Guide to Asylum and Immigration. Birmingham, UK: Venture Press. pp. 65–66.

135. Amnesty International. 2005. *UK: Seeking Asylum Is Not a Crime: Detention of People Who Have Sought Asylum*. London: Amnesty International.

136. Fell and Hayes, 2007: 65–66.

137. Associated Press. 2009b. "Immigrants Face Lengthy Review with Few Rights." Available at http://www.timesrecordnews.com/news/2009/mar/16/immigrants-face-lengthy-detention-few-rights/. (Data obtained from ICE under the Freedom of Information Act.)

138. Siskin, 2004.

139. Australian Human Rights and Equal Opportunity Commission. 2004. *A Last Resort? National Inquiry into Children in Immigration Detention.* Sydney: Australian Human Rights Commission.

140. Ibid.: 68.

141. Don McMaster. 2001. *Asylum Seekers—Australia's Response to Refugees.* Melbourne, Australia: Melbourne University Press.

142. Castles and Miller, 2009: 205.

143. Castles and Miller, 2003: 205.

CHAPTER 6. THE IMPACTS OF MIGRATION

1. Lou Dobbs. 2005. "Border Insecurity; Criminal Illegal Aliens; Deadly Imports; Illegal Alien Amnesty," *CNN Transcript*, 14 April 2005. Available at http://edition.cnn.com/TRANSCRIPTS/0504/14/ldt.01.html.

2. William Drozdiak. 2005. "Europe Braces for New Immigrants;Western Nations Fear Flood of Migrants Will Tax Social Programs," *Washington Post*, 22 October 1990.

3. Matthew Krieger. 2007. "Brain-Drain Threatens to Set Back Hi-Tech," *The Jerusalem Post*, 8 November 2007.

4. Transatlantic Trends. 2008. *Transatlantic Trends: Immigration.* Washington, DC: German Marshall Fund of the United States.

5. Immanuel Ness. 2005. *Immigrants, Unions, and the New U.S. Labor Market.* Philadelphia: Temple University Press.

6. World Bank. 2005. *Global Economic Prospects: Economic Implications of Remittances and Migration.* Washington, DC: World Bank, p. 31.

7. See Roland-Holst 2009, cited in United Nations Development Programme. 2009. *Human Development Report 2009 Overcoming Barriers: Human Mobility and Development.* New York: UNDP, p. 109.

8. Kym Anderson and Bjorn Lomborg. 2008. "Free Trade, Free Labor, Free Growth," Project Syndicate. Available at http://www.project-syndicate.org/commentary/anderson1.

9. Lant Pritchett. 2006. Let Their People Come: Breaking the Deadlock on Global Mobility. Washington, DC: Center for Global Development, p. 3.

10. George J. Borjas. 1994. "The Economics of Immigration," *Journal of Economic Literature* XXXII: 1667–1717.

11. Centre for Economics and Business Research. 2007. *Future Flows: Forecasting the Current and Future Economic Impact of Highly Skilled Migrants.* London: CEBR.

12. Francesc Ortega and Giovanni Peri. 2009. "The Causes and Effects of International Migrations: Evidence from OECD Countries 1980–2005," *NBER Working Paper 14833.* Cambridge, MA: NBER.

13. Karen McVeigh. 2008. "Skilled Migrants Are Vital to Economy, Study Says," *The Guardian*, 25 March 2008, p. 10.

14. George J. Borjas. 1999b. "Immigration," *NBER Reporter*, Fall. Available at http://www.nber.org/reporter/fall99/borjas.html.

15. Stephen Castles and Mark J. Miller. 2009. *The Age of Migration: International Population Movement in the Modern World*, 4th ed. Basingstoke, UK: Palgrave MacMillan, p. 224.

16. Ibid.: 224.

17. Giovanni Peri and Chad Sparber. 2008. "Task Specialization, Immigration, and Wages," *CDP No 02/08*, Centre for Research and Analysis of Migration, University College London.

18. *The Economist*. 2008a. "Of Bedsheets and Bison Grass Vodka," 3 January 2008.

19. Jonathan Coppel, Jean-Christophe Dumond, and Ignazio Visco. 2001. "Trends in Immigration and Economic Consequences," *OECD Economics Department Working Paper No. 284*. Paris: OECD.

20. Ray Barrell, John FitzGerald, and Rebecca Riley. 2007. "EU Enlargement and Migration: Assessing the Macroeconomic Impacts," *Discussion Paper No. 292*, National Institute of Economic and Social Research.

21. Gordon H. Hanson. 2008. "The Economic Consequences of the International Migration of Labor," *NBER Working Paper 14490*. Cambridge, MA: NBER.

22. Barrell, FitzGerald, and Riley, 2007.

23. George J. Borjas. 2003. "The Labour Demand Curve Is Downward Sloping: Reexamining the Impact of Immigration on the Labor Market," *Quarterly Journal of Economics* 118(4): 1335–1374, p. 1335.

24. George J. Borjas. 1999a. Heaven's Door: Immigration Policy and the American Economy. Princeton, NJ: Princeton University Press.

25. Hanson, 2008: 22.

26. David Card. 2005. "Is the New Immigration Really So Bad?" *The Economic Journal* 115(507): 300–323.

27. James P. Smith and Barry Edmonston, eds. 1997. *The New Americans: Economic, Demographic, and Fiscal Effects of Immigration*. Washington, DC: National Academy Press.

28. Fareed Zakaria. 2009. *The Post American World*. London: Penguin, p. 198.

29. Ibid.: 199.

30. Robert D. Putnam. 2007. "E Pluribus Unum: Diversity and Community in the Twenty-first Century, The 2006 Johan Skytte Prize Lecture," *Scandinavian Political Studies* 30(2): 137–174.

31. Vivek Wadhwa, AnnaLee Saxenian, Richard Freeman, Gary Gereffi, and Alex Salkever. 2009. "America's Loss Is the World's Gain: America's New Immigrant Entrepreneurs, Part IV," 2 March 2009. Available at SSRN: http://ssrn.com/abstract=1348616.

32. William R. Kerr and William F. Lincoln. 2008. "The Supply Side of Innovation: H-1B Visa Reforms and US Ethnic Invention," *Harvard Business School Working Paper 09-005*.

33. Ibid.

34. Wadhwa, 2009.

35. Ibid.

36. Richard Florida. 2002. "The Economic Geography of Talent," *Annals of the Association of American Geographers* 92(4): 743–755.

37. Scott E. Page. 2007. *The Difference: How the Power of Diversity Creates Better Groups, Firms, Schools, and Societies.* Princeton, NJ: Princeton University Press.

38. Kerr and Lincoln 2008.

39. Jennifer Hunt and Marjolaine Gauthier-Loiselle. 2008. "How Much Does Immigration Boost Innovation?" *NBER Working Paper 14312*. Cambridge, MA: NBER.

40. Robert Rowthorn. 2008. "The Fiscal Impact of Immigration on the Advanced Economies," *Oxford Review of Economic Policy* 24: 560–580, p. 577.

41. Michael Baker and Dwayne Benjamin. 1995. "The Receipt of Transfer Payments by Immigrants to Canada," *Journal of Human Resources* 30(4): 650–676

42. Felix Büchel and Joachim Frick. 2003. "Immigrants' Economic Performance across Europe: Does Immigration Policy Matter?" *EPAC Working Paper 42*, University of Colchester.

43. Kraen Blume, Bjorn Gustafsson, Peder J. Pedersen, and Mette Verner. 2003. "A Tale of Two Countries: Poverty among Immigrants in Denmark and Sweden since 1984," *UNU-WIDER Research Paper DP2003/36*, United Nations University.

44. Sari Pekkala Kerr and William R. Kerr. 2008. "Economic Impacts of Immigration: A Survey," *Harvard Business School Working Paper 09-013*.

45. International Labour Organization. 2004. *Towards a Fair Deal for Migrant Workers in the Global Economy*. Geneva: ILO, p. 7.

46. *Financial Times*, 23 July 2009, citing a report by the Centre for Research and Analysis of Migration, University College, London.

47. Jacoby, 2006.

48. IPPR. 2007. *Britain's Immigrants: An Economic Profile*. London: IPPR, p. 44.

49. IPPR, 2007.

50. House of Lords. 2008. *The Economic Impact of Immigration*. London: The Stationery Office Limited, p. 42.

51. Quoting Professor Rowthorn. See House of Lords, 2008: 41.

52. Jacoby, 2006.

53. ILO, 2004.

54. Jacoby, 2006.

55. Organization for Economic Cooperation and Development. 2008. *International Migration Outlook 2008—SOPEMI*. Paris: OECD, p. 335.

56. Max Nathan. 2008. *Your Place or Mine? The Local Economics of Migration*. London: Institute for Public Policy Research, p. 24.

57. Smith and Edmunston, 1997: 12.

58. United Nations. 2004a. *World Economic and Social Survey 2004: International Migration*. New York: United Nations, p. 121.

59. ILO, 2004: 7.

60. Will Wilkinson. 2009. "The Immigration Fallacy," *The Week Newsletter*, 27 April 2009.

61. T. H. Marshall. 1950. "Citizenship and Social Class," in T. H. Marshall and T. Bottomore (eds.), *Citizenship and Social Class*. London: Pluto Press, p. 8.

62. Putnam, 2007.

63. Ibid.: 164.

64. Castles and Miller, 2009: 274.

65. Alesina and Glaeser, quoted in Stephen Castles and Carl-Ulrik Schierup. 2010. "Migration and Ethnic Minorities," in Francis G. Castles, Stephan Leibfried, Jane Lewis, Herbert Obinger, and Christopher Pierson (eds.), *The Oxford Handbook of the Welfare State*. Oxford, UK: Oxford University Press.

66. Marshall, 1950: 8.

67. Stuart Soroka, Keith Banting, and Richard Johnston. 2006. "Immigration and Redistribution in the Global Era," in Pranab Bardhan, Samuel Bowles, and Michael Wallerstein (eds.), *Globalization and Egalitarian Redistribution*. Princeton, NJ: Princeton University Press, pp. 261–288.

68. Keith Banting and Will Kymlicka. 2004. "Do Multiculturalism Policies Erode the Welfare State?" in Philippe van Parijs (ed.), *Cultural Diversity versus Economic Solidarity*. Brussels: Deboeck Université Press.

69. Dietlind Stolle, Stuart Soroka, and Richard Johnston. 2008. "When Does Diversity Erode Trust? Neighborhood Diversity, Interpersonal Trust and the Mediating Effect of Social Interactions," *Political Studies* 56: 57–75, p. 58.

70. Francisco Herreros and Henar Criado. 2009. "Social Trust, Social Capital and Perceptions of Immigration," *Political Studies* 57: 335–357, p. 335.

71. Castles and Miller, 2009: 264.

72. Ibid.: 265.

73. Ellie Vasta. 2007. "Accommodating Diversity: Why Current Critiques of Multiculturalism Miss the Point," *COMPAS Working Paper No. 53*, Centre on Migration, Policy and Society, University of Oxford.

74. Ibid.

75. Putnam, 2007: 139.

76. Stephen Castles. 1998. "The Process of Integration of Migrant Communities," in *United Nations, Population Distribution and Migration, Proceedings of the United Nations Expert Meeting on Population Distribution and Migration, Sant Cruz, Bolivia, 18–22 January 1993* (convened in preparation for the International Conference on Population and Development, Cairo, 5–14 September 1994). New York: United Nations, pp. 247–265.

77. Florida, 2002: 745.

78. Page, 2004: xv.

79. Charlan J. Nemeth. 1986. "Differential Contributions of Majority and Minority Influence," *Psychological Review* 93(1): 23–32.

80. Gianmarco I. P. Ottaviano and Giovanni Peri. 2004. "The Economic Value of Cultural Diversity: Evidence from US Cities," *NBER Working Paper No. 10904*. Cambridge, MA: NBER, pp. 2–3.

81. Ibid.

82. Philippe Legrain. 2006. *Immigrants: Your Country Needs Them*. London: Little Brown.

83. United Nations. 2006. "Report of the Secretary-General, International Migration and Development, UN General Assembly, 60th Session," *UN Doc. A/60/871*, 18 May 2006.

84. Ian Goldin and Kenneth Reinert. 2007. *Globalization for Development: Trade, Finance, Aid, Migration and Policy*, 2nd ed. Basingstoke, UK: Palgrave MacMillan.

85. World Bank. 1995. *World Development Report 1995: Workers in an Integrating World*. Oxford, UK: Oxford University Press, p. 64.

86. These percentages reflect the proportion of a country's university-educated population that emigrates. William J. Carrington and Enrica Detragiache. 1999. "How Extensive Is the Brain Drain?" *Finance and Development: A Quarterly Magazine of the IMF* 36(2); Richard H. Adams Jr. 2003. "International Migration, Remittances, and the Brain Drain: A Study of 24 Labor Exporting countries," *Policy Research Working Paper Series 3069*. Washington, DC: The World Bank.

87. J. Dayton Johnson et al. 2007. *Policy Coherence for Development: Migration and Developing Countries*. Paris: OECD.

88. Excluding South Africa.

89. Caglar Ozden and Maurice Schiff, eds. 2006. *International Migration, Remittances, and the Brain Drain*. Basingstoke, UK: Palgrave MacMillan and World Bank.

90. Ibid.: 10–11.

91. Celia W. Dugger. 2004. "Where Doctors Are Scarce, Africa Deploys Substitutes," *New York Times*, 23 November 2004, sec. A, p. 4, col. 3.

92. Hein de Haas et al. 2009. "Mobility and Human Development," *Working Paper 14*, International Migration Institute, James Martin 21st Century School, University of Oxford, p. 33.

93. de Haas et al., 2009: 33.

94. Oded Stark. 2005. "The New Economics of Brain Drain," *World Economics* 6(2): 137–140.

95. Ibid.: 138.

96. Michael Clemens. 2008. "Immigrants Are an Engine of Prosperity," *Atlanta Journal-Constitution*, 27 November 2008.

97. Satish Chand and Michael Clemens. 2008. "Skilled Emigration and Skill Creation: A Quasi-Experiment," *CGD Working Paper Number 152*, Center for Global Development.

98. This example is drawn from Yevgeny N. Kuznetsov, ed. 2006. *Diaspora Networks and the International Migration of Skills: How Countries Can Draw on Their Talent Abroad.* Washington, DC: World Bank Institute, p. 10.

99. Peggy Levitt. 1998. "Social Remittances: Migration Driven Local-Level Forms of Cultural Diffusion," *International Migration Review* 32(4): 926–948, p. 927.

100. Kuznetsov, 2006: 6.

101. AnnaLee Saxenian. 2005. "From Brain Drain to Brain Circulation: Transnational Communities and Regional Upgrading in India and China," *Studies in Comparative International Development* 40(2), p. 3.

102. Ibid.

103. Kuznetzov, 2006: 4.

104. de Haas, 2008: 50.

105. Saxenian, 2005: 19.

106. World Bank, 2005: 67.

107. International Organization for Migration. 2005. *World Migration 2005: Costs and Benefits of International Migration.* Geneva: IOM, p. 228.

108. Ibid.: 228.

109. Ibid.: 228.

110. Alan Gamlen. 2008. "Why Engage Diasporas?" *COMPAS Working Paper 63*, Centre on Migration, Policy and Society, University of Oxford, p. 4.

111. Ibid.: 4.

112. *Financial Times.* 2009a. "Diaspora Fuels War Crimes in Congo, Says UN," 25 November 2009.

113. Rainer Baübock. 2005. "Expansive Citizenship: Voting beyond Territory and Membership," *Political Science and Politics* 38: 683–687.

114. Khalid Koser and Nicholas Van Hear. 2003. "Asylum Migration and Implications for Countries of Origin," *WIDER Discussion Paper No. 2003/20*, United Nations University, p. 12.

115. Liz Olivier. 2009. "Legal and Regulatory Frameworks and Scientific Mobility Giving Something Back: Exploring Making a Contribution at a Distance Policy and Practice," *ResIST Thematic Paper 1*, January 2009.

116. Personal communication with Judith McNeill at Comic Relief UK.

117. Hein de Haas. 2007b. "Remittances, Migration, and Social Development: A Conceptual Review of the Literature," *Social Policy and Development Programme Paper No. 34.* New York: United Nations Research Institute for Social Development, p. 1; Dilip Ratha, Sanket Mohapatra, and Ani Silwal. 2010. "Outlook for Remittance Flows 2010–2011: Remittance Flows to Developing Countries Remained Resilient in 2009, Expected to Recover during 2010–11," *Migration and Development Brief No. 12.* Washington, DC: World Bank.

118. United Nations, 2004: 54.

119. Ibid.: 54.

120. Ratha, 2007: 2.

121. Ibid.

122. Ratha, Mohapatra, and Silwal, 2010; de Haas, 2007: 9.

123. Ratha, Mohapatra, and Silwal, 2010.

124. *Financial Times.* 2009b. "Downturn Deals Blow to US Immigrants," 18 November 2009, p. 10.

125. de Haas, 2007: 10, citing Richard H. Adams and John Page. 2005. "Do International Migration and Remittances Reduce Poverty in Developing Countries?" *World Development* 33(10): 1645–1669.

126. Ratha, 2007: 5.

127. Ibid.: 5.

128. de Haas, 2007: 8.

129. Bimal Ghosh. 2006. *Migrants' Remittances and Development: Myths, Rhetoric and Realities.* Geneva: IOM, p. 51.

130. Ibid.: 51.

131. Ibid.: 51.

132. Koser and Van Hear, 2003:,10.

133. Thanks to Kathleen Newland for clarifying this example.

134. de Haas, 2007: 17.

135. Ratha, 2007: 6.

136. United Nations, 2004: 109.

137. Ghosh, 2006: 52.

138. Ibid.: 53.

139. Hillel Rapoport and Frédéric Docquier. 2005. "The Economics of Migrants' Remittances," *IZA DP No. 1531E.* Bonn, Germany: Institute for the Study of Labor (IZA).

140. United Nations, 2006: 55.

141. Jorge Durand, William Kandel, Emilio A. Parrado, and Douglas S. Massey. 1996. "International Migration and Development in Mexican Communities," *Demography* 33(2): 249–264.

142. Castles and Miller, 2009: 61.

143. Steven Vertovec. 2009. *Transnationalism.* London: Routledge, p. 111–112.

144. Alejandro Portes. 2008. "Migration and Development: A Conceptual Review of the Evidence," in Stephen Castles and Raul Delgado Wise (eds.), *Migration and Development: Perspectives from the South.* Geneva: IOM, p. 25.

145. Vertovec, 2009: 113.

146. de Haas, 2007: 16.

147. United Nations, 2006: 55.

148. United Nations, 2004: 110.

149. United Nations, 2006: 56.

150. Ghosh, 2006: 54.

151. World Bank estimates cited in International Organization for Migration. 2008. *World Migration 2008: Managing Labour Mobility in the Evolving Global Economy.* Geneva: IOM, p. 533.

152. Ghosh, 2006: 57.

153. This paragraph draws on IOM, 2008: 152–153.

154. Michael A. Clemens, Claudio E. Montenegro, and Lant Pritchett. 2009. "The Place Premium: Wage Differences for Identical Workers across the US Border," *Harvard Kennedy School Faculty Research Working Paper Series RWP 09-004.*

155. Purchasing power parity adjusted US dollars.

156. Clemens, Montenegro, and Pritchett, 2009: 2–3.

157. Rosalia Sciortino and Sureeporn Punpuing. 2009. *International Migration in Thailand 2009.* Geneva: IOM.

158. Irina Ivakhnyuk. 2009. "Russian Migration Policy in the Soviet and Post-Soviet Periods and Its Impact on Human Development in the Region," *UNDP Human Development Report 2009 Background Paper 14,* p. 34.

159. Michael A. Clemens. 2009b. "Skill Flow: A Fundamental Reconsideration of Skilled-Worker Mobility and Development," *UNDP Human Development Report 2009 Background Paper 8,* p. 63.

160. Aged 25 years or older. Steven A. Camarota and Karen Jensenius. 2009. "Immigrant Unemployment at Record High: Rate Now Exceeds Native-Born, a Change from Recent Past," Center for Immigration Studies Announcement, April 2009; Steven A. Camarota. 2007. "Immigrants in the United States 2007: A Profile of America's Foreign-Born Population," *Center for Immigration Studies Backgrounder,* November 2007.

161. Camarota, 2007

162. Quoted in Castles and Miller, 2009: 235.

163. Castles and Miller, 2009: 237.

164. OECD, 2007: 76.

165. Ibid.: 76.

166. Jeffrey G. Reitz. 2005. "Tapping Immigrants' Skills: New Directions for Canadian Immigration Policy in the Knowledge Economy," *IRPP Choices* 11(1): 3.

167. Reitz, 2005: 3.

168. Aaditya Mattoo, Ileana Cristina Neagu, and Çağlar Özden. 2005. "Brain Waste? Educated Immigrants in the U.S. Labor Market," *World Bank Policy Research Working Paper 3581.*

169. The Observer. 2010. "A Portrait of the New UK Migrant," 17 January 2010, pp. 16–17.

170. *Financial Times.* 2009b. "Downturn Deals Blow to US Migrants," 18 November 2009, p. 10.

171. *Financial Times.* 2009d. "The Hidden Victims of Recession," 5 November 2009, p. 12.

172. Guillermina Jasso, Douglas S. Massey, Mark R. Rosenzweig, and James P. Smith. 2004. "Immigrant Health—Selectivity and Acculturation," *Labor and Demography 0412002, EconWPA.*

173. Ibid.

174. Minnesota Department of Health. 2003. "Eliminating Health Disparities Initiative: 2003 Report to the Legislature." Available at http://www.health.state.mn.us/ommh/legrpt012103.pdf.

175. Ilene Hyman. 2001. "Immigration and Health," *Health Policy Working Paper 01-05*. Ottawa: Health Canada.

176. Samuel Noh and Violet Kaspar. 2003. *Diversity and Immigrant Health*. Toronto: University of Toronto, p. 25.

177. IOM, 2005: 334.

178. Ibid.: 13.

179. World Health Organization. 2003. *International Migration, Health and Human Rights*. Geneva: WHO.

180. Human Development Index.

181. Barry R. Chiswick and Noyna DebBurman. 2004. "Educational Attainment: Analysis by Immigrant Generation," *Economics of Education Review* 23: 361–379.

182. Ibid., 2004.

183. Maurice Crul and Hans Vermeulen. 2003. "The Second Generation in Europe," *International Migration Review* 37(4): 965–986.

184. Anthony F. Heath, Catherine Rothon, and Elina Kilpi. 2008. "The Second Generation in Western Europe: Education, Unemployment, and Occupational Attainment," *Annual Review of Sociology* 38: 211–235, p. 229.

185. Crul and Vermuelen, 2003: 984.

186. Chiswick and DebBurman, 2004: 375.

187. Teresa Abada, Feng Hou, and Bali Ram. 2008. "Group Differences in Educational Attainment among the Children of Immigrants," *Analytical Studies Branch Research Paper Series*. Ottawa: Statistics Canada, p. 18.

188. Loren B. Landau and Aurelia Wa Kabwe Segatti. 2009. "Human Development Impacts of Migration: South Africa," *UNDP Human Development Report 2009 Background Paper 05*.

189. Darshan Vigneswaran. 2008. "Enduring Territoriality: South African Immigration Control," *Political Geography* 27: 783–801.

190. Jonathan Crush. 2000. "The Dark Side of Democracy: Migration, Xenophobia and Human Rights in South Africa," *International Migration* 38(6): 103–119, pp. 108–112.

191. International Organization for Migration. 2009. *Towards Tolerance, Law, and Dignity: Addressing Violence against Foreign Nationals in South Africa*. Geneva: IOM, p. 2.

192. Francesca Mereu. 2001. "Russia: Moscow Markets Present Troubled Tableau of Life of City's Immigrants," *Radio Free Europe/Radio Liberty*, 14 November 2001. Available at http://www.rferl.org/content/article/1097984.html.

193. Amnesty International. 2006. *Amnesty International Report 2006—Russian Federation*, 23 May 2006. London: Amnesty International.

194. N. E. Hansen and I. McClure. 1998. "Protecting Migrants and Ethnic Minorities from Discrimination in Employment: The Danish Experience," *ILO International Migration Papers, No. 25*, p. 2.

195. Roger Zegers de Beijl. 1999. Migrant Discrimination in the Labour Market: A Comparative Study of Four European Countries. Geneva: ILO.

196. Mahmood Arai, Moa Bursell, and Lena Nekby. 2008. "Between Meritocracy and Ethnic Discrimination: The Gender Difference," *Working Paper*, The Stockholm University Linnaeus Center for Integration Studies (SULCIS), p. 2.

197. Philip Oreopoulos. 2009. "Why Do Skilled Immigrants Struggle in the Labor Market? A Field Experiment with Six Thousand Resumes," *Metropolis Working Paper 09-03*. Vancouver: Metropolis British Columbia.

198. Portes, 2008.

199. Heath, Rothon, and Kilpi, 2008: 229.

200. Wayne Cornelius. 2001. "Death at the Border: The Efficacy and 'Unintended' Consequences of the US Immigration Control Policy 1993–2000," *Working Paper 27*, Center for Comparative Immigration Studies, University of California, San Diego.

201. *The Sunday Times*. 2009. "A Generation Lost to the Deep," 22 November 2009, pp. 10–11.

202. United Nations, 2004: 160.

203. Ibid.: 160.

204. Human Rights Watch. 2004. *Bad Dreams: Exploitation of Migrant Workers in Saudi Arabia*. New York: Human Rights Watch.

205. HRW, 2004.

206. Available at http://news.bbc.co.uk/1/hi/england/lancashire/3464203.stm.

207. Available at http://www.oxfam.org.uk/applications/blogs/pressoffice/?p=3541.

208. International Labour Organization. 2007. *Forced Labour Statistics Factsheet*. Geneva: ILO.

209. Moises Naim. 2005. *Illicit: How Smugglers, Traffickers, and Copycats Are Hijacking the Global Economy*. New York: Doubleday, p. 89.

210. Ibid.: 89.

211. United Nations Office on Drugs and Crime. 2009. *The Global Report on Trafficking in Persons*. Vienna: UNODC.

212. *The Economist*. 2009a. "Bartered Brides," 12 March 2009.

213. Ma Guihua. 2002. "Trade in Vietnamese Brides a Boon for Chinese," *Asia Times*, 14 November 2002.

214. Neil Howard and Mumtaz Lalani. 2008. "The Politics of Human Trafficking," *St Antony's International Review* 4(1): 5–15.

215. IOM, 2005: 335.

216. UNICEF. 2006. *State of the World's Children: Excluded and Invisible*. New York: UNICEF.

217. Ibid.

218. UNHCR. 2006. *State of the World's Refugees 2006*. New York: UNHCR, p. 129.

219. Ibid.: 117.

CHAPTER 7. THE FUTURE OF MIGRATION

1. Stephen Castles. 2002b. "Migration and Community Formation under Conditions of Globalization," *International Migration Review* 36(4): 1143–1168, p. 1168.

2. See Robert Wright. 2001. *Nonzero: The Logic of Human Destiny*. London: Vintage, p. 4.

3. Ian Goldin and Kenneth Reinert. 2007. *Globalization for Development: Trade, Finance, Aid, Migration and Policy*, 2nd ed. Basingstoke, UK: Palgrave MacMillan.

4. Arvind Subramaniana and Shang-Jin Wei. 2007. "The WTO Promotes Trade, Strongly but unevenly," *Journal of International Economics* 72(1): 151–175.

5. This point is made by Pritchett in Lant Pritchett. 2006. *Let Their People Come: Breaking the Deadlock on Global Mobility*. Washington, DC: Center for Global Development.

6. Wright, 2001.

7. Pritchett, 2006: 31.

8. World Bank. 1995. *World Development Report 1995: Workers in an Integrating World*. Oxford, UK: Oxford University Press.

9. World Bank. 2008. *World Development Report 2009: Reshaping Economic Geography*. Washington, DC: World Bank; United Nations Development Programme. 2009. *Human Development Report 2009 Overcoming Barriers: Human Mobility and Development*. New York: UNDP; Organization for Economic Cooperation and Development. 2008. *International Migration Outlook 2008—SOPEMI*. Paris. OECD.

10. Global Commission on International Migration. 2005. *Migration in an Interconnected World: New Directions for Action*. Geneva: GCIM.

11. Jan Aart Scholte. 2000. *Globalization: A Critical Introduction*. Basingstoke, UK: Palgrave MacMillan.

12. On Internet data, see http://www.internetworldstats.com/stats.htm. Estimated Internet users were 1,596,270,108 on 31 March 2009. On mobile phone use, see Associated Press. 2009a. "Developing World Embraces Mobile Phones: UN Report," 2 March 2009.

13. Michael D. Bordo, Alan M. Taylor, and Jeffrey G. Williamson. 2005. *Globalization in Historical Perspective*. Chicago: University of Chicago Press, p. 50.

14. Peggy Levitt. 2009. "Roots and Routes: Understanding the Lives of the Second Generation Transnationally," *Journal of Ethnic and Racial Studies* 35(7): 1225–1242.

15. Steven Vertovec. 2004. "Migration Transnationalism and Modes of Transformation," *International Migration Review* 38(3): 970–1001, p. 992.

16. Vertovec, 2004: 992–993.

17. Pritchett, 2006: 32. See also World Bank. 2005. *Global Economic Prospects: Economic Implications of Remittances and Migration.* Washington, DC: World Bank.

18. Ibid.: 24.

19. Ibid.: 23.

20. Ibid.: 24.

21. Lant Pritchett. 1997. "Divergence, Big Time," *Journal of Economic Perspectives* 11(3): 3–17.

22. Branko Milanovic. 2003. "The Two Faces of Globalization: Against Globalization as We Know It," *World Development* 31(4): 667–683, p. 670.

23. Peter H. Lindert and Jeffrey G. Williamson. 2003. "Does Globalization Make the World More Unequal?" in Michael D. Bordo, Alan M. Taylor, and Jeffrey G. Williamson (eds.), *Globalization in Historical Perspective.* Chicago: University of Chicago Press, pp. 227–271, p. 227.

24. This is the mean for wage ratios for identical workers born in each country of origin and (likely) educated there, having arrived in the United States at or after age 20. Michael A. Clemens, Claudio E. Montenegro, and Lant Pritchett. 2009. "The Place Premium: Wage Differences for Identical Workers across the US Border," *Harvard Kennedy School Faculty Research Working Paper Series RWP 09-004.*

25. Ibid.: 56.

26. Timothy J. Hatton and Jeffrey G. Williamson. 2009. "Vanishing Third World Emigrants?" *NBER Working Paper No. w14785.* Cambridge, MA: NBER, p. 4.

27. Ibid.: 28.

28. World Bank. 2009. *Prospects for the Global Economy.* Available at http://go.worldbank.org/PF6VWYXS10.

29. Hein de Haas. 2007c. "Turning the Tide? Why Development Will Not Stop Migration," *Development and Change* 38(5): 819–841, p. 832.

30. Ibid.: 835.

31. Ibid.: 836.

32. Philip Martin, Susan Martin, and Patrick Weil. 2006. *Managing Migration: The Promise of Cooperation.* Oxford, UK: Lexington Books; Philip Martin and J. Edward Taylor. 2001. "Managing Migration: The Role of Economic Policies," in Aristide R. Zolberg and Peter M. Benda (eds.), *Global Migrants, Global Refugees: Problems and Solutions.* Oxford, UK: Berghahn Books, pp. 95–120, p. 101.

33. This paragraph summarizes an example from Martin, Martin, and Weil, 2006: 206–217.

34. Global Commission on International Migration. 2004. "Global Migration Futures Workshop Report," 10 December 2004, St Antony's College, Oxford, UK.

35. Bruno Losch. 2008. "Migrations and the Challenge of Demographic and Economic Transitions in the New Globalization Era," *SSRC Migration & Development Conference Paper No. 12.*

36. United Nations Department of Economic and Social Affairs (UNDESA). 2008. *World Urbanization Prospects: The 2007 Revision.* New York: United Nations.

37. G. J. Lewis. 1983. *Human Migration: A Geographical Perspective*. New York: Taylor and Francis.

38. Barbara Bruns, Alain Mingat, and Ramahatra Rakotomalala. 2003. *Achieving Universal Primary Education by 2015: A Chance for Every Child*. Washington, DC: World Bank, p. 42.

39. Sajitha Bashir. 2007. *Trends in International Trade in Higher Education: Implications and Options for Developing Countries*. Washington, DC: World Bank, p. 21.

40. UNESCO. 2004. *Gender and Education for All: The Leap to Equality*. Paris: UNESCO, chapter 2; Bashir, 2007: 38.

41. Bashir, 2007: 35.

42. Rodrigo Lluberas. 2007. "The Untapped Skilled Labour of Latin America," *Watson Wyatt Worldwide Technical Paper*, December 2007, p. 14.

43. Wolfgang Lutz, Warren Sanderson, Sergei Scherbov, and Samir K.C. 2008. *Demographic and Human Capital Trends in Eastern Europe and Sub-Saharan Africa*. Washington, DC: Migration Policy Institute, p. 22.

44. Bashir, 2007: 38.

45. Philip G. Altbach. 2004. "Higher Education Crosses Borders," *Change* (March–April 2004).

46. Ibid.

47. International Organization for Migration. 2008. *World Migration 2008: Managing Labour Mobility in the Evolving Global Economy*. Geneva: IOM, p. 122.

48. Examples are drawn from Philip G. Altbach and Jane Knight. 2006. "The Internationalization of Higher Education: Motivations and Realities," in *The NEA 2006 Almanac of Higher Education*. Washington, DC: National Education Association.

49. IOM, 2008: 106.

50. Our thanks to Wolfgang Lutz for this clarification.

51. This paragraph summarizes the overview provided in Hania Zlotnik. 2008. "Migration, Mobility, Urbanization, and Development," *SSRC Migration and Development Conference Paper No.22*, p. 2.

52. Ibid.

53. Jose Antonio Ortega. 2005. "What Are the Implications of the Demographic Transitions Process for 21st Century European Population?" presented at Eurostat/UNECE Work Session on Demographic Projection, Vienna, September.

54. Ibid.: 5.

55. Ibid.: 5.

56. Hatton and Williamson, 2009: 25.

57. Afghanistan, Bangladesh, Bhutan, India, Iran (Islamic Republic of), Kazakhstan, Kyrgyzstan, Maldives, Nepal, Pakistan, Sri Lanka, Tajikistan, Turkmenistan, and Uzbekistan.

58. Losch, 2008: 10.

59. Ibid.: 9.

60. Lant Pritchett. 2004. "Boom Towns and Ghost Countries: Geography, Agglomeration, and Population Mobility," *CGD Working Paper 36*, Center for Global Development.

61. Nicholas Stern, ed. 2006. *The Economics of Climate Change: The Stern Review*. Cambridge, UK: Cambridge University Press.

62. These statistics were helpfully summarized in Oli Brown. 2007. "Climate Change and Forced Migration: Observations, Projections and Implications," *Human Development Report Office Occasional Paper 2007/17*, pp. 9–10.

63. Quoted in Stephen Castles. 2002a. "Environmental Change and Forced Migration: Making Sense of the Debate," *UNHCR New Issues in Refugee Research, Working Paper No. 70*, p. 4.

64. Ibid.

65. Camillo Boana, Roger Zitter, and Tim Morris. 2008. "Environmentally Displaced People," *Forced Migration Policy Briefing 1*. Oxford, UK: Refugee Studies Centre, pp. 7–8.

66. Brown, 2007. See also Richard Black. 2001. "Environmental Refugees: Myth or Reality," *UNHCR New Issues in Refugee Research Working Paper No. 34*.

67. Koko Warner, Tamer Afifi, Olivia Dun, Marc Stal, and Sophia Schmidl. 2008. "Human Security, Climate Change, and Environmentally Induced Migration," *United Nations University Institute for Environment and Human Security, Report*, United Nations University, p. 6.

68. Black, 2001: 6.

69. Brown, 2007: 16.

70. Sam Knight. 2009. "The Human Tsunami," *Financial Times*, 19 June 2009.

71. Black, 2001: 4.

72. Knight, 2009.

73. Thomas F. Homer-Dixon. 1991. "On the Threshold: Environmental Changes as Causes of Acute Conflict," *International Security* 16(2): 76–116.

74. Robin McKie. 2009. "Scientists to Issue Stark Warning over Dramatic New Sea Level Figures," *The Observer*, 8 March 2009.

75. John Vidal. 2008. "UK Gives £50m to Bangladesh Climate Change Fund," *The Guardian*, 8 September 2008.

76. Ministry of Environment and Forests. 2008. *Bangladesh Climate Change Strategy and Action Plan 2008*. Dhaka, Bangladesh: Ministry of Environment and Forests, Government of the People's Republic of Bangladesh.

77. Brown, 2007: 11.

78. See Amartya Sen. 1981. *Poverty and Famines: An Essay on Entitlement and Deprivation*. Oxford, UK: Oxford University Press.

79. Brown, 2007: 11–12.

80. Quoted in Julia Preston. 2009. "Mexican Data Show Migration to U.S. in Decline," *New York Times*, 14 May 2009.

81. Ibid.

82. James Boxell. 2009. "Recession Spurs Migrant Workers to Leave," *Financial Times*, 21 May 2009.

83. United Nations, 2009.

84. Ibid.

85. It is equal to the total number of people under 15 and over 65, divided by those between 15 and 65 (multiplied by 100).

86. See Jean-Philippe Cotis. 2003. "Population Ageing: Facing the Challenge," *OECD Observer No. 239*, September 2003.

87. United Nations. 2000. *Replacement Migration: Is It a Solution to Declining and Aging Populations?* New York: United Nations.

88. Ibid.: 9.

89. Katharina Kloss. 2008. "Jacques Barrot on Immigration: 'Member States Are Compelled to Solidarity,'" *Café Babel*, 18 October 2008.

90. European Parliament. 2009. "Answer Given by Mr Barrot on Behalf of the Commission," *Parliamentary Questions* E-5971/2008, 12 January 2009. Available at http://www.europarl.europa.eu/sides/getAllAnswers.do?reference=E-2008-5971&language=EN.

91. United Nations, 2000.

92. Sarah Harper. 2009. "20th Century—Last Century of Youth?" presentation at Oxford Institute of Ageing, 22 April 2009. (Mimeo.)

93. National Research Council. 2008. *Research on Future Skill Demands: A Workshop Summary*, Margaret Hilton, Rapporteur, Center for Education, Division of Behavioral and Social Sciences and Education. Washington, DC: The National Academies Press.

94. Stéphan Vincent-Lancrin. 2009. "How the Crisis Might Transform Higher Education: Some Scenarios," presented at Higher Education at a Time of Crisis: Challenges and Opportunities, Copenhagen Business School, 29–30 June 2009.

95. Nicholas Keung. 2009. "Wanted: Plumbers. Must Not Be Foreign," *Toronto Star*, 29 April 2009.

96. OECD, 2008: 130, 132.

97. Ibid.: 127.

98. See *Southern Metropolis Daily*. 2008. "'Chocolate City'—Africans Seek Their Dreams in China," January 2008. Translated copy available at http://blog.foolsmountain.com/2008/06/14/chocolate-city-africans-seek-their-dreams-in-china/.

99. Lynn A. Karoly and Constantijn W. A. Panis. 2009. "Supply of and Demand for Skilled Labor in the United States," in Jagdish Bhagwati and Gordon Hanson (eds.), *Skilled Immigration Today: Prospects, Problems and Policies*. Oxford, UK: Oxford University Press, pp. 15–52.

100. Bernard Salt. 2008. "The Global Skills Convergence," *KPMG International*, September 2008: 41. Available at http://www.bernardsalt.com.au/media/Global_Skills_Convergence.pdf.

101. James Goldsborough. 2000. "Out-of-Control Immigration," *Foreign Affairs* 79: 89–101.

102. Devesh Kapur and John McHale. 2005. *Give Us Your Best and Brightest: The Global Hunt for Talent and Its Impact on the Developing World*. Washington, DC: Center for Global Development.

103. Ibid.: 37.

104. Ibid.: 37.

105. Diane Gershon. 2000. "US Congress Encouraged to Lay Out the Welcome Mat for Skilled Foreigners," *Nature* 405: 597–598.

106. Declan McCullagh. 2005. "Gates Wants to Scrap H-1B Visa Restrictions," *ZDNet News*, 27 April 2005. Available at http://news.zdnet.com/2100-3513_22 -142533.html.

107. As reported by the Center for Responsive Politics. 2009. "Lobbying: Computers/Internet, Industry Profile 2008." Available at http://www.opensecrets.org/ lobby/indusclient.php?lname=B12&year=2008.

108. Ibid.

109. See http://www.nasscom.in/Nasscom/templates/NormalPage.aspx?id=55981.

110. Giovanni Facchini, Anna Maria Mayda, and Prachi Mishra. 2009. "Do Interest Groups Affect US Immigration Policy?" *CReAM Discussion Paper No. 04/09*, Center for Research and Analysis of Migration.

111. Ron Hira. 2004. "U.S. Immigration Regulations and India's Information Technology Industry," *Technological Forecasting and Social Change* 71: 837–854.

112. Ibid.: 838.

113. Kapur and McHale, 2005: 38.

114. Robert L. Smith. 2009. "Waves of Immigrants Now Calling Philadelphia Home; New Welcoming Center Idea behind the Lure," *The Plain Dealer* (Cleveland), 20 May 2009.

115. Ibid.

116. William R. Kerr and William F. Lincoln. 2008. "The Supply Side of Innovation: H-1B Visa Reforms and US Ethnic Invention," *Harvard Business School Working Paper 09-005*.

117. Quotation attributed to Simone Weil.

118. Castles, 2002a: 1151.

119. Our thanks to Robin Cohen for framing this dilemma with such clarity.

Chapter 8. A Global Migration Agenda

1. John Kenneth Galbraith. 1979. *The Nature of Mass Poverty*. Cambridge, MA: Harvard University Press.

2. Stephen Castles. 2004. "The Factors That Make and Unmake Migration Policies," *International Migration Review* 38(3): 852–884.

3. Bob Rowthorn. 2006. "Numbers Matter: It Is Time for Mainstream Politics to Debate the Scale of British Immigration," *Prospect Magazine* 125, August 2006. See also Robin Cohen. 1987. *Global Diasporas*. London: Routledge, pp. 70–74.

4. *Financial Times*. 2010. "Cameron Backs Immigration Cap to Curb Population Rise," 11 January 2010.

5. Thanks to Kathleen Newland for noting this development.

6. Stephen Nickell, 2009. "Migration Watch." *Prospect Magazine*, 23 July 2009, issue 161.

7. Laurie Garrett. 2005. "The Next Pandemic?" *Foreign Affairs* 84 (4); Michael T. Osterholm. 2005. "Preparing for the Next Pandemic," *New York Times*, 21 June 2005.

8. See Alan Dowty. 1989. *Closed Borders: The Contemporary Assault on Freedom of Movement*. London: Yale University Press, pp. 68–76.

9. Hiroyuki Tanaka. 2008. "North Korea: Understanding Migration to and from a Closed Country," Migration Policy Institute. Available at http://www.migration information.org/Profiles/display.cfm?id=668.

10. International Crisis Group. 2006. "Perilous Journeys. The Plight of North Koreans in China and Beyond," *Asia Report No. 122*, October 26, 2006.

11. Choe Sang-Hun. 2005. "North Koreans Escape—For a Price," *International Herald Tribune*, 29 April 2005.

12. Timothy J. Hatton and Jeffrey G. Williamson. 2003. "What Fundamentals Drive World Migration?" *WIDER Discussion Paper No. 2003/23*, United Nations University, pp. 6–7.

13. William J. Stern. 2003. "What *Gangs of New York* Misses," *City Journal*, 14 January 2003.

14. Estonia, Latvia, Lithuania, Poland, Czech Republic, Slovakia, Hungary, and Slovenia.

15. Christian Dustmann, M. Casanova, M. Fertig, I. Preston, and C. M. Schmidt. 2003. "The Impact of EU Enlargement on Migration Flows," *Online Report 25/03*. London: Home Office. Available at www.homeoffice.gov.uk/rds/pdfo2/rdoolr2503 .pdf.

16. Naomi Pollard, Maria Latorre, and Dhananjayan Sriskandarajah. 2008. *Floodgates or Turnstiles? Post-EU Enlargement Migration Flows to (and from) the UK*. London: IPPR, pp. 54–55.

17. Christian Dustmann, Tommaso Frattini, and Caroline Halls. 2009. "Assessing the Fiscal Costs and Benefits of A8 Migration to the UK," *CReAM Discussion Paper No. 18/09*, Centre for Research and Analysis of Migration, University College London.

18. Gareth Jones and Kuba Jaworowski. 2008. "In Parts of Europe, Migrant Workers Head Home," *Reuters*, June 16, 2008.

19. Henry Chu. 2009. "Britain Loses Its Allure for Polish Migrants," *LA Times*, 31 March 2009.

20. David G. Blanchflower, Jumana Salheen, and Chris Shadforth. 2007. "The Impact of the Recent Migration from Eastern Europe on the UK Economy," *IZA Discussion Paper No. 2615*, Institute for the Study of Labor, Berlin.

21. See Steve Vertovec. 2009. *Transnationalism*. Abingdon, UK: Routledge.

22. From Jefferson's instructions to Virginia delegates to the 1774 Continental Congress. Cited in Alan Dowty. 1989. *Closed Borders: The Contemporary Assault on Freedom of Movement*. London: Yale University Press, p. 47.

23. Michael Walzer. 1983. Spheres of Justice. New York: Basic Books, p. 61.

24. Ibid.: 61.

25. Joseph H. Carens. 1987. "Aliens and Citizens: The Case for Open Borders," *The Review of Politics* 49(2): 251–273, pp. 265–270.

26. Joseph H. Carens. 2009. "The Case for Amnesty," *Boston Review*, May/June 2009.

27. Seyla Benhabib. 2005. "Borders, Boundaries, and Citizenship," *PS: Political Science and Politics* 38: 673–677.

28. This point is raised in Carens, 1987: 267.

29. United Nations Development Programme. 2009. *Human Development Report 2009 Overcoming Barriers: Human Mobility and Development*. New York: UNDP, pp. 15–16.

30. Galbraith, 1979.

31. Carens, 1987: 270.

32. Kym Anderson and Bjorn Lomborg. 2008. "Free Trade, Free Labour, Free Growth," Project Syndicate. Available at http://www.project-syndicate.org/commentary/anderson1.

33. L. Alan Winters, Terrie L. Walmsley, Zhen Kun Wang, and Roman Grynberg. 2003. "Liberalising Temporary Movement of Natural Persons: An Agenda for the Development Round," *World Economy* 26: 1137–1161.

34. Lant Pritchett. 2004. "Boom Towns and Ghost Countries: Geography, Agglomeration, and Population Mobility," *CGD Working Paper 36*, Center for Global Development.

35. Kerry Howley. 2009. "Ideas: Fixing the World; Welcome Guestworkers," *The Atlantic*, July/August 2009.

36. Jagdish Bhagwati. 2003. "Borders beyond Control," *Foreign Affairs* 82: 98–104.

37. Thomas Straubhaar. 2001. "Why Do We Need a General Agreement on the Movements of People (GAMP)?" in Bimal Ghosh (ed.), *Managed Migration: Time for a New International Regime?* Oxford, UK: Oxford University Press, pp. 110–136.

38. Bimal Ghosh. 2001. "New International Regime for Orderly Movements of People: What Will It Look Like?" in Bimal Ghosh (ed.), *Managed Migration: Time for a New International Regime?* Oxford, UK: Oxford University Press, pp. 220–247.

39. Rey Koslowski. 2008. "Global Mobility and the Quest for an International Migration Regime," in Joseph Chamie and Luca Dall'Oglio (eds.), *International Migration and Development: Continuing the Dialogue: Legal and Policy Perspectives*. Geneva: International Organization for Migration.

40. Steven Vertovec. 2009. *Transnationalism*. London: Routledge, p. 2.

41. Robert Holzmann, Johannes Koettl, and Taras Chernetsky. 2005. "Portability Regimes of Pension and Health Care Benefits for International Migrants: An Analysis of Issues and Good Practices," *Social Protection Discussion Paper Series No. 0519*, The World Bank, p. 2

42. Ibid.: 13.

43. Ibid.

44. Philip Martin and Susan Martin. 2006. "GCIM: A New Global Migration Facility," *International Migration* 44(1): 5–12, p. 6.

45. Tim Harford, Michael Klein, Klaus Tilmes. 2005. "The Future of Aid 1," *Public Policy for the Private Sector Note No. 284*. Washington, DC. The World Bank. It is important to note the range of intermediaries in remittances, many of which are informal. As governments, especially since 11 September 2001, focus more on closing unofficial channels, agencies such as MoneyGram and Western Union (which has over 350,000 outlets) have flourished.

46. Rainer Baübock. 2005. "Expansive Citizenship. Voting beyond Territory and Membership," *Political Science and Politics*, 38: 683–687.

47. Our thanks to Stephen Castles for offering this insightful comment.

48. Angel Gurría. 2009. "Creating Opportunities—Integration, Employment and Social Mobility: European Experiences and Scope for Manoeuvre," in *Comments at the International Symposium on Integration, Employment and Social Mobility*, 26 January 2009. Available at http://www.oecd.org/document/38/0,3343 ,en_2649_33931_42053286_1_1_1_1,00.html.

49. Mina Fazel and Alan Stein. 2004. "UK Immigration Law Disregards the Best interests of Children," *The Lancet* 363(9423): 1749–1750.

50. We are grateful to Robin Cohen and Kathleen Newland for their thoughts on this matter.

51. Global Commission on International Migration. 2005. *Migration in an Interconnected World: New Directions for Action*. Geneva: GCIM, p. 85.

52. *Financial Times*. 2009c. "Economic Fillip Predicted from Migrant Amnesty," 16 June 2009, p. 4.

53. The first point is one made by Joseph H. Carens in Carens, 2009. He also argues that liberal democratic states should institutionalize "an automatic transition to legal status for [undocumented] migrants who have settled in a state for an extended period."

54. Available at http://www.bia.homeoffice.gov.uk/managingborders/managing migration/earned-citizenship/.

55. Winters, Walmsley, Wang, and Grynberg, 2003.

56. IRCA, 1986.

57. Castles, 2004.

58. *The Economist*. 2009e. "This Skeptical Isle," 5 December 2009, p. 36.

59. We gratefully acknowledge Stephen Castles's comments on this point.

60. Ellie Vasta. 2007. "Accommodating Diversity: Why Current Critiques of Multiculturalism Miss the Point," *COMPAS Working Paper No. 53*, Centre on Migration, Policy and Society, University of Oxford.

61. Michael Clemens. 2009a. *CGD Migration Data Scorecard*. Washington, DC: Center for Global Development.

62. Commission on International Migration Data for Development Research and Policy. 2009. *Migrants Count: Five Steps toward Better Migration Data*. Washington, DC: Center for Global Development, p. 1.

63. Commission on International Migration Data for Development Research and Policy, 2009: 9–10.

64. International Labour Organization; International Organization for Migration; Office of the High Commissioner for Human Rights; United Nations Conference on Trade and Development; United Nations Development Programme; United Nations Department of Economic and Social Affairs; United Nations Educational, Scientific and Cultural Organization; United Nations Population Fund; United Nations High Commissioner for Refugees; United Nations Children's Fund; United Nations Institute for Training and Research; United Nations Office on Drugs and Crime; World Bank; and UN Regional Commissions.

65. Timothy J. Hatton. 2007. "Should We Have a WTO for International Migration?" *Economic Policy* 22(50): 339–383, p. 368.

66. Charles Kindleberger. 1986. "International Public Goods without International Government," *American Economic Review* 76(1): 1–13, p. 8.

67. Hatton, 2007; Koslowski, 2008.

68. Kindleberger, 1986: 4.

69. Ibid.: 4.

References

Abada, Teresa, Feng Hou, and Bali Ram. 2008. "Group Differences in Educational Attainment among the Children of Immigrants," *Analytical Studies Branch Research Paper Series*. Ottawa: Statistics Canada.

Abella, Manolo I. 2004. "The Role of Recruiters in Labour Migration," in Douglas S. Massey and J. Edward Taylor (eds.), *International Migration: Prospects and Policies in a Global Market*. Oxford, UK: Oxford University Press, pp. 201–211.

Acemoglu, Daron, Simon Johnson, and James Robinson. 2001. "The Colonial Origins of Comparative Development: An Empirical Investigation," *The American Economic Review* 91(5): 1369–1401.

Adams, Richard H. 2003. "International Migration, Remittances, and the Brain Drain: A Study of 24 Labor Exporting Countries," *Policy Research Working Paper Series 3069*. Washington, DC: World Bank.

Adams, Richard H., and John Page. 2005. "Do International Migration and Remittances Reduce Poverty in Developing Countries?" *World Development* 33(10): 1645–1669.

Adamson, Fiona B. 2006. "Crossing Borders: International Migration and National Security," *International Security* 31(1): 165–199.

Aiken, Linda H., James Buchan, Julie Sochalski, Barbara Nichols, and Mary Powell. 2004. "Trends in International Nurse Migration," *Health Affairs* 23(3): 69–77.

Altbach, Philip G. 2004. "Higher Education Crosses Borders," *Change* 36: 18–25.

Altbach, Philip G., and Jane Knight. 2006. "The Internationalization of Higher Education: Motivations and Realities," in *The NEA 2006 Almanac of Higher Education*. Washington, DC: National Education Association, pp. 1–11. Available at http://www.bc.edu/bc_org/avp/soe/cihe/pga/pdf/Internationalization_2006.pdf.

Amnesty International. 1995. *Prisoners without a Voice. Asylum-Seekers Detained in the United Kingdom*. London: Amnesty International.

———. 2005. *UK: Seeking Asylum Is Not a Crime: Detention of People Who Have Sought Asylum*. London: Amnesty International.

———. 2006. *Amnesty International Report 2006—Russian Federation*. London: Amnesty International.

Anderson, Kym, and Bjorn Lomborg. 2008. "Free Trade, Free Labour, Free Growth," *Project Syndicate*. Available at: http://www.project-syndicate.org/commentary/anderson1.

Andreas, Peter, and Timothy Snyder, eds. 2000. *The Wall around the West: State Borders and Immigration Controls in North America and Europe.* Oxford, UK: Rowan and Littlefield Publishers, Inc.

Arai, Mahmood, Moa Bursell, and Lena Nekby. 2008. "Between Meritocracy and Ethnic Discrimination: The Gender Difference," *Working Paper*, The Stockholm University Linnaeus Center for Integration Studies. Stockholm: SULCIS.

The Asian Age. 2001. "Professor Amartya Sen in India," 28 February 2001. Available at http://www.tata.com/company/Media/inside.aspx?artid=mWEoPvKEFew=.

Associated Press. 2009a. "Developing World Embraces Mobile Phones: UN Report," 2 March 2009.

———. 2009b. "Immigrants Face Lengthy Review with Few Rights." Available at http://www.timesrecordnews.com/news/2009/mar/16/immigrants-face -lengthy-detention-few-rights/.

Australia Department of Citizenship and Immigration. 2008. *Population Flows: Immigration Aspects, 2007–8.* Canberra, Australia: Australian Government.

Australian Human Rights and Equal Opportunity Commission. 2004. *A Last Resort? National Inquiry into Children in Immigration Detention.* Sydney, Australia: Australian Human Rights Commission.

Bach, Stephen. 2006. "International Mobility of Health Professionals Brain Drain or Brain Exchange?" *UNU-WIDER Research Paper No. 2006/82*, United Nations University. Helsinki, Finland: UNU-WIDER.

Baker, Michael, and Dwayne Benjamin. 1995. "The Receipt of Transfer Payments by Immigrants to Canada," *Journal of Human Resources* 30(4): 650–676.

Banting, Keith, and Will Kymlicka. 2004. "Do Multiculturalism Policies Erode the Welfare State?" in Philippe van Parijs (ed.), *Cultural Diversity versus Economic Solidarity.* Brussels: Deboeck Université Press.

Barnett, Laura. 2002. "Global Governance and the Evolution of the International Refugee Regime," *International Journal of Refugee Law* 14(2/3): 238–262.

Barrell, Ray, John FitzGerald, and Rebecca Riley. 2007. "EU Enlargement and Migration: Assessing the Macroeconomic Impacts," *Discussion Paper No. 292.* London: National Institute of Economic and Social Research.

Bashir, Sajitha. 2007. *Trends in International Trade in Higher Education: Implications and Options for Developing Countries.* Washington, DC: World Bank.

Baübock, Rainer. 2005. "Expansive Citizenship: Voting Beyond Territory and Membership," *Political Science and Politics* 38: 683–687.

BBC News. 2008. "Migrant Numbers 'Must Be Reduced,'" 18 October 2008. Available at http://news.bbc.co.uk/1/hi/uk_politics/7677419.stm.

Benhabib, Seyla. 2005. "Borders, Boundaries, and Citizenship," *PS: Political Science and Politics* 38: 673–677.

Bentley, Jerry H. 1993. *Old World Encounters, Cross-Cultural Contacts and Exchange in Pre-Modern Times.* Oxford, UK: Oxford University Press.

———. 1998. "Hemispheric Integration, 500–1500 CE," *Journal of World History* 9(2): 237–254.

Bhagwati, Jagdish. 2003. "Borders beyond Control," *Foreign Affairs* 82: 98–104.

Bharadwaj, Prashant, Asim Ijaz Khwaja, and Atif R. Mian. 2008. "The Big March: Migratory Flows after the Partition of India." *HKS Working Paper No. RWP08-029*. Available at SSRN: http://ssrn.com/abstract=1124093.

Black, Richard. 2001. "Environmental Refugees: Myth or Reality," *UNHCR New Issues in Refugee Research Working Paper No. 34*. Geneva: UNHCR.

Blanchflower, David G., Jumana Salheen, and Chris Shadforth. 2007. "The Impact of the Recent Migration from Eastern Europe on the UK Economy," *IZA Discussion Paper No. 2615*. Berlin: Institute for the Study of Labor.

Blume, Kraen, Bjorn Gustafsson, Peder J. Pedersen, and Mette Verner. 2003. "A Tale of Two Countries: Poverty among Immigrants in Denmark and Sweden since 1984," *UNU-WIDER Research Paper DP2003/36*, United Nations University. Helsinki, Finland: UNU-WIDER.

Boana, Camillo, Roger Zetter, and Tim Morris. 2008. "Environmentally Displaced People," *Forced Migration Policy Briefing 1*. Oxford, UK: Refugee Studies Centre.

Bordo, Michael D., Alan M. Taylor, Jeffrey G. Williamson. 2005. *Globalization in Historical Perspective*. Chicago: University of Chicago Press.

Borjas, George J. 1989. "Economic Theory and International Migration," *International Migration Review*, 23(3): 457–485.

———. 1994. "The Economics of Immigration," *Journal of Economic Literature* XXXII: 1667–1717.

———. 1999a. *Heaven's Door: Immigration Policy and the American Economy*. Princeton, NJ: Princeton University Press.

———. 1999b. "Immigration," *NBER Reporter*, Fall. Available at: http://www.nber.org/reporter/fall99/borjas.html.

———. 2003. "The Labor Demand Curve Is Downward Sloping: Reexamining the Impact of Immigration on the Labor Market," *Quarterly Journal of Economics* 118(4): 1335–1374.

Borjas, George J., and Stephen G. Bronars. 1991. "Immigration and the Family," *Journal of Labour Economics* 9(2): 123–148.

Boxell, James. 2009. "Recession Spurs Migrant Workers to Leave," *Financial Times*, 21 May 2009.

Boyd, Monica. 1989. "Family and Personal Networks in International Migration: Recent Developments and New Agendas," *International Migration Review* 23(3): 638–670.

Brinkley, Joel. 1991. "Ethiopian Jews and Israelis Exult as Airlift Is Completed," *New York Times*, 26 May 1991. Available at: http://www.nytimes.com/1991/05/26/world/ethiopian-jews-and-israelis-exult-as-airlift-is-completed.html?sec=&spon=&pagewanted=all.

Brown, Oli. 2007. "Climate Change and Forced Migration: Observations, Projections and Implications," *Human Development Report Office Occasional Paper 2007/17*. New York: United Nations Development Programme, Human Development Report Office.

Bruns, Barbara, Alain Mingat, and Ramahatra Rakotomalala. 2003. *Achieving Universal Primary Education by 2015: A Chance for Every Child.* Washington, DC: World Bank.

Büchel, Felix, and Joachim Frick. 2005. "Immigrants' Economic Performance across Europe: Does Immigration Policy Matter?" *Population Research and Policy Review* 24(2): 175–212.

Bundy, Colin. 1988. *The Rise and Fall of the South African Peasantry.* London: James Currey.

Burgess, Greg. 2008. *Refuge in the Land of Liberty. France and Its Refugees, from the Revolution to the End of Asylum, 1787–1939.* Basingstoke, UK: Palgrave MacMillan.

Camarota, Steven A. 2007. "Immigrants in the United States 2007: A Profile of America's Foreign-Born Population," *Center for Immigration Studies Backgrounder,* November 2007. Washington, DC: Center for Immigration Studies.

Camarota, Steven A., and Karen Jensenius. 2009. "Trends in Immigrant and Native Employment," *Center for Immigration Studies Backgrounder,* May 2009. Washington, DC: Center for Immigration Studies.

Card, David. 2005. "Is the New Immigration Really So Bad?" *The Economic Journal* 115(507): 300–323.

Carens, Joseph H. 1987. "Aliens and Citizens: The Case for Open Borders," *The Review of Politics* 49(2): 251–273.

———. 2009. "The Case for Amnesty," *Boston Review,* May/June 2009.

Carrington, William J., and Enrica Detragiache. 1999. "How Extensive Is the Brain Drain?" *Finance and Development: A Quarterly Magazine of the IMF,* 36(2). Available at http://www.imf.org/external/pubs/ft/fandd/1999/06/carringt.htm.

Castles, Stephen. 1989. "Migrant Workers and the Transformation of Western Societies," *Western Societies Program Occasional Paper No. 22.* Ithaca, NY: Cornell University Press.

———. 1998. "The Process of Integration of Migrant Communities," in *United Nations, Population Distribution and Migration, Proceedings of the United Nations Expert Meeting on Population Distribution and Migration, Sant Cruz, Bolivia, 18–22 January 1993* (convened in preparation for the International Conference on Population and Development, Cairo, 5–14 September 1994), pp. 247–265. New York: United Nations.

———. 2002a. "Environmental Change and Forced Migration: Making Sense of the Debate," *UNHCR New Issues in Refugee Research, Working Paper No. 70.* Geneva: UNHCR.

———. 2002b. "Migration and Community Formation under Conditions of Globalization," *International Migration Review* 36(4): 1143–1168.

———. 2004. "The Factors That Make and Unmake Migration Policies," *International Migration Review* 38(3): 852–884.

———. 2006. "Guestworkers in Europe: A Resurrection?" *International Migration Review* 40(4): 741–766.

———. 2007. "Comparing the Experience of Five Major Emigration Countries," *Working Paper 7*, International Migration Institute, James Martin 21st Century School, University of Oxford. Oxford, UK: International Migration Institute.

Castles, Stephen, and Godula Kosack. 1974. "How the Trade Unions Try to Control and Integrate Immigrant Workers in the German Federal Republic," *Race and Class* 15(4): 497–514.

———. 1984. *Immigrant Workers and Class Structure in Western Europe*, 2nd ed. Oxford, UK: Oxford University Press.

Castles, Stephen, and Sean Loughna. 2003. "Trends in Asylum Migration to Industrialized Countries: 1990–2001," *UNU-WIDER Discussion Paper No. 2003/31*. Available at: http://www.wider.unu.edu/stc/repec/pdfs/rp2003/dp2003-31.pdf.

Castles, Stephen, and Mark J. Miller. 2003. *The Age of Migration: International Population Movements in the Modern World*, 3rd ed. New York: Palgrave MacMillan.

———. 2009. *The Age of Migration: International Population Movements in the Modern World*, 4th ed. New York: Palgrave MacMillan.

Castles, Stephen, and Carl-Ulrik Schierup. 2010. "Migration and Ethnic Minorities," in Francis G. Castles, Stephan Leibfried, Jane Lewis, Herbert Obinger, and Christopher Pierson (eds.), *The Oxford Handbook of the Welfare State*. Oxford, UK: Oxford University Press.

Center for Responsive Politics. 2009. "Lobbying: Computers/Internet, Industry Profile 2008." Available at http://www.opensecrets.org/lobby/indusclient.php?lname=B12&year=2008.

Centre for Economics and Business Research. 2007. *Future Flows: Forecasting the Current and Future Economic Impact of Highly Skilled Migrants*. London: CEBR.

Chand, Satish, and Michael A. Clemens. 2008. "Skilled Emigration and Skill Creation: A Quasi-Experiment," *CGD Working Paper Number 152*. Washington, DC: Center for Global Development.

Chappell, Laura, Dhananjayan Sriskandarajah, and Tracy K Swinburn. 2008. "Building a New Home: Migration in the UK Construction Sector," *Economics of Migration Project, Working Paper 2*. London: Institute for Public Policy Research.

Chiswick, Barry R., and Noyna DebBurman. 2004. "Educational Attainment: Analysis by Immigrant Generation," *Economics of Education Review* 23: 361–379.

Christian, David. 2005. *Maps of Time: An Introduction to Big History*. Berkeley and Los Angeles: University of California Press.

Chu, Henry. 2009. "Britain Loses Its Allure for Polish Migrants," *LA Times*, 31 March 2009.

Cleland, John, Stan Bernstein, Alex Ezeh, Anibal Faundes, Anna Glasier, and Jolene Innis. 2006. "Family Planning: The Unfinished Agenda," *The Lancet* 368(954): 1810–1827.

Clemens, Michael A. 2008. "Immigrants Are an Engine of Prosperity," *Atlanta Journal-Constitution*, 27 November 2008.

———. 2009a. *CGD Migration Data Scorecard*. Washington, DC: Center for Global Development.

Clemens, Michael A. 2009b. "Skill Flow: A Fundamental Reconsideration of Skilled-Worker Mobility and Development," *UNDP Human Development Report 2009 Background Paper 8*. New York: United Nations Development Programme, Human Development Report Office.

Clemens, Michael A., Claudio E. Montenegro, and Lant Pritchett. 2009. "The Place Premium: Wage Differences for Identical Workers across the US Border," *Harvard Kennedy School Faculty Research Working Paper Series RWP 09-004*. Cambridge, MA: Harvard Kennedy School.

Cohen, Robin. 1987. *Global Diasporas: An Introduction*. London: Routledge.

———. 2006. *Migration and Its Enemies: Global Capital, Migrant Labour and the Nation-State*. London: Ashgate.

———. 2008. *Global Diasporas: An Introduction*. London: Routledge.

Collinson, Sarah. 1993. *Europe and International Migration*. London: Pinter Publishers.

———. 2009. "The Political Economy of Migration Processes: An Agenda for Migration Research and Analysis," *Working Paper 12*, International Migration Institute, James Martin 21st Century School, University of Oxford. Oxford, UK: International Migration Institute.

Commission on International Migration Data for Development Research and Policy. 2009. *Migrants Count: Five Steps toward Better Migration Data*. Washington, DC: Center for Global Development.

Coppel, Jonathan, Jean-Christophe Dumond, and Ignazio Visco. 2001. "Trends in Immigration and Economic Consequences," *OECD Economics Department Working Paper No. 284*. Paris: OECD.

Cornelius, Wayne. 2001. "Death at the Border: The Efficacy and 'Unintended' Consequences of the US Immigration Control Policy 1993–2000," *Center for Comparative Immigration Studies Working Paper 27*. San Diego: University of California.

Cotis, Jean-Philippe. 2003. "Population Ageing: Facing the Challenge," *OECD Observer No. 239*, September 2003. Paris: OECD.

Crul, Maurice, and Hans Vermeulen. 2003. "The Second Generation in Europe," *International Migration Review* 37(4): 965–986.

Crush, Jonathan. 2000. "The Dark Side of Democracy: Migration, Xenophobia, and Human Rights in South Africa," *International Migration* 38(6): 103–119.

Curtin, Philip D. 1984. *Cross-Cultural Trade in World History*. Cambridge, UK: Cambridge University Press.

Dayton-Johnson, Jeff, Louka T. Katseli, Anna di Mattia, and Theodora Xenogiani. 2007. *Policy Coherence for Development: Migration and Developing Countries*. Paris: OECD.

de Haas, Hein. 2007a. "North African Migration Systems: Evolutions, Transformations, and Development Linkages," *Working Paper 6*, International Migration Institute, James Martin 21st Century School, University of Oxford. Oxford, UK: International Migration Institute.

————. 2007b. "Remittances, Migration, and Social Development: A Conceptual Review of the Literature," *Social Policy and Development Programme Paper No.34.* New York: United Nations Research Institute for Social Development.

————. 2007c. "Turning the Tide? Why Development Will Not Stop Migration," *Development and Change* 38(5): 819–841.

————. 2008a. "The Internal Dynamics of Migration Processes," presented at IMSCOE Conference on Theories of Migration and Social Change, 1–3 July 2008, Oxford University.

————. 2008b. "Migration and Development: A Theoretical Perspective," *Working Paper 9,* International Migration Institute, James Martin 21st Century School, University of Oxford. Oxford, UK: International Migration Institute.

————. 2009. *Migration System Formation and Decline: A Theoretical Inquiry into the Self-Perpetuating and Self Undermining Dynamics of Migration Processes.* IMI Working Paper Series. International Migration Institute, James Martin 21st Century School, University of Oxford. Oxford, UK: International Migration Institute.

————. 2010. *Migration Transitions: A Theoretical and Empirical Inquiry into the Developmental Drivers of International Migration.* IMI Working Paper Series. International Migration Institute, James Martin 21st Century School, University of Oxford. Oxford, UK: International Migration Institute.

de Haas, Hein, Oliver Bakewell, Stephen Castles, Gunvor Jónsson, and Simona Vezzoli. 2009. "Mobility and Human Development," *Working Paper 14,* International Migration Institute, James Martin 21st Century School, University of Oxford. Oxford, UK: International Migration Institute.

Demeny, Paul. 2004. "Population Policy Dilemmas in Europe at the Dawn of the Twenty-First Century," *Population and Development Review* 29(1): 1–28.

Diamond, Jared. 1998. *Guns, Germs and Steel.* Vintage. London.

Dobbs, Lou. 2005. "Border Insecurity; Criminal Illegal Aliens; Deadly Imports; Illegal Alien Amnesty," *CNN Transcript,* 14 April 2005. Available at http://edition.cnn.com/TRANSCRIPTS/0504/14/ldt.01.html.

Docquier, Frederic, and Abdeslam Marfouk. 2006. "International Migration by Education Attainment, 1990–2000," in Caglar Ozden and Maurice Schiff (eds.), *International Migration, Remittances and Brain Drain.* Basingstoke, UK: World Bank and Palgrave MacMillan, pp. 151–199.

Dowty, Alan. 1989. *Closed Borders: The Contemporary Assault on Freedom of Movement.* London: Yale University Press.

Drozdiak, William. 2005. "Europe Braces for New Immigrants; Western Nations Fear Flood of Migrants Will Tax Social Programs," *Washington Post,* 22 October 1990.

Duffield, Mark. 2001. *Global Governance and the New Wars. The Merging of Development and Security.* London: Zed Books.

Dugger, Celia W. 2004. "Where Doctors Are Scarce, Africa Deploys Substitutes," *New York Times,* 23 November 2004.

Durand, Jorge, William Kandel, Emilio A. Parrado, and Douglas S. Massey. 1996. "International Migration and Development in Mexican Communities," *Demography* 33(2): 249–264.

Dustmann, Christian, M. Casanova, M. Fertig, I. Preston, and C. M. Schmidt. 2003. *The Impact of EU Enlargement on Migration Flows, Online Report 25/03*. London: Home Office. Available at www.homeoffice.gov.uk/rds/pdfs2/rdsolr2503.pdf.

Dustmann, Christian, Tommaso Frattini, and Caroline Halls. 2009. "Assessing the Fiscal Costs and Benefits of A8 Migration to the UK," *CReAM Discussion Paper No. 18/09*, Centre for Research and Analysis of Migration, University College London. London: CReAM.

Düvell, Franck. 2009. "Irregular Migration in Northern Europe: Overview and Comparison," Clandestino Project Conference, London, 27 March 2009. Available at: http://clandestino.eliamep.gr/wp-content/uploads/2009/04/key_note_28_3_09_fd.pdf.

The Economist. 2008a. "Of Bedsheets and Bison Grass Vodka," 3 January 2008.

———. 2008b. "Tough Times," 29 November 2009.

———. 2009a. "Bartered Brides," 12 March 2009.

———. 2009b. "Economics Focus: Give Me Your Scientists," 7 March 2009.

———. 2009c. "The Immigration Superhighway," 18 April 2009.

———. 2009d. "The People Crunch," 17 January 2009.

———. 2009e. "This Skeptical Isle," 5 December 2009.

Eltis, David. 2002. "Introduction: Migration and Agency in Global History," in David Eltis (ed.), *Coerced and Free Migration: Global Perspectives*. Stanford, CA: Stanford University Press.

Epstein, Gil S. 2008. "Herd and Network Effects in Migration Decision-Making," *Journal of Ethnic and Migration Studies* 34: 567–583.

European Parliament. 2009. "Answer Given by Mr Barrot on Behalf of the Commission," *Parliamentary Questions E-5971/2008*, 12 January 2009. Available at http://www.europarl.europa.eu/sides/getAllAnswers.do?reference =E-2008-5971&language=EN.

Facchini, Giovanni, Anna Maria Mayda, and Prachi Mishra. 2009. "Do Interest Groups Affect US Immigration Policy?" *CReAM Discussion Paper No 04/09*, Center for Research and Analysis of Migration, University College London. London: CReAM.

Fagan, Brian. 2007. *People of the Earth: An Introduction to World Prehistory*. London: Prentice Hall.

Faist, Thomas. 2000. *The Volume and Dynamics of International Migration and Transnational Social Spaces*. Oxford, UK: Oxford University Press.

Fazel, Mina, and Alan Stein. 2004. "UK Immigration Law Disregards the Best Interests of Children," *The Lancet* 363(9423): 1749–1750.

Fell, Peter, and Debra Hayes. 2007. *What Are They Doing Here? A Critical Guide to Asylum and Immigration*. Birmingham, UK: Venture Press.

Fernandez-Armesto, Felipe. 2006. *Pathfinders: A Global History of Exploration*. Oxford, UK: Oxford University Press.

Financial Times. 2009a. "Diaspora Fuels War Crimes in Congo, Says UN," 25 November 2009.

———. 2009b. "Downturn Deals Blow to US Immigrants," 18 November 2009.

———. 2009c. "Economic Fillip Predicted from Migrant Amnesty," 16 June2009.

——— 2009d. "The Hidden Victims of Recession," 5 November 2009.

———. 2010. "Cameron Backs Immigration Cap to Curb Population Rise," 11 January 2010.

Finn, Michael. 2005. "Stay Rates of Foreign Doctorate Recipients from U.S. Universities, 2005," Division of Science Resources Statistics of the National Science Foundation. Available at http://orise.orau.gov/scp/files/stayrate07.pdf.

Florida, Richard. 2002. "The Economic Geography of Talent," *Annals of the Association of American Geographers* 92(4): 743–755.

Florida, Richard, Charlotta Mellander, and Kevin Stolarick. 2008. "Inside the Black Box of Regional Development—Human Capital, the Creative Class and Tolerance," *Journal of Economic Geography* 8(5): 615–649.

Gabbard, Susan, Rick Mines, and Beatriz Boccalandro. 1994. "Migrant Farmworkers: Pursuing Security in an Unstable Labor Market," *Research Report No. 5*, U.S. Department of Labor, Office of the Assistant Secretary for Policy, Office of Program Economics. Washington DC: U.S. Department of Labor.

Galbraith, John Kenneth. 1979. *The Nature of Mass Poverty.* Cambridge, MA: Harvard University Press.

Gamlen, Alan. 2006. "Diaspora Engagement Policies: What Are They, and What Kinds of States Use Them?" *COMPAS Working Paper No. 32,* Centre on Migration, Policy and Society, University of Oxford. Oxford, UK: COMPAS.

———. 2008. "Why Engage Diasporas?" *COMPAS Working Paper 63,* Centre on Migration, Policy and Society, University of Oxford. Oxford, UK: COMPAS.

Garrett, Laurie. 2005. "The Next Pandemic?" *Foreign Affairs* 84(4): 3–23.

Gershon, Diane. 2000. "US Congress Encouraged to Lay Out the Welcome Mat for Skilled Foreigners," *Nature* 405: 597–598.

Ghosh, Bimal. 2001. "New International Regime for Orderly Movements of People: What Will It Look Like?" in Bimal Ghosh (ed.), *Managed Migration: Time for a New International Regime?* Oxford, UK: Oxford University Press, pp. 220–247.

———. 2006. *Migrants' Remittances and Development: Myths, Rhetoric and Realities.* Geneva: IOM.

Global Commission on International Migration. 2004. "Global Migration Futures Workshop Report," 10 December 2004, St Antony's College, Oxford. Available at http://www.gcim.org/attachements/Global%20Migration%20Futures%20Workshop.pdf.

———. 2005. *Migration in an Interconnected World: New Directions for Action.* Geneva: GCIM.

Goebel, Ted, Michael R. Waters, and Dennis H. O'Rourke. 2008. "The Late Pleistocene Dispersal of Modern Humans in the Americas," *Science* 319(5869):1497–1502.

Goldin, Ian. 1987. *Making Race: The Politics and Economics of Coloured Identity in South Africa*. London: Longman.

Goldin, Ian, and Kenneth Reinert. 2007. *Globalization for Development: Trade, Finance, Aid, Migration and Policy*, 2nd ed. Basingstoke, UK: Palgrave MacMillan.

Goldsborough, James. 2000. "Out-of-Control Immigration," *Foreign Affairs* 79: 89–101.

Gordon, Ian. 1995. "Migration in a Segmented Labor Market," *Transactions of the Institute of British Geographers* 20(2): 139–155.

The Guardian. "Net Migration Falls by a Third as Departures from UK Soar," 27 November 2009.

Guarnizo, Luis Eduardo. 2003. "The Economics of Transnational Living," *International Migration Review* 37(3): 666–699.

Guihua, Ma. 2002. "Trade in Vietnamese Brides a Boon for Chinese," *Asia Times*, 14 November 2002.

Gurría, Angel. 2009. "Creating Opportunities—Integration, Employment and Social Mobility: European Experiences and Scope for Manoeuvre," *Comments at the International Symposium on Integration, Employment and Social Mobility*, 26 January 2009. Available at http://www.oecd.org/document/38/0,3343 ,en_2649_33931_42053286_1_1_1_1,00.html.

Hansen, N. E, and I. McClure. 1998. "Protecting Migrants and Ethnic Minorities from Discrimination in Employment: The Danish Experience," *ILO International Migration Papers, No. 25*. Geneva: ILO.

Hansen, Randall. 2000. *Citizenship and Immigration in Post-War Britain: The Institutional Origins of a Multicultural Nation*. Oxford, UK: Oxford University Press.

Hanson, Gordon H. 2008. "The Economic Consequences of the International Migration of Labor," *NBER Working Paper 14490*. Cambridge, MA: NBER.

Harford, Tim, Michael Klein, and Klaus Tilmes. 2005. "The Future of Aid 1," *Public Policy for the Private Sector Note No. 284*. Washington, DC: World Bank.

Harper, Sarah. 2009. "20th Century—Last Century of Youth?" Presentation at Oxford Institute of Ageing, 22 April 2009. (Mimeo.)

Harris, John R., and Michael P. Todaro. 1970. "Migration, Unemployment & Development: A Two-Sector Analysis," *American Economic Review* 60(1): 126–142.

Harzig, Christiane, Dirk Hoerder, and Donna Gabaccia. 2009. *What Is Migration History?* Cambridge, UK: Polity Press.

Hatton, Timothy J. 2007. "Should We Have a WTO for International Migration?" *Economic Policy* 22(50): 339–383.

Hatton, Timothy J., and Jeffrey G. Williamson. 1994. "What Drove the Mass Migrations from Europe in the Late Nineteenth Century," *Population and Development Review* 20(3): 533–557.

———. 1998. *The Age of Mass Migration*. Oxford, UK: Oxford University Press.

———. 2003. "What Fundamentals Drive World Migration?" *WIDER Discussion Paper No. 2003/23*, United Nations University. Helsinki, Finland: UNU-WIDER.

————. 2005. *Global Migration and the World Economy: Two Centuries of Policy and Performance.* Boston: MIT Press.

————. 2009. "Vanishing Third World Emigrants?" *NBER Working Paper No. w14785.* Cambridge, MA: NBER.

Haug, Sonja. 2008. "Migration Networks and Migration Decision-Making," *Journal of Ethnic and Migration Studies* 34(4): 585–605.

Heath, Anthony F., Catherine Rothon, and Elina Kilpi. 2008. "The Second Generation in Western Europe: Education, Unemployment, and Occupational Attainment," *Annual Review of Sociology* 38: 211–235.

Herreros, Francisco, and Henar Criado. 2009. "Social Trust, Social Capital, and Perceptions of Immigration," *Political Studies* 57: 335–357.

Hira, Ron. 2004. "U.S. Immigration Regulations and India's Information Technology Industry," *Technological Forecasting & Social Change* 71: 837–854.

Hoefer, Michael, Nancy Rytina, and Christopher Campbell. 2007. "Estimates of the Unauthorized Immigrant Population Residing in the United States: January 2006," *Population Estimates 2007.* Washington, DC: Office of Immigration Statistics Policy Directorate.

Hoerder, Dirk. 2002. *Cultures in Contact: World Migrations in the Second Millennium.* London: Duke University Press.

Hoffman, Jaco. 2009. "Ageing in Africa," Oxford Institute of Ageing, James Martin 21st Century School, University of Oxford. (Mimeo.)

Hogondorn, Jan S. 1984. "Review Essay: The Economics of the African Slave Trade," *Journal of American History* 70(4): 854–861.

Holmes, Colin. 1995. "Jewish Economic and Refugee Migrations, 1880–1950," in Robin Cohen (eds.), *The Cambridge Survey of World Migration.* Cambridge, UK: Cambridge University Press, pp. 148–153.

Holzmann, Robert, Johannes Koettl, and Taras Chernetsky. 2005. "Portability Regimes of Pension and Health Care Benefits for International Migrants: An Analysis of Issues and Good Practices," *World Bank Social Protection Discussion Paper Series No. 0519.* Washington, DC: World Bank.

Homer-Dixon, Thomas F. 1991. "On the Threshold: Environmental Changes as Causes of Acute Conflict," *International Security* 16(2): 76–116.

House of Lords. 2008. *The Economic Impact of Immigration.* London: The Stationery Office Limited.

Howard, Neil, and Mumtaz Lalani. 2008. "The Politics of Human Trafficking," *St Antony's International Review* 4(1): 5–15.

Howley, Kerry. 2009. "Ideas: Fixing the World; Welcome Guestworkers," *The Atlantic,* July/August 2009.

Hugo, Graeme. 2005. "Migrants in Society: Diversity and Cohesion," *Global Commission on Migration,* September 2005. Available at http://www.gcim.org/attachments/TP6.pdf.

Human Rights Watch. 2004. *Bad Dreams: Exploitation of Migrant Workers in Saudi Arabia.* New York: Human Rights Watch.

Human Security Centre. 2005. *Human Security Report.* Oxford, UK: Oxford University Press.

Hunt, Jennifer. 1992. "The Impact of the 1962 Repatriates from Algeria on the French Labor Market," *Industrial and Labor Relations Review* 45(3): 556–572.

Hunt, Jennifer, and Marjolaine Gauthier-Loiselle. 2008. "How Much Does Immigration Boost Innovation?" *NBER Working Paper 14312.* Cambridge, MA: NBER.

Huntington, Samuel P. 1996. *The Clash of Civilizations and the Remaking of World Order.* New York: Simon and Schuster.

Hyman, Ilene. 2001. "Immigration and Health," *Health Policy Working Paper 01-05.* Ottawa: Health Canada.

Institute for International Education. 2009. *Open Doors 2008: Report on International Education Exchange.* Washington, DC: Institute for International Education.

Institute for Public Policy Research. 2007. *Britain's Immigrants: An Economic Profile.* London: IPPR.

International Crisis Group. 2006. "Perilous Journeys: The Plight of North Koreans in China and Beyond," *Asia Report No. 122,* 26 October 2006. Seoul/Brussels: International Crisis Group.

International Labour Organization. 2004. *Towards a Fair Deal for Migrant Workers in the Global Economy.* Geneva: ILO.

———. 2007. *Forced Labor Statistics Factsheet.* Geneva: ILO.

International Migration Institute. 2008. "Global Migration Futures: Towards a Comprehensive Perspective," presentation at James Martin 21st Century School, 22 April 2008. (Mimeo.)

International Organization for Migration. 2000. *World Migration Report.* Geneva: IOM.

———. 2005. *World Migration 2005: Costs and Benefits of International Migration.* Geneva: IOM.

———. 2008. *World Migration 2008: Managing Labour Mobility in the Evolving Global Economy.* Geneva: IOM.

———. 2009. *Towards Tolerance, Law, and Dignity: Addressing Violence against Foreign Nationals in South Africa.* Geneva: IOM.

Ivakhnyuk, Irina. 2009. "The Russian Migration Policy in the Soviet and Post-Soviet Periods and Its Impact on Human Development in the Region," *UNDP Human Development Report 2009 Background Paper 14.* New York: United Nations Development Programme, Human Development Report Office.

Jacoby, Tamar. 2006. "Immigration Nation," *Foreign Affairs,* November/December 2006.

Jandl, Michael. 2003. "Estimates of the Number of Illegal and Smuggled Immigrants in Europe," presented at 8th International Metropolis Conference, Vienna, Austria, 17 September 2003.

Jaspers, Karl. 1951. *Way to Wisdom: An Introduction to Philosophy.* New Haven, CT: Yale University Press.

Jasso, Guillermina, Douglas S. Massey, Mark R. Rosenzweig, and James P. Smith. 2004. "Immigrant Health—Selectivity and Acculturation," *Labor and Demography*. Available at http://ideas.repec.org/p/wpa/wuwpla/0412002.html.

Jasso, Guillermina, and Mark R. Rosenzweig. 1986. "Family Reunification and the Immigration Multiplier: US Immigration Law, Origin Country Conditions, and the Reproduction of Immigrants," *Demography* 23: 291–311.

Jasso, Guillermina, Mark R. Rosenzweig, and James P. Smith. 2003. "The Earnings of US Immigrants: World Skill Prices, Skill Transferability, and Selectivity." Available at http://econwpa.wustl.edu:80/eps/lab/papers/0312/0312007.pdf.

Jones, Gareth, and Kuba Jaworowski. 2000. "In Parts of Europe, Migrant Workers Head Home," *Reuters*, June 16, 2008.

Joppke, Christian, and Zeev Roshenhek. 2001. "Ethnic-Priority Immigration in Israel and Germany: Resilience versus Demise," *Center for Comparative Immigration Studies Working Paper 45*. San Diego: University of California.

Kaplan, Robert D. 2001. *Soldiers of God: With Islamic Warriors in Afghanistan and Pakistan*. New York: Vintage.

Kapur, Devesh, and John McHale. 2005. *Give Us Your Best and Brightest: The Global Hunt for Talent and Its Impact on the Developing World*. Washington, DC: Center for Global Development.

Karoly, Lynn A., and Constantijn W. A. Panis. 2009. "Supply of and Demand for Skilled Labor in the United States," in Jagdish Bhagwati and Gordon Hanson (eds.), *Skilled Immigration Today: Prospects, Problems and Policies*. Oxford, UK: Oxford University Press, pp. 15–52.

Kashiwazaki, Chikako. 2002. "Japan's Resilient Demand for Foreign Workers," *Migration Information Source* (Migration Policy Institute). Available at http://www.migrationinformation.org/feature/display.cfm.

Kay, Diana. 1995. "The Resettlement of Displaced Persons in Europe, 1946–1951," in Robin Cohen (ed.), *Cambridge World Survey of World Migration*. Cambridge, UK: Cambridge University Press.

Keeley, Charles B. 2001. "The International Refugee Regime(s): The End of the Cold War Matters," *International Migration Review* 35(1): 303–314.

Kerr, Sari Pekkala, and William R. Kerr. 2008. "Economic Impacts of Immigration: A Survey," *Harvard Business School Working Paper 09-013*. Cambridge, MA: Harvard Business School.

Kerr, William R., and William F. Lincoln. 2008. "The Supply Side of Innovation: H-1B Visa Reforms and US Ethnic Invention," *Harvard Business School Working Paper 09-005*. Cambridge, MA: Harvard Business School.

Keung, Nicholas. 2009. "Wanted: Plumbers. Must Not Be Foreign," *Toronto Star*, 29 April 2009.

Kindleberger, Charles. 1986. "International Public Goods without International Government," *American Economic Review* 76(1): 1–13.

King, Desmond. 2000. *Making Americans: Immigration, Race, and the Origins of a Diverse Democracy*. London: Harvard University Press.

Klein, Herbert S. 1995. "European and Asian Migrations to Brazil," in Robin Cohen (ed.), *The Cambridge Survey of World Migration*. Cambridge, UK: Cambridge University Press, pp. 208–214.

———. 1999. *The Atlantic Slave Trade*. Cambridge, UK: Cambridge University Press.

Klein, Sidney, ed. 1987. *The Economics of Mass Migration in the Twentieth Century*. New York: Paragon Books.

Kloss, Katharina. 2008. "Jacques Barrot on Immigration: 'Member States Are Compelled to Solidarity,'" *Café Babel*, 18 October 2008.

Knight, Sam. 2009. "The Human Tsunami," *Financial Times*, 19 June 2009.

Kofman, Eleonore, and Veena Meetoo. 2008. "Family Migration," in International Organization for Migration, *World Migration 2008: Managing Labour Mobility in the Evolving Global Economy*. Geneva: IOM, pp. 151–172.

Koslowski, Rey. 2002. "Human Migration and Pre-Modern World Politics," *International Studies Quarterly* 46(3): 375–399.

———. 2008. "Global Mobility and the Quest for an International Migration Regime," in Joseph Chamie and Luca Dall'Oglio (eds.), *International Migration and Development: Continuing the Dialogue: Legal and Policy Perspectives*. Geneva: IOM.

Krieger, Matthew. 2007. "Brain-Drain Threatens to Set Back Hi-Tech," *The Jerusalem Post*, 8 November 2007.

Kritz, Mary M., and Hania Zlotnik. 1992. "Global Interactions: Migration Systems, Processes, and Policies," in Mary M. Kritz, Lin Lean Lim, and Hania Zlotnik (eds.), *International Migration Systems: A Global Approach*. Oxford, UK: Oxford University Press, pp. 1–16.

Kuznetsov, Yevgeny N., ed. 2006. *Diaspora Networks and the International Migration of Skills: How Countries Can Draw on Their Talent Abroad*. Washington, DC: World Bank Institute.

Lahav, Gallya. 2003a. "Migration and Security: The Role of Non-State Actors and Civil Liberties in Liberal Democracies." Available at http://www.pfcmc.com/esa/population/meetings/secoord2003/ITT_COOR2_CH16_Lahav.pdf.

———. 2003b. "The Rise of Non-State Actors in Migration Regulation in the United States and Europe: Changing the Gatekeepers or 'Bringing the State Back In'?" in Nancy Foner, Rubén G. Rumbaut, and Steven James Gold (eds.), *Immigration Research for a New Century: Multidisciplinary Perspectives*. London: Russell Sage Foundation.

Landau, Loren B., and Aurelia Wa Kabwe Segatti. 2009. "Human Development Impacts of Migration: South Africa," *UNDP Human Development Report 2009 Background Paper 05*. New York: United Nations Development Programme, Human Development Report Office.

Legrain, Philippe. 2006. *Immigrants: Your Country Needs Them*. London: Little Brown.

Levitt, Peggy. 1998. "Social Remittances: Migration Driven Local-Level Forms of Cultural Diffusion," *International Migration Review* 32(4): 926–948.

———. 2001. *The Transnational Villagers*. Stanford: University of California Press.

———. 2009. "Roots and Routes: Understanding the Lives of the Second Generation Transnationally," *Journal of Ethnic and Racial Studies* 35(7): 1225–1242.

Lewis, G. J. 1983. *Human Migration: A Geographical Perspective.* New York: Taylor and Francis.

Lindert, Peter H., and Jeffrey G. Williamson. 2003. "Does Globalization Make the World More Unequal?" in Michael D. Bordo, Alan M. Taylor, and Jeffrey G. Williamson (eds.), *Globalization in Historical Perspective.* Chicago: University of Chicago Press, pp. 227–271.

Lindley, Anna. 2008. "Conflict-Induced Migration and Remittances: Exploring Conceptual Frameworks," *Working Paper Series No. 17,* Refugee Studies Centre, University of Oxford. Oxford, UK: Refugee Studies Centre.

Lluberas, Rodrigo. 2007. "The Untapped Skilled Labour of Latin America," *Towers Watson Technical Paper.* Available at http://papers.ssrn.com/sol3/papers.cfm?abstract_id=1261978.

Losch, Bruno. 2008. "Migrations and the Challenge of Demographic and Economic Transitions in the New Globalization Era," *SSRC Migration & Development Conference Paper No. 12.* Brooklyn, NY: SSRC.

Lowell, Lindsay. 2008. "Highly Skilled Migration," in *World Migration 2008: Managing Labour Mobility in the Evolving Global Economy.* Geneva: International Organization for Migration.

Lucas, Robert E. B. 2005. *International Migration and Economic Development: Lessons from Low-Income Countries.* Cheltenham, UK: Edward Elgar.

Lucassen, Jan, and Leo Lucassen, eds. 1997. *Migration, Migration History, History: Old Paradigms and New Perspectives.* Bern: Peter Lang.

Lutz, Wolfgang, Warren Sanderson, Sergei Scherbov, and Samir K.C. 2008. *Demographic and Human Capital Trends in Eastern Europe and Sub-Saharan Africa.* Washington, DC: Migration Policy Institute.

Madhaven, M. 1987. "Indian Emigration," in Sidney Klein (ed.), *The Economics of Mass Migration in the Twentieth Century.* New York: Dragon House.

Manning, Patrick. 2005. *Migration in World History.* London: Routledge.

———. 2006. "*Homo sapiens* Populates the Earth: A Provisional Synthesis, Privileging Linguistic Evidence," *Journal of World History* 17(2): 115–158.

Marrus, Michael R. 2002. *The Unwanted: European Refugees from the First World War through the Cold War.* Philadelphia: Temple University Press.

Marshall, T. H. 1950. "Citizenship and Social Class," in T. H. Marshall and T. Bottomore (eds.), *Citizenship and Social Class.* London: Pluto Press.

Martin, Philip L. 1993. *Trade and Migration: NAFTA and Agriculture.* Washington, DC: Institute for International Economics.

———. 2002. "Mexican Workers and U.S. Agriculture: The Revolving Door," *International Migration Review* 36(4): 1124–1142.

———. 2008. "Low and Semi-Skilled Workers Abroad," in International Organization for Migration, *World Migration 2008: Managing Labor Mobility in the Evolving Global Economy.* Geneva: IOM, pp. 77–104.

Martin, Philip L., Manolo Abella, and Christiane Kuptsch. 2006. *Managing Labor Migration in the Twenty-first Century.* London: Yale University Press.

Martin, Philip L., and Susan Martin. 2006. "GCIM: A New Global Migration Facility," *International Migration* 44(1): 5–12.

Martin, Philip L., Susan Martin, and Patrick Weil. 2006. *Managing Migration: The Promise of Cooperation.* Oxford, UK: Lexington Books.

Martin, Philip L., and J. Edward Taylor. 2001. "Managing Migration: The Role of Economic Policies," in Aristide R. Zolberg and Peter M. Benda (eds.), *Global Migrants Global Refugees: Problems and Solutions.* Oxford, UK: Berghahn Books, pp. 95–120.

Martin, Steve I. 1999. *Britain's Slave Trade.* London: Channel 4 Books.

Marx, Karl. 1976. *Capital: A Critique of Political Economy,* vol. 1, trans. Ben Fowles. Hammondsworth, UK: Penguin.

Massey, Douglas S., Joaquin Arango, Graeme Hugo, Ali Kouaouci, Adela Pellegrino, and J. Edward Taylor. 1993. "Theories of International Migration: A Review and Appraisal," *Population and Development Review* 19(3): 431–466.

———. 2002. *Worlds in Motion: Understanding International Migration at the End of the Millennium.* Oxford, UK: Oxford University Press.

Massey, Douglas S., Jorge Durand, and Nolan J. Malone. 2002. *Beyond Smoke and Mirrors: Mexican Immigration in an Era of Economic Integration.* New York: Russell Sage Foundation.

Massey, Douglas S., and J. Edward Taylor. 2004. "Back to the Future: Immigration Research, Immigration Policy, and Globalization in the Twenty-First Century," in Douglas S. Massey and J. Edward Taylor (eds.), *International Migration: Prospects and Policies in a Global Market.* Oxford, UK: Oxford University Press, pp. 373–387.

Mattoo, Aaditya, Ileana Cristina Neagu, and Çağlar Özden. 2005. "Brain Waste? Educated Immigrants in the U.S. Labor Market," *World Bank Policy Research Working Paper 3581.* Washington, DC: World Bank.

McCullagh, Declan. 2005. "Gates Wants to Scrap H-1B Visa Restrictions," *ZDNet News,* 27 April 2005. Available at http://news.zdnet.com/2100-3513_22-142533.html.

McKeown, Adam. 2003. "Ritualization of Regulation: The Enforcement of Chinese Exclusion in the United States and China," *The American Historical Review* 108(2): 377–403.

———. 2004. "Global Migration, 1846–1940," *Journal of World History* 15(2): 155–189.

McKie, Robin. 2009. "Scientists to Issue Stark Warning over Dramatic New Sea Level Figures," *The Observer,* 8 March 2009.

McLaughlan, Gail, and John Salt. 2002. "Migration Policies toward Highly Skilled Foreign Workers," *Report to the UK Home Office,* March 2002. Available at http://rds.homeoffice.gov.uk/rds/pdfs2/migrationpolicies.pdf.

McMaster, Don. 2001. *Asylum Seekers—Australia's Response to Refugees*. Melbourne, Australia: Melbourne University Press.

McNeill, John R. 2001. "Biological Exchange and Biological Invasion in World History," in Solvi Sogner (ed.), *Making Sense of Global History*. Oslo: Universitetsforlaget, pp. 106–119.

McNeill, William H. 1963 [1991]. *The Rise of the West: A History of the Human Community* [with a retrospective essay]. Chicago: University of Chicago Press.

———. 1967. *A World History*. Oxford, UK: Oxford University Press.

———. 1978. "Human Migration: A Historical Overview," in William H. McNeill and Ruth S Adams (eds), *Human Migration: Patterns and Policies*. Bloomington: Indiana University Press.

———. 1982. *The Pursuit of Power: Technology, Armed Force, and Society since AD 1000*. Oxford, UK: Blackwell.

———. 1984. "Human Migration in Historical Perspective," *Population and Development Review* 10(1): 1–18.

———. 1998. "World History and the Rise and Fall of the West," *Journal of World History* 9(2): 215–236.

McVeigh, Karen. 2008. "Skilled Migrants Are Vital to Economy, Study Says," *The Guardian*, 25 March 2008.

Mereu, Francesca. 2001. "Russia: Moscow Markets Present Troubled Tableau of Life of City's Immigrants," *Radio Free Europe/Radio Liberty*, 14 November 2001. Available at http://www.rferl.org/content/article/1097984.html.

Messina, Anthony M., and Gallya Lahav, eds. 2006. *The Migration Reader: Exploring Politics and Policies*. London: Lynne Rienner Publishers.

Meyer, Jean-Baptiste. 2001. "Network Approach versus Brain Drain: Lessons from the Diaspora," *International Migration Quarterly Review* 39(5): 91–110.

Milanovic, Branko. 2003. "The Two Faces of Globalization: Against Globalization as We Know It," *World Development* 31(4): 667–683.

Ministry of Environment and Forests. 2008. *Bangladesh Climate Change Strategy and Action Plan 2008*. Dhaka, Bangladesh: Ministry of Environment and Forests, Government of the People's Republic of Bangladesh.

Minnesota Department of Health. 2003. *Eliminating Health Disparities Initiative: 2003 Report to the Legislature*. Available at http://www.health.state.mn.us/ommh/legrpt012103.pdf.

Money, Jeannette. 1999. *Fences and Neighbors: The Political Geography of Immigration Control*. Ithaca, NY: Cornell University Press.

Moses, Jonathon W. 2006. *International Migration: Globalization's Last Frontier*. London: Zed Books.

Naim, Moises. 2005. *Illicit: How Smugglers, Traffickers, and Copycats Are Hijacking the Global Economy*. New York: Doubleday.

Nathan, Max. 2008. *Your Place or Mine? The Local Economics of Migration*. London: Institute for Public Policy Research.

National Foundation for American Policy. 2006. "Nearly 40 Asian American and Pacific Island Organizations Unite to Demand Fair and Humane Integration Program," Press Release 19 May 2006. Available at http://www.apalc.org/pdffiles/Immigration%20Reform%20Press%20Release%200506.pdf.

National Research Council. 2008. "Research on Future Skill Demands: A Workshop Summary," Center for Education, Division of Behavioral and Social Sciences and Education. Washington, DC: The National Academies Press.

Nemeth, Charlan J. 1986. "Differential Contributions of Majority and Minority Influence," *Psychological Review* 93(1): 23–32.

Ness, Immanuel. 2005. *Immigrants, Unions, and the New U.S. Labor Market*. Philadelphia: Temple University Press.

New Scientist. 2009. "French Immigrants Founded British Farms," 5 December 2009.
———. 2010. "Robo-guards and the Borders of the Future," 9 January 2010.

Nickell, Stephen. 2009. "Migration Watch," *Prospect Magazine*, 23 July 2009, issue 161.

Noh, Samuel, and Violet Kaspar. 2003. *Diversity and Immigrant Health*. Toronto: University of Toronto.

Northrup, David. 1995. *Indentured Labor in the Age of Imperialism: 1834–1922*. Cambridge, UK: Cambridge University Press.
———. 1998. "Vasco da Gama and Africa: An Era of Mutual Discovery, 1497–1800," *Journal of World History* 9(2): 189–211.
———. 2003. "Free and Unfree Labor Migration, 1600–1900: An Introduction," *Journal of World History* 14(2): 125–130.

Nunn, Nathan. 2008. "The Long-Term Effects of Africa's Slave Trade," *The Quarterly Journal of Economics* 123(1): 139–176.

The Observer. 2010. "A Portrait of the New UK Migrant," 17 January 2010.

Olivier, Liz. 2009. "Legal and Regulatory Frameworks and Scientific Mobility Giving Something Back: Exploring Making a Contribution at a Distance Policy and Practice," *ResIST Thematic Paper 1*, January 2009. Available at http://www.resist-research.net/paperslibrary/full-and-final-results.aspx.

Olson, Steve. 2002. *Mapping Human History*. Boston: Mariner.

Oreopoulos, Philip. 2009. "Why Do Skilled Immigrants Struggle in the Labor Market? A Field Experiment with Six Thousand Resumes," *Metropolis Working Paper 09-03*. Vancouver: Metropolis British Columbia.

Organization for Economic Cooperation and Development. 2007. *International Migration Outlook 2007—SOPEMI*. Paris: OECD.
———. 2008. *International Migration Outlook 2008—SOPEMI*. Paris: OECD.

Ortega, Francesc, and Giovanni Peri. 2009. "The Causes and Effects of International Migrations: Evidence from OECD Countries 1980–2005," *Working Paper 14833*. Cambridge, MA: NBER.

Ortega, Jose Antonio. 2005. "What Are the Implications of the Demographic Transitions Process for 21st Century European Population?" Available at: http://circa.europa.eu/irc/dsis/jointestatunece/info/data/paper_ortega.pdf.

Osterholm, Michael T. 2005. "Preparing for the Next Pandemic," *New York Times*, 21 June 2005.

O'Sullivan, Dan. 1984. *The Age of Discovery, 1400–1550*. London: Longman.

Ottaviano, Gianmarco I. P., and Giovanni Peri. 2004. "The Economic Value of Cultural Diversity: Evidence from US Cities," *NBER Working Paper No. 10904*, Cambridge, MA: NBER.

Ozden, Caglar, and Maurice Schiff, eds. 2006. *International Migration, Remittances, and the Brain Drain*. Basingstoke, UK: Palgrave MacMillan.

Page, Scott E. 2007. *The Difference: How the Power of Diversity Creates Better Groups, Firms, Schools, and Societies*. Princeton, NJ. Princeton University Press.

Papademetriou, Demetrios. 2003. "Managing Rapid and Deep Change in the Newest Age of Migration," *Political Quarterly* 74(1): 39–58.

Parry, John H. 1981. *The Discovery of the Sea*. Berkeley: University of California Press.

Parsons, Christopher R., Ronald Skeldon, Terrie L. Walmsley, and L. Alan Winters. 2007. "Quantifying International Migration: A Database of Bilateral Migrant Stocks," *World Bank Policy Research Working Paper 4165*, March 2007. Washington, DC: World Bank.

Pasternak, Charles. 2004. *Quest: The Essence of Humanity*. Chichester, UK: John Wiley and Sons, Ltd.

Percept, Adeline, and Clément Perrouault. 2009. "Spain Offers Immigrants an Incentive to Leave," *France 24*, 22 January 2009. Available at http://www.france24 .com/en/20090122-spain-immigration-zapatero-financial-crisis-unemployment.

Peri, Giovanni, and Chad Sparber. 2008. "Task Specialization, Immigration, and Wages," *CDP No 02/08*, Centre for Research and Analysis of Migration, University College London. London: CReAM.

Plotkin, Norman. 1987. "Latin America after World War II," in Sidney Klein (ed.), *The Economics of Mass Migration in the Twentieth Century*. New York: Paragon Books

Pollard, Naomi, Maria Latorre, and Dhananjayan Sriskandarajah. 2008. *Floodgates or Turnstiles? Post-EU Enlargement Migration Flows to (and from) the UK*. London: IPPR.

Pomerantz, Kenneth. 2000. *China, Europe, and the Making of the Modern Economy*. Princeton, NJ: Princeton University Press.

Portes, Alejandro. 1997. "Immigration Theory for a New Century: Some Problems and Opportunities," *International Migration Review* 31: 799–825.

———. 2008. "Migration and Development: A Conceptual Review of the Evidence," in Stephen Castles and Raul Delgado Wise (eds.), *Migration and Development: Perspectives from the South*. Geneva: IOM, pp.17–42.

Portes, Alejandro, and Jozsef Borocz. 1989. "Contemporary Immigration: Theoretical Perspectives on Its Determinants and Modes of Incorporation," *International Migration Review* 23(3): 606–630.

Portes, Alejandro, and Josh DeWind. 2004. "A Cross-Atlantic Dialogue: The Progress of Research and Theory in the Study of International Migration," *International Migration Review* 38(3): 828–851.

Potts, Lydia. 1990. *A World Labour Market: A History of Migration*. London: Zed Books.

Preston, Julia. 2009. "Mexican Data Show Migration to U.S. in Decline," *New York Times*, 14 May 2009.

Pritchett, Lant. 1997. "Divergence, Big Time," *Journal of Economic Perspectives* 11(3): 3–17.

———. 2004. "Boom Towns and Ghost Countries: Geography, Agglomeration, and Population Mobility," *CGD Working Paper 36*. Washington, DC: Center for Global Development.

———. 2006. *Let Their People Come: Breaking the Gridlock on Global Labor Mobility*. Washington, DC: Center for Global Development.

Putnam, Robert D. 2007. "E Pluribus Unum: Diversity and Community in the Twenty-first Century, The 2006 Johan Skytte Prize Lecture," *Scandinavian Political Studies* 30(2): 137–174.

Rapoport, Hillel, and Frédéric Docquier. 2005. "The Economics of Migrants' Remittances," *IZA DP No. 1531E*. Bonn, Germany: Institute for the Study of Labor (IZA).

Ratha, Dilip. 2007. "Leveraging Remittances for Development," *Migration Policy Institute Policy Brief, June 2007*. Washington, DC: Migration Policy Institute.

Ratha, Dilip, Sanket Mohapatra, and Ani Silwal. 2009. "Outlook for Remittance Flows 2009–2011: Remittances Expected to Fall by 7–10 Percent in 2009," *Migration and Development Brief No. 10*. Washington, DC: World Bank.

———. 2010. "Outlook for Remittance Flows 2010–2011: Remittance Flows to Developing Countries Remained Resilient in 2009, Expected to Recover during 2010–11," *Migration and Development Brief No.12*. Washington, DC: World Bank.

Ratha, Dilip, Sanket Mohapatra, and Zhimei Xu. 2008. "Outlook for Remittance Flows 2008–2010: Growth Expected to Moderate Significantly, but Flows to Remain Resilient," *Migration and Development Brief No. 8*. Washington, DC: World Bank.

Recchi, Ettore, Damian Tambini, Emiliana Baldoni, David Williams, Kristin Surak, and Adrian Favell. 2003. "Intra–EU Migration: A Socio-Demographic Overview," *Working Paper 3*, Pioneur Project. Available at: http://www.obets.ua.es/pioneur/documentos_public.php.

Reitz, Jeffrey G. 2005. "Tapping Immigrants' Skills: New Directions for Canadian Immigration Policy in the Knowledge Economy," *IRPP Choices* 11(1).

Reyes, Belinda T., and Hans Johnson. 2000. *Holding the Line? The Effect of Recent Border Build-up on Unauthorized Immigration*. San Francisco: Public Policy Institute of California.

Richards, John F. 1997. "Early Modern India and World History," *Journal of World History* 8(2): 197–209.

Robinson, Vaughan. 1995. "The Migration of East African Asians to the UK," in Robin Cohen (ed.), *The Cambridge Survey of World Migration*. Cambridge, UK: Cambridge University Press, pp. 331–336.

Robinson, Vaughan, and Jeremy Segrott. 2002. "Understanding the Decision-Making of Asylum-Seekers," *Home Office Research Study 243*, Home Office Research, Development and Statistics Directorate, July 2002. London: UK Home Office.

Rodenberg, Janet. 1993. *Emancipation or Subordination? Consequences of Female Migration for Migrants and Their Families in Internal Migration of Women in Developing Countries.* New York: United Nations.

Rodrik, Dani. 2002. "Final remarks," in T. Boeri, G. Hanson, and B. McCormick (eds.), *Immigration Policy and the Welfare System.* Oxford, UK: Oxford University Press, pp. 314–317.

Rowthorn, Robert. 2006. "Numbers Matter: It Is Time for Mainstream Politics to Debate the Scale of British Immigration," *Prospect Magazine* 125, August 2006.

———. 2008. "The Fiscal Impact of Immigration on the Advanced Economies," *Oxford Review of Economic Policy*, 24: 560–580.

Salt, Bernard. 2008. "The Global Skills Convergence," *KPMG International*, September 2008. Available at http://www.bernardsalt.com.au/media/Global_Skills_Convergence.pdf.

Salt, John. 2005. "Types of Migration in Europe: Implications and Policy Concerns," presented at European Population Conference 2005: Demographic Challenges for Social Cohesion, 7–8 April 2005, Strasbourg.

Salt, John, and Jane Millar. 2006. "Foreign Labour in the United Kingdom: Current Patterns and Trends," Office for National Statistics, Labour Market Trends, October 2006.

Salter, Mark B. 2004. "Passports, Mobility, and Security: How Smart Can a Border Be?" *International Studies Perspectives* 5: 71–91.

Sang-Hun, Choe. 2005. "North Koreans Escape—For a Price" *International Herald Tribune*, 29 April 2005.

Sassen, Saskia. 1988. *The Mobility of Labour and Capital: A Study of International Investment and Labor Flow.* Cambridge, UK: Cambridge University Press.

———. 1996. *Losing Control?* New York: Columbia University Press.

———. 1999. *Guests and Aliens.* New York: The Free Press.

Saxenian, AnnaLee. 2005. "From Brain Drain to Brain Circulation: Transnational Communities and Regional Upgrading in India and China," *Studies in Comparative International Development* 40(2).

Scholte, Jan Aart. 2000. *Globalization: A Critical Introduction.* Basingstoke, UK: Palgrave MacMillan.

Schumpeter, Joseph. 1942 [1975]. *Capitalism, Socialism and Democracy.* New York: Harper.

Sciortino, Rosalia, and Sureeporn Punpuing. 2009. *International Migration in Thailand 2009.* Geneva: IOM.

Semino, Ornella, Giuseppe Passarino et al. 2000. "The Genetic Legacy of Paleolithic *Homo sapiens sapiens* in Extant Europeans: A Y-Chromosome Perspective," *Science* 290: 1155–1159.

Sen, Amartya. 1981. *Poverty and Famines: An Essay on Entitlement and Depriva-tion*. Oxford, UK: Oxford University Press.

———. 1999. *Development as Freedom*. New York: Anchor Books.

Shafir, Gershon. 1995. "Zionist Immigration and Colonization in Palestine in 1948," in Robin Cohen (ed.), *The Cambridge Survey of World Migration*. Cambridge, UK: Cambridge University Press, pp. 405–409.

Shah, Nasra M. 1998. "The Role of Social Networks among South Asian Male Mi-grants in Kuwait," in Reginald Appleyard (ed.), *Emigration Dynamics in De-veloping Countries. Vol. II: South Asia*. Aldershot, UK: Ashgate Publishing, pp. 30–70.

Shah, Nasra M., and Indu Menon. 1999. "Chain Migration through the Social Net-work: Experience of Labour Migrants in Kuwait," *International Migration* 37(2): 361–382.

Shogren, Jason, Richard Horan, and Erwin Bulte. 2005. "How Trade Saved Human-ity from Biological Exclusion: An Economic Theory of Neanderthal Extinction," *Journal of Economic Behavior and Organization* 58: 1–29.

Siskin, Alison. 2004. "Immigration-Related Detention: Current Legislative Issues," *CRS Report for Congress*, 28 April 2004. Washington, DC: Congressional Re-search Service.

Smith, James P., and Barry Edmonston, eds. 1997. *The New Americans: Economic, Demographic, and Fiscal Effects of Immigration*. Washington, DC: National Academy Press.

Smith, Michael E. 1984. "The Aztlan Migrations of the Nuhuatl: Myth or History?" *Ethnohistory* 31(3): 153–186.

Smith, Robert L. 2009. "Waves of Immigrants Now Calling Philadelphia Home; New Welcoming Center Idea behind the Lure," *The Plain Dealer* (Cleveland), 20 May 2009.

Solberg, Carl. 1978. "Mass Migrations in Argentina, 1870–1970," in William H. Mc-Neill and Ruth Adams (eds.), *Human Migration: Patterns and Policies*. London: Indiana University Press, pp. 146–166.

Solow, Barbara L. 2001. "The Transatlantic Slave Trade: A New Census," *The William and Mary Quarterly* 58(1): 9–16.

Soroka, Stuart, Keith Banting, and Richard Johnston. 2006. "Immigration and Re-distribution in the Global Era," in Pranab Bardhan, Samuel Bowles, and Michael Wallerstein (eds.), *Globalization and Egalitarian Redistribution*. Princeton, NJ: Princeton University Press, pp. 261–288.

Southern Metropolis Daily. 2008. "'Chocolate City'—Africans Seek Their dreams in China," 23 January 2008. Translated copy available at http://blog.foolsmountain .com/2008/06/14/chocolate-city-africans-seek-their-dreams-in-china/.

Spencer, Ian R. G. 1997. *British Immigration Policy since 1939: The Making of Multi-Racial Britain*. London: Routledge.

Stalker, Peter. 2000. *Workers without Frontiers*. New York: ILO/Lynne Rienner.

Stark, Oded. 2005. "The New Economics of Brain Drain," World Economics 6(2): 137–140.

Stark, Oded, and David E. Bloom. 1985. "The New Economics of Labour Migration," *The American Economic Review* 75(2): 173–178.

Stern, Nicholas, ed. 2006. *The Economics of Climate Change: The Stern Review.* Cambridge, UK: Cambridge University Press.

Stern, William J. 2003. "What *Gangs of New York* Misses," *City Journal*, 14 January 2003.

Stolle, Dietlind, Stuart Soroka, and Richard Johnston. 2008. "When Does Diversity Erode Trust? Neighborhood Diversity, Interpersonal Trust and the Mediating Effect of Social Interactions," *Political Studies* 56: 57–75.

Straubhaar, Thomas. 2001. "Why Do We Need a General Agreement on the Movements of People (GAMP)?" in Bimal Ghosh (ed.), *Managed Migration: Time for a New International Regime?* Oxford, UK: Oxford University Press, pp. 110–136.

Strikwerda, Carl. 1999. "Tides of Migration, Currents of History: The State, Economy, and the Transatlantic Movement of Labour in the Nineteenth and Twentieth Centuries," *International Review of Social History* 44: 367–394.

Subramaniana, Arvind, and Shang-Jin Wei. 2007. "The WTO Promotes Trade, Strongly but Unevenly," *Journal of International Economics* 72(1): 151–175.

Sumption, Madeleine, and Will Somerville. 2009. *The UK's New Europeans Progress and Challenges Five Years after Accession.* London: Equality and Human Rights Commission and Migration Policy Institute.

The Sunday Times. 2009. "A Generation Lost to the Deep," 22 November 2009.

Sykes, Brian. 2001. *The Seven Daughters of Eve.* London: Corgi Books.

Tanaka, Hiroyuki. 2008. "North Korea: Understanding Migration to and from a Closed Country," *Migration Policy Institute.* Available at http://www.migration information.org/Profiles/display.cfm?id=668.

Thomas, Rebekah. 2005. "Biometrics, International Migrants and Human Rights," *European Journal of Migration and Law* 7: 377–411.

Tilly, Charles. 1990. "Transplanted Networks," in Virginia Yans-McLaughlin (ed), *Immigration Reconsidered: History, Sociology, and Politics.* Oxford, UK: Oxford University Press, pp. 79–95.

———. 2006. "Migration in Modern European History," in Anthony M. Messina and Gallya Lahav (eds.), *The Migration Reader: Exploring Politics and Policies.* London: Lynne Rienner.

Torpey, John. 2000a. *The Invention of the Passport: Surveillance, Citizenship and the State.* Cambridge, UK: Cambridge University Press.

———. 2000b. "States and the Regulation of Migration in the Twentieth-Century North Atlantic World," in Peter Andreas and Timothy Snyder (eds.), *The Wall around the West: State Borders and Immigration Controls in North America and Europe.* Oxford, UK: Rowan and Littlefield Publishers, Inc., pp. 31–54.

Transatlantic Trends. 2008. *Transatlantic Trends: Immigration*. Washington, DC: German Marshall Fund of the United States.

Traven, B. 1934 [1991]. *Death Ship: The Story of an American Sailor*. Knopf: New York, republished by Lawrence Books: New York.

Travis, Alan. 2009. "East Europeans Seeking Work in UK down 47%," *The Guardian*, 25 February 2009.

Tremblay, Karine. 2005. "Academic Mobility and Immigration," *Journal of Studies in International Education* 9(3): 196–228.

UNESCO. 2004. *Gender and Education for All: The Leap to Equality*. Paris: UNESCO.

UNHCR. 2005. *State of the World's Refugees*. Oxford, UK: Oxford University Press.

———. 2006. *State of the World's Refugees 2006*. New York: UNHCR.

———. 2008a. *2007 Global Trends: Refugees, Asylum-Seekers, Returnees, Internally Displaced and Stateless Persons*. Geneva: UNHCR.

———. 2008b. *2007 UNHCR Statistical Annex*. Geneva: UNHRC.

———. 2009. *2008 Global Trends: Refugees, Asylum-Seekers, Returnees, Internally Displaced and Stateless Persons*. UNHCR: Geneva.

UNICEF. 2006. *State of the World's Children: Excluded and Invisible*. New York: UNICEF.

United Nations. 2000. *Replacement Migration: Is It a Solution to Declining and Ageing Populations?* New York: United Nations.

———. 2004a. *World Economic and Social Survey 2004: International Migration*. New York: United Nations.

———. 2004b. *World Population Prospects: 2004 Revision*. New York: United Nations.

———. 2006. "Report of the Secretary-General, International Migration and Development, UN General Assembly, 60th Session," *UN Doc. A/60/871*, 18 May 2006. New York: United Nations.

———. 2009. *Population Prospects: The 2008 Revision*. Available at http://esa.un .org/unpp.

United Nations Department of Economic and Social Affairs. 2008. *World Urbanization Prospects: The 2007 Revision*. New York: United Nations.

United Nations Development Programme. 2009. *Human Development Report 2009 Overcoming Barriers: Human Mobility and Development*. New York: UNDP.

United Nations Office on Drugs and Crime. 2006. *Organized Crime and Irregular Migration from Africa to Europe*. Vienna: UNODC.

———. 2009. *The Global Report on Trafficking in Persons*. Vienna: UNODC.

United Nations Population Division. 2004. "Seminar on the Relevance of Population Aspects for the Achievement of the Millennium Development Goals," New York, 17–19 November 2004. Available at http://www.un.org/esa/population/publications/PopAspectsMDG/.

———. 2006. *Trends in Total Migrant Stock: The 2005 Revision*. New York: United Nations.

United Nations Press Centre. 2009. "Maldives: Climate Change Threatens Right to Housing, Says UN Expert," 26 February 2009. Available at http://www.un.org/apps/news/story.asp?NewsID=30026&Cr=housing&Cr1=climate.

U.S. Committee for Refugees and Immigrants. 2008. *World Refugee Survey 2008*. Washington, DC: USCRI.

U.S. Government. 1993. *Statistical Yearbook and Naturalization Service*. Washington, DC: Government Printing Office.

U.S. Immigration and Customs Enforcement. 2007. *Fiscal Year 2007 Annual Report: Protecting National Security and Upholding Public Safety*. Available at http://www.ice.gov/doclib/about/ice07ar_final.pdf.

Vacca, John R. 2007. *Biometric Technologies and Verification System*. Oxford, UK: Butterworth-Heinemann.

Vasta, Ellie. 2007. "Accommodating Diversity: Why Current Critiques of Multiculturalism Miss the Point," *COMPAS Working Paper No. 53*, Centre on Migration, Policy and Society, University of Oxford. Oxford, UK: COMPAS.

Vertovec, Steven. 2003. "Migration and Other Modes of Transnationalism: Towards Conceptual Cross-Fertilization," *International Migration Review* 37(3): 641–665.

———. 2004. "Migration Transnationalism and Modes of Transformation," *International Migration Review* 38(3): 970–1001.

———. 2009. *Transnationalism*. London: Routledge.

Vidal, John. 2008. "UK Gives £50m to Bangladesh Climate Change Fund," *The Guardian*, 8 September 2008.

Vigneswaran, Darshan. 2008. "Enduring Territoriality: South African Immigration Control," *Political Geography* 27: 783–801.

Vincent-Lancrin, Stéphan. 2008. "Student Mobility, Internationalization of Higher Education and Skilled Migration," in International Organization for Migration, *World Migration 2008: Managing Labor Mobility in the Evolving Global Economy*. Geneva: IOM.

———. 2009. "How the Crisis Might Transform Higher Education: Some Scenarios," presented at Higher Education at a Time of Crisis: Challenges and Opportunities, Copenhagen Business School, 29–30 June 2009.

Wadhwa, Vivek. 2009. "A Reverse Brain Drain," *Issues in Science and Technology* 25(3). Available at http://www.issues.org/25.3/wadhwa.html

Wadhwa, Vivek, AnnaLee Saxenian, Richard Freeman, Gary Gereffi, and Alex Salkever. 2009. "America's Loss Is the World's Gain: America's New Immigrant Entrepreneurs, Part IV," 2 March 2009. Available at SSRN: http://ssrn.com/abstract=1348616

Walker, John. 1987. "Migration to Australia and New Zealand," in Sidney Klein (ed.), *The Economics of Mass Migration in the Twentieth Century*. New York: Dragon House.

Walzer, Michael. 1983. *Spheres of Justice*. New York: Basic Books.

Warner, Koko, Tamer Afifi, Olivia Dun, Marc Stal, and Sophia Schmidl. 2008. "Human Security, Climate Change and Environmentally Induced Migration,"

United Nations University Institute for Environment and Human Security Report. Bonn, Germany: UNU-EHS.

Watson, Andrew. 1983. *Agricultural Innovation in the Early Islamic World: The Diffusion of Crops and Farming Techniques, 700–1100.* Cambridge, UK: Cambridge University Press.

Weatherford, Jack. 2004. *Genghis Khan and the Making of the Modern World.* New York: Three Rivers Press.

Wells, Spencer. 2002. *The Journey of Man: A Genetic Odyssey.* Princeton, NJ: Princeton University Press.

Wertheimer, Jack. 1987. *Unwelcome Strangers: East European Jews in Imperial Germany.* Oxford, UK: Oxford University Press.

Wilkinson, Will. 2009. "The Immigration Fallacy," *The Week Newsletter,* 27 April 2009.

Williamson, Jeffrey. 2004. "The Political Economy of World Mass Migration: Comparing Two Global Centuries," *American Enterprise Institute,* 11 May 2004.

Winder, Robert. 2004. *Bloody Foreigners: The Story of Immigration to Britain.* London: Abacus.

Winters, L. Alan, Terrie L. Walmsley, Zhen Kun Wang, and Roman Grynberg. 2003. "Liberalising Temporary Movement of Natural Persons: An Agenda for the Development Round," *World Economy* 26: 1137–1161.

Wise, Raul Delgado. 2008. "The Mexico–United States Migratory System: Dilemmas of Regional Integration, Development, and Emigration," in Stephen Castles and Raul Delgado Wise (eds.), *Migration and Development: Perspectives from the South.* Geneva: IOM, pp. 113–142.

World Bank. 1995. *World Development Report 1995: Workers in an Integrating World.* Oxford, UK: Oxford University Press.

———. 2005. *Global Economic Prospects: Economic Implications of Remittances and Migration.* Washington, DC: World Bank.

———. 2008. *World Development Report 2009: Reshaping Economic Geography.* Washington, DC: World Bank.

———. 2009. *Prospects for the Global Econom.* Available at http://go.worldbank.org/PF6VWYXS10.

World Health Organization. 2003. *International Migration, Health and Human Rights.* Geneva: WHO.

Wright, Robert. 2001. *Nonzero: The Logic of Human Destiny.* London: Vintage.

Yakobson, Alexander, and Amnon Rubinstein. 2005. *Democratic Norms, Diasporas, and Israel's Law of Return.* New York: American Jewish Committee.

Yasuo, Wakatsuki. 1995. *Sengo hikiage no kiroku.* Tokyo: Jiji Tsoshinsha.

Zakaria, Fareed. 2009. *The Post-American World and The Rise of the Rest.* London: Penguin.

Zegers de Beijl, Roger. 1999. *Migrant Discrimination in the Labour Market: A Comparative Study of Four European Countries.* Geneva: ILO.

Zlotnik, Hania. 2004. "Population Growth and International Migration," in Douglas S. Massey and J. Edward Taylor (eds.), *International Migration: Prospects and Policies in a Global Market*. Oxford, UK: Oxford University Press, pp. 15–34.

———. 2005. "International Migration Trends since 1980," presented at International Migration and the Millennium Development Goals: Selected Papers of the UNFPA Expert Group Meeting, Marrakech, Morocco, 11–12 May 2005.

———. 2008. "Migration, Mobility, Urbanization, and Development," *SSRC Migration and Development Conference Paper No. 22*. Brooklyn, NY: SSRC.

Zolberg, Aristide R. 1997. "Global Movements, Global Walls: Responses to Migration, 1885 1925," in Wang Gungwu (ed.), *Global History and Migrations*. Boulder, Colorado: Westview Press, pp. 279–303.

———. 2006. "Patterns of International Migration Policy," in Anthony M. Messina and Gallya Lahav (eds.), *The Migration Reader: Exploring Politics and Policies*. London: Lynne Rienner Publishers, pp. 110–125.

Index